ISRAEL HOROVITZ
Biography

ISRAEL HOROVITZ was born in Wakefield, Massachusetts, in 1939. His first play, *The Comeback*, was written at age 17. In the years that have followed, nearly 50 Horovitz plays have been translated and performed in as many as 30 languages, worldwide. Among the best-known Horovitz early plays are: *The Indian Wants The Bronx*, which introduced Al Pacino and John Cazale to the American stage; *Line*, which introduced Richard Dryfuss (a NYC revival of "Line: is now entering its 19th year, and is off-Broadway's longest-running play); *It's Called The Sugar Plum*, which introduced Marsha Mason and, subsequently, Jill Clayburgh (and was featured, last season, on A&E Cable Network, starring Ione Skye and Fisher Stevens); *Rats*, which introduced Scott Glenn; *Morning* of the Horovitz-McNally-Melfi Broadway triptych *Morning, Noon and Night*; *The Wakefield Plays*, a seven-play cycle including *Hopscotch, The 75th, Alfred the Great, Our Father's Failing, Alfred Dies, Stage Directions and Spared* (which Horovitz is now directing in NYC, starring William Hickey, and will again direct, next season, in French, in Paris; *Mackerel*; *The Primary English Class*, which starred Diane Keaton in its NYC premiere; *The Good Parts*, and many others.

For the past several years, Mr. Horovitz has been at work on a cycle of plays set in his adopted hometown, Gloucester, Massachusetts, all of which have had their world premieres at The Gloucester Stage Company, a theatre founded by Horovitz 15 years ago, and which he still serves as its Artistic Director and Producer. Among Horovitz's Gloucester plays are: *The Widow's Blind Date*, which played to SRO audiences for several months at the Gloucester Stage Company, and re-opened in NYC, off-Broadway, in December, 1989 (and is currently being performed in France, Germany, Spain and Israel); *Park Your Car In Harvard Yard*, which was workshopped at the Manhattan Theatre Club with Burgess Meredith and Ellen Burstyn, and was a triumph in Paris at Théâtre des Bouffes-Parisiens (and enjoyed a highly successful run on Broadway, starring Jason Robards and Judith Ivey); *Henry Lumper*, which was a success, off-Broadway; *North Shore Fish*, which was a hit at the WPA theatre, off-Broadway, and is slated for major productions in Los Angeles, and in Paris, next season; 1988's Hudson Guild Theatre entry, *Year Of The Duck*; *Firebird At Dogtown*; *Sunday Runners In The Rain*, which was produced by Joseph Papp at The N.Y. Shakespeare Festival; and *Fighting Over Beverley*, which had its world premiere at Gloucester Stage and will open in NYC in 1995; *Strong-Man's Weak Child*, which premiered at the Los Angeles Theatre Center and, subsequently, at Gloucester Stage, in a critically-acclaimed LATC/Gloucester Stage co-production of the world premiere. The feature-film rights to *Strong-Man's Weak Child* have been purchased by Tri-Star Pictures. Horovitz has recently completed the screenplay.

Other Horovitz plays include *The Former One-On-One Basketball Champion*, which was produced in Seattle, starring former Boston Celtics great, Bill Russell; and Horovitz's successful off-Broadway *Sault Ste. Marie Trilogy*: *Today, I Am A Fountain Pen*; *A Rosen By Any Other Name*; and *The Chopin Playoffs*. Horovitz's short comedy, *Faith,* was seen off-Broadway, in the Horovitz-McNally-Melfi reunion triptych *Faith, Hope and Charity*. Horovitz's newest play *Unexpected Tenderness*, will open in NYC at the WPA theatre in September, 1994.

In the past few years, Horovitz has written several original screenplays, including: *The Deuce* (a/k/a *The Gloucester Waterfront*); *Payofski's Discovery*; *The Pan*; *Barbers In Love*; *Letters To Iris* and *Strong-Man*. Other films written by Horovitz include the prize-winning *The Strawberry Statement*; *Believe In Me*; *Author! Author!*, which starred Al Pacino; and *A Man In Love* (written with Diane Kurys). He is currently writing three screenplays for Warner Brothers: the first, *With Honors*; the second, based on the life of James Dean; and the third, a remake of *A Star Is Born*. He has completed *Without A Word*, a dance-movie that will star Patrick Swayze.

In 1975, Horovitz founded the New York Playwrights Lab, a weekly workshop for full-time, professionally-produced playwrights. Still active, the NYPL is now a project of the Joseph Papp Public Theatre. Mr. Horovitz still serves the Lab as its artistic director.

Horovitz has won numerous awards, including the OBIE (twice), the EMMY, Prix du Plaisir de Théâtre (for *Line* in Paris), Prix du Jury (Cannes Film Festival), the NY Drama Desk Award, an Award in

Literature of The American Academy of Arts and Letters, The Eliot Norton Prize, and many others. In spring, 1991, he was awarded a Doctor of Humanities degree by Salem State College, Massachusetts.

Israel Horovitz is America's most-produced playwright in France. In French theatre history, no other American has had more plays translated and produced in French language. Five Horovitz plays are currently running in Paris, in productions directed by Mr. Horovitz.

As a director, Israel Horovitz has created world premiere productions of many of his plays, including *Strong-Man's Weak Child*; *Spared*, starring Lenny Baker in productions here and in France; *Hopscotch*, starring Swoosie Kurtz and Lenny Baker; the Gloucester and New York productions of *The Widow's Blind Date*; the French premiere of *Line* (*le ler*, directed by Horovitz with Michel Fagadau); and many others.

He is married to Gillian Adams, the current British National Marathon Champion; and is the father of five children, film-producer Rachael Horovitz, novelist Matthew Horovitz, Beastie Boys star/actor Adam Horovitz, and unemployed 8-year-old twins, Hannah and Oliver Horovitz.

The Horovitz family divides its time among homes in Gloucester, Massachusetts, NYC's Greenwich Village, and London's Dulwich Village.

ISRAEL HOROVITZ
Collected Works: Volume I
Sixteen Short Plays

Contemporary Playwrights Series

SK
A Smith and Kraus Book

Published by Smith and Kraus, Inc.
Lyme, New Hampshire

Special thanks from Israel Horovitz to Jana Mestecky for her countless hours of proofreading.

Manufactured in the United States of America
First Edition: June 1994
10 9 8 7 6 5 4 3 2

Library of Congress Cataloging-in-Publication Data
Horovitz, Israel.
Israel Horovitz : 17 short plays. --1st ed.
p. cm. --(Plays for actors series)
ISBN 1-880399-51-2
I. Title. II. Title: 17 short plays. III. Title: Seventeen short plays.
IV. Series: Plays for actors.
PS3558.069I76 1993
812'.54--dc20 93-46378
CIP

For my five artist-children:
Rachael, Matthew, Adam, Hannah, and Oliver Horovitz;
and for my French God-child, Marie-Solen Anouilh d'Harcourt ...
May they progress from where I stop.

CONTENTS

PREFACE

Israel Horovitz is a young man, really nice, really charming -- a tender American hoodlum. Sweet. As soon as you see him, you can't help but love him. Like all the tender ones, like all the sweet ones, he writes the cruelest things one can imagine. And these are the works that ring of the truth.

Israel Horovitz is both a sentimentalist and a realist. One can only imagine, therefore, to what degree he can be ferocious.

I'm not going to present to you -- *explain* to you -- his play *Line.* Rest assured. I'll only say that it's unique -- that there's no action -- nothing happens, nothing but everything.

Everything? What? Well, *Line* illustrates the themes of conflict. More precisely, competition. Put two men together -- strangers ... then, three, then, four, then, five -- then, introduce a woman among them. Conflict will erupt.

These strangers know each other at heart, and because they know each other, they hate each other -- they *despise* each other! They'll battle for first place, which, of course, they'll lose and regain and re-lose -- because of the woman, who is, of course, *also* fighting for first place. I think that they would even be willing to kill each other, and that they would even be willing to die in the first place, if there is no other way to end up first. Of course, first place is an illusion. There's no head to any line. We need to believe that there's a first place. Otherwise, how could we possibly have competition?

In this play, Israel tells us all, which means he says nothing. I won't tell you how much I love this play. I will let you discover it on your own. Because we might not agree -- especially, if I were the first one to have said it!

—*Eugène Ionesco*

ISRAEL HOROVITZ
Collected Works: Volume I
Sixteen Short Plays

LINE

For my father

ACROBATS and LINE were first presented by The New Comedy Theatre (Jerry Schlossberg, James Hammerstein, Israel Horovitz, Albert Poland) at the Theatre de Lys, in New York City, on February 15, 1971. They were directed by James Hammerstein; the production was designed by Neil Peter Jampolis; additional staging was by Grover Dale, and the production stage manager was Robert Vandergriff. The cast, in order of appearance, was as follows:

FLEMING .... John Randolph
STEPHEN .... Richard Dreyfuss
MOLLY .... Ann Wedgeworth
DOLAN .... John Cazale
ARNALL .... Barnard Hughes

LINE, in an earlier, version, was presented by Ellen Stewart on November 29, 1967, at Cafe LaMama ETC, in New York City. It was directed by James Hammerstein with the following cast:

FLEMING .... Paul Haller
STEPHEN .... Israel Horovitz
MOLLY .... Ann Wedgeworth
DOLAN .... John Cazale
ARNALL .... Michael Del Medico

Introduction

Line was my first play to be produced in New York City. Thanks to Leonard Melfi, who talked Ellen Stewart into taking me and my play, on faith, *Line* was scheduled to run for six consecutive nights at Cafè LaMama, at its original original original location on 2nd Avenue. In those days, LaMama was, arguably, the hottest showcase in the country for a beginning playwright. If you had a play on at LaMama, it was reviewed. And you were either In or Out.

Thus, the premiere of *Line* was, simply, terrifying. James Hammerstein and I assembled a sublime cast of talented friends ... all willing to work without pay. Each production was given a budget of $80, in cash, handed over by Ellen Stewart (LaMama, herself), who said "The money's yours, honey. If you don't spend it all on scenery and props, you can keep the difference." I'd brought John Cazale and Ann Wedgeworth into the cast; Jimmy brought the others. Cazale and I had grown up in neighboring Massachusettts towns: he, in Winchester; me, in Wakefield. I'd stage-managed a Tennessee Williams play with Ann Wedgeworth, at the Paper Mill Playhouse in New Jersey, two years before. Except for Hammerstein, who had worked on Broadway, none of us had had any particular prior success in NYC. We all took *Line* and LaMama very, very seriously. We rehearsed, endlessly.

Our dress rehearsal was wonderful ... hilarious and frightening. We seemed to be, in a word, unstoppable. And then, the bomb fell. The young actor who was playing Stephen announced—after the dress rehearsal—that he'd gotten a role in a TV series pilot and was going from the theatre to the airport, where he would fly away, forever. He did. All of the above.

I turned to Hammerstein and told him that it was obvious that he would have to take over the role. In those days, LaMama was booked solid for a year. I was certain that postponing *Line* would mean postponing our careers—for a year.

James Hammerstein, talented and dear, was and is 6'8" tall, feet stockinged or unstockinged. There was no way he'd fit into the little quitter's costume. All eyes were suddenly on me.

We stayed in the theatre, rehearsing through the night and through the next day. At 8pm, I walked out on stage as Stephen in *Line*, facing an auditorium no longer empty and safe, but, now filled to the brim with NEW YORK DRAMA CRITICS! ... One look at their faces and I forgot who I was, where I was ...

Horrified, I did what any actor in my shoes (*especially* in my shoes) would have done: I yelled "Line!". Bonnie Frindel Morris, my life-long friend and then-stage manager, yelled back at me with the first line of the play "Is this a line?". I then, dutifully, repeated what she'd said: "Is this a line?". As it was the 60's, the audience, understandably, assumed that *Line* was "that kind of play". They laughed at our rapid-fire exchange of "lines", and they applauded. My stage-fright soared to uncharted heights. My heart shifted into Automatic Pilot, and I sailed through the rest of the play, word-perfect—almost—until John Cazale, with his flawless North Shore Massachusetts "Pahk Yo'r Cah" accent, looked me straight in the panic-stricken eye, upstage-center, and whispered, proudly, "Yo'r doin' great, Ah'tie!" (Artie was my nickname, diminutive for my middle name, Arthur.) As soon as I heard the word "Ah'tie", I, once again, forgot who I was, where I was ...

Jerry Tallmer, reviewing *Line* for the New York Post, gave me my first review in New York City ... as a playwright and as an actor. The review's headline was "WELCOME MR. HOROVITZ".

Two years later, a commercial production of *Line* in NYC, fared less well. I'd replaced myself with Richard Dreyfuss, a then-unknown young actor I'd seen in Gordon Davidson's brilliant L.A. production of *Line*, at the Mark Taper Forum. Richard had played in *Rats*, there, as well. He was wonderful in both of my plays. On my return to NYC, I was so enthusiastic about Dreyfuss, Hammerstein agreed to take him as Stephen in *Line*, sight unseen.

Alas, I'd been talked into putting a curtain-raiser with *Line*, which, on its own, only ran an hour or so. The reviews for *Line* were stunning. But, the reviews for it curtain-raiser, *Acrobats*, were far less than stunning. In fact, the word on the street was "Skip the first play; don't miss the second play"... We ran for only a few months, playing to half-houses, and then, we closed. I had expected much more, and I was devastated.

A few years later, Edith O'Hara, who ran the 13th St. Repertory Theatre, asked me if she could do a revival of *Line*. I said yes, but, with one condition: that *Line* be done on its own. The 13th St. Repertory Theater's production of *Line* has been, at this writing, running for 19 consecutive years, and is off-Broadway's longest-running play (as distinguished from *The Fantasticks*, which is off-Broadway's longest-running MUSICAL).

Eugène Ionesco's preface to *Line*, printed elsewhere in this edition, represents a another kind of turning-point in my life. I'd had some plays performed in Paris, with some success, prior to *Line*, but, I was totally unprepared for what would happen with *Line*, itself. The Paris production opened well after the play's commercial failure in NYC, but, before its 13th St. Repertory Theatre revival. Essentially, I worked on the Paris production for the pure fun of being in France, and working with French actors. Speaking French that was, like Jean-Paul Sartre, *tout charmant, mais, jamais correct*, I co-directed the French-language premiere of *Line*. I was teamed with my friend Michel Fagadau, who'd guided the French premieres of *The Indian Wants The Bronx*, and *It's Called The Sugar Plum*, two years earlier.

Lucky for me, the French translation of *Line* had been done by Claude Roy, who was, and is, two things: an angel and a genius. On the opening night of *Line* in Paris, Claude and I went together to a festival of Marx Brothers movies in a tiny cinema on Rue d'Ombre. We watched four consecutive hours of Marx Brothers antics. The event was hilarious and humbling, and, as we'd hoped, totally distracting. We passed by Théâtre de Poche-Montparnasse, at 10pm, to see if there was any hint of what had happened, there, earlier. We found Michel, alone, waiting for us on the sidewalk in front of the darkened theatre. Cautiously, Claude asked him how it went. We both liked his answer: *C'était une triomphe!* It seems that Jean-

Jacques Gauthier had stood, at the end, and yelled "Bravo!". Gauthier was *le Figaro's* drama critic, and the most respected drama critic in Paris, during the 1970's. That production ran for eleven years, and *Line* (*le 1er*) is almost constantly in production in French language.

In fact, like *The Indian Wants The Bronx*, *Line* has been translated and played in nearly thirty languages, worldwide.

Why one play succeeds and another play does not, is, really, the mystery of mysteries. I love to hear people explain successes and failures. I always eavesdrop. It's always funny, gorgeously pretentious dialogue: "See, *Line* is cheap to produce ... nice acting roles ...". The truth be told, both *The Indian Wants The Bronx* and *Line* have enjoyed similar success, around the globe, and Lord only knows why. The plays are as different as different can be. By all that's Holy, they should appeal to totally different audiences.

But, as Euripides so often said, when asked about the success, or failure, of any his 126 plays: "Go figure!" ...

Characters

STEPHEN
FLEMING
MOLLY
DOLAN
ARNALL

Setting

A line. Now.

LINE

As the audience enters the theatre, Fleming is standing behind a fat, white strip of adhesive tape that is fixed to the stage floor. The play has begun.
He is waiting . . . waiting . . . waiting.
The stage is without decoration other than Fleming and the line.
The lighting is of that moment when late night turns to early morning: all pinks and oranges and, finally, steel-gray blue.
Fleming checks and rechecks his feet in relation to the line. He is clearly first there, in first place.
He steps straight back now and again, testing his legs and the straightness of the line that will follow.
Fleming has carried a large war-surplus duffel with him, full of beer, potato chips, whatever he might need for a long-awaited long wait.
Back to the audience, he reaches into the bag and takes something out. He stands, hands penis-high, in a small pantomime of urination. He turns again to the line and reveals that he has peeled a banana. He eats it.
His feet are planted solidly at the line now, yet his body breaks the rigidity, revealing his exhaustion. He is waiting . . . waiting . . . waiting.
He dips again into the bag and produces a bag of potato chips, a can of beer (flip-top) and a rather nice cloth napkin, which he tucks into his shirt-top. He opens the beer, eats the chips, drinks, belches and does it all again. His feet never move from the mark now.
He leans back and sings, softly at first, "Take Me Out To The Ball Game," possibly confusing the lyrics. He drinks, belches and spills potato chips all over the place, then continues singing again to end of song. Stephen enters quietly. He watches Fleming carefully. Fleming senses Stephen's presence. He stops singing and, waiting for Stephen to speak, does nothing. Neither does Stephen. Fleming gets on with it. Singing carefully now. Stephen cuts him off with a soft question.*

STEPHEN: Is this a line? (*Fleming stares directly into Stephen's eyes, but doesn't answer.*) Excuse me, mister. Is this a line? (*After studying*

*See note on copyright page.

Stephen's clothing and manner, Fleming rechecks his feet and turns from Stephen, facing straight ahead.) Is this a line, huh?

FLEMING: (*Does a long, false take.*) What's it look like?

STEPHEN: (*Walking over, leaning between Fleming's legs, he literally caresses the tape.*) Oh, yeah. There it is. It's a line all right. It's a beautiful line, isn't it? *I couldn't* tell from back there. I would have been earlier if I had started out earlier. You wouldn't think anyone would be damn fool enough to get up this early. Or not go to bed. Depending on how you look at it. (*Fleming stares at Stephen incredulously.*) Oh, I didn't mean you were a damn fool. (*Pauses.*) Not yet. Nice line. Just the two of us, huh?

FLEMING: What's it look like? What's it look like?

STEPHEN That's all you ever say, huh? "What's it look like?" – "What's it look like?" (*Pause.*) Must be nice.

FLEMING: Huh?

STEPHEN: Being first. Right up front of the line like that. Singing away. Singing your damn fool heart out. I could hear you from back there. Singing your damn fool heart out. You like music? (*Fleming turns his back to Stephen, who now begins to talk with incredible speed.*) I'm a music nut myself. Mozart. He's the one. I've got all his records. Started out on seventy-eight. Moved on up to forty-fives. Then I moved on to thirty-three and a third when I got to be thirteen or so. Now I've got him on hi-fi, stereo cartridges, and, of course, compact discs. (*Displays a portable CD player.*) I've got him on everything he's on. (*Pause.*) Must be nice. (*Pauses.*) Want to trade places?

FLEMING: You yak like that all the time?

STEPHEN: (*Peeks over Fleming's shoulder at the line.*) That's a good solid line. I've seen some skimpy little lines in my day, but that one's a beauty. (*Whistles a strain from "The Magic Flute."*) That's Mozart. Want me to whistle some more? Or we could sing your song. "Take Me Out To The Ball Game." I know most of your pop songs from your twenties, your thirties, your forties, your fifties and your sixties. I'm bad on your seventies, eighties and nineties. That's when I started composing. And, of course, that's when Mozart really started getting in the way. But, have it like you will – just name that tune. 'Course, don't get me wrong. I'd rather be whistling my own songs any day of the week. Any night, for that matter. Or whistle Mozart. "The Magic Flute." "Marriage of Figaro." Go on. Just "Name That Tune." I can sing it in Italian, German, French, or your Basic English. Hell, if he could knock them out at seven, I should be able to whistle at thirty, right? Christ, I am thirty-five. Around the age of Christ. What hath God wrought? (*Pauses, arms out and feet pinned together as in crucifixion.*) God hath wrought iron! (*Pauses. Waits to see if Fleming has crumbled yet. Sees Fleming is confused, but still on his feet, so Stephen continues.*) Thirty-five. That's how old he was. He thought he was writing his funeral music all right. He was, too. Isn't that something, to have that kind of premonition? That's what you call your young genius. The only real genius ever to walk on this earth, mister. Wolfgang Amadeus Mozart. W-A-M. (*Yells at Fleming's face.*) WAM! WAM! WAM! (*Fleming, thunderstruck, turns and overtly snubs Stephen, who is perched, ready to take first position, if Fleming falls. Fleming stays afloat, so Stephen takes his wallet out of his pocket and studies its contents carefully. He pokes Fleming.*) You want to read my wallet?

FLEMING: Huh?

STEPHEN: (*Begins to unfold an enormous credit-card case.*) You want to read my wallet? You can read my wallet and I'll read your wallet. You can learn a lot about people from their wallets. Avis cards. Hertz cards. American Express. Air Travel. Bloomingdale's. Saks'. Old phone numbers. Bits and scraps. Contraceptives. Locks of hair. Baby pictures. Calendars. Business cards. And the ladies. Businessladies have cards. ID cards. Not the ladies, I mean. I mean the men who own the wallets who you're learning about, right? (*Fleming sings two bars of "Take Me Out To The Ball Game."*) Hey. Don't turn your back on me, huh? Let me read your wallet. I've read mine before. I read my wallet all the time. Hey, will you? Here. Take my wallet, then. You don't even have to let me read yours. (*Forces his wallet into Fleming's hands. Fleming is absolutely astonished.*) That's it. Go on. Read. (*Fleming obeys, wide-eyed.*) There. See that ID card? That lets you know who I am, right away. See? Stephen. Steve. Or Stevie. Gives you a choice, even. And where I work. See that? Now look at the pictures. My kids. That one's dead. That one's dead. That one's dead. That one's dead. There are more. Don't stop. More pictures. (*Stephen leaves the wallet in Fleming's hand and begins a wide circle around him, almost forcing Fleming out of line.*)

FLEMING: How'd you lose all those kids?

STEPHEN: Lose the kids?

FLEMING: Dead. All these dead kids? (*Sees that the pictures are lithographs of Mozart.*) Hey! Those are drawings!

STEPHEN: Who said they were kids?

FLEMING: (*Waits, staring.*) Oh, boy. Here we go. (*Sings three bars of "Take Me Out To The Ball Game," after jamming Stephen's wallet back into Stephen's pocket. Stephen joins in for one bar. In unison. Fleming stops.*)

STEPHEN: (*Sings another bar, then stops, asks.*) Do you really think this line is for a ball game? Huh? There's no ball game around here. I mean, I wouldn't be here if there was a ball game. Ball games aren't my kind of stuff. I loathe ball games, myself. You like ball games?

FLEMING: (*At this point, the situation has gone beyond Fleming's comprehension, and his confusion surfaces as a rubber duck.*) Who are you?

STEPHEN: That's why I gave you my wallet. If everybody would just pass their wallets around, sooner or later something would happen, right?

FLEMING: Yeah.

STEPHEN: Can you imagine if you met the President and he gave you his wallet to read? You'd know everything about him. Or the Mayor. Kings. Ballplayers, even. Read THEIR wallets. Boy, would you know it all soon enough. Scraps of paper that held secrets they forgot were secrets. Meetings they were supposed to make. Locks of hair. Pictures of babies they forgot they had. Names. Addresses. ID cards. Secret money hidden in secret places. You'd know everything, wouldn't you? (*Stephen has Fleming going now. He increases the speed of his delivery, eyes flickering, hands waving, watching Fleming's terrified responses.*) You see, friend, all those up-front people are fakes. Fakes. There's never been a real first place . . . never a real leader. Except you know *who*.

FLEMING: Who?

STEPHEN: War heroes? All frauds. If there had been one really efficient war, we wouldn't be here, would we?

FLEMING: I'm first. All I know is I'm first.

STEPHEN: First. It's just a word. Twist the letters around, you get strif. God backwards. Dog. Split the first three letters off the word therapist, you get two words: the rapist. Spell Hannah backwards, you get Hannah. Spell backwards backwards, you get sdrawkcab. I tell you, show me one of your so-called winners, and let me have one look at his wallet; just one. I'll never have to count the money, either. There's never been a real first before. Never. I know, friend. I know. See that line? Turn it on end, you know what you've got? A number one. But how do you hang on to it? How do you really hold it, so you're not one of those wallet-carrying, secret compartment fakes like all of them? Answer that question and I'd let you follow me in. You could be second.

FLEMING: What do you mean "second"? I'm first. I'm right at the front.

STEPHEN: For the moment.

FLEMING: Don't get any smart ideas.

STEPHEN: The only conclusions I draw are on men's-room walls. Now if you'd shut up for a while, I'll sing my wallet. (*Stephen sings his Hertz card lyric to "Eine Kleine Nachtmusik."*) "This non-transferable Hertz charge card entitles the person named to use Hertz Rent A Car service under the terms of the Hertz Rental Agreement on a credit basis. Where you desire to make immediate payments, the card enables you to rent without deposit. Payment for rentals charged is due within ten days after the billing date. This card is subject to invalidation and modification without notice and is the property of the Hertz system . . . " (*Molly, a voluptuous woman, wanders onto the stage. When Stephen sees her, he continues to sing the Hertz lyric, but changes the melody to a tacky love song. Stephen stops Molly as she crosses the stage.*) Hey. You looking for a line, lady?

MOLLY: Line?

STEPHEN: That's right. This is a line. You're third. Number three. There used to be just two of us here. Me and Fleming. This is Fleming. Who are you?

FLEMING: How'd you know my name, huh? How'd you know my name?

STEPHEN: (*To Fleming.*) I read your wallet. (*To Molly.*) You're third. That's not too bad. You won't have to wait long.

FLEMING: (*Checks to see if Stephen has stolen his wallet, then screams.*) You didn't read my wallet! Nobody's read my wallet, except me!

MOLLY: (*Joining the line.*) Third? I'm third, huh? How long have you been waiting?

STEPHEN: About nine and a half minutes. Fleming must have been here all night. Were you here all night, Fleming? He looks it, huh?

FLEMING: How the hell did you know my name? How'd you know?

MOLLY: Third place. How soon do they open?

STEPHEN: You'll probably see a crowd before that. There's always a crowd. The crowd that says, "Maybe there won't be a crowd, let's go anyway." That crowd. You'll see that crowd, won't she, Fleming?

FLEMING: How'd you know my name? How'd you know my name?

STEPHEN: Fleming, don't be a bore! What's your name? Mine's Stephen.

MOLLY: Molly. I'm Molly.

STEPHEN: Hello, Molly. Glad you're third. Fleming, this is Molly.

MOLLY: Hello.

FLEMING: Hey, kid. Hold our places in line. Come here, ma'am. (*Takes her aside, whispers.*) That kid's crazy. Watch out. He's one of them freaky weirdoes. He's been saying crazy things to me.

STEPHEN: (*Moves into first position.*) I can't guarantee your places. The crowd's going to come sure as hell and I can't guarantee anybody's place. The fact is, Fleming, I'm first now.

FLEMING: What?

STEPHEN: I'm first. (*Straddles the line.*) Look at me. I'm up first. Up front. Front of the line. (*Molly jumps into second position.*)

MOLLY: You could have held our places. Nobody else is here.

STEPHEN: It's just not right. Besides, Fleming wouldn't hold anybody's place. You can tell that just from looking at him. He's never held anybody's place in his life.

FLEMING: (*Enraged, but trying to maintain control.*) Kid, I've been standing there all night. All night. Waiting. Waiting in the front of the line. The very front. Now I think you'd better let me get right back up there. (*As Fleming continues, Dolan enters and walks toward the line. he carries a canvas-topped, artist's portable stool.*) Just step back one pace and let me in there. (*Dolan quietly steps into line behind Molly. To Dolan.*) I'm up front.

DOLAN: (*Sitting.*) Huh?

FLEMING: I'm first. That kid just took my spot. You're fourth.

DOLAN: I don't mean to argue, but I count third. You're fourth.

FLEMING: Hey. Listen. That kid grabbed my place. I waited all night up front. Right at the front of the line.

DOLAN: I don't want to argue, but you're not getting in front of me, pal, so skip it.

FLEMING: Skip it? Bull, I'll skip it. (*Walks up to Stephen.*) Give me back my place, kid, or I'll knock you out of it. (*Stephen drops to the floor in the lotus-position. Fleming stares, again astonished.*) Get up!

DOLAN: I hate to argue, but get out of the front, Mac! The kid was up front and I'm third. The lady's second.

MOLLY: He was up front, actually.

DOLAN: Well, he can go second if you want him to, lady. I'm third. (*Arnall enters and walks directly into the line.*)

ARNALL: Molly?

MOLLY: Arnall. Here I am.

ARNALL: You think I can't see you? You saved my place?

MOLLY: (*To Dolan.*) I was saving his place, sir. We had an arrangement.

DOLAN: Not that I want to run things, but that's too bad. No place was saved. He can go fourth.

FLEMING: I'm fourth! For Christ's sake what am I saying? I'm first.

ARNALL: (*Jumps into fourth position.*) I'm fourth.

MOLLY: I'm second.

STEPHEN: (*After the stampede, to Dolan.*) Obviously, I'm first. My name's Stephen. Who are you?

DOLAN: (*Shaking Stephen's hand.*) Dolan's what they call me. How long you been waiting?

STEPHEN: About twelve and a half minutes.

ARNALL: Jesus. If I could have found my clean shirts, Molly . . . If I could have found where you hid them . . . I would have been here half an hour ago. I would have been first.

FLEMING: I've been here all night.

ARNALL: (*Considers it.*) How come you're fifth? (*Pause for a "take" from Fleming.*) You're not even in line. Why aren't you first?

FLEMING: I AM first. God damn it! I AM first. That crazy kid grabbed my place. How'd you know my name, kid?

ARNALL: Fleming?

FLEMING: How the hell do you know?

ARNALL: (*Pulls Fleming's T-shirt neck to his eyes.*) It's written on your undershirt. (*Fleming spins around trying to read the label.*)

STEPHEN: I read your undershirt.

FLEMING: (*To Dolan.*) Look, I've been here all night. I've been standing right at the front of the line all night. You know that's true. (*To Molly.*) You saw me here, lady. You know I was first.

MOLLY: You stepped out of line. (*To Arnall.*) He stepped out of line, Arnall.

ARNALL: Serves you right, then, Fleming. If I could have found my clean shirt, I would have been first. My dumb wife hides my dumb shirts. Isn't that terrific? She hides my shirts. I could have been first by half an hour. But she hid my shirt. You know where I found it? (*Simply.*) I couldn't find it.

FLEMING: (*After rapt attention to Arnall's shaggy-shirt story. Furiously.*) This is ridiculous. I was first. All night. (*To Arnall.*) I just took your wife aside to warn her about that crazy kid. He jumped the line. He jumped in front. That's not fair, is it? I was here all night.

DOLAN: You're fifth. There's plenty here for five. You'll get your chance.

FLEMING: (*To Arnall.*) That's not the point. God damn it. There's only one first and I waited up all night. All night in the line all by myself. And he took it away from me. Now that is definitely unfair.

ARNALL: (*Completely against Fleming's problem.*) I hate to go anywhere at night with the shirt from the day still on. You never know what kind of germs you come in contact with during the day. You never can tell, can you?

STEPHEN: Life's full of dirt.

ARNALL: Our place is full of dirt. My wife never cleans. If it were up to her, we'd be up to our lips in dirt. Day and night. That's why I'm late. What movie's playing?

FLEMING: (*He's had it!*) Movie?

ARNALL: I thought we were going to the movies, Molly?

MOLLY: Arnall, don't cause a scene!

STEPHEN: Your shirt looks terrific, Arnall.

ARNALL: Looks are deceptive. Hospitals look clean, don't they? But if you ever ran a check for germcount, oh boy, wouldn't you get a score? After all, people come there – to hospitals – because they're ridden with germs. Take an old building full of germridden people, paint it stark white, you got yourself a place that looks clean, but underneath that look, there's just a white hospital – full of germridden people.

STEPHEN: How do you feel about that, Fleming? Do germridden people disturb you too?

FLEMING: Don't get smart with me, kid. I was waiting here a long time before you, and you know it. (*To Dolan.*) He's trying to distract your attention from the fact that he took first place . . . he didn't earn it. No, sir. *I* earned it. I waited up for that place. He took it!

DOLAN: Well, I don't want to be the one who starts any arguments, but he *is* in first place, and he was in first place when I first got here.

STEPHEN: Fair *is* fair, Fleming!

FLEMING: (*Yells.*) Don't "fair" me, kid, or you'll have a fat lip to worry about!

DOLAN: Now listen to me, Fleming.

FLEMING: (*Screams.*) What do *you* want?

DOLAN: (*Screams.*) Lower your voice!

ARNALL: Easy, Dolan, easy. Easy, easy, easy . . .

DOLAN: (*To Fleming.*) Look, I don't want to start any trouble, but it seems to me if you want to be first, be first. Move the kid. If you want to be second, be second. Move his old lady. (*And with that, Dolan [Mister Niceguy] nearly strangles Arnall. He catches himself before Arnall dies. He brushes Arnall's jacket and smiles. To Arnall.*) And don't you – God damn it! – "easy" me. I'm nice and easy all the time. I'm Mister Niceguy. Get it? Mister Niceguy.

ARNALL: Move *who*?

DOLAN: Your old lady.

FLEMING: Your old lady.

ARNALL: You can't do that.

DOLAN: And why not?

FLEMING: And "why not" is right.

ARNALL: (*Archly.*) She's second. She's in line. That's the way things are. She's in second place. She can beat you there.

FLEMING: (*Has an original thought.*) Hell, she did! I spent the night in first. Right up there at the white line. Got my sack here with food and drink. I'm prepared. Prepared to be first. God damn it! Not second. Not third. Not fifth. I'm prepared for first. But, mind you, if I want to move your old lady and be second, I'll just move your old lady and be second. Just like that. (*Arnall steps out of line into Fleming's way, as Fleming pretends to move to shove Molly. Fleming quickly jumps into line in Arnall's spot. Fleming is now fourth.*)

ARNALL: (*Stunned.*) Hey. Hey, you dirty sonofabitch! Sonofabitch! You took my place. He took my place. What the hell is this? Get out of line, Fleming. Move out, Fleming. You took my place!

FLEMING: (*Laughing.*) That's what a woman does to you, what'syourname. That's what a woman does.

ARNALL: (*Humiliated.*) Stop laughing, you sonofabitch!

FLEMING: (*A mule giggling.*) That's what a woman does to you.

ARNALL: (*Walks up to Molly, squares off.*) He's right! (*He slaps Molly on the hand.*)

MOLLY: (*Amazed and furious.*) Arnall. Arnall. Damn you. How could you? (*She chases him, slapping his head. Dolan and Fleming quickly move up one space, laughing.*)

DOLAN: (*A jock's scream of victory.*) I'm second. I'm second.

FLEMING: (*A neat imitation.*) I'm right behind you.

ARNALL: (*Giving the proof of the pudding.*) Now look, you bitch. Now look. We're both out. They moved up. You moved up, you sons of bitches. You snuck up.

DOLAN: You stepped out.

STEPHEN: (*Whispers.*) Out of line, out of luck!

DOLAN: (*Picks it up.*) Out of line, out of luck!

FLEMING: (*Instinct.*) Out of line, out of luck.

ARNALL: Out of line, out of luck? That supposed to be funny, huh? That's supposed to be a joke? Out of line, out of luck?

FLEMING: Who said that?

ARNALL: You said that. "Out of line, out of luck!"

FLEMING: (*A bit boggled, but giddy.*) Well, then . . . that's right! That's what a woman does to you, Arnall. You lose your place.

MOLLY: You made me do that, Arnall. You made me do that.

ARNALL: Shut up, you bitch! You start first with the shirts, now my place, now your place. Just shut up . . . I've got to think.

STEPHEN: (*Sings.*) "Se voul venire nella – " I'm first.

FLEMING: Don't be smart, kid. I don't forget easily. You'll get yours.

STEPHEN: I got mine. I'm first! (*Sings.*)

Se vuol venire nella mia scuola,
La capriolo le insegnero.

That's a song my mother taught me. I'll never forget it, either. (*Sings.*)

Se vuol venire . . . etc.

FLEMING: Forget it.

MOLLY: (*Sidling up to Stephen.*) Your mother?

ARNALL: Stay away from him, Molly.

MOLLY: Shut your dumb mouth, Arnall. Just shut up. (*To Stephen.*) Is she young? (*She puts a foot on Fleming's bag. Her leg is Mrs. Robinson's.*)

STEPHEN: (*A sweaty Benjamin.*) Metza-Metz" (*He sings.*)

Se vuol venire nella mia . . .

MOLLY: (*Interrupts.*) You've got a pretty face, you know that?

ARNALL: Molly! For crying out loud.

MOLLY: (*To Stephen.*) Don't pay any attention to him. (*Arnall walks to the other side of the stage and sits.*)

STEPHEN: I'll pay attention to whom I choose. To who I choose? Whatever I choose. You know what I mean.

MOLLY: I was saying that you have a pretty face.

STEPHEN: Yes, you were.

MOLLY: Good bones. Strong bones in your face. Like James Dean.

STEPHEN: James Dean?

MOLLY: The movie star. The one who got killed in his Porsche. That's who you look like. James Dean.

FLEMING: Who's James Dean? A movie star?

DOLAN: Killed in his what?

STEPHEN: Is James Dean still dead?

MOLLY: Don't make jokes about James Dean. He was a beautiful boy. And I'm telling you that you remind me of him.

STEPHEN: I wasn't trying to be funny.

MOLLY: I always wanted to make love with James Dean.

FLEMING: Holy Jesus!

DOLAN: Shut up. (*He wants to hear.*)

STEPHEN: Why didn't you?

MOLLY: I never met him, silly. He's a movie star. And then he got killed. If I could have met him, I would have made love to him. If I had been Marilyn Monroe, I'd have played with him.

FLEMING: Monroe? Joltin' Joe's missus?

MOLLY: I could have made him happy. (*Pauses.*) I could make you happy.

STEPHEN: I don't have a Porsche.

MOLLY: It's very warm here, don't you think? Don't you think it's very warm here?

STEPHEN: (*Unbuttoning his shirt, just a few buttons.*) Yeah. I can't remember a time this hot. It makes you want to take all your clothes off, doesn't it?

MOLLY: (*She takes his hand in hers.*) All your clothes.

STEPHEN: Unbearable.

MOLLY: Unbearable.

MOLLY AND STEPHEN: Torture. (*They kiss, a long deep passionate kiss. Suddenly, they break apart and dance off, in a polite minuet.*)

STEPHEN: (*Sings. Optional: he sings in German, French, Italian or English, although Italian is preferred.*)

Should he, for instance, wish to go dancing,

He'll face the music, I'll lead the band, yes.
I'll lead the band.
And then I'll take my cue, without ado,
And slyly, very, very, very, very, very slyly.
Using discretion, I shall uncover his secret plan.
Subtly outwitting, innocent seeming,
Cleverly hitting, planning and scheming,
I'll get the best of the hypocrite yet,
I'll beat him yet!

(*As Stephen sings, Dolan and Fleming talk. Arnall walks forward quietly to watch Molly and Stephen as they dance. All are astonished.*)

FLEMING: (*Almost a whisper.*) You've got to hand it to that kid.

DOLAN: Shh. Her old man's watching.

FLEMING: It's disgusting.

DOLAN: (*Watching the lovers.*) What's disgusting?

FLEMING: Her old man watching like that. It ain't natural.

DOLAN: Yeah. It certainly ain't natural.

FLEMING: Sonofabitch. You've got to hand it to that kid. I never would have guessed.

DOLAN: I had a woman once in a car.

FLEMING: What happened?

(*By now, their attitudes should reveal that Molly and Stephen are copulating-by-dance.*)

DOLAN: The usual thing.

FLEMING: That's all?

DOLAN: Yeah.

FLEMING: Oh.

DOLAN: I've never had a woman in a line.

FLEMING: Me neither.

DOLAN: It's funny watching like this, ain't it?

FLEMING: Yeah.

DOLAN: I'd rather be doing it.

FLEMING: Yeah. (*They both continue to stare goggle-eyed.*)

DOLAN: I'm getting horny.

FLEMING: Yeah.

DOLAN: Yeah.

FLEMING: Yeah.

(*The "yeah's" start to build in a crescendo as the lovers reach their first climax.*)

ARNALL: (*From nowhere.*) Yeah.

DOLAN: Yeah. Yeah.

ALL: Yeah! Yeah! Yeah! *Yeah!!! Yeah!!!*

STEPHEN: (*Sings his orgasm.*) "Piano . . . Piano . . . Piano . . . "!

(*After they dance, Molly takes first! Stephen sings again, exhausted, but "dances her" out of first place, tired, but not to be undone.*)

FLEMING: He's doing it again!

DOLAN: I can't take much more of this!

FLEMING: What are we going to do?

DOLAN: You figure it out, pal. I know what I want. (*He jumps forward and grabs Molly. Sings "I Want a Girl Just Like the Girl That Married Dear Old Dad."* Arnall tries to jump into first position, but Stephen does a terrific baseball slide into first. Arnall is forced into the slot Dolan vacated: second. Fleming is stunned.*)

STEPHEN: I'm still first. I'm still first!

ARNALL: (*To Molly.*) Bitch. Bitch. You bitch!

STEPHEN: (*To Arnall.*) You're second. You were nowhere. You were nowhere.

FLEMING: What happened?

ARNALL: He slid into first.

FLEMING: Yeah. But what happened? (*In the meantime, Dolan and Molly are dancing as Dolan sings. Note: after this "dance," Molly calmly will return to first and brush her hair. Dolan continues singing happily. Over his song, the dialogue continues. Fleming, finally, realizing.*) This is terrible. I forgot to move up.

STEPHEN: You didn't move up. You didn't move in. Fleming, you disappoint me. (*He lies down on the floor, goes to sleep.*)

FLEMING: (*To Arnall.*) You just let your old lady do that? I mean, does she do it all the time?

ARNALL: All the time. All the time.

FLEMING: That's terrible. That's a terrible thing. You must get embarrassed.

ARNALL: It doesn't hurt any more. Not after all these years.

FLEMING: Why don't you throw her out?

ARNALL: Why? She's predictable.

FLEMING: Predictable?

ARNALL: Consistent. I never have any surprises with Molly. She's pure. All bad.

FLEMING: That's good?

ARNALL: Right. My philosophy is quite simple. Never ever leave yourself open for surprises, and you'll never be surprised. Surprise brings pain, pain is bad. No surprise, no pain. No pain, no bad. No bad, all good. (*Proudly.*) I've got it made.

DOLAN: Da-ah-aahd!

ARNALL: (*After, a pause.*) They're finished now. Want to take a whack at it?

FLEMING: What?

ARNALL: Go on. Go ahead. Have a bash. Have a go at it. It'll do you good. Go on. I don't mind.

FLEMING: You sure?

ARNALL: Positive.

FLEMING: Do you mind if Dolan holds my place in line?

ARNALL: Of course not.

FLEMING: Hey, Dolan.

DOLAN: What?

FLEMING: Hold my place in line, will you. I'd like to have a bash.

DOLAN: Have a what?

FLEMING: Have a go at it. That's what her old man calls it. Hey, Dolan. Hold my place, will you?

DOLAN: (*Slides into Fleming's place and falls there.*) Go get it. (*Fleming stares at Dolan, Molly, Arnall, and the lot again. He grabs Molly and drags her upstage slightly, he "counts" a fox trot beat. He sings his song and they dance.*)

FLEMING: One two three – one two three – one two three – and – (*Sings "Take Me Out To The Ball Game." As he continues his song, the dialogue does not stop.*)

DOLAN: I like the way you think, Arnold.

ARNALL: You mean my little philosophy?

DOLAN: (*A bit confused.*) Yeah, I guess you could call it that. Your little philosophy. I like the way you think, Arnold.

ARNALL: Arn*all.* (*Spells it, then, goes on like a house-on-fire.*) A-R-N-A-L-L. My mother wanted to call me Arthur. My father liked Nathan. Thought it was strong. My grandmother liked Lloyd, after Harold Lloyd. So they took the A-R from Arthur, the N-A from Nathan, the L-L from Lloyd, and called me Arn*all.* What do you want?

DOLAN: I like the way you think, Arnold. I want to tell you how touched I am. I have a little philosophy myself; I call it the Under*dog* philosophy.

ARNALL: Under*dog?*

DOLAN: Did you ever hear of Arnold Palmer? Arnold Palmer is the world's richest golfer. He always looks like he is going to lose, but he almost never loses. He's the world's richest golfer.

ARNALL: I don't get it.

DOLAN: Everybody wants to be first, right?

ARNALL: Right.

DOLAN: Now you can be obvious about it. Just jump in like the kid and yell and brag about being first. Or about deserving to be first. What I mean is you got to stand back a little. (*Dolan has walked Arnall around in a circle and is about to take second place.*) Maybe be in second place for a while. Then when nobody's looking, you kind of sneak into first place. But first you got to build up everybody's confidence that you're really one hell of a nice guy. You smile a lot. You say nice things all the time like, "Great night for a line," or, "Terrific wife you've got there, Arnall, kid." Then, when everybody likes you . . . you sneak up.

ARNALL: I still don't get it.

DOLAN: (*Now in second place.*) You notice I'm second in line? You notice I was second to make it with your wife. Second in this line to make it . . . right?

ARNALL: Right.

DOLAN: There you are.

ARNALL: Why do you call that Under*dog?*

DOLAN: The easiest way to kick a dog in the balls is to be underneath him. Let him walk on top of you for a while. Take good aim. And . . .

ARNALL: I get it. (*Fleming and Molly waltz into view, and then off.*)

DOLAN: Good boy. Terrific wife you got there, Arnall. Kid. Great night for a line. (*Arnall is crying.*) What's the matter?

ARNALL: My philosophy is quite simple. Never ever leave yourself open for surprise and you'll never be surprised. Surprise brings pain. Pain is bad. No pain, no bad. No bad all good. I've got it made. (*Weeping now.*) I've got it made.

DOLAN: You've got to learn to take it easy, Arnall. You're making a wreck of yourself with all that unhappiness. You got to get happy.

ARNALL: I have a real philosophy, real philosophy. I'm supposed to be gleeful. All the time. I didn't know. I really didn't know. I knew she had friends.

DOLAN: Certainly she had friends. She's very friendly.

ARNALL: But I thought they were just friends.

DOLAN: (*Checking Fleming.*) They'll be done soon.

ARNALL: I can't stand it. I can't stand it. (*Arnall rushes to Fleming and Molly. He taps Fleming on the shoulder, "cutting in." Fleming nods and moves into line.*)

FLEMING: (*Realizing.*) Hey, I didn't finish. I didn't finish. I didn't finish. I didn't finish.

DOLAN: Hop in line. You can be third.

FLEMING: But I didn't finish! Didn't you see?

DOLAN: See? Of course I saw. You were doing it with his old lady. Right in front of his eyes!!!

FLEMING: *You* did it in front of his eyes.

DOLAN: Jesus, don't remind me.

FLEMING: I didn't finish. For Christ's sake, I'm hornier than ever.

STEPHEN: What took you so long?

FLEMING: Shut up, kid. Shut up before I finish with *you*.

ARNALL: (*Tapping out a bunny hop beat.*) Molly. It's me, Arnall. Your husband.

MOLLY: (*Shocked.*) Arnall? What the hell are you doing?

ARNALL: (*Dancing the bunny hop.*) I'm doing it. With you. My wife. A surprise, Molly! A surprise!

MOLLY: You've lost your place in line. You stepped out of line!

ARNALL: (*Tapping away.*) I couldn't stand it. Watching all those others doing it with you. It drove me crazy. It made me want you, Molly. I really want you.

MOLLY: (*Tapping with him.*) Oh, Arnall. You're such a bore.

ARNALL: (*Humming "Tiptoe Through The Tulips"* before he speaks.*) Please, Molly. Please.

MOLLY: (*They're dancing now.*) Well, you're doing it, aren't you?

ARNALL: (*Hums "Tiptoe" and dances a bit.*) I am. Oh. I am. Oh, I like it, Molly. I like it.

MOLLY: (*Bored sick.*) Hurry up, Arnall. Hurry up.

ARNALL: (*Stops.*) Shall I sing?

MOLLY: (*Angry.*) Just hurry up, Arnall. Just hurry up. (*Arnall sings "Tiptoe Through the Tulips," picking it up in the middle and continuing to end of song. Exits.*)

DOLAN: (*Pauses.*) Now that's the way it should be. A man and his wife. That's a beautiful thing. Great night, huh? (*Stephen, helping Arnall and Molly gain speed, sings his wallet.*)

STEPHEN: (*To "Tiptoe" tune.*)

Saks' card and a Hertz card and an Avis card
And a Un-ih-Card Card
Diners Club and a Chemical New York.

DOLAN: That's a beautiful sight, isn't it?

FLEMING: It's terrible. *Terrible.* I never finished.

DOLAN: Just wait, Fleming. Let the husband finish first. That's decent enough. Then you can finish. You can start from scratch.

MOLLY: Hurry up, Arnall.

FLEMING: Yeah, Arnall. Hurry up. (*Arnall's erection and song begin to "die" offstage.*)

STEPHEN: (*A dirge, sings:*)
That's one's dead. That's one's dead.
That's one's dead. That's one's dead.

DOLAN: Sing a happy song, kid. For Christ's sake. That part of your wallet depresses the hell out of me.

STEPHEN: (*He sings again.*)
Henry Brown, insurance man.
Harry Schwartz, the tailor.
Alvin Krantz, delivery service.
My Uncle Max, the sailor.
Franklin National Saving Bank.
(*Molly and Arnall bunny hop onto stage with gusto.*)
Doyle, and Dane and Bernbach.

DOLAN: That's nice. That's got a beat.

STEPHEN: (*Stops. Speaks.*) He's ready! He's ready!

ARNALL: (*Screams.*) Surprise, Molly! Surprise!

DOLAN: That's a beautiful thing. (*Arnall collapses in Molly's arms.*)

ARNALL: Were you surprised, Molly?

MOLLY: Let me go, Arnall.

FLEMING: No. Not yet. Not yet. I never finished. (*Fleming grabs Molly.*)

MOLLY: Hey.

FLEMING: (*Explaining, a whiny child.*) I never finished.

MOLLY: Take the gum out of your mouth.

FLEMING: Oh. (*Puts gum behind ear.*)

ARNALL: What place am I in?

DOLAN: Third.

STEPHEN: Last.

ARNALL: I'd rather be third.

STEPHEN: You're in last place.

DOLAN: Shut up, kid. Don't listen to the kid. You're third. Two from the front. You did very well. I watched you all the way.

ARNALL: It's been a long time. My legs are all rubbery. I'm very nauseous. I've got to practice up a little, maybe. A little practice and I'd be better.

DOLAN: You did good.

ARNALL: I'll practice up some. (*Fleming sings "Take Me Out To The Ball Game."* They dance off.*) Oh, God! Him again.

DOLAN: Don't watch. You'll feel better. (*Pours beer into Arnall's mouth. Fleming, offstage, continues song at a more rapid speed.*) You feeling any better now?

ARNALL: (*Screams.*) I want it again.

DOLAN: You what?

ARNALL: I want it again. Molly's mine. I want it again. I liked it.

DOLAN: You'll get sick again, pal. You know it makes you sick.

ARNALL: I like it. I like it. (*Fleming and Molly dance back on – past Arnall. They stop in front of Dolan.*)

DOLAN: Fleming. (*No answer.*) Fleming! (*No answer.*) Fleming. (*Dolan reaches over with his foot and kicks Fleming a hard one in the behind. Fleming wheels around, dazzled.*)

FLEMING: What's the matter!

DOLAN: (*Flatly.*) Her old man wants it again.

FLEMING: (*Overlapping.*) He had it already.

DOLAN: (*Overlapping.*) He wants it again.

STEPHEN: (*Wiseass.*) He wants it again.

FLEMING: (*Angrily.*) I heard Dolan.

DOLAN: (*Flatly.*) He wants it again.

ARNALL: (*Cockily.*) I want it again.

FLEMING: (*As though no one knows. To Molly.*) Your old man wants it again.

MOLLY: (*A pronouncement.*) I want the boy.

DOLAN: (*Senses the unjust.*) But your old man wants it.

MOLLY: (*A solid pronounce.*) I want the boy.

DOLAN: (*Realizes he might move up the Big Space.*) She wants you.

STEPHEN: (*Exhausted with the understanding of this complicated moment.*) I heard her.

MOLLY: (*Moving in.*) I want you, boy.

STEPHEN: (*Holding his eyes.*) I heard you.

ARNALL: (*Overlapping.*) She likes them young.

FLEMING: (*Overlapping.*) What about me?

DOLAN: You had two chances.

FLEMING: I didn't finish.

DOLAN: You had two chances.

FLEMING: I was almost finished. Some bastard kicked me!

DOLAN: Two chances. I only had one. The kid only had one.

FLEMING: The kid took two.

DOLAN: Two on one chance. *He's a kid.*

ARNALL: She likes the young ones. She always likes the young ones.

MOLLY: Come here, boy.

STEPHEN: (*Pretends to be engrossed in his wallet.*) American Express. Chemical New York. VISA card. My library card! (*Stephen is pulled out by Molly. Dolan jumps up into first position. Fleming jumps over Arnall.*)

DOLAN: I'm first! I'm first.

STEPHEN: You've made me lose my place.

MOLLY: You have such a wonderful bone structure.

ARNALL: She always always likes them young. (*Stephen knows he's out for now. He laughs. He and Molly dance off, singing together in harmony.*) I'm last, last, last. Last dammit!

DOLAN: You're third. (*To Fleming.*) Tell him he's third.

FLEMING: You're third.

ARNALL: I'm last. There are only three of us. One, two, three. Three is me. I'm last.

DOLAN: Two over there. Those two. The kid and your terrific wife.

FLEMING: (*Counting on his fingers.*) That makes five.

DOLAN: You're two from the front and two from the back. Two from the first and two from the last. You're the average. (*Stephen sings lightly now as he and Molly dance. Arnall tells his story to the world.*)

ARNALL: I would like to tell the story of my marriage. I worked hard every night. I knew she had friends, but I never knew they were doing it. (*Pauses.*) That's the story of my marriage. (*There is a shaggy-dog silence.*)

DOLAN: As first man, I say that Arnall gets a chance to do it again as soon as the kid is finished. (*Stephen screams the ending of his song: "Piano."*) The kid is finished.

FLEMING: Have a bash, Arnall.

ARNALL: I'll lose my place in line. Never mind.

DOLAN: Stay put, then. Fleming? You want a whack at it? You want a third, uh, try?

FLEMING: I'm second. It ain't worth it now. You want another one,

Dolan? Huh? Why don't you have a go at it? Give it another bash.

DOLAN: You're pretty obvious, Fleming. Pretty obvious. Did anybody every tell you how dumb you are? Did anybody ever take the time to tell you just how really dumb and stupid you really are?

FLEMING: (*After a hideously long pause.*) You think I don't know? You think I'm too stupid to know how dumb I am? Brains ain't everything, you know? I ain't exactly at the end of the line. It ain't over yet. (*Stephen walks to the opposite side of the line and squares off with Dolan, eye to eye. Stephen speaks with simple authority.*)

STEPHEN: The line's facing the wrong way.

DOLAN: (*Incredulously.*) What the hell are you talking about, kid?

STEPHEN: (*To all, an announcement.*) The line's facing the wrong way. (*To Dolan.*) The line's facing the wrong way. I'm first. (*Stephen and Dolan eye each other for a full half-minute with terrifying tension. Nobody moves. Stephen smiles a frozen smile. Dolan wipes his hands with a handkerchief, checking everyone in line. As Dolan checks to one side, Molly quickly snakes around into Second Place, behind Stephen. Dolan does a take. Arnall quickly slides around, following Molly. He's now Third in Stephen's line. Dolan does a full take. Then Dolan turns to Fleming and signals Fleming to "take it easy," to wait, to rest. Fleming nods agreement. Suddenly, as soon as Fleming's settled down, Dolan races into Fourth Place in Stephen's line. Fleming sees and races after him, ending up last. When Stephen's line is settled, the very instant, in fact, that Stephen's line is full, Stephen steps over the Line into the true First position. He smiles. All others freeze, staring at him. Molly breaks and jumps into second.*)

MOLLY: I'm second! (*Dolan bolts into third.*)

DOLAN: I'm third!

FLEMING: (*Leaping into fourth.*) I'm fourth!

ARNALL: (*Limping into last.*) I'm last. Bitch-damn-crap! I'm really last now.

DOLAN: (*Overlapping.*) Oh, man. That was rotten, kid. Really and truly filthy rotten.

FLEMING: (*Overlapping.*) That kid is no good. I told you that kid was no good.

ARNALL: (*Overlapping.*) Always the young ones. I'm sick of it. Sick of it. Sick of the young ones getting to be first.

DOLAN: (*Screams.*) We'll get him, Arnall.

FLEMING: Not finished. Not first! We'll get him. (*Screams.*) We're gonna get you, kid!

ARNALL: (*Whining.*) Cuckolded. Cuckolded. I'm a buffoon. (*Screams.*) A buffoon!!!

MOLLY: (*Desperately sexual, caressing with her voice.*) You have the face of a president. A movie star. A senator. You have a Kennedy's face. A beautiful face.

FLEMING: (*Overlapping.*) Breathe the air now, kid. Breathe it deep! We're gonna get you!

DOLAN: (*Overlapping.*) Third. First to goddam third!

ARNALL: (*Overlapping.*) Last. Really last. This time there's no question.

STEPHEN: (*A maniacal scream.*) SHUT UP, IDIOTS!!!

FLEMING: Who the hell are you calling "idiot"???

STEPHEN: All of you. Idiots. Fools. Lemmings. Pigs. Lint.

DOLAN: Lint?

MOLLY: Lint?

ARNALL: Lint?

FLEMING: Lint?

STEPHEN: Lint!

FLEMING: Oh boy. Oh boy. That's the limit. We're gonna' have your ass, kid.

STEPHEN: It's too late, idiots. I've won. I'm in first and anyone who isn't in first is an idiot. We've got nothing in common, so why talk about it?

DOLAN: We've all got something in common, kid. And don't you forget it, either.

STEPHEN: What's that, Dolan???

DOLAN: We've all been at his terrific wife. Whatever she's got, we've got.

FLEMING: That's true. We're like a club. Whatever she's got, we've got. (*Does a huge "take" to Arnall.*) What's she got?

STEPHEN: They're right, damn you. You let them all have you. Even your husband.

ARNALL: (*Hopefully.*) Molly?

MOLLY: Nobody had me.

FLEMING: Nobody but all of us!

MOLLY: Nobody had me.

STEPHEN: (*Turns sharply about to Molly.*) Everybody had you . . . everybody.

MOLLY: Nobody had me.

DOLAN: She's crazy, too. (*To Arnall.*) You've got a crazy wife, Mister.

MOLLY: Nobody had me, get it? Nobody. *I* had all of you. *I* did the doing. Not you. *I* made the choices. You all wanted to be first, what kept you from it, huh? What kept you? (*Pushes Stephen over the line, out of first place, viciously. He falls to one side, D.L. Shocked.*) I'm first now. *Me!*

STEPHEN: (*Wandering, confused.*) You pushed me. She pushed me.

MOLLY: I'm first now!

DOLAN: She's crazy. You've got a crazy wife, Mister. This is a terrible night.

STEPHEN: Don't flatter yourself, Molly. Not for a second. You've screwed your way to first and you'll be screwed right out of first. That's the way it's always been and that's the way it's always going to be. This line's my last, Molly. You really think I'm going to let you come in first?

MOLLY: I am first. I am first. And I'm not moving. I screwed my way to first and now I'm resting. Maybe this is my last line too. Look who's first. Just look who's first. Me. Molly. Just where I knew I'd be from the moment I saw this line.

FLEMING: You got yourself a real bitch for a wife there, Arnall. A real bitch.

ARNALL: I know. I know.

MOLLY: I know what you've been thinking all night. Here we are, four big shots. One woman in line. Might as well roll her over, just to kill time. That's what you're always thinking. That's what every line's about, right? And you think in any other place you'd never give me a look . . . but . . . as long as we're all killing time together . . . why not? 'Course, under *normal* conditions, she'd never be good enough for me. Well, I've got a piece of news for you all: under any conditions, none of you is good enough for me. Not a one of you!

STEPHEN: (*Crosses to her.*) Molly. You're good enough for me.

MOLLY: Go to the back of the line, boy. You didn't satisfy me. You didn't make it. You didn't thrill me. You need experience. You make love like a child.

STEPHEN: What about my beautiful bones?

MOLLY: Go to the back of the line.

DOLAN: That's telling the wise-ass kid. Go to the back of the line, kid. You heard the lady.

MOLLY: Don't gloat. Don't lick your lips. I could have done better with an ape than with you.

FLEMING: Terrific, Molly. An ape, Dolan. An ape.

MOLLY: Are you the one with the beer and the gum who's too old and tired to finish?

FLEMING: What's that supposed to mean?

ARNALL: Molly? Molly? Is it me?

MOLLY: Don't be a bore, Arnall. You couldn't satisfy a canary.

DOLAN: You've run out. If none of us satisfied you, who did?

MOLLY: None of you. Simple as that. I am an unsatisfied woman still looking for a man. You all failed.

DOLAN: I've had better than you, tubby, and I mean some real beauties. And they've screamed for more. Screamed for more!

MOLLY: More money? Okay. Sure. I can understand that.

FLEMING: I've had models.

DOLAN: Screw your models. I had one in a car once.

FLEMING: Yeah. You told me.

MOLLY: I'm first. I'm unsatisfied. I've had four men. One three times. One unfinished. And I'm unsatisfied.

ARNALL: Don't let her get to you. Don't let her get you going. She'll drive you all crazy. Make surprises. Ruin all your philosophies. She'll hide your shirts.

MOLLY: Arnall, you're such a bore.

STEPHEN: (*Crosses to her. Whispers.*) I've got something to tell you.

MOLLY: To the back of the line, sonny. You lost. You're last . . . move.

DOLAN: You're out of line completely, kid. She's right. When the crowds come, you'll be left out altogether. (*Stephen wanders to R. portal.*)

MOLLY: I hope there's a man in the *crowd*. One man.

ARNALL: You see what I mean? She won't let up now. Now that she's first, she'll just keep pouring it on.

DOLAN: She's worse than *my* old lady. Much worse. My old lady's a dog, but nothing like yours. Yours is the biggest dog of all. Queen dog. Yeah. She's the biggest dog of all. How'd you get stuck with her, anyway?

ARNALL: She picked me up at a party. I was at a party. The lights were dim. I felt a hand sneak between my legs. I was only fifteen. It was Molly. She taught me everything I know. I don't know anything either.

STEPHEN: (*A proclamation.*) When I make love to a woman, I never shut my eyes. Never. I watch. I watch and I listen to every movement she makes.

FLEMING: (*Embarrassed.*) Shut up.

DOLAN: (*Wants to hear Stephen's "secret."*) You shut up, Fleming.

STEPHEN: I listen to every movement she makes. So that every time I move, I understand her response. One little wiggle to the left, one little wiggle to the right and I get a response I remember. I make notes. I have a whole loose-leaf binder filled with notes and half another filled as well. All kinds of notes. How to wiggle front and back. How short women respond. How tall women respond. How certain ethnic groups respond.

MOLLY: What did you learn from me, little boy?

STEPHEN: (*His guise has worked. He knows it. He sets up his next line carefully, ready to strike. He moves into position close to Molly.*) Never screw an ugly, greedy, slob like you. Always to follow my natural desire. Only screw who I want, when I want. If I had followed my natural desire, I never would have screwed you. Not once. Not twice, certainly. Not three times. It was all an incredible waste of my incredibly valuable time. That's what I wanted to tell you.

MOLLY: (*Explodes.*) You little squirt. You little jerk. (*She charges at him in a rage. He knocks her aside and regains first position . . . Molly is out of line.*)

STEPHEN: (*With a flourish.*) Gentlemen, I am first again.

FLEMING: You've really got to hand it to that kid. Go on, Dolan. Hand it to the kid.

DOLAN: (*He is standing on Stephen's toes.*) Nice work, kid.

ARNALL: (*A small bitch.*) I'm not last. You're last, Molly. I'm ahead of you. You're last.

DOLAN: (*Ruefully.*) Nice work, kid.

STEPHEN: Say it again, Dolan.

DOLAN: Nice work, kid. (*He pushes Stephen violently off-stage. Dolan takes first. Stephen falls into the audience.*) Look who's first now, will you?

STEPHEN: You pushed me. He pushed me. Hey, he pushed. Did you see him? That's not fair, Dolan.

DOLAN: I'm first.

FLEMING: (*Jumps forward.*) I'm second.

ARNALL: (*Jumps forward.*) I'm third.

MOLLY: I'm fourth.

STEPHEN: (*Starts walking up the aisle.*) I'm out.

DOLAN: In every crowd, there's a winner. A winner. I waited back there. I hung in. Look at me now.

STEPHEN: (*From the back of the theatre.*) You broke the rules, Dolan.

DOLAN: What rules?

STEPHEN: (*From another aisle.*) He pushed me.

DOLAN: She pushed you.

STEPHEN: (*Screaming.*) She's a woman. That's different.

FLEMING: That's true, Dolan. It's different when it's a woman. Especially that woman.

ARNALL: You see, Molly's always breaking rules. She breaks everything. Dishes. Cups. Saucers.

MOLLY: Just shut your dumb mouth, Arnall.

FLEMING: Yeah. Shut up, Arnall. We got to figure this out.

DOLAN: What's to figure out? I'm up front. Head of the line. I won. That's pretty simple.

FLEMING: Yeah, but you pushed the kid. We sort of had an unwritten rule here. I mean, none of us did any pushing.

DOLAN: You want to push me, Fleming?

FLEMING: Hey, look. Don't start that stuff! I'm a hell of a lot tougher than you, pal. You want to start that stuff and that's the kind of stuff you'll get. You know what I mean?

STEPHEN: (*Walking back to the stage.*) I'd hate to see you start a fight over me, Fleming. It's probably better that I just stay right out of line. You people can handle things on your own. You don't need me.

FLEMING: Yeah, I suppose.

DOLAN: What the hell are you trying to do, kid? You're gonna' just let me stay in First? You ain't gonna' trick me out of it?

STEPHEN: (*Standing, facing the stage.*) You don't trust people. That's your trouble, Dolan. You think everybody's out to get you all the time, don't you?

DOLAN: I don't think of anybody but NUMBER ONE. I hung in back there in second all that time. I knew what I was doing. I've watched you up there. I knew when to strike. I knew when my iron was hot. I waited it out. I'm first. That's simple, isn't it?

STEPHEN: (*Leaning on the stage.*) There are ways of getting to first that are acceptable and ways of getting to first that are unacceptable. Women and children, excluded, of course.

FLEMING: That's right.

DOLAN: What's right?

FLEMING: The thing he said about women and children. That's always the way about women and children.

STEPHEN: Women and children first.

FLEMING: Women and children first.

STEPHEN: Dolan's not a women.

FLEMING: Dolan's not a children.

ARNALL: Dolan's none of those things.

MOLLY: Dolan's nothing.

STEPHEN: Everybody's something.

FLEMING: Not Dolan!!! (*Fleming pushes Dolan violently off-stage, and takes first!*) Holy Christ! I'm in first place!

ARNALL: I'm second.

MOLLY: (*Jumping up.*) I'm third.

DOLAN: (*Crawling back on stage.*) For Christ's sakes. For crying out loud. Fleming pushed me.

STEPHEN: You changed the rules. You pushed first.

DOLAN: She pushed first.

FLEMING: Holy Christ! I'm really in first place. I'm first guy. Top dog. (*And he pushes Dolan off-stage again.*)

DOLAN: He pushed me right out of first place.

MOLLY: (*She pushes Arnall.*) Be a winner, Arnall. (*She pushes Arnall so hard, he clobbers Fleming right out of first place. Arnall is first now.*)

FLEMING: Hey. Hey. Hey. (*Dolan crawls back on to the stage and Fleming crashes into him – Dolan flies off-stage again.*)

ARNALL: I didn't do that. She did that. She pushed me so hard I pushed you. I didn't push you. Honest to God, I didn't push you. Here. Take it back. (*Arnall walks right out of first place, trembling. He leads Fleming by the hand back into first place. Molly stands frozen. Astonished. Dolan crawls back on stage and into second.*)

FLEMING: I'm first again.

DOLAN: I'm second. Hah! I'm second.

ARNALL: (*Slipping, mincing into third, in front of an astonished Molly, he says simply:*) I'm third.

MOLLY: Arnall, you damn dumb fool. Look what you did. Look what you did, you damn dumb dummy.

ARNALL: I gave that to you, Fleming. I gave you first. But you've got to protect me!

FLEMING: From what?

ARNALL: Her.

FLEMING: Why?

ARNALL: Please, Fleming?

FLEMING: Why?

MOLLY: Damn you, Arnall. Damn you. (*She beats him, as a child swatting a mosquito.*)

ARNALL: See? See what I mean? I need help, Fleming. Help me, Fleming.

FLEMING: (*He walks to Molly and talks to her, reasonably.*) Now look, ma'am. I don't want to hurt a lady. I've never hurt a lady.

ARNALL: She's no lady.

DOLAN: (*Jumps into first, incredulously.*) I'm first again! (*Everybody freezes, out of line, as Dolan stands alone.*)

FLEMING: Now just wait a God-damned minute!

DOLAN: I'm first, first! (*Fleming clobbers Dolan.*)

ARNALL: This is awful. (*Jumps in first.*)

MOLLY: This is your fault, Arnall. (*Pushes Arnall out.*)

STEPHEN: (*From the audience, giggling.*) I'd say it was Dolan's fault.

DOLAN: Knock it off, kid.

STEPHEN: Hell, I'll knock it off. If you hadn't broken the rules and pushed me, we'd be in a perfectly straight line. This is chaos, friends. Chaos. (*Arnall dashes into first place.*)

ARNALL: I'm first. I'm first! (*Dolan slams Arnall to the ground.*)

DOLAN: No, you're not. I am. I'm First.

MOLLY: (*Attacking Dolan, she kicks his testicles.*) Move out of there. Move. (*They all end up in a horrible fist fight, ending with Dolan hitting Molly fiercely . . . Arnall crawls in and bites Molly's leg.*)

FLEMING: (*Astonished.*) You hit her. You hit her!

STEPHEN: See? See what you have? Chaos. Pure, plain and simple. Chaos.

FLEMING: You're God damned right it is, kid. God damned right. (*Fleming has Dolan's arm pinned.*) Help the kid back in the line. Go on.

DOLAN: Are you crazy?

FLEMING: I've seen this happen before. Help him back!

STEPHEN: (*Walking into line, into first.*) Anybody mind my being First?

DOLAN: I held back, dammit! I waited! What is this????

FLEMING: (*Screams at Dolan.*) Don't!

DOLAN: (*Frightened.*) Okay. Okay. (*Dolan suddenly lurches for First.*

Fleming grabs him and beats him with three quick terrifying punches.) Ughhh. Ahhh. Ughhh.

FLEMING: I said "don't" and I mean "don't"! Everybody hear me? Huh? Everybody hear me clear.

DOLAN: (*Whipped.*) I'm second.

FLEMING: Okay. I'll stay in Third. 'Til we get straightened out. You, Arnall. You get Fourth. And you, you fat bitch, you started this pushing business. You get in Fifth.

ARNALL: (*As a 3-year-old child.*) I'm not last. You're last, Molly. I'm ahead of you. You're last.

FLEMING: Everybody shut up! (*Pauses.*) Okay, kid. What do we do now?

STEPHEN: Shut up and listen. (*He presses the "on" button on his CD player and Mozart's "Eine Kleine Nachtmusik" fills the theatre.*) Can you feel him? Mozart. "Eine Kleine Nachtmusik." The Allegro. He was younger than me when he wrote this. A baby. The Allegro. Then Andante. Then Minuet. Then Rondo.

ARNALL: Austrian, right? Isn't he Austrian, Stephen?

STEPHEN: That's Mozart, for Christ's sakes! It's Mozart. I'm not first. I'm second. Stop. Please. This is crazy. This is a crazy thing. (*Stephen turns off the CD player.*)

FLEMING: You're the crazy thing.

ARNALL: (*Really spooky.*) You know how he died, Stephen? Singers came in and sang him to death. His Requiem, Stephen. They sang while he died.

STEPHEN: (*Staring at the Mozart he sees ahead of him.*) It's not true. It's not true.

ARNALL: But I was there, Stephen. I saw it. I heard it.

STEPHEN: (*Weeping.*) Stop it. Stop it.

ARNALL: I was there, Stephen. He was writing the percussion up until the last. Boom-boom. Boom-boom. (*Arnall marches singing "boom-boom."*)

STEPHEN: I'm losing my mind.

MOLLY: Arnall. You weasel, Arnall.

ARNALL: Boom-boom. Just shut up, you bitch. Just shut up. Boom-boom.

STEPHEN: No! This isn't happening! I'm first. Look at me. I'm first. I earned this, I know I did!

FLEMING: Bullshit, you did! We'll get you, kid.

DOLAN: We'll get you, kid.

ARNALL: Want me to sing it, Stephen? The Requiem? Want me to sing The Requiem now? (*He sings as a choirboy: "La-ah cree-mo-sa, Ita-es-eela. etc." He continues The Requiem and Stephen seems totally hypnotized. He walks towards Stephen and then past him. He moves around past Dolan and Fleming, who stare wide-eyed. He swings around again, softly singing, heading straight for first place.*) Boom-boom. Boom-boom. It could be lovely, Stephen. Lovely. I'll sing . . . (*Checks, sees.*) . . . and Dolan . . . boom-boom . . .

DOLAN: (*Taking a nod from Arnall.*) Boom-boom . . . boom-boom . . .

ARNALL: . . . and Fleming . . . boom-boom . . .

FLEMING: (*Confused, follows with his voice.*) Boom-boom . . . boom-boom . . .

ARNALL: will do their work . . . BOOM BOOM . . . BOOM BOOM . . . BOOM BOOM . . .

DOLAN AND FLEMING: BOOM BOOM . . . BOOM BOOM . . .

ARNALL: BOOM BOOM . . . BOOM . . . BOOM . . . BOOM BOOM . . . (*Stephen grabs his neck in anguished pain. He screams a most hideous scream and falls forward onto his face. He writhes on the floor, sobbing in agony. Arnall walks quietly into first place.*)

FLEMING: (*After a huge pause.*) That's terrible. I'll never sing with you again, Arnall.

DOLAN: Holy Jesus Christ!! Will you look at that???? (*Stephen is silently staring from the floor. He sees Arnall. He stands slowly, almost berserk now. He lunges at Arnall, grabbing his throat.*)

STEPHEN: You little twirp. You little plucked-chicken. You step back, Arnall. You're playing with fire, Arnall. Fire. You move now or I'm going to strangle you, Arnall. You'll be dead, Arnall.

ARNALL: Please, Stephen. Please. I only want Molly. I don't want first. Only Molly. Please, Stephen. Please??? (*But, Stephen's too far gone. He squeezes Arnall's throat.*)

STEPHEN: You move or I'll kill you, Arnall. Do you believe me? (*Arnall and Stephen stare at each other. A long hold.*)

ARNALL: (*Defeated.*) Yes.

STEPHEN: Back of the line, Arnall.

FLEMING: Yeah, Arnall. Back of the line. I can't see what the kid is saying when you're standing there. You're blocking me from the kid.

DOLAN: That ain't right, Arnall. Move back, Arnall.

FLEMING: Move back, Arnall.

MOLLY: (*Fiercely.*) You heard them! Move!!!

(*Arnall walks slowly to the end of the line. Broken. Defeated.*)

FLEMING: (*Breaking the horrific silence of Arnall's total humiliation.*) What's next, kid?

STEPHEN: The end. I beat all of you, not with luck, but with genius. There's only one person to beat, and you can't see him in this line. I can see him in this line. (*Stephen is now screaming at the place in front of him.*) I'll beat you. I'll die youngest, the best. And after I'm gone you'll see I can take it with me! (*Stephen turns on the CD player to an unbearable volume and slides the machine across the stage. It lands, blaring and staring up at a startled Arnall. Music fills the auditorium. Lighting shifts to red—it is a mad scene. Slowly, carefully, Stephen picks up the line – that white piece of tape that is first place itself – and eats it, as a berserk strand of spaghetti. Arnall picks up the CD player and smashes the "off" button: killing it, as though he were swatting an insect.*)

ARNALL: (*In the now-deafening silence, carefully.*) You are crazy! You are an insane, horrible child. (*Arnall draws a deep, deep breath.*)

STEPHEN: (*He's swallowed the tape by now.*) How dare you, you cuckolded little nothing!!! You let your wife – your fat horrible wife – screw on the street while you do nothing more than watch. She screws and you watch. And tomorrow you'll crawl in bed beside her with your chubby clean-but-sweaty little body begging for a whore's kiss!!!

MOLLY: You animal! You animal! Hit him, Arnall! Hit him!

ARNALL: We're much older than you are, son. You could show some respect.

STEPHEN: (*The final insult follows.*) Maybe I hate you most, Arnall. Just maybe. (*Like a bullet.*) You're a loser, Arnall.

FLEMING: It's okay, Arnall, you can hit him. Boom Boom. Boom Boom.

STEPHEN: I won! I did it! I did it. I did it. I won. I won. (*Chasing them all.*) Come on, Arnall. It's okay now. Hit me. Scratch my eyes out. Kill me.

ARNALL: Me?

STEPHEN: You. Anybody. Come on. Let's get on with it.

DOLAN: We're gonna get you, kid.

STEPHEN: Do it, Dolan. Do it.

FLEMING: Go on, Arnall. Get him. Boom Boom.

MOLLY: Hit him, Arnall. Boom Boom. (*Molly gets the recorder and gives it to Arnall.)*

ARNALL: Me?

DOLAN: Kill him, Arnall. Boom Boom.

ARNALL: Me?

DOLAN AND FLEMING: Kill him, Arnall. Boom Boom.

STEPHEN: (*He laughs maniacally.*) I can take it with me. I finally won! (*Stephen kneels, head up, eyes closed – waiting to be killed. Dolan, Fleming and Molly chant "Boom Boom" over and over, urging Arnall to kill Stephen.*)

ARNALL: You son of a bitch. You son of a bitch!!! (*Arnall takes tape recorder and raises it to kill Stephen. He stops, as Molly shrieks.*)

MOLLY: (*Scream. They all stop and jump back one step.*)

STEPHEN: (*Opens his eyes, stands, amazed.*) What's wrong? Why are you stopping? Somebody's got to kill me.

ARNALL: Us?

FLEMING: Kill him?

MOLLY: Kill him?

STEPHEN: You've got to kill me. I've got to die first. Please . . . please . . . please . . . please . . . please . . . (*Dolan walks into first position, but of course the line is gone. Dolan is astonished.*)

DOLAN: (*A whine.*) Where's the line?

FLEMING: The line! Where is it?

ARNALL: The line!

MOLLY: Arnall! The line's gone.

ARNALL: Where'd it go?

STEPHEN: (*Burps a little, smiles.*) I ate it.

FLEMING: What?

STEPHEN: I ate it. (*He groans.*)

MOLLY: He ate it. He ate it?

FLEMING: He ate it. He ate it?

DOLAN: He ate it?

ARNALL: He *ate* it?

STEPHEN: I ate it.

MOLLY: See? I'm right. He is crazy. He's really crazy.

FLEMING: I told you that, lady. I told you that the second you walked up. He's really crazy.

STEPHEN: What is this? I'm supposed to die! (*He's stunned, as it appears that he isn't going to die after all.*)

MOLLY: He wanted us to beat him so he'd die so there'd be a dead kid in first. And we were supposed to just watch.

ARNALL: How could we watch a thing like that?

FLEMING: Why not? We've been watching everything else.

MOLLY: Oh, my God! What if I'm pregnant?

ARNALL: Pregnant? Molly. A son? A son, Molly?

FLEMING: (*Thrilled, laughs a relieved laugh.*) I never finished.

MOLLY: He finished. The way it counts.

FLEMING: (*Pointing to Stephen.*) You see, Arnall? They never really forget the first one.

ARNALL: What?

DOLAN: Jesus! What a wife you've got there. What a rotten night! (*To Stephen.*) Give us back the line, kid. They're going to open soon and we need a line.

MOLLY: They'll open and we won't have a line. (*Steps behind Stephen.*) And I'm only second.

ARNALL: I'm right beside you.

FLEMING: Me too.

DOLAN: For crying out loud! We're all second!

FLEMING: This looks very phony. Give us back our line, Steve.

MOLLY: Please, Stephie. Please.

ARNALL: Give it back, Steven.

DOLAN: Cough it up, *Stephen.* Steve, Stevie. Cough it up. (*Stephen begins to gag and choke. The line begins to appear from his lips.*)

FLEMING: Hey. The line.

DOLAN: There it is!

MOLLY: The line.

ARNALL: He *did* eat it. (*Dolan grabs the line from Stephen's mouth and runs across stage.*)

DOLAN: He took it with him. (*Stephen rises, dazzled. Dolan runs downstage-left. Fleming runs to Stephen.*)

STEPHEN: I didn't take it with me. I didn't go anywhere. Damn it all. I'm not dead. (*Stephen begins to go through a series of contortions as a woman in labor.*)

DOLAN: (*Standing victoriously, his own line on the floor.*) I'm first. I had to wait for my chance, but I'm first. Had to wait. Wait. Hang back. But I'm first. (*Stephen gags again and a second piece of tape appears: another line. Fleming grabs the line and stares at it as a moron might, then follows Dolan's example, setting his line, downstage-right.*)

FLEMING: I'm first! Finally, I'm first! I should be first. I was the first one here. Fair's fair. (*Stephen retches as he stands up. Molly steps forward and kisses Stephen full on the lips. She comes away with a piece of line as her reward, between her teeth. Stephen is now a dispenser. He walks mechanically, emitting sounds like a berserk Coca-Cola machine.*)

MOLLY: (*Setting her line down: her first.*) He gave me first. He made me first. he gave me first place. (*Fleming, Molly and Dolan now stare, dreamy-eyed with victory. All of them will continue repeating their victory speeches until Arnall's final line, which he will repeat alone in the silence. Arnall slaps Stephen on the back and a line falls into his hands.*)

ARNALL: (*After placing his line upstage-right.*) Molly. Darling. I'm first. I didn't want to be first. I never wanted first. But I'm first. And I like it, Molly! First is good. (*Stephen still walks as a machine, puking up a final scrap of line. He grabs it and just as he places it on the floor downstage-center, but then he sees the others in their victory stances. He understands. He throws his line away, into the audience. As he turns to leave,* THE LIGHTS SWITCH OFF.)

THE PLAY IS OVER.

IT'S CALLED THE SUGAR PLUM

"The killing of the nurses in Chicago
was a quantity killing, not a quality killing."
—Newspaper interview with Truman Capote,
author of In Cold Blood

IT'S CALLED THE SUGAR PLUM was first presented at the Astor Place Theatre in New York City (along with THE INDIAN WANTS THE BRONX) on January 17, 1968 by Ruth Newton Productions in association with Diana Mathews. It was directed by James Hammerstein and designed by Fred Voelpel. The cast was as follows, in order of appearance:

WALLACE ZUCKERMAN .... John Pleshette
JOANNA DIBBLE .... Marsha Mason

Introduction

It's Called The Sugar Plum was one my of earliest plays, written and produced when I was 18 years old, under the title *This Play Is About Me.* The play involved three teenaged friends fighting to be the most significant among the survivors of a recently deceased friend (killed, in Harvard Square, while skateboarding in the rain). Ultimately, the play reveals that each of the three survivors is willing to take the blame for their friend's death, as long as they will be considered The Most Significant Friend. The play ends with the lines "This play is about me, isn't it? ISN'T IT?" ...

When looking for a curtain-raiser for *The Indian Wants The Bronx,* several years later, I came upon a script of *This Play Is About Me,* and set about doing a major overhaul. (No self-respecting 25-year-old could ever allow a play he'd written at age 18 to hit the boards without a major overhaul!) Thus, *Sugar Plum,* as it now exists, was first written. When I finished the first draft, I quickly gave it over to Tullio Garzone, who'd directed an early version of *Indian.* He fell in love with *It's Called The Sugar Plum* and insisted that it was the perfect companion for *Indian.*

I'm sure he was incorrect. *It's Called The Sugar Plum* is a sweet, fragile play. By contrast, *The Indian Wants The Bronx* has the sweetness and fragility of a sledgehammer. When the two plays were initially done, off-Broadway, *Sugar Plum* suffered terribly in comparison to *Indian.* At Intermission, the audience loved *It's Called The Sugar Plum.* At the end of the evening, however, after they'd been terrified and beaten up, emotionally, by *The Indian Wants The Bronx,* the curtain-raiser, *It's Called The Sugar Plum,* had virtually been forgotten. The critics were kind to *It's Called The Sugar Plum,* but, clearly, they preferred *The Indian Wants The Bronx.*

To my amazement, and my delight, when the show closed in NYC, and the two plays were offered for production around the country,

It's Called The Sugar Plum found nearly as many productions as *The Indian Wants The Bronx.* Internationally, as well. 25 years later, both plays are still being done. (I have just approved a new French translation of *It's Called The Sugar Plum,* that will be performed in Paris, next season, nearly 30 years after *Sugar Plum* first opened in NYC! This, for me, defines the word thrilling.)

It's Called The Sugar Plum was first cast with Marsha Mason playing Joanna Dibble. Let me say it, quickly and clearly, Marsha was wonderful. She was 21 years old, and movie-star beautiful. Also, talented, big-time. But, somehow, our erstwhile Producer (the same woman who refused to cast Al Pacino in *Indian*) wanted Marsha out of the show. For the life of me, I cannot remember how this sordid act was executed, but, we were suddenly faced with finding a replacement for the role of Joanna Dibble in *It's Called The Sugar Plum.*

"Al has a new girl-friend who acts."

That is precisely the way Jill Clayburgh was first introduced to me—by John Cazale. You can imagine how excited I was to meet Jill. I'd adored Marsha and was deeply upset that she'd left the cast of *It's Called The Sugar Plum.* Needless to say, for me, Jill Clayburgh was what the French call a *coup de foudre* ... love at first sight. Jill was instantly brilliant in *It's Called The Sugar Plum* ... funny, scary, totally nuts. She wowed the critics and audiences in Italy, that summer, at the Spoleto Festival. So strong and positive is my memory of Jill's work in *It's Called The Sugar Plum,* I can almost forgive her for marrying another playwright.

Sugar Plum has always managed to attract exciting actresses. Maureen Lipmann was unforgettable in the play's London premiere, as was Collette Castel, playing opposite Laurent Terzieff in the play's Paris premiere. Another bit of exciting casting for *Sugar Plum* occurred, recently, when Ione Skye (my son has a wife who acts) was cast opposite Fisher Stevens in A&E (Television) Network's recent, superb production of *It's Called The Sugar Plum.*

About *It's Called The Sugar Plum,* c.Now. When A&E announced *Sugar Plum* in their line-up, I was really quite surprised by my own negative reaction. The prospect of providing a play for my son and daughter-in-law to perform was a pleasant one. But, when Push came to Shove, Adam was off shooting a movie, and couldn't meet A&E's schedule. For me, suddenly, the prospect being fiftysomething years old and allowing the Country to watch a play I'd (essentially) written at age 18, became, well, daunting.

I have, at least in recent years, taken pride in letting go of my work (as opposed to The Old Days, when I was rather well known for slugging directors and producers, once or twice a season). But, somehow, this fragile, innocent play—light years away from what I'd been writing in the last two decades—worried me. Was it too soft? Was it too sweet? Was its innocence embarrassing? I'd actually considered pulling the play ... I'd rehearsed a reasonable speech to make to the producer. But, in the end, as a courtesy to my daughter-in-law, really, I visited a rehearsal ... and not a great one. I watched Fisher and Ione, with immeasurable talent and charm, breath life into young people I knew so well, so many years past ... and there and then, I thought to myself: What is this business of playwriting, finally, if not to create a record of what Life was like, in our time, on our little dot on the planet Earth? As serious playwrights, we can do no more. We can do no less.

And so, the show, like life, went on.

Characters

WALLACE ZUCKERMAN
JOANNA DIBBLE

Setting

A cramped, one-room flat in Cambridge, Massachusetts.
Late afternoon,
the present.

IT'S CALLED THE SUGAR PLUM

The setting is a dormitory-styled, one-room, student flat in Cambridge, Massachusetts.

The furnishing is scruffy, second-hand. A wooden table with three chairs is set stage left. A single bed, stage right. The walls are covered with mementos of college life: a school blanket, odd photographs, etc. A second bed is used for storage of books, etc. There are some books and magazines scattered about. A stack of newspapers is on the table.

Wallace Zuckerman scans the newspapers. He is 22 years old, rather thin, dressed with a planned sloppiness.

He studies the newspapers carefully, stopping to re-read articles, snips them out, and pastes them into a scrapbook.

A transistor radio is heard in the background.

Open in blackout . . . music and commercial on radio. Radio is covered by newspapers.

The Announcer's voice is heard, faintly. Wallace now starts throwing papers behind bed, uncovering radio.

Lights begin to fade. Action is seen as described above.

ANNOUNCER: How much meat do you think you can get for $39.95? Ten pounds? Twenty pounds? Boston Freezer Plan gives you MORE MEAT THAN YOU EVER BELIEVED POSSIBLE! That's right, folks. For just $39.95 Boston Freezer Plan will give you more meat than your butcher. (*Zuckerman finds and picks up the radio and switches stations quickly, so there is an inter-dispersing of the radio commercial with bits of the news broadcast and music. He checks his wristwatch. On cue, there is a thunk at the door, as a newspaper is thrown against it. Wallace rises, crosses to door, opens it, gets paper, closes door. He leaves paper on stove, listens to radio. As he begins to scan the front page of the newspaper, the commercial ends with . . .*)

NEW ANNOUNCER: . . . dollars down, just ten extra pennies a day. Boston Freezer Plan will supply a spanking new Rhotostatic 28-cubic-foot freezer right in your kitchen or pantry. (*He switches the dial.*)

ANNOUNCER: . . . There is speculation that the soil purchased last month to refertilize the Common is the very soil that's been missing. (*He switches the dial again. Music is heard.*)

SINGERS: Lonely streets. Lonely streets. Lonelier when you're all alone. Lovely when you want to be alone . . . (*He switches the dial once more, then scans the front page again, setting the radio on the table.*)

NEW ANNOUNCER: Don't even think once. Call your good neighbor from . . . (*Chorus sings.*) "Boston Freezer . . . that's the Plan!" (*Just as Zuckerman is about to turn the page, the newscaster comes back on.*)

ANNOUNCER: Cambridge. Frank Weeks Simpson, 21 . . . (*Zuckerman throws down the newspaper and runs to the radio, kneeling, he turns up the volume.*) . . . was pronounced dead on arrival last night at Massachusetts General Hospital. He was run down and killed as he slipped under the wheels of a passing automobile on Mount Auburn Street in Cambridge. The pavement was wet from last night's heavy rainfall and Simpson, riding a skateboard, slipped and fell, just as the moving car was upon him. The driver of the car was 22-year-old Harvard student Wallace Zuckerman . . . (*Announcer pronounces Zuckerman like "suckerman." Zuckerman corrects the radio, pronouncing Zuckerman like "Zoo-ker-man."*)

ZUCKERMAN: Zuckerman.

ANNOUNCER: . . . The tragedy was witnessed by Judge Herman Lee of the Cambridge District Court. Judge Lee issued a statement at the scene of the accident that Zuckerman . . .

ZUCKERMAN: (*Corrects the radio again.*) Zuckerman.

ANNOUNCER: . . . was not, repeat, NOT speeding and not at fault. Judge Lee again confirmed his statement this morning and suggested the formation of an official committee banning the use of skateboards on the streets of Cambridge. A date has not as yet been set for the final hearing. Zuckerman . . .

ZUCKERMAN: (*Correcting, this time in disgust.*) Zuckerman!!!

ANNOUNCER: . . . released without bail, faces a possible, but highly improbable manslaughter charge. Worcester. A fire swept through the deserted Wearever Knitting Mills early this morning . . . (*Zuckerman switches dials one last time. Music again.*)

SINGERS: Lonely streets. Lonely streets. Lovely when you want to be alone. (*Zuckerman switches off the radio in disgust. He pastes two more clippings onto one of the blank pages of his scrapbook. Suddenly, there is a knock at the door. The knock is ferocious, loud. Zuckerman springs to his feet and looks about the room carefully. He takes two steps and then freezes in one position. The knock sounds again. Even louder than before. Zuckerman begins to talk, but his words are barely audible.)*

ZUCKERMAN: Who is it? (*After first knock Wallace rises, crosses R. with radio and scrapbook to desk, leaves radio on desk, puts scrapbook on floor behind bed, takes clothes from back of chair, tosses them over book. After third knock, Wallace crosses L. to door to listen at it.*) Who is it? (*There is silence. Zuckerman moves to the door, quietly. He steps back, puzzled and frightened. He looks about his room once more, without moving. The knock sounds again. Incredibly loud. Almost as the door might be kicked in any moment. Zuckerman is clearly shaken. He attempts to speak again, but his voice cracks, weaker than the first time.*) Can I help you? (*Clears his throat.*) Can you help me? (*Silence again.*) Who is it? (*There is no answer.*) Who's there? (*Still no answer. He walks to the door and calls again.*) Yes? (*No answer.*) I hear you, who are you? Who's there? (*He cracks open the door cautiously, as Joanna Dibble enters, closing door behind her. She sweeps into the room wearing black tights, black skirt, black sweater, black shoes. A fraternity pin is pinned to her sweater. She is wide-eyed, with long straight hair. Joanna is Zuckerman's age.*) Joanna Dibble, right? (*Wallace backs into room.*)

JOANNA: (*Crosses down to face Wallace. Enraged.*) Killer! Murderer!

ZUCKERMAN: Jesus, I'm sorry. It was an accident . . .

JOANNA: (*Stepping in closer.*) So this is what a killer looks like, Fascinating. You don't even show any signs of a tear. Killer. Murderer. Not even a tear. Killer-Murderer. Not even a tear.

ZUCKERMAN: (*Backing R.*) I cried all night.

JOANNA: (*Tosses purse on bed.*) You're free! It's incredible! You're free! They didn't beat you. They didn't lock you up. You're free.

ZUCKERMAN: (*Backed against R. bed.*) He was on a skateboard. He slipped under the car. It wasn't my fault. There was a witness. He slipped.

JOANNA: (*Crossing in on Wallace.*) Oh, my God! He slipped under the car. That sets you free. That excuses you. That lets you wander the streets tonight. And tomorrow. (*Pauses.*) Tell me something, Zuckerman.

ZUCKERMAN: Zuckerman . . .

JOANNA: Tell me something, killer. What sets me free? What sets me free?

ZUCKERMAN: You're not arrested for anything.

JOANNA: (*Her act runs out of gas.*) Arrested? Of course, I'm not arrested. It's not a crime to be in love. It's not a crime to give yourself totally to another. It's not even a crime, it seems, to drive your car over a man's body. Oh, God. What sets me free?

ZUCKERMAN: Here. Sit down. (*He offers the chair.*)

JOANNA: (*Not noticing.*) The plans. The dreams. The *commitment!* (*As if a revelation.*) How about the commitment? It was total. Total. Did you know that we were getting married in May, right after graduation?

ZUCKERMAN: No.

JOANNA: Well, now you know. Now you know. (*Turns, faces Wallace.*) And you can stand there facing me as though I've come for tea. As though I've come to borrow a pencil. Or a cup of . . . something. Jesus, God! Are you flesh or are you a machine? (*As the scene plays, she forces him to walk backwards as she attacks. Finally, he trips and falls to the floor behind stove.*) How symbolic. How symbolic. Why don't I have my car now. I could drive over your body. I could drive right over you and squeeze the life out of you. Oh. Oh. (*She cries. And cries.*)

ZUCKERMAN: (*Rises, crosses with chair. Seats Joanna, back to audience.*) Oh, please, Joanna. Sit down. You'll feel better. I'll get you a cup of coffee. You want a cup of coffee?

JOANNA: (*Whimpers.*) Yes. Please. I promised I wouldn't cry. Yes.

ZUCKERMAN: (*Starts to kitchen. Remembering.*) I don't have any coffee. You want some water? (*No response.*) Peanut butter?

JOANNA: (*Without looking at him.*) We were getting married in May. May twentieth. You know that?

ZUCKERMAN: (*To her back.*) Joanna, it was an accident. An accident. I wasn't speeding or anything. He fell right under my car. He slipped. (*Crosses to face Joanna.*) He could have fallen under anybody's car. Even your car.

JOANNA: (*She looks.*) I don't have a car.

ZUCKERMAN: If you did, he could have. Anybody's.

JOANNA: Then why yours? Why yours?

ZUCKERMAN: (*To God.*) That's what I've been asking myself all night. Why mine?

JOANNA: (*Rises.*) It means nothing, does it? An accident. Anybody's car. So you're free and I'm alone. (*Crosses past Wallace to bed.*) My commitment is gone. My love is gone. My life is gone.

ZUCKERMAN: (*Crosses to Joanna.*) You're young, Joanna. You're young. There'll be others.

JOANNA: (*Forces Wallace.*) That's what they all say. That's what they all say. You, too? You, too? Even the one who kills? That's what you say, too?

ZUCKERMAN: (*Flustered.*) I didn't mean it the way it sounded.

JOANNA: What do you mean, then? What do you mean? You think I'll love again. (*Crosses behind bed.*) You think my life will continue? With what? Why? My life. My work. It's ended.

ZUCKERMAN: (*Follows Joanna.*) Your work?

JOANNA: That's gone too.

ZUCKERMAN: Where do you work?

JOANNA: My painting. My career. It's over now. There's no reason to continue.

ZUCKERMAN: I saw two of your paintings in the Common – in the Arts Festival. One was a play poster, right? Hey, that's right. I saw you in a play, too. The one about the lesbian. You were terrific.

JOANNA: (*Stronger than ever.*) So you know. You've seen my work. You killed *that* too. How do you feel about the fact that you've killed *that* as well? Are you crying now? Are there tears welling up in your eyes?

ZUCKERMAN: (*Long pause. He's rattled at this point and slightly annoyed.*) Just what the hell are you talking about?

JOANNA: (*Turns on Wallace, forcing him against the bed.*) My career, killer. You didn't just run over a *thing* last night. You didn't snuff out a candle. You killed more than one person. You killed TWO, Zuckerman. You drove your car over two lives!

ZUCKERMAN: Look, Miss Dibble, I didn't . . .

JOANNA: (*Hates her name. Simply.*) Call me "Joanna."

ZUCKERMAN: Look, Joanna. I didn't kill anybody. (*Follows Joanna.*) That's not what I mean. Yeah. Sure. I killed whatshisname, (*Joanna looks at Wallace.*) Simpson. And I know he was your husband. I mean he was gonna be your husband. And I'm sorry. *I Goddamned well am sorry!* But it was an accident. An accident. You think I'm just a clod without a heart. *I* was the one who did it. *I'm* the one who's got to remember what the wheels sounded like. What the cops accused me of. *I'm* the one who's got to suffer for all of that. It hurts *me* too, you know. (*And that's Zuckerman's strength, exhausted for the moment, as Joanna recoups her position for the attack.*)

JOANNA: (*Turns on Wallace, forces him to chair.*) You heard the wheels. You heard the wheels. Oh Jesus Christ. YOU heard the wheels! And you suffer. You poor suffering bastard. You poor suffering bastard. My heart is yours. I feel only pity. (*Pauses.*) You skinny little fink. You took your God damned car and murdered my man . . . yes, my *man!* You think I run around falling in love every day? Frank and I had been pinned for five months. (*Pacing.*) Five months. Five whole months of my life snuffed out. Five months burned away. A life is gone. A career is gone. Yes, a career! (*Forces Wallace. Holding chair to defend himself.*) Who do you think I worked for? For myself? Hah! You've seen my painting. Was that the work of a child? Hah! That was the work of a woman. A whole woman. Not a child, but a woman in love. Love.

ZUCKERMAN: (*Raises chair between them. Fiercely – he musters all his energy.*) *Shut up!* That's right. Shut up and listen to me. (*She starts for the door.*)

JOANNA: Let me out of here, you pig. Let me out of here.

ZUCKERMAN: (*Raises chair as if to hit Joanna. Screams.*) No. No, God damn it! Not until you've heard me. (*As she tries to push him aside, he picks up a chair and motions as though he might hit her with it. She pulls back.*) Now shut up!

JOANNA: What are you going to do?

ZUCKERMAN: (*Crosses to door. Sits in chair.*) I'm going to talk. Just for a minute. You're going to listen. Then you can go.

JOANNA: Why are you doing this?

ZUCKERMAN: (*Strongly, but, indeed, he's frightened.*) Because you've got to listen to me. Please, Joanna. Please. I'm begging you. Please listen to me.

JOANNA: What could *you* say? What do you *want?*

ZUCKERMAN: Miss Dibble, I don't know what to say. I'm sorry. I didn't want to hurt you. And I certainly didn't want what happened last night. For God's sakes. Someone's got to believe that. It was an accident. Maybe I could have stopped it. I don't have a clue. But it happened. And it happened to me, too. Not just you. You're sorry. I believe you. Now please believe me, too. I've never hurt anyone or anything in my life. I protest against war. I work against poverty. I do everything I can so nobody will be unhappy. I *couldn't* hurt anybody. Except by accident. (*Almost weeping.*) For God's sakes. Please believe. (*Pauses.*) OK. I guess that's all. You can go, if you want. (*Rises.*)

JOANNA: Oh, damn it. I'm so confused. I don't know what to believe. (*Wallace closes door.*)

ZUCKERMAN: (*Moving the chair to center stage.*) Please sit down. (*Crosses to Joanna. He reaches for her hand. She pulls back violently.*)

JOANNA: (*Over-reacts violently.*) Don't you touch me! Oh, you would touch me!

ZUCKERMAN: Look, Miss Dibble, I don't want to touch you. I just want you to sit down before you faint or something. You're terribly tense. I can see that and I feel awful about the whole thing. Just sit down.

JOANNA: Maybe you'd like to make some tea? Or turn on the phonograph, so we could dance? The killer is so calm. So matter-of-fact!

ZUCKERMAN: Don't call me a killer.

JOANNA: And why not?

ZUCKERMAN: Because it's . . . cruel . . . yes, it's definitely cruel. That's why, I didn't do it on purpose. Supposing you did it. How would you like me coming around up your place and calling you a "killer" or a "murderer" or names like that. You think I'm not upset now.

JOANNA: (*That hurt her.*) You insensitive pig. Oh! How I hate you.

ZUCKERMAN: Well, I don't hate you.

JOANNA: Why should you hate me?

ZUCKERMAN: You're pretty insensitive too, when you get right down to it. You lack empathy. (*Sits at stove, feet on chair.*)

JOANNA: (*That really hurt her.*) Empathy?

ZUCKERMAN: (*Sits on stove. He mimes the scene, casually.*) Sure. Put yourself in my shoes. You're driving home, right? It's late. It's raining like hell. You're not a crazy kid, right? In fact, you're a nice kid. Almost everybody likes you, except a couple of guys and they're jerks, OK? You haven't been doing anything special, just riding in the rain. You're alone, OK?

JOANNA: All right.

ZUCKERMAN: Good. Now picture this. You feel a bump. Not even a thump. Just a little bump. You think it's maybe a flat tire. You stop. And it's Frank Weeks Simpson.

JOANNA: Oh, dear God. Is that how it happened?

ZUCKERMAN: Yes, that's exactly how it happened.

JOANNA: (*Crosses to Wallace.*) You weren't watching. You weren't studying the road. You were just speeding along, not watching a thing. Practically asleep at the wheel. And you ran Frank down. You didn't even slow down first?

ZUCKERMAN: That's not what I said at all!

JOANNA: You didn't even touch the brakes.

ZUCKERMAN: Wait a minute. Now wait a minute. He slipped. Or tripped. Maybe he skated under the car. Yeah – maybe he skated under intentionally to kill himself, for all I know.

JOANNA: (*Turns to Wallace. She goes after him fiercely.*) That's a lie and you know it!

ZUCKERMAN: I didn't say it was positively true. I just said it was a possibility. You're supposed to be in my shoes.

JOANNA: I am in your shoes. I am in your shoes.

ZUCKERMAN: Then how come you don't understand?

JOANNA: I understand that I was supposed to be with Frank last night, but I was too busy. I understand that Frank went somewhere by himself. I understand that I was waiting outside for him for twenty minutes before it became quite evident that he was not going to pick me up like we had planned. I went and had a drink for a couple of hours. I was sitting alone with a sculptor who was almost a complete stranger when someone walks right up and announces that Frank was dead. Dead. (*Spells the word.*) D.E.A.D. Dead. That I understand. (*Joanna sits on chair by stove.*)

ZUCKERMAN: (*As he clips another clipping.*) Miss Dibble, if I could live my life over it never would happen, believe me. They've taken away my car. They've taken away my license. Do you think this is what I like?

JOANNA: Pleasure??? Like??? You're not only a killer, you're a complete psychotic.

ZUCKERMAN: Everything I say, you twist around.

JOANNA: (*Rises, sees papers.*) You're interested enough to buy all the newspapers, I see.

ZUCKERMAN: (*Nervously.*) Yeah. Sure. I always buy papers. What the hell. I mean, I'm an English Major.

JOANNA: (*Behind bed, sees the scrapbook.*) Oh my God! (*Picks up scrapbook.*) A scrapbook. you're making a scrapbook.

ZUCKERMAN: That's no scrapbook!

JOANNA: Yes it is!

ZUCKERMAN: You can't just come running in here and invade my privacy.

JOANNA: Oh dear God. A scrapbook.

ZUCKERMAN: That is not a scrapbook.

JOANNA: You're collecting things to show your grandchildren. You're enjoying this, Killer. Murderer. Assassin.

ZUCKERMAN: (*Leaps across bed.*) Give me my scrapbook. (*He lunges for it.*)

JOANNA: (*Evades Wallace.*) Every word of it that's in print, you have. You're making a collection. How many other people are you planning to run over? Look at all these blank pages. How are you going to fill them up?

ZUCKERMAN: Jesus, that's not fair!

JOANNA: (*Steps to Wallace.*) Fair! Fair! (*Throws book at his feet.*) Get into my shoes. Go ahead. Get into my shoes.

ZUCKERMAN: (*Picks up book, sits on bed, putting book down.*) All right.

JOANNA: Yesterday. I was a whole person. A total being. I had my work. I had my man. I had my mind. (*Wallace gets cigarette.*) I had my LOVE. Do you know what love is?

ZUCKERMAN: Well, yeah. Sort of, I've been in love.

JOANNA: With who? (*Joanna gets cigarette from purse.*)

ZUCKERMAN: Oh, lots of times. I'm always in love with somebody. (*Wallace lights cigarette.*) There was Marylin. That was love. Nothing too big, but it sure was love. Of course, right now I'm sort of between things. But I've been around. Yes, sir. I've been around plenty. Love . . .

JOANNA: (*Cuts him off like Zorro with:*) I said LOVE!!!

ZUCKERMAN: (*Wallace rises.*) Yeah. Well. I hear you. Love.

JOANNA: Love. Communication between two people. Truth. Beauty. Total commitment. Poetry. Hands on my breasts. Trees. Flowers.

ZUCKERMAN: (*Stares incredulously in open fascination, peppered with his interpretation of what she is free associating, i.e.: his sexual fantasy begins.*) Hands on your breasts?

JOANNA: Love. Real love. Communication between two very real souls. Sensibilities that mesh into one. Bodies that join in love. Love. Simplicity. Simplicity like candy and fruit. Candy and fruit. Two artists living together. Totally. Like Sartre and Simone de Bou . . . de Bou – the name like Jackie Kennedy's. Do you understand at all? Do you understand any speck of what I'm saying?

ZUCKERMAN: Sure I do. Sure. Love. Real love. Like Sartre and Jackie Kennedy. (*Lights her cigarette. Not wanting the fantasy to end. He moves closer.*) Tell me more about you and him.

JOANNA: We met. It was in the Fall. School had just begun. Frank was tall, you know.

ZUCKERMAN: About my height.

JOANNA: A little taller.

ZUCKERMAN: Not too much, though.

JOANNA: He was a thinker. A scholar. He was a Math Major, but *potentially* a great artist. We met at a party. Frank was at the party. He was the tallest person there.

ZUCKERMAN: There must have been a lot of short people, 'cause I'm no giant and he was not that much taller than me.

JOANNA: He asked me to go to the mountains with him.

ZUCKERMAN: What mountains?

JOANNA: He had a cabin. In New Hampshire. A hunting lodge.

ZUCKERMAN: Did you go?

JOANNA: He told me about his hunting lodge. How the winters were. About the animals. His eyes were soft. Frank loved animals. (*By bed.*)

ZUCKERMAN: I like animals. I had a dog once. (*He remembers.*) Shit.

JOANNA: (*Turns.*) What's the matter?

ZUCKERMAN: I had a dog and I killed him by accident.

JOANNA: You killed your dog?

ZUCKERMAN: Why didn't I think of that before? I killed my dog. I ran over him. I had him since I was a kid, too. One night I drove into the driveway and he ran right under the car. He was dead, too.

JOANNA: You killed him with your car?

ZUCKERMAN: I ran right over him. I didn't even see him. (*Pauses.*) I've got a knack for this kind of thing. Why didn't I remember?

JOANNA: What else have you killed?

ZUCKERMAN: My own dog. He was a great dog, too. Right over him with my car. First the front wheels. Then the back wheels. He was squashed. How could I forget a thing like that?

JOANNA: (*Returns to reverie. Dead center, straight front.*) We finally went up to his cabin.

ZUCKERMAN: (*Confused.*) What cabin?

JOANNA: Frank's cabin. In the mountains.

ZUCKERMAN: You went up there, huh?

JOANNA: It was like a dream. Just Frank and me and the mountains. As far as you could see there was just trees and sky. Green and blue.

ZUCKERMAN: What was the cabin like?

JOANNA: (*Elephant tears.*) Split logs. Frank built it with his father. Split logs. Trees that they had taken down together. (*Crosses L. and sits at L. end of bed.*) It was a beautiful place.

ZUCKERMAN: Did they all live there?

JOANNA: Who?

ZUCKERMAN: Frank's family. His father.

JOANNA: No. It was their hunting lodge. No heat or water or anything. Just pure. We burned things to keep warm. We made love . . . And hot chocolate.

ZUCKERMAN: Did you go up there often?

JOANNA: Very often.

ZUCKERMAN: (*Simply, like a pal.*) I'd love to go up there sometime. I've never really been up in the mountains like that. Oh, I've never been . . . you know.

JOANNA: Not many people have.

ZUCKERMAN: You want some hot chocolate? I've got hot chocolate.

JOANNA: No. Not now. Not so soon. It wouldn't be right.

ZUCKERMAN: (*Walks to the table.*) Wheat thin?

JOANNA: No, thank you. I'm stuffed.

ZUCKERMAN: Want some Rosé? (*Joanna rises. Wallace takes purse from her. Tosses it on bed. Starts for the locker.*) Please stay. I mean, don't go away. I mean, keep talking. I can hear you. (*Crosses to kitchen. He calls.*) I can hear you.

JOANNA: (*Crosses to chess board.*) How long have you lived here? (*She inspects the flat again.*)

ZUCKERMAN: (*In kitchen.*) What?

JOANNA: (*She walks to the chess board and "jumps" four white men as in checkers.*) How long have you lived here? (*Joanna puts chessmen on desk.*)

ZUCKERMAN: Oh. About six months. Since school began. I used to have a roommate but he . . . (*A crash sounds in the kitchen.*) Christ! I spilled the wine. (*Wally mops up wine. Pause.*) He was named Charles.

JOANNA: Who?

ZUCKERMAN: My dog. He had a funny little tail. It got cut off in the screen door. There are people who bite dogs' tails off for a living, you know that?

JOANNA: They bite dogs' tails?

ZUCKERMAN: (*Re-considers.*) That's probably not true. (*Pauses.*) I remember once he licked my father's face when he was asleep in the hammock. When I was little I used to hide cookies behind my back and offer Charles a little bit. He used to come behind me and eat the big piece and I'd be left with the little piece. (*Pauses.*) And I ran him right over with my car. Right over. How the Hell did I forget *that?*

JOANNA: Have you ever thought of getting another dog? You can get dogs for nothing at the rescue league place.

ZUCKERMAN: I turned the car into the driveway and the stupid Goddamned dog came running up with his tongue hanging out. (*Mimics the dog.*)

JOANNA: (*Dead center again.*) Do you live here alone?

ZUCKERMAN: (*Returns to kitchen. Loads tray.*) Yeah.

JOANNA: Don't you have a roommate?

ZUCKERMAN: He flunked out. I'm looking for a roommate, but everybody seems to be settled in. You know what I mean? I ran an ad, but nobody answered. I'll probably get one next semester.

JOANNA: Why don't you live in a dorm?

ZUCKERMAN: (*Enters with a tray of beer, wheat thins, wine, olives, etc. Crosses to footlocker, pushes it with his foot to in front of bed, sets tray on footlocker.*) Here.

JOANNA: Oh, my goodness.

ZUCKERMAN: You're probably hungry.

JOANNA: I adore olives.

ZUCKERMAN: Go on. Take some. That's what it's there for. Go on.

JOANNA: (*She does.*) Thank you. Umm, it's good.

ZUCKERMAN: Rosé? (*Holds up bottle, inspects it, crosses to window to get Heinekens, leaves Rosé on desk, picks up bottle opener from desk.*) Or Heinekens? Or I've got some warm soda water if you'd like.

JOANNA: Heinekens' fine.

ZUCKERMAN: (*Opens beer, measures it into two glasses.*) Me, too. I like beer a lot. I don't drink too much. Don't get me wrong. But I like to relax with a good foreign beer.

JOANNA: (*Wallace gives her glass, sits in chair.*) Why don't you live in a dorm?

ZUCKERMAN: I like to be alone. The dorms are stupid.

JOANNA: I thought there was a rule about apartments.

ZUCKERMAN: That's just for out-of-staters. It's very complex. I'm a native. I told them that I live at home. It's OK.

JOANNA: Don't your folks care?

ZUCKERMAN: Naw. They don't care. I pay for this place myself. Why should they care?

JOANNA: Do you work?

ZUCKERMAN: Sure. I load meat.

JOANNA: You load meat?

ZUCKERMAN: My uncle owns a meat market. It's a stupid job.

JOANNA: Meat. I adore meat. It's so basic.

ZUCKERMAN: You wouldn't "adore" it, if you had to handle it every day.

JOANNA: I think it's very beautiful that you handle meat.

ZUCKERMAN: Beautiful? You don't understand. I have to mop the trucks. Trim up lamb chops. Run cheap meat up and in the thing that makes hamburg. What's so beautiful about that?

JOANNA: Meat. Don't you understand? Meat is even more basic than bread or wine. It's the essence of life. It's terribly symbolic.

ZUCKERMAN: I never really thought of it that way.

JOANNA: It's absolutely primitive.

ZUCKERMAN: I guess you just don't think of it that way when it's your stupid uncle's meat in your stupid uncle's meat market.

JOANNA: I think it's really beautiful that you don't work in a shoe store or something. You handle meat.

ZUCKERMAN: (*Realizing he's got a good thing going.*) Well, some people are cut out for shoes. I'm just cut out for meat. You know what I mean?

JOANNA: Do you make a lot of money?

ZUCKERMAN: They pay seven-fifty a morning. Oh, yeah. The trucks come in with the meat every morning at five o'clock. They need people to carry the meat in off the trucks. It's wild. (*Rises. He now begins to pantomime the fantasy, the seduction is on.*) You take a hook and stand with your back to the truck. Then the guy drops a whole side of beef onto your hook. You walk it into the door and kind of lift up with your back. There's a chain going around with a whole batch of hooks and you wait until one of the hooks grabs ahold of your meat. Then you go out and get another one. (*He pauses dreaming up a decent climax for his lie.*) You follow me?

JOANNA: You do this every day?

ZUCKERMAN: Sure. Every day. Seven days a week. There's nothing to it. I get back here around six and sack out for a couple of hours. They don't take out any income tax or nothing. I clear fifty-two-fifty a week. Almost two-fifty a month. That pays tuition, rent, food, the works. (*He's strutting now.*) 'Course, I get a scholarship. But the meat pays for everything else.

JOANNA: Wally, you have certain potential qualities that are really . . unique. What's your major?

ZUCKERMAN: Lit. That's how I got to see you in the lesbian thing. We all went. The whole class. You were really terrific.

JOANNA: What's your minor?

ZUCKERMAN: Ed. My art history ed. class all went to the Common. That's how I saw your paintings. That's some accident – coincidence. (*Pause.*) Lit. major, ed. minor.

JOANNA: What do you write?

ZUCKERMAN: I don't. I'm going to teach.

JOANNA: Where?

ZUCKERMAN: Back home. In the high school. In Wakefield.

JOANNA: Have you ever tried writing?

ZUCKERMAN: Ten thousand poems for creative poetry 201. Nothing any good, though.

JOANNA: I'd love to read some of your work.

ZUCKERMAN: (*Wallace puts tray on bed.*) Really? I'll get them if you'd like.

JOANNA: What time is it?

ZUCKERMAN: Quarter to three. It's early. Have you got a date? (*Realizes what this means.*) Wow! I'm sorry, Joanna.

JOANNA: I know. I know. (*Sucks in her breath.*) Poetry?

ZUCKERMAN: They're not much, really.

JOANNA: I don't want to put you to any trouble.

ZUCKERMAN: Oh. It's no trouble. None at all. I've got them right over here in the thing. (*He runs to the footlocker and pulls out a sheaf of papers. Opens locker, gets papers, closes locker.*) See? I never read them to anyone. They're really kind of stupid.

JOANNA: I'd love to read them.

ZUCKERMAN: Here. I'll read one to you.

JOANNA: No. Let me read. I can never understand poetry unless I read it aloud.

ZUCKERMAN: I'll read it *slowly*.

JOANNA: No. Really. You don't understand. Let me read it.

ZUCKERMAN: How about if I read the first one and you read the next one?

JOANNA: No. Please. Let me read.

ZUCKERMAN: OK. Here. This one's . . . (*He scans the papers.*) Naw. That's stupid. (*Finds one he likes.*) Here. Here's one. You might like it. It's sort of "yogi."

JOANNA: (*She takes the paper and reads.*)

Very quiet,
Cleansed of any passion,
The true yogi knows that Brahman
Is his highest ecstasy.

That's lovely. It's so familiar.

ZUCKERMAN: Yeah. I based it on something. Actually, it's not completely mine. I sort of paraphrased a thing.

JOANNA: It's just lovely.

(*Reads.*)

His heart is with Brahman,
His eye in all things
Sees only Brahman,
Equally present,
In every creature
And all creation.

That's really good. I really like it. What's Brahman?

ZUCKERMAN: Well, you know. Brahman is sort of a thing . . . You know. From the Swami. (*Moves tray to footlocker.*)

JOANNA: Like Atman?

ZUCKERMAN: Sure. That's right. Like Atman. You know Atman, too, huh? (*Pauses.*) What's Atman?

JOANNA: Atman is like tranquility.

ZUCKERMAN: So's Brahman. Like tranquility. (*Changes the subject. Sits in chair.*) That's a nice word, *tranquility*.

JOANNA: Tranquility.

ZUCKERMAN: I mean, it's one of those words that sounds like it means.

JOANNA: Tranquility. (*Experiments with the sounds.*) Tran. Quil. It. Tee. Tranquility.

ZUCKERMAN: You know what the most beautiful two words are in the whole English language? You know what?

JOANNA: (*Plays the sound.*) The most beautiful.

ZUCKERMAN: Listen. (*He mouths the words carefully.*) Cellar door.

Cellar door. Isn't that something? Cellar door.

JOANNA: (*She doesn't know what the hell he's talking about.*) It sounds French.

ZUCKERMAN: That's right. Cellar door. Name two other words more beautiful. Go on, try. You just can't. Cellar door. (*He's excited again.*) Hey. You want to hear a great story? I mean a *great* story. It happened back home. I used to pass a gourmet shop on my way to Boston. When I came into my Uncle's to work on Sunday. I was just a kid then. I used to come in every Sunday from Wakefield. On the bus. Anyway. There was this gourmet shop. German. They sold pastries and stuff to make your own pastries. Anyway. They had this terrific sign in their window for years advertising dough for strudel. Huge sign. Strudel dough. It was up for years. I used to pass it every Sunday. And I used to think about all those people who had to keep staring at it every day. They never ever changed the sign. I mean, it just *hung* there, taped to the window getting old and sort of yellow and terrible. Strudel dough. Get it? So one day, I got off the bus near the pastry shop; and I took a magic marker and right under "strudel dough" I wrote "strudel dee!!!" Isn't that beautiful? (*She's been laughing, but goes deadpan. He's laughing.*) Strudel dough. Strudel dee. Can you imagine what all those poor people said when they saw it? After all those years of passing that sign, all of a sudden it's funny. Strudel dough. Strudel dee. You think that's funny, don't you?

JOANNA: (*Seriously, intensely.*) You'll be a marvelous writer.

ZUCKERMAN: You think so?

JOANNA: You love words, don't you?

ZUCKERMAN: (*Puzzled.*) What do you mean?

JOANNA: Words. Word sounds. Like strudel dough – strudel dee – cellar door. You're right. I can't think of a more beautiful word. It's silly, yet you're absolutely right. Cellar-door. Cellar-door. (*Still doesn't know.*)

ZUCKERMAN: You're right about their sounding French. Wanna' read some more poems?

JOANNA: (*Plays the word sounds.*) More poems.

ZUCKERMAN: Do you know Zen questions?

JOANNA: (*Again.*) Zen questions.

ZUCKERMAN: (*He's really excited now.*) Yeah. Zen questions. Like "If you were hanging by your teeth from the limb of a tree over a cliff and there were jagged rocks below, and your hands were tied." Get it? "Then some guy shows up at the bottom of the tree and asks, 'What is Zen?' What would you answer?" (*Wallace pauses as she poses, staring at her bosom.*)

JOANNA: (*She waits, considering.*) That's beautiful.

ZUCKERMAN: Yeah. I've got this place all fixed up for Zen.

JOANNA: How? (*Wallace rises, puts tray on book shelf, begins to go into a series of Zen exercises as Joanna finds his sheaf of poems and begins to sketch him as he talks. He snaps from pose to pose, demonstrating.*)

ZUCKERMAN: There are rules. You can't just meditate *anywhere*. For beginners, you need a clean quiet place with a comfortable temperature. I'm getting a Puritron.

JOANNA: Puritron. (*Playing the word-sound.*)

ZUCKERMAN: Your place should be well ventilated. No problem there. There are things about your body. A true Zen keeps a certain kind of physical condition. Exercises. They hurt at first, (*Does "Lotus" pose.*) but you get used to them. No associations with men of fame or those who like to argue or those who enjoy competitive sports. "If you can't beat 'em, Zen-out," that's what I always say. (*Joanna goes to footlocker, sits, begins sketching in blue book.*) And no view that distracts the mind. Usually I don't have that kind of problem. (*They giggle. He giggles at his joke. Checks Joanna for a laugh. Nothing. Goes on.*) That's all I can remember. I've got the rules written down. You're drawing on them. (*She looks up.*) That's OK. It's just an old blue-book. If you ever want to cheat, buy blank blue-books and write lists out in the back with the same pen you bring into the test. When they pass out the blue-books, ask for two. Then switch one quick, while they're still passing out. (*Pauses.*) I don't cheat much. Just when the tests are dumb.

JOANNA: (*Sketching.*) That's brilliant.

ZUCKERMAN: You're the first person I've ever told, you know that? I'll bet I could tell anybody else and the whole city would be buying blue-books tomorrow. It's incredible that nobody ever thought of that before, (*Drops pose, crosses to Joanna.*) isn't it? You want something? Food? A pillow? Do you want anything at all?

JOANNA: (*Hands olive pit to Wallace. He tosses it into waste basket.*) You're very attentive. Very loving. Very gentle. You're almost virginal. You know that?

ZUCKERMAN: (*Struck down, he tries to act cool.*) Virginal? *Virginal?* Listen. I've been in love plenty. Real love. Like you say. Sensibilities and stuff like Sartre. If you'll pardon my saying it, I've had my hands on plenty of breasts. You think I'm just a kid, right? Well, let me tell you a little bit of news, Miss Dibble, I've been around. And I mean *around.* I've got a list as long as your hair. Rachael. Marylin. Shirley. Doris. Bonnie. (*Thinks.*) Did I say Marylin?

JOANNA: Yes.

ZUCKERMAN: (*Continues.*) Yeah. Marylin. And Bonnie. Maybe I haven't slept around all over the place, but I've been pretty close. Pretty close. (*Takes blue book, crosses R. to bed.*) There was Marylin. Yes, sir. There certainly was. (*Now he's shaken. He pauses. Back to the papers. Reading.*) Here's one I never understood. "Do not waste your time writing poems and essays about Zen."

JOANNA: Are you sure that's right?

ZUCKERMAN: I copied it right out of the book. (*As he explains the "message," she does a "take" saying "oh." He knows now.*) I mean, the message of the man hanging by his teeth is not to open your mouth, right? And they tell you not to argue. Maybe they lost something in the translation. "Mah-nish-ta-noh. Ha li-loh ha-zeh. Mikol ha-lay-los."

JOANNA: Do you translate?

ZUCKERMAN: (*Very proud, very cool.*) Oh, a little bit.

JOANNA: You're really a thinker, aren't you?

ZUCKERMAN: (*Honestly.*) I never really have anybody to talk to. Those guys down at the market laugh at me.

JOANNA: What do they know?

ZUCKERMAN: (*Classic paranoia.*) Oh, I don't put them down. I mean, they're REAL people. You know what I mean? They don't go to school or anything. They're definitely *real.* It's sort of crazy, but sometimes I think I'm more comfortable with them than with anyone else. It's crazy, especially since they hate me. They don't even talk to me. Not for two years. They really hate me.

JOANNA: No. I understand. Just being with kids all the time. It drives me crazy. I envy you.

ZUCKERMAN: You envy *me?*

JOANNA: Sure. I'd love to carry meat like you do. I have to take money from home, you know what I mean?

ZUCKERMAN: You couldn't carry meat.

JOANNA: That's the point. There's so little a woman can do. Alone, I mean. Artists belong together. Don't you think so? I can paint all right. But I can't make a living from it. Not yet, anyway. All that there's for me is some silly job selling dresses or something. I'd like to be able to do some real work. To meet some real people. Like you do. Every day. Not just once in a while. (*Pauses for the greatest line ever written.*) Could I come down to the market with you?

ZUCKERMAN: Would you like to?

JOANNA: I'd adore it. Oh, could I?

ZUCKERMAN: Sure. You could come down whenever you like. It's not too exciting, though. But we could walk around the waterfront. Have you ever walked around the waterfront?

JOANNA: A few times.

ZUCKERMAN: You ought to walk around down there at 5:15 every morning. That's when it's great. At dawn. I go there all the time, when we break from the meat. I go off by myself. You've got to see it. The men like to break alone, so I walk over to the harbor. When we break from the meat.

JOANNA: I'd love to.

ZUCKERMAN: There are fishing boats. And real fishermen. Honest to God. Real fishermen. They make their living fishing. You'd never think there were any real fishermen left, would you?

JOANNA: Not around here.

ZUCKERMAN: (*He's on the verge of total ecstasy.*) There are. Hundreds of them. They work the docks. They're great. Yellow slickers. Big boots. Paper hats. (*Pauses.*) Oh, yeah. I act kind of different with them though. I have to be sort of one of them.

JOANNA: What do you do?

ZUCKERMAN: (*Crosses to stove, takes paper. Then crosses to footlocker, sits on bed, begins making hat.*) First off, you have to make a hat out of newspaper. To keep the blood and junk out of your hair. (*He demonstrates by taking the newspaper that was delivered before Joanna's entrance. He unfolds the first section and chooses the right shape and size, then begins to fold his hat.*) See. This is a big status thing. I mean, the easiest way to spot a phony is by his paper hat. It took me weeks to figure out how the hell to make this stupid thing. (*He finishes and puts the newspaper hat on his head. Rises.*)

JOANNA: Ohh.

ZUCKERMAN: There you are. Nice, huh? You've got to admit, even after seven years of shlepping meat, I've got clean hair. Right? There's more to it.

JOANNA: What?

ZUCKERMAN: More things you have to do to fit in.

JOANNA: More hats?

ZUCKERMAN: Hell no. That turned out to be the easiest part of it. You've got to walk tough.

JOANNA: Walk tough?

ZUCKERMAN: (*He demonstrates, strutting like crazy, walking "tough."*) See? I walk tough. And I spit a lot. That's really important. You have to spit a lot. They spit all the time. And you have to talk dirty. You might not like that.

JOANNA: (*She jumps up and runs to him, giggling.*) I'd love it. You're wrong. I'd love it. (*They embrace. At first, from Joanna's enthusiasm. Then they embrace, sensing that it has happened. They hold each other childishly. Then they kiss, a long delicious kiss. They break apart as Zuckerman holds Joanna at arms' length.*)

ZUCKERMAN: Joanna. I love you. I love you.

JOANNA: Oh Wally.

ZUCKERMAN: Ever since the play I've loved you. You know that?

JOANNA: Oh Wally. My knees are all "rubbery." I feel funny all over. (*They sit on stove. They kiss again. Their hands search each other's body. Then they embrace, still kissing, as Zuckerman bends her backwards, kissing her as passionately as he can. They break apart. Joanna holds his face in her hands. He stares into her eyes, helpless.*) I love you, Wally. I know I love you. Your face. Your funny hat. (*Suddenly she spies her picture on his hat.*) Oh my God!!! He used that picture.

ZUCKERMAN: Huh? What picture?

JOANNA: It's the paper. The story. The picture. He used a horrible picture.

ZUCKERMAN: That was my high school picture.

JOANNA: No, the one of me.

ZUCKERMAN: (*Pulling the hat from his head, he tears it apart, searching frantically.*) What one of you???? (*NOTE: The play changes here! I.H.*)

JOANNA: (*She points it out.*) How could he? I look ridiculous.

ZUCKERMAN: (*Takes paper.*) Where'd they get that? What's this? How'd they get yours?

JOANNA: A reporter came around last night. He took pictures from me.

ZUCKERMAN: (*Pulls the paper back from her. Reading.*) "Joanna Dibble. 21-year-old artist." Artist??? You're a student. You go to school. What's this crap???

JOANNA: You're an artist.

ZUCKERMAN: I am not.

JOANNA: He came around last night. We talked for a long time and I was upset. He asked personal questions. You know.

ZUCKERMAN: (*Reading.*) "Our love was pure." Pure??? Holy Jesus!!! I'll say he asked personal questions!!!

JOANNA: I was upset, Wally. I never would have given him that picture if I was thinking clearly.

ZUCKERMAN: "We went to his cabin." Jumping Jesus. Jumping Jesus Christ!!! Why did you do this???

JOANNA: I was all calmed down. Now you're making it all awful again. Don't do this, Wally. Don't do this. I'm not going to let you get me going again. I'm staying calm.

ZUCKERMAN: "We went to his cabin!!!" How could you say that??? How could you let that get into the papers??? Tell me!!! What prompted you to tell him??? To tell anybody???

JOANNA: (*Pulls it away.*) I was very upset. "Heartbroken, tearful, full of contempt. She wept for twenty minutes before she could speak. And when she spoke, her words sobbed."

ZUCKERMAN: Who the hell wrote this?

JOANNA: The reporter, silly.

ZUCKERMAN: He came last night?

JOANNA: This morning.

ZUCKERMAN: You said last night.

JOANNA: I meant this morning. What difference does it make?

ZUCKERMAN: (*Cuckolded.*) Nobody came *here* this morning.

JOANNA: Your picture's here.

ZUCKERMAN: That's the same one. Look how little it is.

JOANNA: They had the big one this morning.

ZUCKERMAN: Why didn't you tell me about this?

JOANNA: Why?

ZUCKERMAN: "And when she spoke, her words sobbed." That's the most ridiculous thing I ever read. "Sobbed."

JOANNA: I was very upset.

ZUCKERMAN: "New wrinkle?" You're a "new wrinkle." What does that mean?

JOANNA: That's newspaper talk.

ZUCKERMAN: Newspaper talk? What kind of talk is that?

JOANNA: I was the fiancée. Human interest.

ZUCKERMAN: (*Rises.*) Human interest! You weren't anywhere near the accident. What the hell is all of this about? (*Puts paper on locker, sits on bed.*)

JOANNA: It's only a story. He said that my love was a "new wrinkle."

ZUCKERMAN: But how did he *know* about you? Who told him?

JOANNA: I called the papers.

ZUCKERMAN: You *what?*

JOANNA: I was engaged to be married.

ZUCKERMAN: I know. You were engaged to be married. Swell.

JOANNA: Well, that's enough reason. Isn't it?

ZUCKERMAN: (*Rises.*) Am I crazy or are you crazy? Is this a game?

JOANNA: It's just news. Wally, you know how I feel about you.

ZUCKERMAN: (*Spreads paper on floor.*) How you feel about *me?* This whole thing's about *you.* How the hell did this happen?

JOANNA: Wally, a reporter came to the dorm. He asked me questions about the way I felt. And I answered him. It's news. News. *I* was *engaged* to him. They wanted my statement. Why are you so upset?

ZUCKERMAN: What about MY statement? Doesn't that count? There was a witness. An honest-to-God witness. A judge yet. I didn't even get a second statement. This is terrible.

JOANNA: Look at that horrible picture.

ZUCKERMAN: (*To the world.*) Jesus. She doesn't like her picture. Two inches of my high school picture and you're upset. Look at the pimples. You're upset. That's the most ridiculous thing I ever heard of.

JOANNA: But we both have our pictures in. Look, Wally, our pictures are together. Sort of side by side. (*Dialogue dissolves – overlays as they tear through newspapers.*)

ZUCKERMAN: I had a suspicion that something was wrong. I felt it. I never expected anything like this! Never. You knifed me, that's what. Wally Zuckerman gets knifed again.

JOANNA: I never should have let him use that picture. Aren't they supposed to get a release? Can they just go ahead and print whatever they want? That's such a ridiculous picture.

ZUCKERMAN: I just can't understand it. Not one new picture.

JOANNA: (*Rises, holding paper, tearing her picture from it.*) He didn't bring a photographer. That's probably why. There wasn't time. They *had* to use old pictures.

ZUCKERMAN: You knew it all along. You knew it. You wanted to take this away from me. That's why you came here. To take this from me.

JOANNA: That's not true. That's not true. I don't tell lies. That's not true.

ZUCKERMAN: (*Menacingly.*) Lies? True? I don't believe this. I don't believe it!!! You came here to steal. Steal. Steal it from me. Isn't that right? Huh. Isn't that right??? I've got to be the dumbest dummy ever made. (*Picks up drawing from footlocker. Sees her drawing of him.*) What are you going to call that drawing? "Dumb-Dumb???" (*Rips drawing.*)

JOANNA: He got pictures. He got pictures of the two of us. Old pictures. But pictures of the two of us. Together almost.

ZUCKERMAN: I sat in the police station last night. Not you. I did.

JOANNA: I was engaged to him.

ZUCKERMAN: I carry the goddamned meat. Up with the meat. Down with the meat.

JOANNA: I loved him.

ZUCKERMAN: I walk along that stupid waterfront. Staring at nothing at all!

JOANNA: I was part of his life.

ZUCKERMAN: I sit in the rooms. I cram my head fat with nothing at all. Why? Don't you understand? Something finally happened. What in hell do you think I've been waiting for? Now it's gone. It's gone. It's nothing. (*Rips clippings from bulletin board.*)

JOANNA: You have a life, Wally. You and I. You have your Work. I have my Work.

ZUCKERMAN: You carry the meat tomorrow. You carry the meat. I'll paint trash cans. (*Mimes as well.*) I'll run around playing lesbians. I don't know what I'll do. I'll probably lose my license over this for sure. Why?

JOANNA: You love me.

ZUCKERMAN: Love you? That's more baloney. I don't even know you. Who are you anyway?

JOANNA: It's me, Joanna Dibble. Wally, what's happened?

ZUCKERMAN: Wallace Zuckerman. A schmucky name like that. I was born with a silver knife in my back. How many chances do you think I'll get in my life? Just how many do you think I'll ever get?

JOANNA: How many fiancés will I lose?

ZUCKERMAN: A million. You'll be a widow ten times over. You'll have plenty of chances and you know it. (*Takes book from bed. He walks to the scrapbook.*) Three dollars blown on this. One hundred and seventeen globs of hamburger up and in. (*Throws book on floor.*) This is mine. Not yours. Not a bit of it. You're nothing. Nothing. Now there's complications. Implications. New faces. New story. New wrinkles. Where is Wally? Huh? Where is Wally in all of this? Where am I?

JOANNA: Wally. You love me. You love me, damn it. (*She slaps his face.*)

ZUCKERMAN: (*He slaps her fiercely across the face. The sound is fierce. She steps back and touches her cheek. She slaps him. He slaps her. She slaps him. He slaps her. She slaps him. He slaps her. Finally, she falls on bed.*) Oh, Jesus.

JOANNA: (*Rises.*) Oh, Wally. (*She walks to him and they kiss, passionately.*)

ZUCKERMAN: (*He breaks, after a long kiss.*) Screw it. It's only a story, that's all. It's just a story.

JOANNA: (*Not looking at him.*) Tell me how it's going to be, Wally. He was sweet. But not nearly as sweet as you. Not nearly as gentle. Will you always be gentle, Wally? (*He's caught pulling back the bedspread.*) Do you have something?

ZUCKERMAN: I do.

JOANNA: Oh, good.

ZUCKERMAN: (*Pauses. The lights begin to fade, slowly, until they are pinspotted alone.*) Tomorrow we'll get up just before dawn. We'll walk to the waterfront.

JOANNA: I'd like that. But I'd like to take walks with you when the sun is orange, beside the moon.

ZUCKERMAN: We'll watch the sun break at dawn. Over the harbor. It's pretty there. The fishermen. They're *real* people.

JOANNA: You know when that is, Wally? That's the time I love best of all. At the end of the day and the beginning of the night. When the sun is orange and the moon is just a trace of yellow.

ZUCKERMAN: No, at dawn. I'll load the meat and you can watch me.

JOANNA: (*Sits on bed.*) That's when I know there are two other places . . . Two other places.

ZUCKERMAN: (*Crosses to Joanna.*) When I'm through, we can walk back to the harbor. There's a ship I want you to see. It's really a tugboat. It's called the Sugar Plum.

JOANNA: (*Focuses on Wallace.*) That's right. Candy and fruit. Candy and fruit. That's all I'm looking for. That's all. (*Holds arms out to Wallace.*)

ZUCKERMAN: (*Embracing Joanna.*) No, it's called the Sugar Plum . . . It's called the Sugar Plum.

JOANNA: That's all I'm looking for. That's all.

ZUCKERMAN: (*Looks into audience, quizzically.*) I *think* it's called the Sugar Plum.

LIGHTS SWITCH TO BLACK.

END OF PLAY.

THE INDIAN WANTS THE BRONX

THE INDIAN WANTS THE BRONX was first presented at the Astor Place Theatre in New York City (along with IT'S CALLED THE SUGAR PLUM) on January 17, 1968 by Ruth Newton Productions in association with Diana Mathews. It was directed by James Hammerstein and designed by Fred Voelpel. The cast, in order of appearance, was as follows:

GUPTA, AN EAST INDIAN .... John Cazale
JOEY .... Matthew Cowles
MURPH .... Al Pacino

Introduction

Although *The Indian Wants The Bronx* seems to be born on the streets of New York, the play, in fact, has its roots in England.

In the early 1960's, I lived in London, where I was studying at the Royal Academy of Dramatic Art ... and, of course, writing plays. To say I was poor, back then, is to say the sky had possibilities. The labor laws in England were absurdly biased against foreigners, and I was only allowed to take work that no Englishman would accept. I found such an odious job, as a bartender, in an American Air Force Non-Commissioned Officers' Club in West Ruislip, six miles west of the BBC. For my 45 hours of labor, each week, I took home the equivalent of $35 ... which was precisely what I needed to pay the rent, and not a penny more.

I should add that I was already supporting a family of three ... my daughter Rachael (the film-producer) was already alive and eating food on a regular basis.

I offer all this as background to my particular state of mind during the conception and writing of *The Indian Wants The Bronx.* I was not what you might call a frivolous guy.

Several times a week, I ate the odd meal (on my way to or from school and/or work) in the cafeteria at the Commonwealth Institute on the Kensington High Street. Between normal meal-times, slightly out-of-date, over-cooked food was less expensive to buy in the restaurant, there, than it was to buy in a food-market. It was less than wonderful. Early-morning breakfasts at the Commonwealth Institute cafeteria often featured last night's unserved meals. Curried eggs and veal chops sort of thing.

When I got to the Commonwealth Institute that particular morning, the cafeteria was still shut and locked. At the door, there was already a substantial line of hungry people, waiting to buy a cheap meal. We were a mix of students and older down-and-outers, all colorless, in tan or olive-drab raincoats. Because of his turban and native dress, one young Indian student—a Hindu, 20-ish, my age—was considerably more visible than the rest of us.

We all stood, together, silently, no chat, as Londoners are wont to do, for several minutes ... until the silence was exploded by a carful of Teddy Boys (c.1963 version of Skinheads) screaming racist insults at the young Hindu ... such as:

> Hey, Sahib, move your fookin' elephant!

None of us knew what to do, exactly. We stood there, dumbfounded, listening to heckling that grew more and more obscene, more and more violent, as the Teddy Boys tried to outdo one another.

And then, one by one, we saw that the young Hindu was anything but upset. He was laughing ... nodding ... waving to his verbal assassins. In fact, his friendliness undid the Teddy Boys, who drove off, annoyed and unsatisfied.

We all stood together, silently, watching the Teddy Boys' car disappear into the clot of morning traffic—and then, watching the young Hindu calm his happy giggles down to embarrassed smiles.

We all had the same question burning in our minds: What the hell just happened?

Insofar as finding an answer was concerned, the Brits did nothing. I was American, so, I leaned in and asked him: What the hell just happened? He replied with the most amazing gibberish: flawless Hindi. He didn't speak a word of English. Not a word. He must have been a country boy. He must have arrived in London, the night before, or, that morning, with one address: The Commonwealth Institute. So profound was the young Hindu's loneliness, he was thrilled to have human contact, even from cruel and dangerous aggressors.

When I finished drama school, I left London, and moved to New York, for the first time in my life. I'd grown up in a small town in Massachusetts, and New York City seemed to me like twenty-five Londons. I was lonely and I was terrified.

My second child, Matthew (the novelist) was now alive and eating food, regularly. I had two full-time jobs. (Yes, America was, indeed, the land of Opportunity.) In the middle of the night, I wrote plays. *The Indian Wants The Bronx* was the first new play I finished, after returning to America. It was somehow quite easy to imagine myself a Hindu, lost in Manhattan, trying to reach a child. The first draft of *The Indian Wants The Bronx* came together quickly and surely. I knew exactly what I was writing about, and why.

Al Pacino was acting in a play in somebody's living room, uptown, on Central Park West. The play was called (I think) *Y Is A Crooked Letter.* It was impenetrable. Pacino was great. I was one of eight in the packed audience. There was no question that Pacino was the right actor for my play. I introduced myself and gave him the script, which he read, that night. The next day, we had our first meeting. He was a janitor in a run-down building in the West 60's. (Maybe it wasn't run-down when Al took the job?) His apartment was in the basement. I remember drinking coffee from old orange-juice cans.

I also remember doing a performance of *The Indian Wants The Bronx* in a 3,000-seat ballroom-theatre on Long Island, during our search for a commercial producer to bring our show into New York. Only three people were in their audience—ladies, extremely old, in picture hats. Midway through the show, they left. Al stopped acting, looked out front:

> What do we do, now, Israel?

At risk of turning this already too-long short introduction to *The Indian Wants The Bronx* into a full-length autobiography, I'll offer one more story and than stop.

When Pacino auditioned for the commercial producer we'd finally turned up for an off-Broadway production of *The Indian Wants The Bronx,* she didn't want him. She'd actually never seen Pacino perform the play. She'd only met him. She thought he was too short and not handsome. So, on audition day, she brought in the actor she wanted: blonde, blue-eyed, tall, untalented. I said no, absolutely no. She said, fine, okay, she wouldn't produce the play. I said let both actors audition for us, and then we'll decide, calmly, intelligently. I told Al exactly what was going on. He was furious with me for putting such pressure on him.

Pacino was made to audition during an open call, as he wasn't yet a member of Actors Equity. The play had made the rounds of NYC talent agents, and it seemed like every young, non-union actor in NYC showed up that day ... in addition to the actors who'd auditioned, previously, and were call-backs. First, we endured the Producer's Choice. He was, in a word, boring. And then it was Pacino's turn. (I'd gotten the producer to agree to audition the two front-runners back to back, for what I'd promised her would be easy comparison.)

The theatre was packed with hopeful young actors sitting in the audience, waiting their turns, when Pacino auditioned for the role of Murph in *The Indian Wants The Bronx.* He came out singing ... and then he moved down-stage, center, looked straight through the 4th wall into the house, and bellowed the first lines of the play ... directly into the producer's smiling face:

> Hey, Pussyface, can you hear us? Can
> you hear your babies singin' to ya'?

The producer was startled, terrified. I grabbed her arm.

> Okay, okay, you see it, right?
> ... You can see he's better, right?

She said yes, meekly. I ran on to the stage, in front of all the other hopeful actors, still waiting to audition, and hugged Pacino.

> You got the part, Al! She said yes!

The rest is history. Pacino and John Cazale both did the play, off-Broadway. And they were both brilliant. We all won OBIES—Al won as Best Actor; John won as Distinguished Actor (John won for *Line*, as well as *Indian* ... he'd graced two of my plays, that first glorious season in New York); and I won an OBIE, as well, for Best Play.

In the Summer of 1968, we took *The Indian Wants The Bronx* to the Spoleto Festival in Italy, where we were reviewed by a great number of European critics. In a word, our careers happened.

Characters

GUPTA An East Indian
JOEY
MURPH

Setting

A bus stop on upper Fifth Avenue in New York City.
A chilly, September's night.

THE INDIAN WANTS THE BRONX

As the curtains open, the lights fade up, revealing Gupta, an East Indian. He is standing alone, right of center stage, near a "bus stop" sign. An outdoor telephone booth is to his left; several city owned "litter" baskets to his right.

Gupta is in his fifties. Although he is swarthy in complexion, he is anything but sinister. He is, in fact, meek and visibly frightened by the city.

He is dressed in traditional East Indian garb, appropriately for mid-September. As curtain rises Gupta is in center, looking for a bus. He crosses right.

As Gupta strains to look for a bus on the horizon, the voices of two boys can be heard in the distance, singing. They sing a rock 'n roll song, flatly, trying to harmonize.

JOEY: (*Entering.*)

I walk the lonely streets at night,
A'lookin' for your door,
I look and look and look and look,
But, baby, you don't care.
Baby, you don't care.
Baby, no one cares.

MURPH: (*Following Joey. Murph stops Joey. Interrupting.*) Wait a minute, Joey. I'll take the harmony. Listen. (*He sings.*)

But, baby, you don't care,
Baby, you don't care.
Baby, no one cares.

(*Confident that he has fully captured the correct harmony, he boasts.*) See? I've got a knack for harmony. You take the low part.

BOYS: (*They sing, together.*)

I walk...the lonely, lonely street...
A'listenin' for your heartbeat,
Listening for your love.
But, baby, you don't care.
Baby, you don't care.
Baby, no one cares.

(*They appear on stage. First boy is Joey. Second boy is Murph. Joey is slight, baby-faced, in his early twenties. Murph is stronger, long-haired, the same age.*)

MURPH: (*Circles as Joey crosses to baskets. Singing.*)

. . . The lonely, lonely streets, called out for lovin'
. . . but there was no one to love . . .
'cause, baby, you don't care . . .

JOEY: (*Joins in the singing.*)

Baby, you don't care . . .

MURPH: Baby, you don't care.

Baby, you don't care.
Baby, no one cares.
Baby, no one cares.

(*Calls out into the audience, across to the row of apartment houses opposite the Park.*) Hey, Pussyface! Can you hear your babies singing? Pussyface. We're calling you.

JOEY: (*Joins in.*) Pussyface. Your babies are serenading your loveliness. (*They laugh.*)

MURPH: Baby, no one cares.

MURPH AND JOEY: (*Singing together.*)

Baby, no one cares.
Baby, no one cares.

MURPH: (*Screams.*) Pussyface, you don't care, you Goddamned idiot! (*Murph notices The Indian.*) Hey. Look at the Turk. (*Joey stares at The Indian for a moment, then replies.*)

JOEY: (*Foot on litter basket.*) Just another pretty face. Besides. That's no Turk. It's an Indian.

MURPH: (*Continues to sing.*)

Baby, no one cares.

(*He dances to his song, strutting in The Indian's direction. He then turns back to Joey during the completion of his stanza and feigns a boxing match.*)

I walk the lonely, lonely streets,
A'callin' out for loving . . .
But, baby, you don't give a Christ for
Nothin' . . . Not for nothin'

(*Murph pretends to swing a punch at Joey, who backs off laughing.*) You're nuts. It's a Turk!

JOEY: Bet you a ten spot. It's an Indian.

MURPH: It's a Turk, schmuck. Look at his fancy hat. Indians don't wear fancy hats. (*Calls across the street, again.*) Hey, Pussyface. Joey thinks we got an Indian. (*Back to Joey.*) Give me a cigarette.

JOEY: You owe me a pack already, Murphy.

MURPH: So I owe you a pack. Give me a cigarette.

JOEY: Say "please," maybe?

MURPH: Say "I'll bust your squash if you don't give me a cigarette!"

JOEY: One butt, one noogie.

MURPH: First, the butt.

JOEY: You're a Jap, Murphy. (*As Joey extends the pack, Murph grabs it. Ducks around litter baskets.*)

MURPH: You lost your chance, baby. (*To the apartment block.*) Pussyface! Joey lost his chance!

JOEY: We made a deal. A deal's a deal. You're a Jap, Murphy. A rotten Jap. (*To the apartment.*) Pussyface, listen to me! Murphy's a rotten Jap and just Japped my whole pack. That's unethical, Pussyface. he owes me noogies, too!

MURPH: Now I'll give you twenty noogies, so we'll be even. (*He raps Joey on the arm. The Indian looks up, as Joey squeals.*)

JOEY: Hey. The Indian's watching.

MURPH: (*Raps Joey sharply again on the arm.*) Indian's a Turkie.

JOEY: (*Grabs Murphy's arm and twists it behind his back.*) Gimme my pack and it's an Indian, right?

MURPH: I'll give you your head in a minute, jerkoff.

JOEY: Indian? Indian? Say, Indian! (*Murph twists around. He twists Joey's little finger, slowly. Joey's in pain.*)

MURPH: Turkie? Turkie?

JOEY: Turkie. OK. Let go. (*Murph lets him up and laughs. Joey jumps up and screams.*) Indian! (*He runs a few steps.*) Indian!

MURPH: (*Laughing.*) If your old lady would have you on Thanksgiving you'd know what a turkey was, ya' jerk. (*Hits him on the arm again.*) Here's another noogie, turkie-head! (*The Indian coughs.*)

JOEY: Hey, look. He likes us. Shall I wink?

MURPH: You sexy beast, you'd wink at anything in pants.

JOEY: Come on. Do I look like a Murphy?

MURPH: (*Grabs Joey and twists both of his arms from behind.*) Take that back.

JOEY: Aw! Ya' bastard. I take it back.

MURPH: You're a Turkie-lover, right?

JOEY: Right.

MURPH: Say it.

JOEY: I'm a Turkie-lover.

MURPH: You're a Turkie-humper, right?

JOEY: *You're* a Turkie-humper.

MURPH: Say, *I'm* a Turkie-humper.

JOEY: That's what I said. You're a Turkie-humper. (*Murph twists his arms a bit further.*) OWW, YA' DIRTY BASTARD! All right, I'm a Turkie-humper! Now, leggo! (*Joey pretends to laugh.*)

MURPH: You gonna hug him and kiss him and love him up like a mother?

JOEY: Whose mother?

MURPH: Your mother. She humps Turkies, right?

JOEY: Owww! All right. Yeah. She humps Turkies. Now, leggo!

MURPH: (*He lets go.*) You're free.

JOEY: (*Breaks. Changes the game.*) Where's the bus?

MURPH: Up your mother.

JOEY: My old lady's gonna kill me. It must be late as hell.

MURPH: Maybe we'll get our own place. Yeah. How about that, Joey?

JOEY: Yeah, sure. I move out on her and she starves. You know that.

MURPH: Let her starve, the Turkie-humper.

JOEY: (*Hits Murph on the arm and laughs.*) That's my mother you're desecrating, you nasty bastard.

MURPH: How do you desecrate a whore? Call her a lady?

JOEY: Why don't you ask your mother?

MURPH: (*Hits Joey on the arm.*) Big mouth, huh?

JOEY: Hey! Why don't you pick on som'body your own size, like Turkie, there.

MURPH: Leave Turkie out of this. He's got 6 elephants in his pocket, probably.

JOEY: (*Laughs at the possibility.*) Hey Turkie, you got 6 elephants in your pocket?

MURPH: Hey shut up, Joey. (*He glances in The Indian's direction and The Indian glances back.*) Shut up.

JOEY: Ask him for a match.

MURPH: You ask him.

JOEY: You got the butts.

MURPH: Naw.

JOEY: Chicken. Want some seeds to chew on?

MURPH: I'll give you somethin' to chew on.

JOEY: Go on, ask him. I ain't never heard an Indian talk Turkie-talk.

MURPH: He's a Turkie, I told ya'. Any jerk can see he's a definite Turk!

JOEY: You're a definite jerk, then. 'Cause I see a definite Indian!

MURPH: Yeah?

JOEY: Yeah.

MURPH: I'll show you. (*Murph walks toward The Indian, slowly, taking a full minute to cross the stage. He slithers from side to side and goes through pantomime of looking for matches.*)

JOEY: Hey Murph. You comin' for dinner. We're havin' turkey tonight! Hey! Tell your Turkie to bring his elephants.

MURPH: Schmuck! How's he going to fit 6 elephants in a rickshaw? Quick!

JOEY: (*Flatly.*) Four in front. Three in back. (*He reaches The Indian.*)

MURPH: Excuse me. May I borrow a match? (*Pantomimes looking for matches. Note: The Indian answers in his own language, Hindi, not English, unless noted otherwise.*)

INDIAN: I cannot speak your language. I don't understand.

MURPH: (*To Joey, does a terrific "take," then speaks, incredulous.*) He's got to be kidding. (*Joey and Murph laugh.*)

INDIAN: I'm sorry. I don't understand you.

MURPH: No speak English, huh? (*The Indian looks at him blankly. Louder.*) You can't speak English, huh? (*The Indian stares at him confused by the increase in volume. The Indian smiles.*)

JOEY: (*Flatly.*) Son of a bitch. Hey, Murph. Guess what? Your Turkie only speaks Indian.

MURPH: (*Moves in closer, examining The Indian.*) Say something in Indian, big mouth.

JOEY: (*Holds up his hand.*) How's your teepee? (*The Indian stares at him. He laughs.*) See. (*The Indian welcomes Joey's laugh and smiles. He takes their hands and "shakes" them.*)

MURPH: (*Nodding and smiling as he shakes Indian's hand. Catches on as to why The Indian has joined the smile and feigns a stronger smile until they all laugh aloud. Murph cuts off the laughter with:*) You're a fairy, right?

INDIAN: (*He smiles harder than before.*) I don't understand you. I'm looking for my son's home. We were supposed to meet, but I could not find him. I'm looking for his home. This is his address. Am I headed in the correct direction? (*The Indian produces a slip of paper with an address typed on it. And a photograph.*)

MURPH: (*Takes photo.*) Gupta. In the Bronx. Maybe it is an Indian. Big deal. (*To The Indian.*) Indian, right? You an Indian? Indian? (*Pauses.*) He don't know. (*Murph shakes his head up and down, smiling. The Indian, mistaking this signal for approval of direction, shakes his head and smiles as well.*) This picture must be his kid. Looks like you, Joey.

JOEY: (*Looks at picture. Steps out of Murph's reach.*) Looks Irish to me. (*Hands picture to Murph.*)

BOTH: Ohhh.

MURPH: Yeah. Why'd you rape all those innocent children? (*Pause.*) I think he's the wrong kind of Indian. (*To The Indian.*) You work in a restaurant? (*Pauses. Does an overstated "s" sound with:*) It's such a shame to kill these Indians. They do such superb beaded work. (*Murph shakes his head up and down again, smiling.*)

INDIAN: (*Follows Murph's cue.*) I haven't seen my son all day. Your city is so big and so busy.

JOEY: Ask him to show you his elephants.

MURPH: You ask. You're the one who speaks Turkie-Indian.

JOEY: (*Steps toward them, holds up hand.*) White man fork with tongue. Right? (*Steps toward them, holds up hand.*) Naw, he don't understand me. You ask. You got the right kind of accent. All you foreigners understand each other good. (*Pulls L.*)

MURPH: You want another noogie?

JOEY: Maybe Turkie wants a noogie or six?

MURPH: (*Shaking his head.*) You want a noogie, friend?

INDIAN: (*Agrees.*) I'm sorry. I haven't been here long.

MURPH: Give him his noogie.

JOEY: Naw. He's your friend. You give it to him. That's what friends are for.

MURPH: (*Looks at paper and photograph, gives them back.*) Jesus, look at that for a face. Prem Gupta. In the Bronx. Jesus, this is terrific. The Indian wants the Bronx.

JOEY: He ain't gonna' find no Bronx on this bus.

MURPH: Old Indian, pal. (*Gives Indian card.*) You ain't going to find the Bronx on this bus. Now, I've got a terrific idea for fun and profit.

INDIAN: Excuse me?

MURPH: (*Leans L. basket. Pauses.*) Why don't you come home and meet my mother? (*No response from The Indian.*) Or maybe you'd like to meet Pussyface, huh? (*To Joey.*) Should we bring him over to Pussyface?

JOEY: He don't even know who Pussyface is. You can't just go getting Indians blind dates without giving him a breakdown.

MURPH: (*To Indian.*) OK, Chief. Here's the breakdown on Pussyface. She's a pig. She lives right over there. See that pretty building. (*Points over the audience, to the back row.*) That one. The fancy one. That's Pussyface's hideaway. She's our Social Worker.

JOEY: That's right.

MURPH: Pussyface got assigned to us when we were tykers, right, Joe?

JOEY: Just little fellers.

MURPH: Pussyface was sent to us by the City. To watch over us. And care for us. And love us like a Mother. Not because she wanted to. But because she was paid to. Because we were bad boys. We stole a car.

JOEY: We stole two cars.

MURPH: We stole two cars. And we knifed a kid.

JOEY: You knifed a kid.

MURPH: (*To Joey.*) Tell it to the judge, fella! (*He takes a pocketknife from his pocket and shows it to The Indian who pulls back in fear.*)

JOEY: The Chief thinks you're going to cut him up into a totem pole.

MURPH: Easy, Chief! I've never cut an Indian in my life. (*Puts knife away.*)

JOEY: You've never *seen* an Indian in your life.

MURPH: Anyway, you got a choice. My mother – who happens to have a terrific personality. Or Pussyface, our beloved Social lady.

JOEY: Where's the bus?

MURPH: It's coming.

JOEY: So's Christmas.

MURPH: Hey. Show Turkie my Christmas card for Pussyface. (*To The Indian.*) Pussyface gives us fun projects. I had to make Christmas cards last year. (*Back to Joey.*) Go on. Show the Chief the card. (*Joey fishes through his wallet, finds a "dogeared" photostat, gives it to Murph. He hands it to The Indian, who accepts curiously.*)

INDIAN: What is this?

MURPH: I made that with my own two cheeks. Tell him, Joe.

JOEY: Stupid, he don't speak English.

MURPH: It don't matter. He's interested, ain't he?

JOEY: You're a fink-jerk.

MURPH: Oooo. I'll give you noogies up the kazzooo. This is a Christmas card. I made it. Get me? Pussyface got us Christmas jobs last year. She got me one with the City. With the War on Poverty. I ran the Xerox machine.

JOEY: Jesus. You really are stupid. He don't understand one word you're saying.

MURPH: (*Mimes the entire scene, slowly.*) He's interested, ain't he? That's more than I can say for most of them. (*To The Indian.*) Want to know how you can make your own Christmas cards with your simple Xerox 2400? It's easy. I'll show you. Watch. (*Crosses straight U. C. and begins his act.*) First you lock the door to the stat room, so no one can bust in. Then you turn the machine on. (*Crosses to "machine" turns dial.*) Then you set the dial at the number of people you want to send cards to. 30, 40.

JOEY: 3 or 4.

MURPH: Right, fella'. Then you take off your pants. And your underpants. Them's the one's underneath. You sit on the glass. You push the little button. The lights flash. When the picture's developed you write "Noel" across it! (*Pauses. Crosses to Indian. Indian hands card to Murph.*) That's how you make Christmas cards. (*Murph waits for a reaction from The Indian, then turns back to Joey, dismayed. To Joey.*) He's waiting for the bus. (*Gives him card.*)

JOEY: Me, too. Jesus. Am I ever late!

MURPH: Tell her to stuff it. You're a big boy now.

JOEY: She gets frightened, that's all. She really don't care how late I come in, as long as I tell her when I'm coming. If I tell her One, and I don't get in until One-thirty, she's purple when I finally get in. (*Pauses.*) She's alright. Where's the Goddamned bus, huh? (*Calls across the park.*) Pussyface, did you steal the bus, you dirty old whore? Pussyface, I'm calling you! (*Pauses. Looks for bus.*) She's alright, Murph. Christ, she's my mother. I didn't ask for her. She's alright.

MURPH: Who's alright? That Turkie-humper? (*To The Indian.*) His old lady humps Turkies, you know that? (*Smiles, but The Indian doesn't respond.*) Hey, Turkie's blowin' his cool a little. (*Indian looks for bus.*) Least you got som'body waitin'. My old lady wouldn't know if I was gone a year.

JOEY: What? That Turkie-humper?

MURPH: (*To The Indian – Murph yells.*) "Hey!" (*The Indian jumps, startled, Murph laughs.*) Hey! You got any little Indians runnin' around your teepee? No? Yeah? No? Aw, ya' stupid Indian. Where is the Goddamn bus?

JOEY: Let's walk it.

MURPH: Screw that. A hundred blocks? Besides, we gotta keep this old Turkie company, right? We couldn't let him stand all alone in this big ole' city. Some nasty boys might come along and chew him up, right?

JOEY: We can walk it. Let the Indian starve.

MURPH: (*Crosses to Indian.*) So walk it, jerk. I'm waiting with the chief. (*Murph stands next to The Indian.*)

JOEY: Come on, we'll grab the subway.

MURPH: Joe, the trains are running crazy now. Anyway, I'm waitin' with my friend the chief, here. You wanna' go, go. (*Murmurs.*) Where is it, Chief? Is that it? Here it comes. Huh? (*Looks for the bus, acting it out.*) I think I see it. Sure.

JOEY: (*Considers it.*) Yeah, we gotta' watch out for Turkie. (*Joey stands on the other side of The Indian, who finally walks, slowly, back to the bus stop area.*)

MURPH: See that, Turkie, little Joey's gonna' keep us company. That's nice, huh? (*The Indian looks for the bus. He's still holding I.D. card.*) You know, Joey, this Turkie's kinda' a pain in the ass. He don't look at me when I talk to him. (*Takes card, hands to Joey in front of Indian.*)

JOEY: He oughta' be polite. (*Hands card to Murph behind Indian. They pass the card in a game. The Indian smiles.*)

MURPH: I don't think he learned many smarts in Indiana. Any slob knows enough to look when they're being talked to. Huh? (*Hands card to Joey in front of Indian.*)

JOEY: This ain't just any slob. This is a definite Turkie-Indian slob. (*Hands card to Murph behind Joey, as in a magic act. They fool The Indian.*)

MURPH: He's one of them Iraqi slobs, probably. War mongering bastard. (*Card to Joey in front of Indian. Flatly.*) Saddam, here, rapes all the little kids.

JOEY: Terrible thing. (*Card to Murph.*) Too bad we can't give him some smarts. We'll give 'im plenty of smarts. (*Crosses U. Indian follows. Card to Indian.*) Want some smarts, Chief?

INDIAN: I can't understand you. Please? When is the bus due here? Am I at the right station? (*He contains his dignity, smiling.*)

JOEY: Hey, look. He's talking out of the side of his mouth. Sure, that's right . . . Hey Murph. Ain't Indian broads s'posed to have sideways breezers? Sure.

MURPH: (*Grins.*) You mean Chinks, Joey.

JOEY: Naw. Indian broads too. All them foreign broads. Their breezers are sideways. That's why them foreign cars have the back seats facing the side, right?

MURPH: Is that right, Turkie? Your broads have horizontal snatches?

INDIAN: (*Stares at him nervously.*) I can't understand you.

MURPH: (*Repeating him in the same language.*) I can't understand you.

INDIAN: (*Recognizing the language, finally. He speaks with incredible speed.*) Yes, that's correct. I can't understand your language. I'm sorry, but I've only been in your country for a few days. I haven't had time to understand your language. Please forgive me. I'm separated from my son. He's been living in your country for six years. When his mother died two months ago, he sent for me. I came imme-diately. He's a good son to his father. I'm sorry I haven't learned your language yet, but I shall learn.

MURPH: (*Does a "take." Flatly.*) This Turkie's a real pain in the ass.

JOEY: Naw. I think he's pretty interesting. I never saw an Indian before.

MURPH: (*Crosses to Joey and slaps the back of Joey's head.*) Oh. It's fascinating. It's marvelous. This city's a regular melting pot. Turkies. Kikes like you. (*Pause.*) I even had me a French lady once.

JOEY: A French lady, huh?

MURPH: Yep. A real French broad.

JOEY: You been at your mother again?

MURPH: (*Hits him on the arm.*) Wiseass. Just what nobody likes. A wiseass.

JOEY: Where'd you have this French lady, huh?

MURPH: I found her in the park over there. (*Points.*) Just sitting on a bench. She was great. (*Boasts.*) A real *talent.*

JOEY: Yeah, sure thing. (*Calls into the park.*) Hello, talent. Hello, talent! (*Pauses.*) I had a French girl, too. (*Turns to avoid Murph's eyes, caught in a lie.*) Where the hell's that bus?

MURPH: Sure you did. Like the time you had a mermaid?

JOEY: You better believe I did. She wasn't really French. She just lived there a long time. I went to first grade with her. Geraldine. She was my first girlfriend. (*Talks very quickly.*) Her old man was in the Army or something, 'cause they moved to France. She came back when we were in high school.

MURPH: Then what happened?

JOEY: Nothin'. She just came back, that's all.

MURPH: I thought you said you *had* her?

JOEY: No, she was just my girl-friend.

MURPH: In high school?

JOEY: No, ya' stoop. In the first grade. I just told you.

MURPH: You had her in the first grade?

JOEY: Jesus, you're stupid. She was my girl-friend. That's all.

MURPH: (*Feigns excitement.*) Hey . . . that's a *sweet little story.* (*Flatly.*) What the hell's wrong with you?

JOEY: What do ya' mean?

MURPH: What do you mean, "what do you mean?" First you say you had a French girl, then you say you had a girl-friend in first grade, who went to France. What the hell kind of story's that?

JOEY: It's a true one, that's all. Yours is full of crap.

MURPH: What's full of crap?

JOEY: About the French lady in the park. You never had any French lady unless you been at your own old lady again. Or maybe you've been at Pussyface?

MURPH: Jesus, you're lookin' for it, aren't you?

JOEY: I mean, if you gotta' tell lies to your best buddy, you're in bad shape, that's all.

MURPH: (*Gives Joey a "high-sign."*) Best buddy? You? (*Noogie gesture to Joey. The noogie gesture sign to The Indian. He returns the obscene gesture, thinking it an American sign of welcome.*)

JOEY: Turkie! Is that how it is in Ceylon, sir?

MURPH: Say-lon? What the hell is say-long?

JOEY: See, ya' jerk. Ceylon's part of India. That's where they grow tea.

MURPH: No kiddin'? Boy it's terrific what you can learn just standin' on a corner with a schmuck like you. Tea, huh? (*To The Indian, he screams:*) Hey! (*Looks for bus, crosses to Indian. The Indian turns around, startled, but catches Murph at the game and smiles. Murph returns the smile and asks:*) How's your teabags? (*No response.*) No? (*To Joey.*) Guess you're wrong again. He don't know teabags.

JOEY: Look at the bags under his eyes.

(*Transition scene: Murph screams: "Hey!" – The Indian smiles. They dance a war-dance around him – beating a rhythm on the trashcans, hissing and cat-calling for a full minute. Murph scares*

Indian who retreats. Murph ends the dance with a final "Hey!" The Indian jumps in fear. Murph works Indian around behind litter baskets. Now that they sense his fear, the comedy has ended.)

MURPH: Turkie looks like he's getting bored.

JOEY: Poor old Indian. Maybe he wants to play a game.

MURPH: You know any poor old Indian games?

JOEY: We could burn him at the stake. (*He laughs.*) That ain't such a terrible idea, you know. Maybe make an Indian stew.

MURPH: Naw, we couldn't burn a nice fellow like Turkie. That's nasty.

JOEY: We got to play a game. Pussyface always tells us to play games. (*To the apartment.*) Ain't that right, Pussyface? You always want us to play games.

MURPH: (*Screams.*) Hey! (*The Indian jumps, startled again.*) Hey! I know a game. (*Makes false jump at Indian.*) "Indian – Indian – Where's the Indian?"

JOEY: That's a sweet game. I haven't played that for years.

MURPH: (*Steps toward Joey.*) Wiseass. You want to play a game, don't you?

JOEY: Indian-Indian. Where's the Indian?

MURPH: Sure. It's just like Ring-a-leave-eo. Only with a spin.

JOEY: That sounds terrific.

MURPH: (*Crosses to Joey.*) Look. I spin the hell out of you until you're dizzy. Then you run across the street and get Pussyface. I'll grab the Indian and hide him. Then Pussyface and you come over here and try to find us.

JOEY: We're going to spin, huh?

MURPH: Sure.

JOEY: Who's going to clean up after you? Remember the ferris wheel, big shot? All those happy faces staring up at you?

MURPH: I ain't the spinner. You're the spinner. I'll hide the Chief. Go on. Spin.

JOEY: How about if we set the rules as we go along? (*To The Indian.*) How does that grab you, Chief?

INDIAN: I'm sorry, but I can't understand your language.

MURPH: He's talking Indianna again. He don't understand. Go on. Spin. I'll grab the Chief while you're spinning . . . count to ten . . . hide the Chief, while you're after Pussyface. Go on. Spin.

JOEY: I ain't going to spin. I get sick.

MURPH: Ain't you going to play?

JOEY: I'll play. But I can't spin any better than you can. I get sick.

You know that. How about if you spin and I hide the Chief? You can get Pussyface. She likes you better than me, anyhow.

MURPH: Pussyface ain't home. You know that. She's in New Jersey.

JOEY: Then what the hell's the point of this game, anyway?

MURPH: It's just a game. We can pretend.

JOEY: You can play marbles for all I care. I just ain't going to spin, that's all. And neither are you. So let's forget the whole game.

MURPH: (*Fiercely.*) Spin! Spin!

JOEY: You spin.

MURPH: (*Slaps Joey on arm.*) Hey. I told you to spin. (*Murph squares off against Joey, menacingly. Joey looks Murph straight in the eye for a moment and then says:*)

JOEY: OK. Big deal. So I'll spin. Then I get Pussyface, right? You ready to get the Chief?

MURPH: Will you stop talking and start spinning?

JOEY: Alright. Alright. Here I go. (*Joey spins himself meekly, as Murph grabs The Indian and runs for the trash can. Joey giggles as he spins ever so slowly. Murph glances at Joey as Joey pretends. Murph is confused.*) There. I spun. Is that OK?

MURPH: That's a spin?

JOEY: Well, it wasn't a fox trot.

MURPH: I told you to spin! Any slob knows that ain't no spin! Now spin, God damn it! Spin!

JOEY: (*Crosses to Murph.*) This is stupid. You want to play games. You want a decent spin. (*Strikes at Murph.*) You spin. (*He walks straight to Murph – a challenge. Joey slaps Murph. They freeze.*)

MURPH: (*Circles Joey as if to hit him. He squares off, viciously. Raises his arms. Looks at Joey cruelly and orders:*) Spin me. (*Joey brings Murph's arms behind Murph's back, and holds Murph's wrists firmly, so Murph is helpless. Joey spins him three times. Slowly at first. Then faster. Faster. Joey's hostility is released. Joey laughs.*)

JOEY: You wanted to spin. Spin. Spin. (*Joey spins Murph frantically. The Indian watches in total horror, not knowing what to do. The Indian cuddles next to the Bus Stop sign: his island of safety. Murph screams.*)

MURPH: Enough, you little bastard!

JOEY: (*Continues to spin him.*) Now YOU get Pussyface. Go on. (*He spins Murph all the faster as in a grotesque dance gone berserk.*) I'LL hide the Chief. This is your game! This is your game. YOU get Pussyface. I'll hide the Chief. Go on, Murphy. You want some more spin. (*Joey has stopped the spinning now, as Murph is obviously ill.*) You want to spin some more?

MURPH: Stop it, Joey. I'm sick.

JOEY: (*Spins Murph once more around.*) You want to spin some more or are you going to get Pussyface and come find the Chief and me?

MURPH: You little bastard.

JOEY: (*Spins Murph once again, still holding Murph helpless with his arms behind his back.*) I'LL hide the Chief. YOU get Pussyface and find us. OK? OK? OK?

MURPH: (*Stumbling U. R.*) OK. You bastard. OK.

JOEY: (*Spins Murph once more.*) Here's one more for good luck. (*Joey spins Murph three more times, fiercely, then shoves him off stage. Murphy can be heard retching, about to vomit, during the final spins. Joey first pushes Murph off stage, then grabs The Indian, who pulls back in terror. Murph stumbles off as Joey grabs The Indian, pushes him behind litter baskets.*)

INDIAN: No, please, what are you going to do?

JOEY: Easy, Chief. (*Slaps The Indian.*) It's just a game. Murph spun out on us. It's just a game. I've got to hide you now. (*Murph's final puking sounds can be heard well in the distance.*)

INDIAN: No. No. Please, I beg you.

JOEY: Easy, Chief. Look. I promise you, this ain't for real. This is only a game. A game. Get it? It's all a game! Now I got to count to ten. One. Two. Three. Murphy? (*He laughs.*) Four. Five. Murph? Come get us. Six. Seven. Pussyface is waiting. Eight. Nine. (*Pauses.*) Murphy? Murph? Hey, Buddy. (*Joey stands up. Speaks.*) Ten. Get up. Up. (*No response.*) Get up, Turkie. (*Joey turns, sees Indian is already up. The Indian shakes from fear. Then The Indian shakes from a chill. There is a moment's silence as Joey watches. Joey removes his own sweater and offers it to The Indian.*) Here. Here. Put it on. It's OK. Put it on. (*Joey crosses to Indian, ties sweater around his neck. The Indian stares at the sweater. Joey takes it from his hands and begins to cover The Indian, who is amazed. Joey speaks.*) I hope I didn't hurt you too much. You OK? (*No response.*) You ain't sick too bad, huh? (*Pause.*) Huh? (*Checks the Indian for cuts.*) You look OK. You're OK, huh? (*No response.*) I didn't mean to rough you up like that, but . . . you know. Huh? (*The Indian raises his eyes to meet Joey's. Joey looks down to avoid the stare.*) I hope you ain't mad at me or nothin'. (*Pause.*) Boy, it's gettin' chilly. I mean, it's cold, right? Sure is quiet all of a sudden. Kind of spooky, huh? (*Calls.*) Hey, MURPHY! (*Joey laughs aloud.*) Murph ain't a bad guy. He's my best buddy, see? I mean, he gets kinda' crazy sometimes, but that's all. Everybody gets kind of crazy sometime, right? (*No response.*) Jesus, you're a stupid Indian. Can't you speak any English? No? Why the hell did you come here, anyway? Especially if you can't talk any English. You ought to say something. Can't you even say "Thank you"? (*The Indian recognizes those words, finally, and mimics them, slowly. Painfully.*)

INDIAN: (*In English – very British.*) Thank you.

JOEY: (*Crosses to Indian.*) I'll be Goddamned! You're welcome. (*Slowly, indicating for The Indian to follow.*) You're welcome. (*Waits.*)

INDIAN: (*In English.*) You are welcome.

JOEY: That's terrific. You are welcome. (*Joey smiles, as though all is forgiven. In relief.*) How are you?

INDIAN: You are welcome.

JOEY: No. How are ya? (*Joey is excited. The Indian might be a second friend!!!*)

INDIAN: (*In English—very "Joey."*) How are ya?

JOEY: (*Joyously.*) Jesus. You'll be talking like us in no time!!! You're OK, huh? You ain't bleeding or anything. I didn't wanna' hurt you none. But Murph gets all worked up. You know what I mean. He gets all excited. This ain't the first time, you know. No, sir!

INDIAN: (*In English.*) No, sir.

JOEY: That's right. He's especially crazy around broads.

INDIAN: (*In English.*) Broads.

JOEY: (*Forgetting that The Indian is only mimicking.*) That's right. Broads. (*He pauses and remembers, deeply.*) What am I yakking for? Tell me about India, huh? I'd like to go to India sometime. Maybe I will. You think I'd like India? India? (*No response.*) That's where you're from, ain't it? Jesus, what a stupid Indian. India! (*Spells the word.*) I.N.D.I.A. Nothin'. Schmuck. India.

INDIAN: India.

JOEY: Yeah! Tell me about India! (*Long pause as they stand staring at each other.*) No? You're not talking, huh? Well, what do you want to do? Murph oughta' be back soon. (*Discovers coin in his pocket. Crosses to Indian.*) You wanna' flip for quarters? Flip? No? Look, Kennedy half. (*Joey goes through three magic tricks with the coin:*

No. 1 He palms the coin, offers the obvious choice of hand, then uncovers the coin in his other hand. The Indian raises his hand to his turban in astonishment.) Like that, huh? (*No. 2. Coin slapped on breast.*) Which hand is it under? This hand right? Which hand is it under? Go on, which hand? This hand here! Is it in this hand? This hand. No! It's in this hand. Back to your dumb act? Here's the one you liked! (*Does No. 1. This time The Indian points to the correct hand instantly.*) You're probably some kind of hustler. OK. Double or nothing. (*Flips.*) Heads, you live. Tails, you die. OK? (*Uncovers the coin.*) I'll be a son-of-a-bitch. You got Indian luck. Here. (*Hands coin to Indian.*)

INDIAN: (*Stares in question.*) NO?

JOEY: (*Considers cheating.*) Take it. You won. No, go ahead. Keep it. (*Offers coin to Indian who takes it.*) I ain't no Indian giver. (*Pause. He laughs at his own joke. No response.*) You ain't got no sense of humor, that's what.

INDIAN: Thank you.

JOEY: Murph's my best buddy, you know. Me and him were buddies when we were kids. Me and Murph, all the time. And Maggie. His kid sister. (*Pause.*) I had Maggie once. Sort of. Well, kind of. Yeah, I had her. That's right. Murph don't know. Makes no difference now. She's dead, Maggie. Makes no difference when you're dead. (*Sings.*) The worms crawl in. The worms crawl out. (*Speaks.*) What the hell difference does it make? Right?

INDIAN: (*Steps closer to Joey. In English.*) No sir.

JOEY: (*Without noticing.*) That's why Murph is crazy. That's why he gets crazy, I mean. She dies seventeen, that's all. Seventeen. Just like *that*. Appendix. No one around. There was no one around. His old lady? Forget it! The old man took off years go. All there was really was just Murph and Maggie. That's why he could take it. At home. You think my old lady's bad. She's nothing. His old lady's a pro. You know? She don't even make a living at it, either. That's the bitch of it. Not even a living. She's a dog. I mean, *I* wouldn't even pay her a nickel. Not a nickel. Not that I'd screw around with Murphy's old lady. Oh! Not that she doesn't try. She tries. Plenty. (*His fantasy begins.*) That's why I don't come around to his house much. She tries all the time. She wouldn't charge me anything, probably. But it ain't right screwing your best buddy's old lady, right? I'd feel terrible if I did. She ain't that bad, but it just ain't right. I'd bet she'd even take Murph on. She probably tries it with him, too. That's the bitch of it. She can't even make a living. You think Pussyface is a help? That's the biggest joke yet. (*The Indian is by now thoroughly confused on all counts. He recognizes the name "Pussyface" and reacts slightly. Seeing Joey's anxiety, he cuddles him. For a brief moment, they embrace: an insane father-and-son tableau. Note: Be careful here. I.H.*) Pussyface. There's a brain. You see what she gave us for Christmas. (*He fishes a knife out of his pocket.*) Knives. Brilliant, huh? Murph's up on a rap for slicing a kid and she gives us knives for Christmas. To whittle with. She's crazier than Murphy. Hah. (*Joey flashes his open knife at The Indian, who misinterprets the move as spelling disaster. The Indian waits, carefully scrutinizing Joey, until Joey begins to look away. Joey now wanders to the spot where he pushed Murph off-stage.*) Hey, Murph! (*The Indian moves slowly to the other side of the stage Joey sees his move at once and races after him, thinking The Indian was running away.*) Hey. Where are you going? Don't run away. We got to wait for Murphy. (*The Indian knows he'll be hit. He tries to explain with mute gestures and attitude. It's futile.*) You were gonna' run off. Right. Son of a bitch. You were gonna' tell Murphy. (*Joey punches Indian, left, right, left, right. Indian breaks, runs behind baskets, and thenJoey chases him hitting him with a rabbit punch as Indian rushes against Murph, who has just entered. Indian falls back against booth. The Indian makes one last effort to escape and runs the length of the stage, screaming a bloodcurdling anguished scream. Murph enters. Stops. Stares incredulously as The Indian runs into his open arms. Joey races to The Indian and strikes a karate chop to the back of The Indian's neck, Joey is audibly sobbing. The Indian drops to the stage as a bull in the ring, feeling the final thrust of the sword . . . Joey stands frozen above The Indian. Murph stares, first at Joey, then to The Indian.*)

MURPH: Pussyface isn't home yet. She's still in New Jersey. Ring-a-leave-eo.

JOEY: (*Staring at Indian. Sobbing, senses his error.*) Indians are dumb.

MURPH: Pussyface isn't home. I rang her bell. She don't answer. I guess she's still on vacation. She ruined our game.

JOEY: (*Sobbing.*) Oh, jumping Jesus Christ. Jesus. Jesus. Jesus. Indians are dumb.

MURPH: Pussyface ruins everything. She don't really care about our games. She ruins our games. Just like Indians. They don't know how to play our games either.

JOEY: Indians are dumb. Dumb. (*He sobs.*)

MURPH: (*Crosses to Joey, slaps his arm.*) What the hell's going on?

JOEY: He tried to run. I hit him.

MURPH: Yeah. I saw that. You hit him alright. (*Stares at The Indian.*) Is he alive? (*The Indian groans. Pulls himself to his knees.*)

JOEY: He was fighting. I hit him.

MURPH: OK. You hit him. (*The Indian groans again. Then he speaks in a plea.*)

INDIAN: (*Murph turns to look at Indian.*) Please. Don't hurt me anymore. What have I done? Please don't hurt me.

MURPH: (*To Joey.*) He's begging for something. Maybe he's begging for his life. Maybe he is. Sure, maybe he is.

JOEY: (*Crosses to Indian. Embarrassed, starts to help The Indian to his feet.*) C'mon there, Chief. Get up and face the world. C'mon, Chief. Everything's going to be alright.

MURPH: What's got into you, anyway?

JOEY: C'mon, Chief. Up at the world. Everything's OK. (*The Indian ad libs words of pleading and pain.*)

MURPH: Leave him be. (*But Joey continues to help The Indian.*) Leave him be. What's with you? Hey, Joey! I said "Leave him be!" (*Murph pulls Joey back and The Indian pulls back with fear.*)

JOEY: OK, Murph. Enough's enough.

MURPH: Just tell me what the hell's wrong with you?

JOEY: (*Kicks basket.*) He tried to run away, that's all. Change the subject. Change the subject. It ain't important. I hit him, that's all.

MURPH: OK, so you hit him.

JOEY: (*Rises.*) OK! Where were you? Sick. Were you a little bit sick? I mean, you couldn't have been visiting, 'cause there ain't no one to visit, right?

MURPH: (*Crosses to Joey.*) What *do* you mean?

JOEY: Where the hell were you? (*Looks at Murph and giggles.*) You're a little green there, Irish.

MURPH: You're pretty funny. What the hell's so funny?

JOEY: Nothing's funny. The Chief and I were just having a little pow-wow and we got to wondering where you ran off to. Just natural for us to wonder, ain't it? (*To The Indian.*) Right, Chief?

MURPH: (*Crosses to Indian, feels sweater.*) Hey, look at that. Turkie's got a wooly sweater just like yours. Ain't that a terrific coincidence. You two been playing strip poker?

JOEY: Oh sure. Strip poker. The Chief won my sweater and I won three of his feathers and a broken arrow. (*To The Indian, he feigns a deep authoritative voice. Crosses to Indian.*) You wonder who I am, don't you? Perhaps this silver bullet will help to identify me? (*Joey extends his hand. The Indian peers into Joey's empty palm, quizzically. As he does, Murph quickly taps the underside of Joey's hand, forcing the hand to rise and slap The Indian's chin, sharply. The Indian pulls back at the slap. Joey turns on Murph, quickly:*) What the hell did you do that for, ya' jerk. The Chief didn't do nothing.

MURPH: Jesus, you and your Chief are pretty buddy-buddy ain't you? (*Mimicks Joey.*) "The Chief didn't do nothing." Jesus. You give him your sweater. Maybe you'd like to have him up for a beer . . .

JOEY: (*Grabs sweater.*) Drop it, Murph. You're giving me a pain in the ass.

MURPH: (*Retorts fiercely. Crosses to Joey.*) You little pisser. Who the hell do you think you're talking to? (*The telephone rings in the booth, they are all startled. Especially The Indian, who senses hope.*)

JOEY: (*After a long wait, Joey speaks the obvious, flatly.*) It's the phone.

MURPH: (*To The Indian.*) The kid's a whiz. He guessed that right away. (*Second ring.*)

JOEY: Should we answer it?

MURPH: What for? Who'd be calling here? It's a wrong number. (*The phone rings menacingly. A third time. Suddenly The Indian darts into the phone booth and grabs the receiver. Joey and Murph are too startled to stop him until The Indian has blurted out his hopeless plea, in his own language.*)

INDIAN: Prem? Is this my son? Prem? Please be Prem. Please help me. I'm frightened. Please help me. Two boys are hurting me . . . I'm frightened. Please. Prem? (*The Indian stops talking sharply and listens. He crumbles as the voice drones the wrong reply. He drops the receiver and stares with horror at the boys. Murph realizes The Indian's horror and begins to laugh hysterically. Joey stares silently. The Indian begins to mumble and weep. He walks from the phone booth. The Voice is heard as a drone from the receiver. The action freezes.*)

MURPH: (*Crosses to booth, hangs up receiver. Laughing.*) Hey!!! (*Kicks *him.*) What's the matter, Turkie? Don't you have a dime? (*Steps out of booth.*) Give Turkie a dime, Joe. Give him a dime.

JOEY: Jesus Christ. I'd hate to be an Indian.

MURPH: Hey, the paper! C'mon, Joey, get the paper from him. We'll call the Bronx.

JOEY: Cut it out, Murph. Enough's enough.

MURPH: Get the frigging piece of paper. What's the matter with you anyway?

JOEY: I just don't think it's such a terrific idea, that's all.

MURPH: You're chicken. That's what you are.

JOEY: Suppose his son has called the police? He knows the old man don't speak any English. He called the police. Right? And they'll trace our call.

MURPH: You're nuts. They can't trace any phone calls. Anyway, we'll be gone from here. You're nuts.

JOEY: I don't want to do it.

MURPH: For Christ's sakes. They can't trace nothing to nobody. Who's going to trace? Get the paper.

JOEY: (*Pulls back a step.*) Get it yourself. Go on. Get it yourself. I ain't going to get it.

MURPH: C'mon, Joey. It's not real. This is just a game. It ain't going to hurt anybody. You know that. It's just a game.

JOEY: Why don't we call somebody else? We'll call somebody else and have the Indian talk. That makes sense. Imagine if an Indian called you up and talked to you in Indian. I bet the Chief would go for that alright. Jesus, Murphy.

MURPH: Get the paper and picture.

INDIAN: What are you going to do now? I'm sorry. I thought that was my son, Prem. I thought that it might be Prem calling me on the telephone. Prem. That's who I thought it was. Prem.

MURPH: (*To Indian.*) Prem. That's the name. (*Plays the rhyme.*)

INDIAN: Prem?

MURPH: Yes, Prem. I want to call Prem. Give me the paper with his name.

INDIAN: What are you saying about Prem? Prem is my son. What have you done to Prem? What do you know about him? Do you know where he is?

MURPH: Shut up, already and give me the paper. (*He drags The Indian from the booth.*) Easy. I ain't gonna' hurt you. Easy.

JOEY: Jesus, Murph.

MURPH: (*Turning The Indian around so that they face each other.*) This is ridiculous. (*He searches The Indian, who resists a bit at first, and then not at all. Finally, Murph finds the slip of paper.*) I got it. I got it. Terrific. "Prem Gupta." In the Bronx. In the frigging Bronx. This is terrific. Here. Hold him. (*Indian follows Murph.*)

INDIAN: (*Crosses to Murph.*) What are you doing? Are you going to call my son?

MURPH: Shut him up. (*Joey grabs Indian, holds him. He fishes for a dime.*) Give me a dime, God damn it. This is terrific.

JOEY: (*Finds the coins in his pocket.*) Here's two nickels. (*Hands them over.*) I think this is a rotten idea, that's what I think. (*Murph crosses to booth. Pauses.*) And don't forget to pay me back those two nickels either.

MURPH: (*From booth.*) Just shut up. (*Dials the "Information Operator."*) Hello. Yeah, I want some information. I want a number up in the Bronx. Gupta. G.U.P.T.A. An Indian kid. His first name's Prem. P.R.E.M. No. I can't read the street right. Wait a minute. (*He reads.*) For Christ's sakes. How many Indians are up in the Bronx? There must be only one Indian named Gupta. There are two Indians named Gupta. (*To the Operator.*) Is the both of them names Prem? (*Pauses.*) Well, that's what I told you. Jesus. Wait a minute. OK. OK. Say that again. OK. OK. Right. OK. Thanks. (*Hurries quickly to return the coins to the slot. Gupta mumbles. To Joey.*) Don't talk to me. (*He dials.*) Six. Seven-four. Oh. One. (*Pauses.*) It's ringing. It's ringing. (*Pauses.*) Hello. (*Covers phone with hand.*) I got him! Hello? Is this Prem Gupta? Oh swell. How are you? (*To Joey.*) I got the kid! (*The Indian breaks from Joey's arm and runs to the telephone . . . Murph sticks out his leg and holds The Indian off. The Indian fights but seems weaker than ever.*)

INDIAN: (*Indian breaks partially loose. Joey restrains him. Screams.*) Please let me talk to my son. (*Murph slams The Indian aside, violently. Joey stands frozen watching. The Indian wails and finally talks calmly, as in a trance.*) Please let me talk to my son. Oh Prem. Please, I beg of you. Please. I'll give you anything at all. Just tell me what you want of me. Just let me talk with my son. Won't you, please? (*Murph glares at The Indian, who no longer tries to interfere, as it becomes obvious that he must listen to even the language he cannot understand.*)

MURPH: Just listen to me, will you, Gupta. I don't know where the hell your old man is, that's why I'm calling. We found an old elephant down here in Miami and we thought it must be yours. You can't tell for sure whose elephant is whose. You know what I mean? (*Murph is laughing now.*) What was that? Say that again. I can't hear you too well. All the distance between us, you know what I mean? It's a long way down here, you follow me? No. I ain't got no Indian. I just got an elephant. And he's eating all my peanuts. Gupta, you're talking too fast. Slow down.

INDIAN: Prem! Prem! Please come and get me. Please let me talk to my son, Mister. Why don't you let me talk to my son? (*Indian runs to booth, Murph shoves him, Joey pushes Indian to floor holding him. Joey lays on top of The Indian.*)

MURPH: That was the waiter. I'm in an Indian restaurant. (*Pauses.*) Whoa. Slow down, man. That was nobody. That was just a myth. Your imagination. (*Pauses. Screams into receiver.*) Shut up, damn you! And listen. OK? Ok. Are you listening? (*Murph tastes the moment. He silently clicks the receiver back to the hook. To Joey.*) He was very upset. (*To The Indian.*) He was very upset. (*Pauses.*) Well, what the hell's the matter with you? I only told him we found an elephant, that's all. I thought maybe he lost his elephant. (*The Indian whimpers.*)

INDIAN: Why have you done this? What have you said to my son?

MURPH: (*To Indian.*) You don't have to thank me, Turkie. I only told him your elephant was OK. He was probably worried sick about your elephant. (*Murph laughs. Crosses to Joey.*) This is terrific, Joey. Terrific. You should have heard the guy jabber. He was so excited he started talking in Indian just like the Chief. He said that Turkie here and him got separated today. Turkie's only been in the city one day. You're pretty stupid, Turkie. One day in the city . . . and look at the mess you've made. You're pretty stupid. We'll call again. Sure. (*Murph goes into the phone booth.*) Sure. (*The Indian leaps on Murph, who throws him off, maniacally pounding the booth four times, screaming:*) Get him off of me! (*Murph takes a dime from his pocket, shows it to Joey, and recalls the number. Talking into receiver. He dials number again and waits for reply. Joey puts one-half nelson on Indian.*) Hello? Is this Gupta again? Oh, hello there. I'm calling back to complain about your elephant. Hey, slow down, will you? Let me do the talking. OK? Your elephant is a terrific pain in the balls to me. Get it. Huh? Do you follow me so far? (*Pauses.*) I don't know what you're saying, man. How about if I do the talking, alright. Your elephant scares hell out of me and my pal here. We don't like to see elephants on the street. Spiders and snakes are OK, but elephants scare us. Elephants. Yeah, that's right. Don't you get it, pal? Look, we always see spiders and snakes. But we never expect to see an elephant. What do you mean? "I'm crazy"? I don't know nothing about your old man. I'm talking about your elephant. your elephant offends the hell out of me. So why don't you be a nice Indian kid and come pick him up? That's right. Wait a minute. I'll have to check the street sign. (*Covers the receiver.*) This is terrific. (*Talks again into the telephone.*) Jesus, I'm sorry about that. There don't seem to be no street sign. That's a bitch. I guess you lose your elephant. Well, what do you expect me to do, bring your elephant all the way up to the Bronx? Come off it, pal. You wouldn't ever bring my elephant home. I ain't no kid, you know! I've lost a couple of elephants in my day. (*Listens.*) Jesus, you're boring me now. I don't know what the hell you're talking about. Maybe you want to talk to your elephant. Huh? (*Turns to The Indian.*) Here, come talk to your "papoose." (*Offers the telephone. The Indian stares in disbelief, then grabs the phone from Murph's hands and begins to chatter wildly.*)

INDIAN: Prem? Oh, Prem. Please come and take me away. What? I don't know where I am. Please come and take me to your house. Please? There are two bad people. Two young men. They are dangerous. I cannot protect myself from them. Please. You must come and get me. (*Murph takes his knife from his pocket, cuts the line.*)

MURPH: You've had enough, Chief. (*Murph laughs aloud, showing Indian the dangling cord.*)

INDIAN: (*Not at once realizing the line must be connected, continues to talk into the telephone, in Hindi.*) Prem. Prem. Please come here. The street sign reads . . . (*He now realizes he has been cut off and stares dumbly at the severed receiver as Murph waves the severed cord in his face. To Murph.*) What have you done?

MURPH: There it is, Turkie. Who you talkin' to?

INDIAN: (*To Joey, screaming a father's fury and disgust.*) Why have you done this? Please. Please help me. (*Joey has been standing throughout the entire scene, frozen in terror and disgust. Joey bolts from the stage, muttering one continuous droning sob, as Murph kicks The Indian straight at Joey.)*

MURPH: Go ahead, Joey. Love him. Like a mother. Hey? Joey? What the hell's the matter??? C'mon, buddy??? (*Murph turns to The Indian, takes his hand, upstage, and cuts The Indian's hand, so blood is on the knife.*) Sorry, Chief. This is for my buddy, Joey. And for Pussyface. (*He calls off-stage.*) Joey! Buddy! What the hell's the matter???? (*Murph races from the stage after Joey.*) Joey! Wait up. Joey! I killed the Indian! (*He exits. The Indian stares dumbly at his hand, dripping blood. He then looks to the receiver and talks into it.*)

INDIAN: Prem. Prem. (*He walks center stage, well away from the telephone booth.*) Why can I not hear my son, Prem? Why have you done this to me? (*Suddenly, the telephone rings again. Once. Twice. The Indian is startled. He talks into the receiver, while he holds the dead line in his bleeding hand.*) Prem? Is that you? Prem? (*The telephone rings a third time.*) Prem. Prem? Is that you? (*A fourth ring. The Indian knows the telephone is dead.*) Prem. Prem. Help me. Prem. (*As the telephone rings a second time, in the silence of the night, the sounds of Two Boys' singing is heard:*)

JOEY: I walk the lonely streets at night . . .
A'lookin' for your door . . .

MURPH: I look and look and look and look . . .

TOGETHER: But, baby, you don't care . . .
But, baby, no one cares . . .
But, baby, no one cares . . .

(*Their song continues to build, as they repeat the lyrics, so the effect is one of many, many voices. The telephone continues its unanswered ring.*)

INDIAN: (*In English. He speaks the only words he has learned.*) How are you? You're welcome. You're welcome. How are you? How are you? Thank you. (*To the front.*) Thank you!

LIGHTS SWITCH TO BLACK.

END OF PLAY.

HINDI TRANSLATIONS OF INDIAN'S SPEECHES

1. MAI TOOM-HAREE BO-LEE NAH-HEE BOL SAK-TAH. MAI TUM-HAH REE BAH-SHA NAH-HEE SAH-MAJ-TAH.
2. MOO-JHAY MAHAF KAR-NAH MAI TOOM-HAH-REE BAH-ART NAH-HEE SAH-MAJ SAK-TAH.
3. MAI TOOM-HAREE BAH-AT NAH-HEE SAH-MAJ-TAH. MAI AP-NAY LAR-KAY KAH GHA-R DHOO-ND RAH-HAH HOOH. OOS-NAY MOO-JHAY MIL-NAH TAR PAHR NAH-JAH-NAY WOH CAH-HAH HAI. MAI OOS-KAH MAH-KAN DHOO-ND RAH-HAH HOON. OOS-KAH PAH-TAH YEH RAH-HAH K-YAH MAI SAH-HEE RAH-STAY PAR HOON.
4. MAI-NAY AP-NAY LAR-KAY KOH SU-BAH SAY NAH-HEE DAY-KHA. TOOM-HARA SHAH-HAR BAH-HOOT HEE BARAH HAI.
5. MOO-JHAY MAHAF KAR-NAH. MOO-JHAY YAH-HAN AYE ZYAH-DA SAH-MAY NA-HEE HOO-AH.
6. K-YAH KAH-HA TOOM-NAY.
7. YAH K-YAH HAI.
8. BHA-EE MAI TOOM-HAREE BAH-AT NAH-HEE SAH-MAJ SAK-TAH. BUS YAH-HAN KIS SA-MAY A-TEE-HAI. K-YAH MAI SA-HEE BUS STOP PAR HOON.
9. MAI TOOM-HAREE BAH-AT NAH-HEE SAH-MAJ SAK-TAH.
10. HAH-N. YEH-THEE-KH HAI. MAI TOOM-HAREE BAH-SHA NAH-HEE SAH-MAJ-TAH. MOO-JHAY MAH-AF KAR-NAH PAR AH-BHEE MOO-JHAY TOOM-HA-RAY DESH AYE KUH-CHAH HEE DIN TOH HU-YAY HAIN. MOO-JHAY TOOM-HA-REE BAH-SHA SEE-KH-NAY KAH AH-BHEE SAH-MAI HEE NAH-HEE MILAH. MAI AHP-NAY LAR-KAY SAY BIH-CHUR GAH-YA HOON. OOS-SAY TOH TOOM-HA-RAY DESH MAY RAH-TAY CHAI SAH-AL HOH GAH-YE HAIN. JAH-B DOH MAH-HEE-NAY PAH-LAY OOS-KEE MAH KAH INTH-KAHL HOO-AH TOH OOS-NAY MOO-JHAY YA-HAN BOOH-LAH BHEH-JHA OR MAI AH GAH-HAY. WOH BAH-RA HON-HAR LAR-KA HAI. MOO-JHAY MAH-AF KAR-NAH KEE MAIH-NAY AH-BHEE TOOM-HA-REE BAH-SHA NA-HEE SEE-KHEE PAR MAI SEE-KH LOON-GHA.
11. MOO-JHAY MAH-AF KAR-NAH. MAI TOOM-HAREE BAH-SHA NA-HEE SAH-MAJ SAK-TA.
12. NA-HEE BHA-YEE TOOM AH-B K-YAH KAH-ROGAY.
13. NA-HEE NA-HEE BHA-YEE. MAI MAH-AFEE MAH-NG-TA HOON.

14. NA-HEE.
15. MOO-JHAY OR NAH SAH-TAO. MAIH-NAY TOOM-HARA K-YAH BIGARAH HAI. MOO-JHAY OR NAH SAH-TAO. MOO-JHAY IN-SEH BACHAH-LOH.
16. PREM KYAH WOH MAY-RAH LARKAH HAI. PREM (PRAY-EM) BAY-TAH MOD-JHAY BACHAH-LOW. MAI FAH-NS GA-YAH HOON. YEH DOH GOON-DAY MOO-JHAY MAR RA-HAY HAIN. MAI BA-HOOT GHAH-BARA GAYA HOON. PRAY-EM.
17. AHB TOOM K-YAH KAH-ROGAY. MOO-JHAY MAH-AF KAR-DOH BHA-YEE. MAIH-NAY SOH-CHA TAH KEY WOH MAY-RAH BAY-TAH PRAY-EM HAI. MOO-JHAY TELEPHONE KAR RAHA MAI-NAY SOH-CHAH THAH-SHA-YAHD WOH PRAY-EM HOH.
18. PRAY AIM.
19. TOOM PRAY-AIM KAY BA-RAY MAY K-YAH KAH RA-HAY HO. TOOM-NAY PRAY-AIM KOH KYAH KEY-YAH. TOOM OOS-KAY BAH-RAY MAY K-YAH JAN-TAY HO. K-YAH TOOM JAN-TAY HO WOH KAH-HAN HAI.
20. TOOM K-YAH KAR RA-HAY HO. K-YAH TOOM PRAY-AIM K-OH BOO-LAH RA-HAY HO.
21. CREE-PAYAH MOO-JHAY AP-NAY LAR-KAY SAY BAH-AT KAR-NAY DOH.
22. CREE-PAYAH MOO-JHAY AHP-NAY LAR-KAY SAY BAH-AT KAR-NAY DOH. MAI TOOM-HARAY HAH-TH JOR-TAH HOON. MAI TOOM-HAY JOH MANGO-GAY DOON-GAH. BUS MOO-JHAY OOS-SAY BAH-AT KAR-NAY DOH –
23. PRAY-AIM BHAI-YAH MOO-JHAY AH-KAY LAY JA-OH. MOO-JHAY AP-NAY LAR-KAY SAY BAH-AT KAR-NAY DOH MOO-JHAY OOS-SAY BAH-AT K-YOHN NAH-HEE KAR-NAY DAY-TAY.
24. TOOM-NAY AI-SAW K-YOHN KI-YAH. TOOM-NAY MAY-RAY LAR-KAY KOH K-YAH KA-HAH HAI.
25. PRAY-AIM, BHAI-YAH PRAY-AIM MOO-JHAY AH-KAY LAY JAH-OH K-YAH? MOO-JHAY NAY-HEE PA-TAH MAI KAH-HAN HOO-N. MOO-JHAY AH-HP-NAY GHA-AR LAY CHAH-LOW YA-HAHN DO-OH BAD-MASH LAR-KAY, JO BAH-HOOT KHA-TAR-NAHK HAI – OON-SAY HAI NAH-HEE BAH-CHA SAK-TAH AH-PA-NAY KOH. TOOM AIK-DAM MOO-JHAY AH-KAY LAY JA-OH.
26. PRAY-AIM, PRAY-AIM, YA-HAHN AA-OH. SAH-RAK KAH NAH-AM HAI . . . YEH TOOM-NAY K-YAH KEY-YAH.

27. TOOM-NAY YEH K-YOHN KEY-YAH. CRI-PA-YAH MAY-REE MAH-DAH-D KAH-ROW.
28. PRAY-AIM, PRAY-AIM, MAI AH-PA-NAY LAR-KAY KEY AH-WAH-AZ K-YON NAH-HEE SOON SAK TAH. PRAY-AIM! TOOM-NAY MAY-RAY SAH-AHTH AIH-SAW K-YOHN KEY-YAW. BAY-TAH PRAY-AIM, K-YAH TOOM HO?
29. PRAY-AIM, PRAY-AIM, BAY-TAH K-YAH TOOM HO – PRAY-AIM PRAY-AIM—MOO-JHAY BAH-CHALO PRAY-AIM.

RATS

With love, to Doris

RATS was first presented by Lyn Austin, Hale Mathews and Oliver Smith, as the final piece in an omnibus of short plays entitled COLLISION COURSE, at the Cafe Au Go Go, in New York City, on May 8, 1968. (The production was transferred to the Actor's Playhouse, in New York City, on June 11, 1968.) Directed by Edward Parone; the production was designed by Michael Davidson; and the costumes were by Diedre Cartier. The production stage manager was M. M. Streicher. The cast, in order of appearance, was as follows:

JEBBIE .... Tom Rosqui
BOBBY .... Scott Glenn
BABY .... Tom Scott

Introduction

Rats was first written for inclusion in an evening of a dozen or so short plays, which were produced in NYC, off-Broadway, in the Spring of 1968, under the omnibus title "Collision Course". *Rats* was never intended to be a mainstream play. It is painful to watch, clearly written for an America that could assassinate Bobby Kennedy and Martin Luther King. I never imagined that *Rats* would have a life beyond its time ... that it would ever find an audience, beyond the '60's or '70's. Thus, to be sitting in front of a computer as I am, today, in Paris, in the rainy Winter of 1994, writing an introduction to a new edition of *Rats* is nothing short of amazing to me. But, it is nothing compared to the fact that I am actually here in Paris to direct this 1968 play, in a new French-language production, opening next week at Théâtre du Lucernaire. And, characteristically, I am worried: Will they like *Rats*? Is it too tough? Will it hurt my career in France? ... *Alors, la compétition: c'est une maladie incurable*!

Over the years, *Rats* has been graced by some truly exciting young artists. Scott Glenn was a rat among the 1968 off-Broadway cast, and Richard Dreyfuss played a rat in the L.A. premiere of *Rats*, just one year later. And, the following year, in Florida, Sylvester Stallone put on the fur and ate the cheese. In the early 1970's, I saw a production of *Rats* used as the Sunday sermon in a church at Mount Holyoke College ... directed by Wendy Wasserstein. A few years later, Al Pacino directed an astonishingly ratty production of *Rats* in New York ... and, again, a few years later, in Boston. In fact, *Rats* has been performed in the USA, continuously, since its initial off-Broadway outing. And, like its author, *Rats* seems to enjoy an active life in Europe, as well.

But, when *Rats* was first written and produced in New York City, I was far too busy chasing SUCCESS to enjoy my success. I was in my twenties, and getting myself KNOWN as a NEW YORK PLAYWRIGHT seemed more important to me, at that time, than did LIFE, itself. I was certain that if I FAILED to get FAMOUS, fast, I would be sent back to Massachusetts, to my room, upstairs, in my parents house, where I would surely have to live out my days in SHAME.

I have always been hypochondriacal. Between the age of 25 and 30, when I wrote most of my one-act plays, *Rats*, included, I was at my worst. I was certain that DEATH was near. I had attacks of GREAT PANIC, daily. I had MIGRAINE HEADACHES, almost constantly.

In a great rush to CREATE GREAT PLAYS before being BURIED IN MY GRAVE, I wrote whenever and wherever I could: in cars, in restaurants, at my desk at work. I had two money-paying jobs at the time—one teaching school, part-time; the other writing and directing TV commercials for an advertising agency, full-time. ("Hertz now offers unlimited mileage! Drive yourself crazy for $99!") ... Three of my five children were already alive and eating food.

Two things were certain in my life:

1) Never enough money.
2) Absolutely no sleep.

Understandably, during this early period of my life/career, I tended to write one-act plays, rather than full-length plays, as it was impossible for me to STAY FOCUSED for long periods of time. Short, one-act plays (characterized by ENORMOUS BURSTS OF ENERGY) mirrored my life: my CONDITION.

Four of the plays I wrote between the age of 25 and 30 (when I was first dying)—*Line*, *The Indian Wants The Bronx*, *It's Called the Sugar Plum*, and *Rats*—were all produced, off-Broadway, during 1968, my extraordinary first season as a "promising, young playwright" in New York. All four of the plays worked well. At the season's end, Newsweek Magazine announced: "1968 was the Year of Horovitz". I won a lot of prizes. I got movie-offers. I quit my jobs and began writing for a living, full-time.

My MIGRAINES worsened. My PANIC increased.

I was such a busy boy, working on twenty projects at the same time. I don't recall seeing a single rehearsal of *Rats.* I can only remember seeing two performances of *Rats* ... one, the play's final preview (the night before the critics arrived), when I was terrified beyond description. The only other performance of *Rats* I recall seeing was the play's opening night, when I was beyond terror: I had to leave the theatre to be ill.

Thus, by the time *Rats* had opened in its NYC premiere, I'd found the SUCCESS I so coveted ... but, hadn't witnessed, experienced, or enjoyed in the slightest.

Returning to Paris, as I have been doing for the past several years, to direct my plays in French language, has been a great joy in my life. I come back here, not only to old friends, but, often to old plays that can still thrill and mystify me. To re-discover my early plays, like *Rats*, as I am doing, now, is to be able to, in a sense, re-discover myself ... journey, (somewhat) calmly, through a time in my life filled with great and mysterious energy ... through a time in my life filled with some of my earliest joys and some of my earliest nightmares ... Through plays from that time that are like children to me ... special children ... frozen in time, eternally young.

As a "promising new French director", I must make once again Rats appropriate for today ... for life as it is, now. I must make this play once again startling ... entertaining ... provocative. I think I can ... But, perhaps, I can't? But, will they like this play? Is it too tough? Too '60's? Is it just too ratty? ...

Ahhh, the JOYOUS PANIC OF CREATION returns!

ADDENDUM: I met Samuel Beckett for the first time, in the late '60's, in Paris, at the Closérie des Lilas. Our first meeting was arranged by the actress, Eléanore Hirt. Without my knowing it, Mrs Hirt must have given Mr Beckett a number of my plays to read, prior to our meeting. When I approached him, he was staring into space, lost in a memory. I whispered a nervous "Hello ... Excuse me ... Mr Beckett?" ... He turned, took a few moments to focus his eyes, smiled, and, to my amazement, replied "I prefer Rats".

Characters

JEBBIE
BOBBY
BABY

Setting

A baby's room. With regret, the present.

AUTHOR'S NOTE

It is the Author's intention to NOT limit this play to New York audiences.

It will therefore be necessary for names of suburban communities such as Greenwich, Connecticut, and Upper Montclair, New Jersey, to be changed for each and every production of this play outside of the New York area.

RATS

Lights up on Jebbie, a fat Harlem Rat, who sits, legs crossed, counting money. He wears grey fur vest. We see an oversized chair, dwarfing the old rat. An oversized playpen is set, opposite side of stage, with something hidden, under a large, tattered quilt, inside.

JEBBIE: One Dollar, One Peseta. One Mark. One Kroner. One Shilling. (*Suddenly, he senses the presence of another Rat. He leaps up and runs about the stage frantically. Yelling:*) Where are you??? Who's there??? C'mon out, God damn it. I know you're here. Come out and show yourself. Show yourself. (*A second Rat enters. Bobby. He's younger and thinner than Jebbie. They circle each other cautiously. Jebbie is obviously stronger, Bobby frightened.*) There you are. I knew it!!!

BOBBY: Please. Please. Please don't. (*They continue to circle each other. Jebbie jabs at Bobby who pulls back each time.*) Please help me.

JEBBIE: What do you want?

BOBBY: I want in.

JEBBIE: Out!! Out!!

BOBBY: In. I want in. Please.

JEBBIE: Out, like the rest of them. Out!!!! (*Attacks; traps Bobby.*)

BOBBY: Don't kill me! I've got a secret!

JEBBY: What?

BOBBY: Listen. I'm sorry. I mean, I don't want to interrupt you or trouble you. Bother you. I can see you're busy. (*Pauses.*) You've got to help me.

JEBBIE: Out!! Out!! Out of my place, kid!!! Find your own, kid!!!

BOBBY: Charlie "ratted" on his brother!

JEBBIE: Don't play on my sympathy. Out!!!

BOBBY: He's a dirty rat!!!

JEBBIE: Don't play on my sympathy.

BOBBY: I smell a rat!!!

JEBBIE: Don't play that game with me, kid. I was a kid. I heard all them expressions. They don't affect me now. Find your own way. Find your own place. Out!!!

BOBBY: Rats spelled backwards is star!

JEBBIE: Out!!!!

BOBBY: Please. You gotta' help me. (*They continue to circle each other, but much more slowly now.*) It took me weeks to get up here. Weeks to find you. So I could talk with you. Be with you. Please. You've got to help me!!! Please. You got to!!!

JEBBIE: I don't *gotta'* do anything, pal.

BOBBY: I know that. I know how busy you are. Look, I want in. I want in so much it's killing me. Please don't hate me for not knocking. For just running in on you, but I need help. I really need help.

JEBBIE: (*Assuming the posture of businessman.*) Look, when I was a kid, struggling like a son of a bitch, I needed help, right?

BOBBY: I would have helped you.

JEBBIE: Yeah. Sure.

BOBBY: Listen, please. I would have. I help everybody I can. (*Digs into his pocket. Pulls out a chunk of cheese and offers it to Jebbie.*) Here.

JEBBIE: You've got to be kidding.

BOBBY: (*Finds two other pieces.*) I heard there was a lack of cheeses.

JEBBIE: Cheeses! Maybe you need help, kid, but you ain't getting me into a helpful mood. What do you want?

BOBBY: (*Confused that his gift has been rejected.*) Cheeses from the finest estate in Greenwich, Connecticut.

JEBBIE: (*Enraged.*) That kind of help!!! Another one. Look. I'll hold my temper down. But I gotta' tell you, kid, I'm hip to your problem because I get calls from two hundred little Madras-commuting-blonde-Nazi-God-Bless-America-Mice like you every week. I'm hip to your problem, but I don't want to help and I ain't gonna' help. Where the Christ do you think I was born? The Bronx? Avenue A? I pulled my ass up from Jersey. That's right, Jersey. Not Newark either, so don't get any smart ideas. I started right at the bottom, kid.

BOBBY: South Orange?

JEBBIE: Worse.

BOBBY: Montclair?

JEBBIE: C'mon, that's nothing.

BOBBY: My God, where?

JEBBIE: Now tell me why I should tell you? Huh? I've got friends I've never told. Why should I tell you?

BOBBY: My mother left me those cheeses.

JEBBIE: Huh?

BOBBY: My mother left me those cheeses. In her will.

JEBBIE: Your mother?

BOBBY: She got it. I saw the seeds. I told her not to eat them. I was only a kid, but I knew. "Don't eat them, mama. Please." (*He's weeping now.*) "Don't eat the seeds, mama. I think it's the stuff." It was bad for us. We were all skinny. Hungry. I begged her to eat the cheeses. Begged her. But she was my mother. Things were bad. She said . . . she said . . . (*He breaks down, crying.*)

JEBBIE: (*Walks over and stares at Bobby.*) Okay. Sit down.

BOBBY: I wasn't going to cry. I haven't cried for fifteen months.

JEBBIE: Don't believe that crap about not crying. Men can cry. Go on. Cry your ass off. No one's gonna' know. There's nobody here. No one's gonna' know.

BOBBY: I'm all right now. I'm all right. I can't understand it. I haven't cried for fifteen months. Not since my father told me how things were. What I was. You know what I mean?

JEBBIE: Look, kid. I said it was okay to cry. Go on. Cry like a man. That's what *they* don't know. That's a big thing we've got going on them. It's okay. Whine. Cry. Go on.

BOBBY: (*Weeping, then crying, he reaches out for Jebbie to hold him.*) I'm lonely! I'm scared.

JEBBIE: Don't touch me. Hey. Don't touch me. (*Jebbie pulls back quickly, in a strange frightened move as Bobby threatens to embrace him.*) Go on. Cry. Cry like a man. Get all them tears out good. Just sit over there and cry, kid. It'll do you good. Damn good.

BOBBY: I'm better now. Jesus, just being here with you makes me better. The loneliness started to go away as I started to get closer to this place. I'm okay now.

JEBBIE: Star spelled backwards, huh? When'd you figure that one out?

BOBBY: Hell. When I was thirteen or so. I told my folks and they laughed and laughed and laughed.

JEBBIE: (*Proudly.*) Superstar is Repus-Rats! (*Considers it.*) That don't make any sense.

BOBBY: I'm not normally like this. I got myself kind of worked up. I walked all the way here by myself. All the way from Greenwich. It's a long way. I got myself tired. I got worked up. I saw others like us in the sewers on the way. They got me worked up. Scared that it was all a mistake. I got scared. I got this awful feeling all over me like I just wanted to lay down and cry and maybe die. You know?

JEBBIE: Sure, kid. I know. (*Pauses.*) Let's eat some of those cheeses, huh.

BOBBY: (*Thrilled. Simply.*) Thank you.

JEBBIE: Don't start any of your sweet stuff on me. I'm hungry, that's all.

BOBBY: (*Gives Jebbie his cheese.*) See? Three kinds.

JEBBIE: I ain't gonna' eat alone.

BOBBY: But they're a gift.

JEBBIE: You're a dumb little bastard, you know that? You got to me. Got me going with you. Don't screw it all around trying to brown-nose me now. You're hungry? Eat. You ain't hungry? Take your cheeses and fuck off.

BOBBY: I'm sorry. I'm sorry if you think I'm brown-nosing or sucking around or anything like that. Look, I want to be honest with you. I wouldn't just give you my cheeses if I didn't want something from you, right? That's honest, isn't it?

JEBBIE: (*Delighted.*) You're all right, kid. You're definitely all right. That's straight talk. That's good. That's good cheese, too.

BOBBY: You see, my mother knew it would do me some good someday. Get me out of the mess. You know what I mean? So she ate the seeds.

JEBBIE: Suicide, huh?

BOBBY: No. That's just it. Suicide's beautiful. For us, I mean. (*Pauses.*) I really am paranoid.

JEBBIE: What's that?

BOBBY: Paranoid. That's one of those words you learn . . .

JEBBIE: One of THEM words you learn!

BOBBY: Yeah. One of THEM words you learn when you're on the skids. Greenwich. Anywhere in Fairfield County. It just means that you imagine bad things that maybe aren't entirely true.

JEBBIE: There's your first lesson. You think I don't know what "paranoid" means? Huh? You think I don't know them big words?

BOBBY: I don't get it.

JEBBIE: Listen. (*Pauses for "impact."*) Penis envy.

BOBBY: My God!

JEBBIE: That's nothing. Listen. (*Lays the words out slowly.*) Nursery School, Caviar. Schvatza.

BOBBY: You weren't kidding, were you?

JEBBIE: (*Checks to see if anyone could possibly, overhear him and then speaks, rapidly, as a typewriter.*) Bulls. Bears. Sell short. Capital gains. Account Executive. Copy Supervisor. Underwriter. (*The clincher.*) Pentium microprocessors.

BOBBY: That recently, huh?

JEBBIE: What do you mean?

BOBBY: That recently. Just what I said. You must have been there within the last eighteen months.

JEBBIE: (*Shocked.*) How'd you know????

BOBBY: Pentium Microprocessors. They're fairly new. Not two decades even.

JEBBIE: (*Amazed and delighted, again.*) Hey. You're a pretty smart kid.

BOBBY: I'm no kid.

JEBBIE: You look like a kid.

BOBBY: I'm twenty-five.

JEBBIE: You're kidding.

BOBBY: I know. I've always looked nine.

JEBBIE: Hell, I'm twenty-nine. Twenty-five's a kid in my book.

BOBBY: My grandfather went all the way to thirty-nine.

JEBBIE: (*Incredulously.*) Thirty-nine months old?

BOBBY: Yes. (*Corrects himself.*) Yep. Thirty-nine months and three days to the minute. And he bought it with Barium Chloride too.

JEBBIE: No shit.

BOBBY: (*Delighted by Jebbie's language.*) No shit! 'Course he was down in Georgia. The heat helps.

JEBBIE: Yeah, but thirty-nine.

BOBBY: Terrific, huh?

JEBBIE: He must have come over on the Mayflower.

BOBBY: Way back they did.

JEBBIE: Maybe you ought to stay in Greenwich. (*Bobby, hurt by that insult, withdraws.*) C'mon, kid. You've got to have a sense of humor. Hell. What's your name?

BOBBY: Bobby.

JEBBIE: That's okay. I'm Jebbie.

BOBBY: You think I don't know that?

JEBBIE: (*Extremely pleased.*) That's what you call your modesty. I guess everybody knows me, huh?

BOBBY: You're a legend in Fairfield County.

JEBBIE: I'll give you your first lesson, Bobby. You don't get famous by waiting for somebody to do anything for you. You got to fight it out yourself, kid. You gotta' fight dirty and tough. None of us got to be anything by not playing it dirty, Bobby. You think your Grandfather went to thirty-nine by being a nice-guy? Shit, no! He must have known the game. When to bite and kill. When to play it cool.

BOBBY: He was tough, all right.

JEBBIE: See this scar? You're privileged, Bobby. That scar's from a kid just like you. Wanted to take over, Bobby. Wanted Jebbie's place. But I got him, Bobby.

BOBBY: Oh, wow! Teeth?

JEBBIE: Forget it. Don't think about it. We got it from all sides, kid. If the others don't get you, your own will.

BOBBY: I felt that. I felt it in the sewers coming up here. They scared me, Jebbie. Something awful.

JEBBIE: You fight and you fight and you fight. But one day you wake up and, if you've fought 'em all hard enough, you've made it. You have a place that's all your own. You have money. Food. All the stuff you think you'll never get, you get. If you fight hard enough.

BOBBY: I want to learn. Honest. I want to learn.

JEBBIE: You gotta' learn things nobody ever told you about. Believe me. Things nobody ever told you about.

BOBBY: But I want to. I want to.

JEBBIE: Barium, huh?

BOBBY: Oh yeah. Thirty-nine.

JEBBIE: That's how my old lady got it.

BOBBY: Your mother?

JEBBIE: Naw. My old lady. The Missus. Barium Chloride. Then, they got the kids.

BOBBY: I'm sorry. Big family?

JEBBIE: (*Softly.*) Not huge. Not bad. Just nice. (*Pauses.*) We had sixty kids. (*Pauses, sentimentally.*) That was a beautiful year. Then she got it first. I couldn't handle the kids on my own. Funny the way things happen. I went off for about five minutes. We were in Jersey. I told you that.

BOBBY: You didn't tell me what town.

JEBBIE: Upper Montclair. You were pretty close.

BOBBY: Upper Montclair! Jesus Christ. Upper Montclair is as bad as

Greenwich.

JEBBIE: (*With fury.*) Don't kid yourself. Greenwich is Gary, Indiana, compared to Upper Montclair. At least you've got some water. The ocean. And the place where the maids live. They had nothing, man. Nothing. No garbage. No grease globs. Nothing. Really nothing.

BOBBY: Upper Montclair. Wow!

JEBBIE: I went off for five minutes. That's what it took. Carbon Bisulphide. A rag soaked in it over the door. I could smell death. You ever smell death, Bobby?

BOBBY: There isn't one of us alive who hasn't. You know that.

JEBBIE: (*Challenges.*) Carbon Bisulphide? Your sixty kids? C'mon. (*Remembers.*) I tried to move the rag. I went out for five minutes. Five whole minutes. They were gone. I just ran. I ran and ran and ran.

BOBBY: How'd you get up here?

JEBBIE: In a car. I got right into the bastards' car. Rode right into the city with them.

BOBBY: That's beautiful.

JEBBIE: That's how you've got to push, Bobby. That's how you've got to do it. (*Pauses.*) But you've done it, haven't you? You made into my place. You're all right. God damned all right. (*Hugs Bobby.*) Rats spelled backwards is star!

(*There's a huge, frightening childlike scream. They both dart away.*)

BABY: WAHHHHHHHHHHHHHH!

BOBBY: (*Hiding; terrified.*)What is it? What is it?

JEBBIE: Easy. Go easy. It's the kid.

BOBBY: I could smell it.

JEBBIE: It's just the kid. (*A black "baby", wearing diapers, an adult, rises in playpen from under quilt; continues to cry and whine, but, doesn't yet see the Rats.*)

BOBBY: He's all black! He's a black baby. My grandfather told me about black babies. (*Note: Baby can be female.*)

JEBBIE: (*Nervously trying to change the subject away from Baby.*) I thought he lived in Georgia.

BOBBY: (*Moving toward Baby.*) It's my fantasy. My mother told me. She came up on a train. He told her, but she told me about black babies . . . about my grandfather and the black babies . . . so much I keep believing he told me.

JEBBIE: (*Calls from distance.*) What?

BOBBY: (*Moves back to Jebbie.*) I never met my grandfather. I just heard my mother talk about it so much, it's as though I was really there myself. Jesus. Don't let me get you mad. I'm just excited. A black baby.

JEBBIE: (*Playing it down.*) Yeah. So. Big deal. A black baby. We've been living together for so long, I forget he's here.

BOBBY: Can I eat him?

JEBBIE: Huh?

BOBBY: Can I eat him? Bite him? I've never bitten a black baby. I've never bitten anyone. Not in Greenwich. There's nobody. Nobody. You're from Jersey. You know.

JEBBIE: Lay off, kid. Lay back.

BOBBY: What's the matter? (*The Baby crawls near them, whimpering. They freeze until the Baby crawls back to his original spot across the stage from them.*)

JEBBIE: Just lay back. Take it easy.

BOBBY: I don't get it.

JEBBIE: Don't try to get it. Just shut up.

BOBBY: Do you bite him much?

JEBBIE: (*Caught.*) Yeah. Well sure. I bite him a lot. Not too much. I mean, if I bite him *all* the time, I'd screw everything up, wouldn't I?

BOBBY: (*Is "licking his lips" at the sight of Baby.*) Huh?

JEBBIE: Look. Just pretend he ain't there, that's all.

BOBBY: That's crazy. How can I do that? There he is. Big. Black and delicious. If you knew how long I've been waiting for something like this!!! Jesus, God. One day in the city and look what I've got. This is terrific, Jebbie. Terrific. I'm very happy.

JEBBIE: Don't settle in so fast, kid. This crib here is mine, see. I dragged myself out of Jersey right to the top of the heap. Just 'cause I ate your cheeses and gave you some of my minutes doesn't mean you moved in. Don't get any smart ideas.

BOBBY: Suppose I just scare him a little? You know. Flash my teeth and whimper.

JEBBIE: I told you to lay off.

BOBBY: I'll bite his foot. (*Bobby makes a move toward the Baby. Jebbie suddenly pounces upon Bobby and beats him to the ground.*)

JEBBIE: Keep away from him. Lay off! (*Baby sees the scuffle and begins to cry again.*)

BOBBY: Ughhh. Hey. Hey. Stop it. Ughhh. (*Gets to his knees. He's shocked. He sees the Baby again and goes for him. Jebbie pounces on Bobby again and beats him until he's unconscious. Baby is crying now and crawling about frantically, from corner to corner of playpen. Jebbie checks to see that Bobby is unconscious, then crawls to Baby and embraces him.*)

JEBBIE: Easy, baby. Easy, boy. It's all right. Don't cry now. Want some milk? Want me to get your bottle? It's in the corner.

BABY: (*Talks gibberish babytalk.*) Nooo. Gee gee waa too too meee.

JEBBIE: No milk for my baby? Good baby? (*He cradles the Baby in his arms.*) Good baby, stop crying. Good baby. That's my baby.

BABY: (*Calmed down. Friendly. Recognizes Jebbie.*) Goo gaa gaa meee? Waa waaa tooo too gee.

JEBBIE: I wish you could talk. I wouldn't let him hurt you. Don't worry.

BOBBY: (*Coming to his knees.*) What's going on?

BABY: (*Sees Bobby and gets panicky.*) Waa waa dooo mee mee. Gee too tooo baabaa!!!! (*Jebbie runs to the Baby and then back to Bobby. He stares hopelessly at both. His crisis is clear. Bobby is still stunned. Baby screams again. Frustrated; trying to speak.*) Naw naw nee mee gee gee naw naw nooo nooo no no no.

JEBBIE: Please, Baby. Please don't cry. No one's gonna' hurt you. Not while I'm here, baby. I can take care of you. I've taken care of you all this time, right. Don't cry.

BABY: Naw naw naw naw naw naw naw naw naw.

JEBBIE: Don't make that noise. They'll come in again. They come in. Remember when they almost caught us? (*Baby crawls around the stage, crying and whining, frantically. Jebbie catches Baby and cradles him, again.*) There. Easy. Easy, baby. C'mon now.

BOBBY: (*Fully conscious, again.*) Jebbie. What's happening What's happening? (*Sees Jebbie cradling Baby.*) Hey! Hey! What the hell are you doing?

JEBBIE: Just shut up, kid. Shut up. You'll make a noise and they'll come. They'll put the rag on you. One sniff and you'll buy it. Shut up.

BOBBY: Bite him. Bite him.

JEBBIE: They'll put the rag over the door and your kids will be dead. Sixty kids will be dead. You go out for a whole minute. All the kids you can make in twelve months will be dead. All your two-month-olds. All your six-month-olds. They'll all be dead. One sniff.

BOBBY: Bite him. Bite his throat. (*Bobby runs at Jebbie; stuns him; then, runs into playpen and grabs the Baby, who is screaming in terror.*)

BABY: Waa waa. Too too mee waa waa. Naw naw naw naw. (*Bobby pounces on the Baby and pins him to the floor. Bobby is just about to bite Baby's throat when Jebbie screams.*)

JEBBIE: Please. Bobby. Please. I'm begging you. Please don't hurt him.

BOBBY: (*Shocked. Stops.*) Huh?

JEBBIE: Please don't hurt Baby. Don't hurt Baby. Enough babies are hurt. One sniff. Can't you see? Enough babies are hurt.

BOBBY: What's the matter with you?

JEBBIE: I'll let you in. I'll let you in.

BOBBY: What do you mean?

JEBBIE: I'll let you in. Get you the right connections. Give you money. Give you whatever you want. You'll be in. Uptown. Way up here. You'll be in the castle. With me. Stop. I'll let you in. I have Kroners. Shillings. Colored glass. Grease globs. (*Begging now.*) Please stop. Just leave him be. (*Suddenly, Bobby runs from playpen, his feelings somehow hurt. The baby frantically cries and crawls to Jebbie. Baby cuddles Jebbie's legs and coos.*)

BABY: Gaa gaa gee gee gooo.

BOBBY: I get it. I get it. You're chicken, Jebbie. You're chicken. That's what they meant. That's what they meant.

JEBBIE: Who? (*Moves toward Bobby.*)

BOBBY: I passed them in the sewers on my way up here. I walked for days, Jebbie. Days gone. Just to see you. The famous Jebbie. Jebbie. They told me you were over the hill, Jebbie. I couldn't believe it. All the stories. Since I was a kid. The famous Jebbie. What a crock of shit, huh, Jebbie? Jebbie's a chicken-shit from Upper Montclair. That's what it is, right Jebbie? That's the story, the real story. Jebbie's over the hill.

JEBBIE: I'll let you in, Bobby. Big things can happen.

BOBBY: What did you call me. Madras-commuter? Funny, coming from you, Jebbie. (*Pauses.*) Jebbie?

JEBBIE: What?

BOBBY: (*Suddenly, Bobby overpowers Jebbie, again—scoots inside playpen and captures the terrified, screaming baby.*) Kill him, Jebbie. Bite him on the neck on the vein that makes the blood flow like red piss from an Indian, Jebbie. Find the vein, Jebbie, and eat it up. Chew Baby's vein, Jebbie. Upper-Montclair-Madras-Commuter-Family-Rat-Jebbie. Chew the vein.

JEBBIE: (*Sobbing.*) Your mother died, Bobby. You smelled death, Bobby. Why more?

BOBBY: Who killed her, you chicken shit bastard? Huh?

JEBBIE: I can let you in. I'll let you in.

BOBBY: Chew the vein, Jebbie. Chew the vein or I'll walk back down the sewers and tell them all, Jebbie. Tell them all so they come up here . . . so they come up where Jebbie's got the best place . . . where Jebbie's on top. Where Jebbie's King. Way uptown where the shit's on the streets and nobody cares but us, Jebbie.

JEBBIE: You'd do that? You'd do that?

BOBBY: You've got a choice, Jebbie. You chew the vein or I chew the vein. Which is it? (*Jebbie enters playpen. For a moment, it seems as if Jebbie will kill the baby to save himself. But, then, he pounces on Bobby and grabs Bobby's throat, strangling him with every ounce of strength he can muster. He then bites Bobby—kills him.*)

BABY: (*Screams and runs about in panic.*) Naw naw gee sawsss nawww nawww naww nawwwn naawwwnnn nooooo.

BOBBY: (*Struggling hopelessly for his life.*) Don't. Please. Please. Don't Jebbie. Don't take my cheeses. My cheeses. Cheeses. (*He's dead.*)

BABY: (*Crawls about frantically as Jebbie stares at the dead Bobby. Jebbie is crying. Suddenly Baby stands up and speaks clearly in English.*) Mommy. Daddy. Help me! Rat! Rats! RATS!!!

JEBBIE: (*Helplessly, he stares, weeping, as the lights fade to black.*)

END OF PLAY.

MORNING

With love, to Doris

MORNING was presented by The Eugene O'Neill Memorial Theatre Foundation, Waterford, Connecticut, and The Festival of Two Worlds, Spoleto, Italy under the title CHIAROSCURO, in preparation for its Broadway premiere by Circle in the Square, Theodore Mann, Paul Libin and Gillian Walker; on November 28, 1968, at the Henry Miller's tHeatre, with the following cast:

GERTRUDE .... Charlotte Rae
UPDIKE .... Sorrell Booke
SISSY .... Jane Marla Robbins
JUNIOR .... Robert Klein
TILLICH .... John Heffernan

Introduction

Terrence McNally, Leonard Melfi and I were inseparable friends, way back then. We seemed to see each other, daily, often, in my house on West 11th Street, in the Village. Terrence, in the beginning, lived next door. When he moved, his new digs were just down the street and around the corner. Leonard, in those days, also lived, close by, in the East Village, near Café LaMama, his home base. I had Doris, Rachael, Matthew and Adam. Terrence had Bobby and Jimmy. Leonard had Kevin and Ellen Stewart. We were all deeply involved in each other's lives and careers, giving each other copious notes and immeasurable support.

I had the idea for the triptych ... *Morning, Noon and Night.* We would draw straws to see which play we wrote. As there isn't any straw growing in Greenwich Village, we drew matches. I got the short match. I wrote *Morning.* Terrence got the middle match, for *Noon,* and Leonard, by default, headed into *Night.*

The essential idea was this: we would share five actors in all three plays. We would also share a director and a unit set.

We started writing our plays in late Winter. By late spring, we had drafts that we showed to Ted Mann for the Circle-in-the-Square Theatre's Broadway project. Mann had produced plays by both Leonard and Terrence, before, and I was teaching playwriting in Circle's theatre school on Bleecker Street. So, we were all connected. Mann loved the plays and agreed to produce them in the next Broadway season. He also wanted to direct. We took a vote, and said "Yes".

In July, my wife and kids and I left NYC, headed to Italy and the Spoleto Festival, where *The Indian Wants The Bronx* and *It's Called The Sugar Plum* were being showcased. Once there, I asked permission to give an off-night showing of *Morning.* I cast the play with available actors and non-actors: John Cazale and Matthew Cowles from the *The Indian Wants The Bronx* cast, Lizzie Spender (the poet's daughter, who was visiting Spoleto with her dad), Sudie Bond, who was in Spoleto with Edward Albee and his play *Box-Mao-Box*, Laurent Wesman, a young French banker/artist, who would, the next year, translate and direct *Morning* in its Paris premiere, with a then-unknown actor named Gerard Depardieu in the lead role.

Morning is a shockingly obcene and dangerous play about a black family wilfully taking pills to turn their skin white. They wake up white and spend one day white. Happily, for them, one day is enough.

The audience in Spoleto loved the play. It got a standing ovation. I very nearly fainted from the sheer thrill of it.

I went from Spoleto to the O'Neill Foundation (National Playwrights Conference) in Waterfront, Connecticut, where George White and Lloyd Richards sanctioned an off-Conference staged-reading of *Morning*. While enthusiastic and positive, this first American audience to see *Morning* also saw the danger in the play. How would audiences respond to the pre-Mamet four-letter and eight-letter words? How would my black friends react? The Waterford audience response was less giddy and far more thoughtful than was the audience response at Spoleto. Many of the older, more experienced theatre-people at the O'Neill expressed worry and concern for me and my play in relation to its upcoming Broadway venue. The phrase most often repeated was "You will be killed by the critics!" ... For my part, I couldn't have cared less. I loved my play and I loved Terrence and Leonard's plays. I couldn't imagine caring about what the critics would think. I knew we were opening on Broadway with plays that spoke—with honest voices—for our particular time on Earth. I was quite proud of myself.

In fact, the reviews were astonishingly positive. My friend Ross Wetzsteon, writing in The Village Voice, praised the plays, but, seemed to be condeming the three of us for allowing our work to go to Broadway. Sell-outs. We'd shared a $1500 advance. We'd sold-out cheap.

In the end, *Morning, Noon and Night* failed to find a broad-based audience, and closed, after a modest two-month Broadway run. But, by and large, the entire experience was wonderful for Leonard, Terrence and me. Our plays were seen by a large audience, reviewed and taken seriously by the NY press. And our very special friendship had withstood the test, and deepened.

25 years have passed, and Leonard Melfi, Terrence McNally and I have long gone our mostly-separate ways. But, I often get lost in the memory of *Morning, Noon and Night.* It was time of great energy, of serious political commitment, of social concern ... and of great hopefulness. I will not say, simply, that c.1994 is inferior to c.1969, or, that being 54 years old is less good than being 30 years old. But, I will say this, simply and clearly: being a young and rather successful playwright in 1969 was something really wonderful. Looking back at such a time often gives me the courage to look forward.

Characters

GERTRUDE
UPDIKE
SISSY
JUNIOR
TILLICH

Setting

A room in Harlem.
Now.

NOTE: Music for "*Morning*" can be secured from Samuel French, Inc. Write for particulars.

MORNING

Scene 1

MORNING BEGINS

The lights fade up, an enormous bed, with black sheets and blankets. Updike is in bed dressed in black pajamas. He is barely awake. He is white. All scenery is black. A four-man band is assembled on stage. They watch the action of the play. Gertrude calls to Updike. She is white.

GERTRUDE: (*Fiercely.*) Come on, Updike. You worthless white nigger! Get your black ass out that fucking black bed!

BLACKOUT

Scene 2

THE CREATION OF MAN

In the blackout, Gertrude, Sissy, Junior, and Updike stand across the apron of the stage. The lights fade up. They deliver their lines as television-commercial announcers, smiling empty smiles directly at the audience. The rock group plays soupy-church-rock music softly. The entire family wears black clothing.

GERTRUDE: In the beginning, there was only God on Earth. And the sunshine.

SISSY: Now God walked in the sunshine daily. He walked in the sunshine and sometimes would lie in the sunshine for hours. Dreaming of ways to create man. Dreaming of ways to create trees. Dreaming of ways to kill time. So God wouldn't get bored just hanging around by himself in the sunshine.

JUNIOR: God, being a wise and educated man, realized all that sunshine was causing his skin to burst forth with itchy sun blisters and a scratchy rash, so first God created Coppertone, and then Bain de Soleil.

GERTRUDE: And then God would lie in the sunshine in great comfort.

UPDIKE: When God turned a bronze and beautiful brown, He created man in the image of Himself.

JUNIOR: At first, man was ravaged by itchy skin blisters and scratchy rash, so God gave unto man His Coppertone and Bain de Soleil.

UPDIKE: And when man had turned a bronze and beautiful brown, he prayed to God to create woman. Man was ready.

GERTRUDE: And God created woman.

SISSY: The women of the Earth lay in the sun until their skin burst forth with itchy skin blisters and scratchy rash.

GERTRUDE: So God gave unto woman His Coppertone and Bain de Soleil as well.

SISSY: And once the women of the Earth turned a bronze and beautiful brown, they lay in the sun in great comfort.

UPDIKE: And the men of the Earth lay in the women of the Earth in great comfort as well.

JUNIOR: (*Stepping forward as a preacher.*) So tired did God grow from watching the men of the Earth lay the women of the Earth, He fell asleep.

GERTRUDE: While God was asleep, the women of the Earth gave birth to new men and new women, who lay in the sun until their skin burst forth with itchy skin blisters and scratchy rash. But because God was resting, there was not Coppertone nor Bain de Soleil. So the new men and women of the Earth had to choose between hiding beneath and behind God's new shade trees, or face a life of prickly heat.

UPDIKE: They, being wise and educated men, hid beneath and behind the shade trees until their itchy sun blisters and scratchy rash disappeared, leaving only the first men and women of the Earth to be a bronze and beautiful brown.

GERTRUDE: As time passed, those in the dark did grow lighter.

UPDIKE: And so, beneath and behind the shade trees, the light men lay the light women, and new light men and new light women were born to Earth.

SISSY: As the years passed, the men and women of the shade and the men and women of the sun sought new lands.

JUNIOR: The black men sought lands of clear sun for laying, while the light men sought lands of shady trees and rocks for laying, without threat of prickly heat.

UPDIKE: So happy was the black man laying under God's own sun, he learned to make music and dance.

JUNIOR: So unhappy was the light man in the dark of God's own shade trees, he stopped laying, now and then, and invented the wheel, the automobile, the jet plane, Coppertone, and Bain de Soleil. But while the wheel and the automobile and the jet plane served him well, the Coppertone and Bain de Soleil came too late to ever catch the bronze and beautiful brown, gone to black of the black man.

SISSY: And the light man grew discontent with his machinery and his light white women, and began to lay the bronze and brown-to-black women, who could then only sing and dance and lay. And so discontent did grow the light man when he discovered that the black man sang and danced and lay better than he, with all his intricate machinery, and he hated the black man and put him into captivity.

ALL: But God did not sleep forever!

GERTRUDE: He awoke one morning, but grew so tired of watching the white men lay the black women and the black men lay the white women, not to mention the black men laying the black women, and all those in between . . . he fell back into his deep and holy rest at once.

UPDIKE: And then he awoke again to create Moses and Christ and the Caesars and the Kings and the Kennedys, but the white man had created weapons modeled after the black man's spears, so Moses and Christ and the Caesars and the Kings and the Kennedys were betrayed and dead so quickly, that God could only sleep again.

GERTRUDE: In his sleep, God was reached by a small fat man who runs a pawnshop on East 126th Street, and has a certain secret interest in a store called Bloomingdale's. In God's half-sleep – for although black, God is a light sleeper – this man took His six pills that are antidotes to the original sin of Coppertone and Bain de Soleil. He took these six pills from God and returned to Earth to distribute the pills, at great profit, among the bronze and beautiful brown-turned-to-black, who wished to liken themselves to those who have lingered so long in the dark, beneath and behind the shade trees.

SISSY: In his journey from Heaven to 126th Street, two of the pills spilled from his pocket and were lost forever.

GERTRUDE: He told me so.

ALL: Indeed, sir!

GERTRUDE: And so, with just four pills, he returned to 126th Street, where he sold them to me. One for me and one for my master. (*Pointing to Updike.*) Him. And one for each of my two children. (*Pointing to Sissy and Junior.*) Them. Last night, before we went to rest to lay, my man and I and each of our two children swallowed a pill with a bit of wine, and the wafer-thin curtains of our poor flat held the heat in and the cool breezes out, while we lay in rest and waited to wake. And wake we did as you can see. No longer bronze and brown, but free and ready to face the world this day as those who have lived forever in the shade.

ALL: (*But Gertrude.*) Not a trace of bronze or brown on my skin. Not a trace of bronze or brown in my mind.

GERTRUDE: I can take my place this morning at the complaint window of Toys 'R' Us, and Lord! The man will listen! I can discuss the size of a bedroom in a low-income controlled city flat on 98th and Riverside, and Lord! The man won't stare down my dress and try to lay me on the bedroom floor, on the bedroom floor plans. I can do any*thing* and any*one* my lily-white heart pleases, because I am free of the bronze and the brown. Not a trace of bronze or brown in my mind! God can go straight on sleeping forever, because I'm free of the bronze and the brown.

ALL: Free! Free, forever, Lord! I'm free.

GERTRUDE: Free! Free, forever, Lord! I'm free.

BLACKOUT

Scene 3

WAKING UP WHITE

Gertrude stands beside the bed. Updike pretends to be sleeping. They are alone.

GERTRUDE: (*Disgusted.*) Kiss me. C'mon. Kiss me?

UPDIKE: (*Gruff.*) I ain't even brushed my teeth yet.

GERTRUDE: (*Strong.*) Kiss me.

UPDIKE: (*Surprised, still gruff.*) You ain't asked me to kiss you for twenty years.

GERTRUDE: I know.

UPDIKE: (*Sitting up.*) After twenty years, don't you think I ought to brush my teeth first?

GERTRUDE: (*Angry.*) This is such a special morning and that's all you can think about? "Don't you think I ought to brush my teeth first?" I'll bet I can find plenty of men this morning that'll kiss me without brushing their teeth. Plenty of men that'll kiss me so terrific, they won't even have any teeth left after they get done kissing me, 'cause they'll lose all their teeth in their passion.

UPDIKE: (*Annoyed.*) Gimme the blankets back, huh? I got a couple of minutes left. I could get some more rest for a couple of minutes.

GERTRUDE: Kiss me, or so help me God, I'll beat you black and blue.

UPDIKE: (*Turns away.*) That's a joke, huh? Black and blue, huh?

GERTRUDE: (*Hurt.*) I didn't mean it to be funny.

UPDIKE: (*Wounded.*) Well, it ain't funny.

GERTRUDE: (*Furious.*) Damn you! You haven't kissed me! You haven't said one special word about how special I look! You haven't made one mention of nothing, damn you. Nothing!

UPDIKE: (*Martyred.*) And what's so special about what you've been saying to me? What's so motherfucking special about what you've been sayin' to me? "Get up, Updike! Kiss me, Updike!" Have you said one word about how terrifically terrific I look this morning, huh? One little word?

GERTRUDE: (*Quizzically.*) How the hell would you know what you look like? You been asleep ever since you took the pill. You haven't even seen yourself, let alone taken one little peek at me.

UPDIKE: (*Awake now.*) Buullshit, woman. That's what I got to say to you. Buuuuuuullllllshiiiiiitttt. You just go rappin' on and on about how fantastically terrifically beautifully magnificently wonderfully wonderful you look, right? And you haven't said fuck-all about Updike, have you? Anything about Updike?

GERTRUDE: (*Amazed.*) But you been asleep since you took the pill?

UPDIKE: (*Proud.*) While you was sleeping in bed, woman. This black bed right here? I was up and around and staring at things. Staring out the window at the stars. Staring at the walls. Staring at the blankets and the bed. I even lifted off the blankets.

GERTRUDE: (*Surprised, almost stunned.*) While I was sleeping?

UPDIKE: (*Enormous pride, success.*) I even lifted off the blankets and I sat staring at you. Right there. Right over there I sat. Right there in that chair just staring at you and digging the hell out of you. I didn't stop there either. You got a lipstick kiss on your stomach.

That's how close you looked at yourself. That's how close you were payin' attention to yourself . . . let alone nothin' to me! You got a lipstick kiss on your stomach.

GERTRUDE: (*Laughing, a defense.*) You're crazy.

UPDIKE: (*Strong.*) I'll bet you all my week's gin money against two extra minutes of sleep you got a lipstick kiss on your belly, 'cause I put it there when I got up.

GERTRUDE: (*Honestly curious.*) I'm a light sleeper. I would have heard you let alone feel you. What do you mean a "lipstick kiss" ?

UPDIKE: (*Delighted.*) You think I didn't know how you'd behave this morning, huh? I figured it out! I know my little Gertrude-honey. Twenty-two years don't pass with me learning nothing, Gertrude. I put your lipstick on and I kissed your belly sure as there was a moon last night and sure as the sun beat the hell out of it at dawn.

GERTRUDE: (*Delighted as well.*) That's crazy talk.

UPDIKE: (*Laughing.*) Look at your belly!

GERTRUDE: (*Opens her robe and screams.*) Lipstick!

(*A "lipstick kiss," cut from bright red plastic tape, is seen.*)

UPDIKE: (*Laughing and prancing as a prize pony in the winner's circle.*) Hot shit, Trudy, huh? That's what I told you didn't I? Huh? Ain't that the prettiest lipstick kiss you ever seen?

GERTRUDE: (*Pleased.*) Why'd you do a crazy thing like that?

UPDIKE: (*Sexy.*) Yesterday morning would that lipstick'd shined like that, huh? That's a coming-out present from Updike, Trudy. That's the present I promised you. Beats the hell out of that process job you wanted right?

GERTRUDE: (*Absolutely thrilled.*) I'm gonna' give you a lipstick kiss like that straight back, too.

(*They roll about kissing and hugging, about to make love when their son, Junior, bursts into the room. They jump up sharply.*)

UPDIKE: (*Caught.*) Why the hell ain't you out on the street, Junior?

GERTRUDE: (*Concerned.*) What happened to you?

UPDIKE: (*Angry.*) Answer your mother, Junior. Why ain't you outside?

JUNIOR: (*He's been beaten up.*) I got mugged!

UPDIKE: By who?

JUNIOR: (*Furious.*) I can't count that high. (*Pauses.*) Everybody.

UPDIKE: (*Amazed.*) That's crazy.

JUNIOR: (*Looking out the window to see if he's safe.*) They wouldn't believe me.

GERTRUDE: (*Stunned.*) You told them.

JUNIOR: (*Angry.*) 'Course I told them. They're my brothers.

UPDIKE: (*Furious.*) You're crazy. (*To Gertrude.*) He's crazy.

GERTRUDE: (*Pulls Junior so he faces her.*) Why'd you tell them?

JUNIOR: They're my brothers!

GERTRUDE: (*Horror-struck.*) What did you tell them? The pill? Did you tell them about the pill?

JUNIOR: Yep.

UPDIKE: (*Exasperated.*) Oh, my God. He's crazy. Gertrude. Your son's crazy.

GERTRUDE: (*Tough, strong, angry.*) Say that again, boy. You told them about the pill?

JUNIOR: (*Smart-assed.*) They didn't believe me. It's okay.

UPDIKE: (*Can't believe it.*) What do you mean?

JUNIOR: (*Smart-assed, bitchy.*) What do you mean, "What do you mean?"

UPDIKE: (*Furious.*) Don't get smart with me, Junior. Give me a straight answer.

JUNIOR: (*As angry, hostile.*) I gave you a straight answer, but you didn't listen. I told them about the pill and they didn't believe me.

UPDIKE: (*Amazed.*) How'd they think you got white???

JUNIOR: (*Simply.*) Paint.

GERTRUDE: (*Quickly, a sound.*) Paint?

UPDIKE: (*The same.*) Paint?

GERTRUDE: (*Shocked.*) They figured you *painted* yourself? (*Pauses.*) That's terrific.

JUNIOR: (*Very hostile.*) One morning, white, Uptown, and your Super-Tom skin pills got me mugged, and *washed,* more times in one morning than I would have washed all next year. They stole my wallet, then they washed up one side of my head and right down the other. (*Pauses, humiliated and furious.*) They checked me all over, man. All over.

UPDIKE: (*Curious.*) What did they find?

JUNIOR: (*Disgusted.*) What did they find?

UPDIKE: (*Quickly.*) You heard me!

JUNIOR: (*Whining.*) They pulled off my underpants. What do you think they found?

GERTRUDE: (*Thrilled.*) We're home free, Updike! Home free!

JUNIOR: (*Pulls away.*) You're all crazy, you know that? You're all fuckin' crazy!

UPDIKE: (*Scolding.*) Mind your fuckin' filthy tongue 'round your mother, boy.

GERTRUDE: (*Double checks.*) They didn't believe you, huh?

JUNIOR: (*Annoyed.*) I said that clear enough.

GERTRUDE: (*Joyously.*) We're home free, Updike. Home free. Ain't nobody gonna' believe we was anything 'cept what we look. What you depressed about?

JUNIOR: (*Wants attention.*) I take one fuckin' walk with my sister, man, and I get my ass whupped and my head whupped and my legs and everything scrubbed so clean I'm about to break open . . . and I'm supposed to be overjoyed, right? Well, hot shit. Nobody whupped me yesterday. Nobody whupped Sissy, neither.

UPDIKE: (*Upset.*) Sissy. Where is she?

GERTRUDE: (*Upset.*) Where's Sissy?

JUNIOR: (*Pleased.*) They were whuppin' hell out of her. That's how I got into the middle of it. They knocked her down and stole her pocketbook.

GERTRUDE: (*Frightened.*) Where is she?

JUNIOR: (*Calming.*) She's okay. She ran off like I told her to. She's probably visiting. She's okay.

UPDIKE: (*Disgusted.*) He's nuts. He's plain nuts.

JUNIOR: (*Wants love.*) I need a Band-Aid for my finger.

UPDIKE: (*Curious.*) Let's have a look at it.

(*Junior extends his hurt finger – bloody for his father's careful scrutiny. Updike is delighted.*)

JUNIOR: (*Rather proud, as a soldier.*) There.

UPDIKE: (*Delighted, almost thrilled.*) Ain't that something?

GERTRUDE: (*Amazed.*) It's pretty.

JUNIOR: (*Disgusted, hostile, tense.*) Have you gone loony? That's my blood you're lovin'!

(*Suddenly Tillich screams from behind the audience.*)

TILLICH: Niggers! (*Tillich rushes down the aisle from the back of the theatre screaming.*) Niggers! Black bastards! (*He rushes up on to the stage, sees them and stops, stunned. They all run to hiding positions and freeze for a moment before peeking their heads out at him.*) Hey. What the hell's goin' on here? Where are the niggers?

UPDIKE: (*His accent goes from "black" to "white": almost clipped.*) The what?

TILLICH: (*Regains his fury.*) The niggers. There were four niggers living here yesterday. A man, a woman, and two black kids. A boy and a girl. Where'd they go off to?

UPDIKE: (*Very British now.*) What'd you want them for?

TILLICH: (*Too quickly.*) My daughter's pregnant. The nigger-boy that lives here knocked her up. (*Realizes.*) Oh Jesus. Now I went and said it out loud. You got me so rattled, seeing you here instead of niggers. I never would have said it out loud.

(*The family freezes. The lights fade out on the set and cross fade up on the apron. Tillich takes a hand microphone.*)

Scene 4

TILLICH'S NIGHTMARE

The lights close in to a pin spot on Tillich. He speaks first, then breaks into a talk-sing-song: a straightforward satire of Bob Dylan. The song should build slowly, until the final "angel-chorus," with the family and the rock group joining in sweetly. Tillich walks to the audience and tells his story.

TILLICH: I never would have said it out loud. Never. My name is Tillich. We live Midtown. Near the river. I'm in communications. My daughter, Alice, is pregnant. She's going to have a baby. (*Sucks in his breath and tells the truth.*) A black baby. She goes to school with a black kid. I mean, she used to go to school with him. He hasn't been around the school at all. Not since she told us. I would have gotten him there. But he stopped going to school. That's where they met. At the school. They bussed the little black bastard right into her. (*Very emotional now.*) Look, I know how I stand. I've seen *Guess Who's Coming to Dinner. Twice!* But she's pregnant. Pregnant. I've seen the kid. Seen him maybe twenty or thirty times. I didn't know what to do. I've been coming up here daily. Just staring at this place. Just staring from outside and trying like the dickens to figure something out. But last night she told me. She told me what she felt. What she wanted. She didn't leave me any choice. (*He takes a pistol from his pocket and shows it to the audience.*) I had to buy this. Twenty-nine ninety-five for this.

(*Music vamps in slowly. Tillich begins his song, "Tillich's Nightmare."*)

I am average weight and height.
I have average kids and sight.
I have average means and way.
On the average, I'm okay. Hooray.
My average daughter Alice
Fucks on the average twice a day,
With an average spade named Junior;
Now she's in the family way.
Oh, my God.
In your average shotgun marriage,
You know exactly what to do.
You make an average family wedding.
Then you wipe your hands, you're through.
But when your average dummy daughter
Expects and wants a mocha child,
Forget your average rules, sir.
You're super-average wild
To kill that little black spade rapist
In an awful average way.
You buy a gun to blow his brains out
Then you kill the goddamn day.
Wondering why the hell she did it:
Why she screwed and screwed you up.
Why she layed and then betrayed you.
Why she . . . Why you? Why you? . . .

(*The family steps in as an "angel-chorus." Tillich now has a gun in one hand and a wad of dollars in the other. He sees the money and sings, ever so sweetly.*)

Polytechnics. Basic dynamics.
Positive forward thrust.
I love America.
America.
Oh God, I love America.

(*Really big climax here.*)

ALL: Oh God, I trust!

(BLACKOUT)

Scene 5

IN BIG TROUBLE

Lights up on the set. Tillich walks on, gun and money in hand.

UPDIKE: (*Very British again; pulls Tillich back into the scene.*) Is that loaded? That sidearm. Is that a loaded thing?

TILLICH: (*Furious.*) You bet your ass it is!

JUNIOR: (*Not so "white." Concerned.*) Is she all right? Your daughter? Is she okay?

UPDIKE: (*Pushing Junior fiercely.*) You get the fuck out of here, you Goddamned fool. (*To Tillich.*) The boy's too young for this grownup talk.

GERTRUDE: (*Grand.*) Ain't it time for you to take a walk, Junior? (*She bends Junior's arm. Tillich sees it. Gertrude explains.*) The boy's got a terrible nervous condition. The doctor says he's supposed to take a long walk every morning. So he doesn't get too nervous. What time is it?

TILLICH: (*Quickly.*) Nine-thirty.

GERTRUDE: (*A shove.*) It's time, Junior.

TILLICH: (*The name's familiar. Too familiar.*) Junior?

JUNIOR: (*Thinks he's being asked a question.*) What?

TILLICH: (*Furious.*) Is that your name? Junior?

JUNIOR: (*Tense. A lie.*) No. That's my nickname.

TILLICH: (*Introspective.*) That's a hell of a coincidence.

UPDIKE: (*Interrupting, frightened.*) How so?

TILLICH: (*To all.*) A hell of a coincidence. Strange. Junior.

UPDIKE: (*Reasonably.*) Ain't nothin' strange about a white boy bein' called Junior. John Kennedy's little one's called Junior. Abe Lincoln's boy was called Junior.

TILLICH: (*Turns on Updike.*) Abe Lincoln? He had a son named Junior?

UPDIKE: (*Caught.*) Junior Lincoln. Terrific kid.

TILLICH: (*After a pause, he sits.*) I don't understand this. Excuse me, but I think I'm losing my mind.

JUNIOR: (*Right at Tillich, laughing. Junior's seen enough.*) Hot shit! Terrific!

GERTRUDE: (*Fist in Junior's mouth.*) Don't pay any attention to him. He's strange.

JUNIOR: (*Pulling free.*) Hot shit! Hot shit! Hee-hee. (*Junior dances around the bed, laughing. Updike hits him on the back of his head fiercely, with a slap. Junior stops.)*

UPDIKE: You'll be dead, you jerk. Now shut up! (*To Tillich.*) We told you this boy was strange. We got problems in our house too, mister. This boy's one of them. Doesn't know anything. Stupid. (*Hits Junior.*) You're stupid, right? Tell the man how stupid you are!

TILLICH: Don't make the same mistake I did. I didn't think she knew anything at all. The boy probably knows more than any of us, don't you boy?

JUNIOR: (*Leaps at him.*) What did you call me?

TILLICH: (*Doesn't see or hear.*) It's all very "in" now, you know. The way they mix it up. I wouldn't give a damn if they played cards or something like that. But she's knocked up.

GERTRUDE: (*A real mum.*) How old is she?

TILLICH: (*Crybaby, whines.*) Alice? She's fourteen. That's all she is. Just a baby? Hell, that's what she's having!

GERTRUDE: (*Has an idea.*) How do you know the boy did it?

JUNIOR: (*Can't believe it; to Gertrude.*) You too? Damn it. We got him three to one.

UPDIKE: (*Aside.*) He's got a gun.

TILLICH: (*Hears a sound.*) Huh?

UPDIKE: (*Smiling. Sick with anxiety.*) I was just explaining to the boy that you're upset enough to kill someone, that's all.

TILLICH: (*Angry.*) Goddamned right I am! How'd you feel if your daughter got knocked up by some nigger?

UPDIKE: (*A long, slow, silent stare into space.*) Well . . .

TILLICH: God forgive me for having to say it out loud.

JUNIOR: (*Tough.*) Yeah?

UPDIKE: (*Angry, terrified, trapped.*) That's enough. That's enough. (*Sissy walks slowly down the aisle and into the room, crying.*)

SISSY: Them dirty motherfucking mothers whupped my head. Them dirty motherfucking motherfuckers. (*She sees Tillich.*) Is that an ofay, or you been passing out our pills, boy?

TILLICH: (*Amazed, stands, stares.*) Who's that?

UPDIKE: (*In a sealed box, buying time.*) I'll be damned if I know. Who are you, girl? This is Mr. WHITE. Was that your name?

TILLICH: (*Confused.*) Mr. *Who?* Tillich. Till – icchh. Tillich.

UPDIKE: (*Anxious beyond description.*) This man I just called Mr. WHITE by accident, has a gun, and he's come up here to shoot and kill some dumb-assed little nigger, what's knocked up his little girl, girl. (*Pauses.*) Who are you?

SISSY: (*Rudely.*) What do you mean, "Who are you?"

UPDIKE: (*Out of control, then in.*) What do you mean, "What do you mean?" This here Mr. WHITE . . .

TILLICH: (*Corrects him.*) Tillich.

UPDIKE: (*Lays it out carefully.*) Mr. Tillich . . . here. This Mr. Tillich's little girl, who happens to be about your age, has just been made with child in her stomach by some little black nigger boy, who happens to be about your brother's age. And this here Mr. WHITE, er . . .

TILLICH: Tillich.

UPDIKE: (*A false laugh, then screams.*) . . . Mr. Tillich's got a loaded gun that kills people deader than a couple of whups on the head, you stupid little shit. (*Quickly to Tillich.*) She's our adopted daughter, and she has a terrible filthy mouth. She's crazy, too. We adopted her from a crazy house. Her mother and father were crazies. (*To Gertrude.*) Get her out of here.

TILLICH: (*Thinks he knows.*) Wait a minute! Hey. Wait a goddamn minute. The girl and the boy. The ages. And you two. The same size. The apartment. Wait a minute.

GERTRUDE: (*A try.*) What's going through your head?

TILLICH: (*Sure he knows.*) This apartment. The boy. The girl.

GERTRUDE: (*A grand white lady.*) Mr. Tillich! I've been standing over there just being very quiet and ladylike, and I've been listening to you use some terrible, terrible language on my youngest and my oldest. And worst of all, on ME, Mr. Tillich. Now, I wouldn't want to think of coming around up your place and talking that way on your innocent little children . . . especially the one that got RAPED by some black boy . . . and corrupt their innocent little bellies. Especially the swollen belly. I wouldn't go pointing guns and using filthy language or any of that shit!

TILLICH: (*Can't believe it.*) Something's crazy here.

GERTRUDE: (*Thinks she's got it made, slapping Tillich's face.*) Manners, Mr. Tillich. Mind your manners.

SISSY: (*Overlapping, a sound.*) Manners.

JUNIOR: (*Overlapping, a sound.*) Manners.

TILLICH: (*Overlapping, a sound.*) I heard her.

GERTRUDE: (*Overlapping, a sound.*) Manners.

TILLICH: (*Overlapping, a sound.*) I heard you.

JUNIOR: (*Overlapping, a sound.*) He heard you.

UPDIKE: (*From nowhere, an answer.*) Well, there, Mr. Tillich. I know what's going on here. You gotta be looking for the niggers in Four-B. Four-*Beeee*, Tillich.

TILLICH: (*His brain boggled.*) Huh?

UPDIKE: (*Thrilled, grand, understated.*) You got the wrong apartment. There are niggers in Four-B. A little black boy.

JUNIOR: (*Amazed.*) Jesus? He's a Cuban.

UPDIKE: (*Annoyed at the distraction.*) Cuban, Puerto Rican, Nigger. It's all the same, ain't it, Tillich?

JUNIOR: (*Continues his amazement.*) But Jesus ain't home! He's back in Havana.

UPDIKE: (*Angry.*) He was home when she got pregnant, though wasn't he, Tillich? When did she get pregnant, Tillich?

TILLICH: (*A limp reply.*) Three months ago.

UPDIKE: (*Furiously. To Junior.*) Three months ago, you jerk. (*Back to Tillich, he mimes his answers softly.*) I think I hear him rattling around in there now, Tillich. Yes, I do. Sounds like they're eating grits in there. Eating soul food! You suppose that's the boy you want to talk to, huh?

TILLICH: (*Stunned.*) Jesus? His name is Jesus?

UPDIKE: (*Pours it on.*) That's his nickname. That's what the neighborhood kids call him. Just for the hell of it. What is the kid's name? The kid you're looking for:

TILLICH: (*Simply an explanation.*) Updike.

(*They freeze.*)

UPDIKE: (*Terrified.*) That sounds like Jesus.

TILLICH: (*Can't believe what he's heard.*) What are you talking about?

UPDIKE: (*As a machine – rapid fire.*) You take the *J* in Jesus. The next letter is *K*. There's a *K* in Updike. You take the *S* in Jesus. Two letters over, there's a *U*. Like in Updike. *E* in Jesus comes after *D* in Updike. *J* in Jesus after the *I* in Updike. What's left?

SISSY: (*From nowhere.*) Pee.

UPDIKE: (*Quickly.*) One letter? Kill me for one lousy letter?

TILLICH: (*Overlapping.*) I smell a rat.

UPDIKE: (*Overlapping.*) I know. It's a problem up here.

(*They unfreeze.*)

TILLICH: (*Taunting.*) "Jesus"? My little Alice is knocked up by a black boy named "Jesus"? If I had a sense of humor, I'd think that was pretty funny. Goddamned funny!

UPDIKE: (*Helpless, confused.*) What's so funny?

TILLICH: (*Quiet rage.*) "Jesus." The whole idea of a black boy being called "Jesus" strikes me as being a funny thing. Doesn't it strike you as being a funny thing?

UPDIKE: (*Trapped, a false laugh.*) Oh, yeah. Sure. Strikes me, all right.

TILLICH: (*To Junior.*) How's that strike you?

JUNIOR: (*Spits.*) Dirty motherfucker!

UPDIKE: (*He slaps Junior sharply on the back of his head.*) How does that strike you, the man wants to know?

JUNIOR: (*Vomits.*) Motherfucking bastard!

UPDIKE: (*Hits him again.*) Every time I ask you how that strikes you, I'm gonna strike you again.

TILLICH: (*Boggled again.*) What's going on here?

UPDIKE: (*Threatens.*) Now you answer the man, Junior, or I'll whup your head black and blue boy. Black and blue.

JUNIOR: (*Straight at Updike.*) Black is beautiful, man. Beautiful. (*Updike and Gertrude smile at Tillich as though Junior is insane. Sissy giggles. Junior continues to scream. The tension is incredible.*) Black is beautiful. Black is love. Black is God. Jesus is black. Jesus is black. Jesus is black. Jesus is black. Jesus is black. Jesus is blaaaaaaaaacccccccckkk!!

(*Updike takes a pillow from the bed and slams Junior to the bed. He covers Junior's face with the pillow until Junior's words are muffled. He continues chanting softly under the pillow.*)

UPDIKE: (*Simply.*) The boy is trying to tell you that Jesus is black.

TILLICH: What the hell's going on?

UPDIKE: (*Quickly, smiling helplessly.*) Jesus is black. Jesus. The black boy from Four-B, what's knocked up your little girl, mister.

TILLICH: (*Ferociously.*) I've been watching *this* apartment, not Four-*Bee!* This is the apartment where the niggers live, not Four-*Bee!* Now somebody tell me what got into that boy and what the hell's got into this apartment.

GERTRUDE: (*Simply.*) Ain't no niggers got into this apartment.

UPDIKE: (*As simply.*) Ain't none here. Can you see any here?

JUNIOR: (*Unmuffled for a moment.*) Jesus is black!

UPDIKE: (*Muffling him again.*) Now if you'll listen to my boy carefully, he's been telling you that there's a black boy next door named Jesus. Time and time again this boy of mine's been tellin' you just that. Now you go straight around to Four-B and you knock up *that* door.

TILLICH: (*Shows the gun; a cowboy.*) Take the pillow off of his face, mister.

GERTRUDE: (*Ferociously.*) Now you listen here, mister. I told you that you can't come running into the home of us white people just like you and come busting things up and screaming and pointing guns. (*Pauses.*) You got a permit for that gun? Huh?

TILLICH: (*Strangely frightened.*) Huh?

GERTRUDE: (*Angrily.*) That's a plain enough question. You got a permit for that gun? Or maybe I got to call the fuzz to find out the answer to my question?

TILLICH: (*Strangely concerned.*) What are you driving at?

GERTRUDE: (*Goes with it.*) Sissy, call the fuzz.

SISSY: (*Amazed.*) You gone crazy, woman?

GERTRUDE: (*Strongly.*) Do as your mother tells you, Sissy. This here what's-his-name thinks he can come busting up our place, maybe he can tell the fuzz exactly why. Why he thinks he can do these kind of things.

TILLICH: (*Terrified.*) Wait a minute.

GERTRUDE: (*Goes with it.*) No."wait a minutes." Call them Sissy.

SISSY: (*Begins, but really whispers.*) Fuzz! Help! Fuzz!

UPDIKE: (*Ashen.*) Not so loud, you goddamned fool.

GERTRUDE: (*Confidently.*) Go on, Sissy, Go on.

SISSY: (*Now she screams.*) FUZZZ! FUZZZ! FUUUZZZZZ!

TILLICH: (*A command more than a plea.*) Hold it!

SISSY: FUZZZ!

GERTRUDE: (*Races over and jams her hand over Sissy's mouth. Updike still has Junior pinned under the pillow. They all freeze waiting for Tillich's reply.*) Yes?

TILLICH: (*Quietly.*) Four-B?

UPDIKE: (*A sound.*) Yeah.

TILLICH: (*Simply.*) Next door?

UPDIKE: (*A simple reply, quickly.*) Right next door.

TILLICH: (*Softly.*) You sure?

GERTRUDE: (*Softly.*) Positive.

TILLICH: (*Backing up.*) Jesus?

UPDIKE: (*Quickly.*) That's right.

GERTRUDE: (*Quickly.*) Uh-huh.

TILLICH: (*Softly.*) OK. (*Starts down the aisle, turns back to them.*) "Jesus," then. Next door. (*Runs off, screaming.*) Jesus! You dirty black bastard. I'm coming after you, Jesus, you oversexed buck son-of-a-bitch. (*They slowly come back to life after Tillich's exit. First Sissy screams, then Junior.*)

SISSY: You chicken-shit. . . . (*Gertrude smacks her viciously.*)

JUNIOR: Motherfucker! I'll be a dirty son-of-a-bitch! (*Updike smacks him viciously.*)

GERTRUDE: (*Undone.*) Knock it off. What are we gonna do? (*The lights fade out on the set. Lights cross fade up on the apron of the stage.*)

Scene 6

IN MY SOUL

Junior and Sissy take hand microphones and face the audience. The rock group stands at the microphone behind them.

JUNIOR AND SISSY:

Mum and daddy's in the back room
Stoned out on gin.
Us up front stretched out on grass.
Set our asses at the table and we rap about the gap.
Between us and around us. Between us and around.
All between and all around.

CHORUS: (*Junior and Sissy are "answered" by the rock group.*)

Uncle Martin. Uncle Martin. Uncle Martin's in my soul.
Uncle Martin. Uncle Martin. Uncle Martin's in my soul.

JUNIOR:

I don't want to be a white man,
But, man, I don't want the black.
All I want is for the war to end,
I just want my babies back.
I don't want to be a white man.
But, man, I don't want the black.
All I want is for the war to end.
That's the war that's got to end.
Man, I want my babies back.

CHORUS:

Uncle Martin. Uncle Martin. Uncle Martin's in my soul.
Uncle Martin. Uncle Martin. Uncle Martin's in my soul.

JUNIOR AND SISSY: (*Talk-sing.*)

How do you freak out?
How do you drop out?
How do you work out how you love?
Can't you see it? Can't you see it?

(*Sung.*)

Can't you see it, man, it's real?

CHORUS:

Uncle Martin. Uncle Martin. Uncle Martin's in my soul.
Uncle Martin. Uncle Martin. Uncle Martin's in my soul.
My soul.

(*The lights switch off with Junior and Sissy standing on the apron of the stage, staring into the audience hatefully. They have each chosen separate people in the audience to "fix" on during the song. The song ends abruptly.*)

BLACKOUT

Scene 7

THE MORNING CONTINUES

The lights fade up again in the room. Junior and Sissy re-enter through the front of the set. The play is again "naturalistic." They stare at each other for a brief moment, then speak.

SISSY: (*Furiously.*) I'm going to kill that white cracker bastard.

UPDIKE: (*He's had it.*) You ain't killing nobody, girl. You're as white as that cracker bastard and you ain't got a gun like he's got. That's *power*, girl. Gun power.

JUNIOR: (*A spade cat.*) I'll buy a piece on the street, man, and I'll go up the side of his head and I'll blow his cracker brains out.

UPDIKE: (*A king.*) Fuck, you will boy! You done knocked up his little girl surer than shit. Piece on the street. You had your piece.

GERTRUDE: (*After a huge pause, furiously.*) You been fucking white girls, huh?

JUNIOR: (*The son again; embarrassed.*) Alice? She fucks for everybody, Mama.

GERTRUDE: (*Outraged.*) Goddamn this! Goddamn everybody. Goddamn you, especially. (*To Junior.*) You and your white girls?

White girls!

SISSY: (*Checks herself.*) What do I look like? A tub of shit?

UPDIKE: Mind your mouth, girl.

JUNIOR: (*Explaining.*) Alice's been on her back more times this year than somebody dead in a coffin. And she's just about that good, too.

UPDIKE: (*An idea.*) Hey! Wait a goddamned minute.

GERTRUDE: (*Gigantically disgusted.*) Yeah? What you got to say, you fast-talkin' worthless white nigger?

UPDIKE: (*Disgusted.*) Shut up, woman. If that there Alice girl – Tillich's little honey – if that there Alice been packin' 'em all in like you say, how come Tillich figures you for the one what made her swell up?

JUNIOR: (*Sweet, soft.*) Alice likes me.

GERTRUDE: (*Amazed.*) What?

JUNIOR: (*Softly.*) Alice likes me.

GERTRUDE: (*Wants to be sure.*) Speak up, boy. Speak up loud and clear so you Mamma can hear you!

JUNIOR: (*Loud and clear; proud.*) Alice is in love with me!

UPDIKE: (*Delighted.*) Well, hot shit! At your age. With a cracker girl, too. At your age. (*Pauses.*) How old are you, boy?

JUNIOR: Sixteen.

UPDIKE: (*Hugs Junior confidentially.*) Shee-ittt. When I was ten, I had me my first cracker. And she was like dead fish too. Just laying there, waiting for me to set her afire with my rhythm, man.

JUNIOR: (*Softly, giggling.*) I love Alice.

UPDIKE: (*Shocked.*) Say that again, boy. I think you just said a crazy thing.

JUNIOR: (*Louder.*) I love Alice.

UPDIKE: (*Almost faints.*) Gertrude, your boy's gone crazy.

GERTRUDE: (*Strong.*) What did you say, *boy?*

JUNIOR: (*Angry now.*) Damn it! You all heard me. I love Alice. I don't care what you say. She's got creamy white skin, man, and beautiful boobies. And she talks real pretty. All the time. She's beautiful, man (*To Sissy.*) And you are a tub of shit, man. That's just what you are.

SISSY: (*Clobbering him.*) You motherfucking son-of-a-bitch!

UPDIKE: (*Breaking up the fight.*) No fighting here and none of your fucking filthy language in this here house. Huh? You get me? Just knock off the shit!

SISSY: (*Quickly.*) You hear what that motherfucker called me?

UPDIKE: I heard him. (*To Junior.*) Say you're sorry, boy.

JUNIOR: (*Confused.*) For what?

UPDIKE: (*Quickly.*) For calling your only sister a tub of shit, that's what. Everybody knows she looks just like her mother. That's a bad thing, Junior.

GERTRUDE: (*Leaning at the window, she stands up sharply.*) Apologize, Junior.

SISSY: (*Mocking.*) Yeah, Junior. Let's kiss and make up. I ain't never kissed a cracker before.

UPDIKE: (*Angry.*) Lay off that shit. As if we ain't got enough trouble here already without you actin' like a racist!

SISSY: (*A "take."*) Huh?

UPDIKE: (*Very "black."*) Look, I hate to be the one to say it, but pill or no pill, "ya-all" is acting like a pack of niggers. And that's all there is to that.

GERTRUDE: (*Taunts.*) "Ya-all"?

UPDIKE: (*Caught.*) In varying degrees. Granted, you ain't actin' quite so Nee-grow as your babies. What with Sissy's "them motherfuckin' motherfuckers" every other word out of her mouth. And Junior here acting like the word "boy" wasn't in Webster's Dictionary. And, shee-it, woman. You is actin' a mite tougher than your average white-assed cracker.

GERTRUDE: (*Sits on the bed, disgusted.*) Don't "shee-it, woman" me, you Swaheelee bum.

UPDIKE: (*Insulted.*) Who you callin' bum?

SISSY: (*Uncle Tom, mocking.*) It ain't me, Babe!

UPDIKE: (*Furiously, to Sissy.*) Come off the shit, girl, 'fore I whup you like you never been whupped before.

JUNIOR: (*Dancing.*) Whup. Whup. Whup. That's the way them white folks talk all the time. Whup, whup, whup. I'll whup ya' like ya' never done been whupped before, mother. Yes, zer!

UPDIKE: (*Distressed.*) Well . . . shee-it. That's the appreciation I get for bringing the pill into this house. Well, shee-it.

GERTRUDE: (*Uncle Tom's it like mad.*) You didn't bring no pill into this house, Updike. I washed and scrubbed them floors every Wednesday through Wednesday – yez, ma'am. Sure thing, ma'am. Bet your sweet ass, I scrubbed them floors, baby, not you. I brought them green bucks right into this house surer than shit so's we could buy them wonderful pills. Now didn't I, children?

SISSY: (*Revivalist.*) Oh, yes. Oh, yes!

GERTRUDE: (*Proud, grand, "black."*) Don't sass me, Sissy.

JUNIOR: (*False "white."*) I hear this 'xact conversation taking place in twenty million white homes just like ours all 'cross the country right now.

GERTRUDE: (*Angry.*) Don't sass me with your wise-ass school-talk neither, boy, 'cause I didn't get the benefits what your father and your mother slaved away to get you . . . that don't give you sassin' rights.

JUNIOR: (*As angry; plays rhythm – "Hot shit, Ben-a-fit."*) Well, hot shit, benefit! What'd you do for all I got? You didn't even vote for the mayor what passed the bussin' law so I get bussed.

UPDIKE: (*Almost weeping.*) And a good fuckin' thing too. That cracker bussed you Downtown, man and look at the mess you made. One day, that's all it took. One day Downtown and look at the mess you made. *Ooooooo. Oooooo.*

JUNIOR: (*Imitating him.*) *Ooooo. Ooooo.* (*Pauses.*) Shee-it. (*Walks directly to the audience. A public speaker. He smiles quietly.*) I'm sick all this infightin' and outfightin'. (*Very middle-class "white" speech imitation.*) I'm going to grow up to be just like you, Dad. I'm leaving this impoverished neighborhood so's I can grow up to go to college – maybe Harvard – then become a surgeon. My lifelong desire. Then I'll have a nice apartment on the Lower West Side. (*Suddenly, "street."*) Wid a motherfuckin' view of da ribba', baby! Shee-it! (*Runs back into set.*)

UPDIKE: (*Very "black."*) Hee. Hee. Hee. Hee. The boy's got a good black brain inside that white head of his. And black is beautiful.

JUNIOR: (*As "black."*) Yes, sah!

SISSY: (*The same.*) Indeed, sah!

GERTRUDE: (*The same.*) Shee-it. You all jist puttin' me on, ain't ya?

UPDIKE: (*Laughing.*) Shee-it. We can't 'ford no infightin' or outfightin' like the young man sez. 'Cause we's crackers now! (*They all laugh and slap each other's hands. Junior runs "through" the set and grabs a hand microphone for Gertrude. The lights fade down to a spot on the front apron.*)

Scene 8

GERTRUDE'S DREAM

Gertrude takes the microphone and begins to sing "White Like Me." The family stands behind her, as a chorus. The rock group walks into the play. All dance and sing. Gertrude begins the song very "white." Slowly during the song, she goes through the gradations of gray, from white to black, and completes the song as a soul singer.

GERTRUDE: (*Singing sweet and cool.*)

I'll sashay in Saks'
And the man will say 'GOOD MORNIN'."
Slither into Schrafft's
And have a frappe.
I'll mince my way through Macy's
And get thirty-day credit.
No – *oooooo* no one will give me crap.

(*She struts.*)

Move over, Mrs. Robinson.
You ain't nothin' any more.
Startin' this mornin', chippie-child,
I don't wash another floor!
Fuck off, Selma Robinson.
Honey-chile' can't you see?
You ain't a rat's-ass better.
You're just white like me!

(*The Family steps in with the rock group. They sing the chorus, while Gertrude ad libs.*)

FAMILY:

White like me. White like me. White like me.

(*Repeated while Gertrude sings.*)

GERTRUDE:

White like me.
It ain't like yesterday.
Uh-uh, honey. Nooo.
The world is *mine* today.
Uh-uh.

(*The chorus ends. Gertrude continues.*)

GERTRUDE:

I'll send my boy to Harvard and
My Sissy to the 'Cliffe.
Take Spanish at the New School.
Won't I speak terrific
Phrases in six languages.
Sometimes they rhymes.
I . . . I . . . I'll read *The New York Times*!

(*Strutting.*)

Move over, Mrs. Robinson.
You ain't nothin' any more.
Starting this mornin', chippie-child,
I don't wash another floor.

(*On her knees, swinging.*)

Fuck off! Selma Robinson.
Honey-chile! Can't you see?
You ain't a rat's-ass better,
You're just white like me.

FAMILY: (*As a chorus.*)

White like me. White like me. White like me.

(*Repeated while Gertrude sings.*)

GERTRUDE: (*Ad libbing on top.*)

It ain't like yesterday.
The world is mine today.
The world is mine.
I'll tell ya' why.
I'll tell ya' why.
I'll tell ya' why. Why. Why.
Because I'm White! White! White!

(*Screams a soul scream.*)

W-H-I-T-E!

(*Just a shriek.*)

AHHHHHHHHH!

ALL: (*Soul-brother climax.*)

Oh-oh-oh, Yeah-yeah-yeah.

(*If a reprise is called for, the final chorus, starting with "Move over, Mrs. Robinson . . . ," should be used, through the finish of the song. Then blackout and hold until applause ends.*)

BLACKOUT

Scene 9

NEARING NOON

After the audience applause stops, the lights fade up. The family is dancing. The rock group plays quietly, faintly. The dialogue and accent is very "Amos and Andy" – until Tillich's entrance.

UPDIKE: (*Laughing.*) Dance, woman. You got rhythm.

SISSY: (*Very "black" and happy.*) Somebody gotta tell this mother he's black inside. He's steppin' all over my toes.

UPDIKE: Hee-hee. Hee-hee. This is terrific.

GERTRUDE: (*Screaming her delight.*) You all want to see my lipstick kiss?

UPDIKE: (*Proudly.*) Yeah. Show 'em, Trudy.

(*They continue the dance throughout this scene. The music fades under slightly.*)

SISSY: What you rappin' 'bout?

GERTRUDE: Your Pa done give me a lipstick kiss, that's what. Right down here. (*She opens her robe so Sissy and Junior can see the lipstick mark.*) Ain't that the prettiest damn thing he's ever done?

JUNIOR: (*Enchanted.*) Hee-hee. You did that, Pa?

UPDIKE: (*A bad joke.*) You don't think your mama's got a girlfriend, do ya?

JUNIOR: (*Thrilled.*) Hee-hee. That's a pretty thing, Mama.

SISSY: (*Jealous.*) I want one. Huh? I want one too.

GERTRUDE: Go on, Junior. Give your sister Sissy what your pa gived me. Where's my lipstick, Updike?

UPDIKE: (*Pulls out a tube of lipstick. He throws it to Junior. They all continue to laugh and dance.*) Here ya are, boy!

(*Junior puts on the lipstick and dances to Sissy. He dances down her body.*)

JUNIOR: (*Giggling.*) Hold still, lovely.

SISSY: (*Out of control, overlapping.*) Shee-it. Shee-it!

JUNIOR: (*Surfacing.*) Hee-hee.

SISSY: (*Laughing, thrilled, embarrassed.*) Shee-it! I never been kissed low down or even up by no cracker before. Shee-it. You don't look like my brother.

JUNIOR: (*Delighted.*) Sissy's gettin' hot, Updike.

UPDIKE: (*A sound.*) Hee-hee. Hee-hee.

SISSY: (*Arguing.*) I am not, ya son-of-a-bitch.

JUNIOR: (*Giggling.*) Yes, ya are. Ya are. Admit it.

SISSY: (*Quickly.*) Well, you don't look like the brother I knew yesterday, you white-assed bastard. And you know it.

JUNIOR: (*Runs to the rock group.*) Alice! Holy shit! Alice! Stop the music!

(*The music stops.*)

GERTRUDE: (*Continues to dance.*) What are you doin', Updike? I'm dancing happy.

UPDIKE: (*Tense.*) You're crazy, woman. That cracker's been over with Jesus for a couple of hours now.

JUNIOR: (*Cool.*) Jesus ain't home, man.

UPDIKE: (*Anxious.*) Jesus is too home, ya jerk. He come home wid his folks this mornin'. They all made up and they're back livin' together. Just this mornin'. I seen 'em in the hallway, man. Before you all woke up.

GERTRUDE: (*Still dancing.*) I was dancin' happy.

UPDIKE: (*Disgusted, frightened.*) Kee-riiist! The woman's high on hope! (*He slaps Gertrude lightly.*) Don't hit me, Trudy. You was just high and I had to bring you down.

GERTRUDE: (*Angry, stops dancing.*) What'd you do that for, Updike? Huh? What'd you hit me for?

UPDIKE: (*Helpless.*) 'Splain it to her.

SISSY: (*Not really concerned.*) Pa think the cracker's comin' back to shoot us.

JUNIOR: (*Explaining.*) Jesus come home this mornin'. The cracker's over with him now.

GERTRUDE: The cracker'll shoot Jesus 'stead of you.

JUNIOR: (*Satirically.*) Well, hell. We gotta stop that injustice right now, ain't we? He's killin' the wrong man. Go get the cracker Sissy, so's he can shoot me, 'stead of Jesus. Fair's fair, huh?

UPDIKE: (*Really frightened.*) Don't talk crazy. This here's a serious situation.

(*Tillich reappears down the aisle. Quietly, he answers Updike.*)

TILLICH: (*Tough.*) Very serious, mister.

UPDIKE: (*Ashen.*) Shee-it.

(*They all freeze as Tillich walks into the room.*)

TILLICH: (*Takes a long, angry walk across, staring at each of them – Junior last.*) Why's the boy wearing lipstick?

UPDIKE: (*After they turn to Junior.*) The boy's a bit peculiar.

TILLICH: (*Straight mockery.*) I just has a long long talk with Jesus.

SISSY: (*Revivalist, to Tillich.*) Glory be.

UPDIKE: (*To Sissy.*) Shut your fuckin' mouth.

TILLICH: (*Pours it out.*) Jesus is Cuban.

JUNIOR: (*Hostile.*) Communist, too, probably.

UPDIKE: (*To Junior.*) You shut your fuckin' mouth, too.

TILLICH: (*Keeps rolling.*) Jesus is a black Cuban and his father's blacker still.

UPDIKE: (*Futile.*) Just what I was sayin' to my family. Ain't that the truth?

SISSY: (*Revivalist.*) It's the truth. It's the truth.

TILLICH: (*He knows.*) Jesus is a black Cuban and his father's blacker. I'd say his father is just about the blackest bastard I've ever seen.

JUNIOR: (*He knows he knows.*) Oh, wow!

TILLICH: (*Stopped.*) Huh?

JUNIOR: (*A rapid explanation; a put-down.*) I just said "Oh, wow." I say that a lot. I put on lipstick, see. Once I get the lipstick on, I can't seem to stop myself from sayin' things like "Oh wow." That's all.

UPDIKE: (*Flatly.*) Well, then. You met Jesus.

TILLICH: (*As flatly.*) That's right.

UPDIKE: (*A sound.*) Yep.

TILLICH: (*A sound.*) Yep.

GERTRUDE: (*Politely, simply.*) Nice of you to drop back and tell us.

TILLICH: (*Won't stop now.*) What would you say if I told you that Jesus never laid his eyes on Alice? Jesus never laid his hands on Alice?

UPDIKE: (*Helpless, scared.*) Jesus never laid Alice?

TILLICH: (*A wicked smile.*) That's right.

UPDIKE: (*The last try.*) That rules Jesus out, don't it? What other sex-crazed friends you got, Junior?

TILLICH: (*Taking out the pistol. He steps back and aims it at Updike's head.*) Come here.

GERTRUDE: (*Her last try.*) You can't come bustin' in here and . . .

TILLICH: (*Fiercely.*) SHUT UP! I'm gonna blow his brains out if I don't get a straight answer. (*He walks to Updike and puts the end of the pistol in Updike's left ear. Updike is not happy.*) Now what is going on here?

UPDIKE: (*An aphorism.*) You've got that gun in my ear.

TILLICH: (*A greater truth.*) Yes, I do.

UPDIKE: (*A plea.*) Gertrude?

GERTRUDE: (*Feebly.*) You just can't come bustin' in like this. Sissy call the fuzz.

TILLICH: (*He isn't kidding.*) If you do, I'll blow his head off.

UPDIKE: (*He knows.*) Don't call them, Sissy. Let it go. (*Tries to cool it.*) Now, Tillich. Let's be reasonable.

TILLICH: (*Tillich knows he knows.*) I'm a reasonable man, Updike. Reasonable enough to listen to my little Alice. I listened to my little Alice tell me about Junior and Sissy and Updike and Junior's mother, Gertrude. Alice says that Junior likes you a lot, Gertrude.

GERTRUDE: (*An attempt.*) We like Alice a lot, too.

UPDIKE: (*Terrified.*) Are you crazy, woman? Shee-it.

TILLICH: (*Archly.*) How do you say that? "Shee-it"? Is that right?

UPDIKE: (*A simple reply.*) That's about it. Yeah.

TILLICH: (*The nitty-gritty.*) How'd you get white?

JUNIOR: (*Getting furious.*) Fuck. Let me throw this son-of-a-bitch right out . . .

TILLICH: (*Fiercely.*) I'll blow your Pa's head off if you as much as open your mouth, boy.

UPDIKE: (*Simply, terrified.*) Please don't open your mouth, Junior. Please.

TILLICH: (*Again.*) Now let's answer some questions. How'd you get white?

SISSY: (*Furious, ashamed.*) We was born white. Same as you. You're makin' one hell of a mistake. (*To Junior.*) Motherfucker.

TILLICH: (*Taunting.*) Jesus says different. Jesus says you was born black as coal. Jesus says you was all born black. And you turned white. Now I believe him. He's a good boy, Jesus. He's been away.

JUNIOR: (*An angry reaction.*) I love Alice.

UPDIKE: (*Undone.*) Shut your mouth.

TILLICH: (*Pleased.*) Now we're gettin' somewhere. Go on, boy.

JUNIOR: (*Can't get the words back.*) I didn't say nothin'.

TILLICH: (*Won't let up.*) I said, go on, boy!

JUNIOR: (*Introverted.*) There's nothin' to go on with.

UPDIKE: (*Flatly, ashen.*) The boy tells the truth.

TILLICH: (*Presses.*) Why are you wearing lipstick?

SISSY: (*Pauses, gets an idea. Pulling up her skirt.*) 'Cause he gave me a lipstick kiss right here.

(*Tillich stares, stunned.*)

GERTRUDE: (*Sees what's happening.*) I got a lipstick kiss right here.

(*She pulls up her skirt as well. Tillich drops his guard. Updike simply takes the gun out of his hand.*)

UPDIKE: (*Amazed.*) I got the fuckin' gun!

TILLICH: (*Panic. He screams.*) Help! Police! The nigger's got a gun! (*Junior runs and takes the gun from Updike and shoves it into Tillich's ear. Tillich continues to scream for help until he slowly realizes there's a gun in his ear.*) Help! Help! Help! Police! Help! (*Pauses.*) You've put the gun in my ear.

JUNIOR: (*A cat.*) No shit. You're a whiz.

TILLICH: (*Terrified.*) What are you going to do?

GERTRUDE: (*Tension is relieved.*) Shee-it. Hee-hee. Shee-it! That school's done that child a world of good.

UPDIKE: (*Faints.*) Oooooowwwwww.

GERTRUDE: (*Strongly, quickly.*) Push the piece further in his ear, and you, Tillich, you shut your mouth. Sissy, get your Pa some water. He fainted.

SISSY: (*Walks over to Updike and slaps his face gently.*) Pa? Pa? You okay?

UPDIKE: Am I dead? (*Stares at his hands.*) Holy Christ, I've turned fucking white. I'm dead. Sissy! You're all white too.

SISSY: (*Slaps him, fiercely.*) Hey!

UPDIKE: What you hit me like that for, girl? You just like your Ma. (*Sees what's happening.*) Well, hot shee-it. We done got ourselves a captive. (*Pauses.*) What we gonna do wid him?

JUNIOR: (*Taunting.*) Maybe we'll blow his brains out, huh?

SISSY: (*Joining quickly.*) He ain't go no brains.

TILLICH: (*Pleads.*) I didn't mean to . . .

JUNIOR: (*Softly, viciously.*) Shut the fuck up, cracker.

TILLICH: (*Flatly.*) Yes. Of course.

UPDIKE: (*Pressing.*) The worm's turned, ain't it cracker?

TILLICH: (*A sound.*) Yes.

JUNIOR: (*Quickly.*) I told you to shut your mouth, man.

TILLICH: (*A plea.*) That gun is loaded, you know. You could kill somebody.

JUNIOR: (*A sound, a laugh.*) Who?

TILLICH: (*Falls to his knees.*) Please.

SISSY: (*Tough.*) Push the piece in a little harder, Junior. Cracker needs to get his ear bent the way he's been bending ours.

UPDIKE: (*Laughing.*) Hee-hee. We done got ourselves one hell of a prisoner.

GERTRUDE: (*From nowhere, fiercely.*) SHUT UP! (*Takes a long pause. Everybody freezes. Silence. She speaks.*) What were you gonna do, cracker? Huh? Were you gonna blow our brains out? Were you gonna shoot Pa's head off? Then Junior? Maybe grab a little ass from me and the little girl before you went home? Huh, cracker?

TILLICH: (*Almost sobbing.*) No. Of course not.

JUNIOR: (*Quickly.*) Was you planning to integrate our neigh-borhood, man? Is that what you came up for?

SISSY: (*Overlapping.*) He was gonna fuck up the neighborhood.

JUNIOR: (*Overlapping.*) Real estate prices would sky-rocket!

GERTRUDE: (*Overlapping.*) Hee-hee. That school's done the boy a world of good, Updike. I told you I was right!

UPDIKE: (*Overlapping.*) Shee-it. Hee-hee. Shee-it!

TILLICH: (*Clearly.*) I'm sorry. Please. I'm really sorry.

JUNIOR: (*A cat.*) Man, I got a piece of real power in my hands, ain't I? If I pull this thing . . . what do you call it? A trigger, rhymes with "nigger," mister? If I pull the *trigger* on this piece of power, will you believe me like you believe Alice, mister?

TILLICH: (*Great sincerity.*) I believe you. I believe you.

JUNIOR: (*Savors his position.*) But I ain't told you nothin' yet! What's to believe?

SISSY: (*A sound.*) Power, baby.

UPDIKE: (*Overlapping. A sound.*) Hee-hee. Power.

TILLICH: (*Babbling, sobbing.*) Look. I'm a very liberal guy. I want to help you people. It's just that my Alice got pregnant that way. I've been donating money and working on fair-housing committees . . . Hell, I never would act like this.

GERTRUDE: (*With tremendous authority.*) Stand over there, cracker. Over there. There. Stop. Right there. That's just where I want you. (*Walking over to Tillich and inspecting him.*) Let's see your white skin, mister. (*To Junior.*) I want to see a little skin. (*Junior stares at his mother blankly.*)

JUNIOR: (*Wise-ass.*) Roll over nice for my Mama, cracker. (*Tillich rolls.*)

GERTRUDE: (*Fiercely, pauses.*) Looks pretty stupid, don't it? Looks pretty stupid when all that white skin's down on its knees just beggin' for mercy.

JUNIOR: (*Taunting.*) Right, Mama. It looks pretty dumb to me.

TILLICH: (*Terrified.*) Please. What are you going to do to me?

GERTRUDE: (*Stranger still.*) I think you better keep your mouth tight-up closed.

TILLICH: (*Flatly, softly.*) Sure. Yes. Sure.

GERTRUDE: (*Laughing.*) That's the stuff.

SISSY: (*Overlapping.*) Cracker's scared shit, ain't he?

UPDIKE: (*Proudly.*) Well, hot shit. You figured it out, Trudy. (*To Tillich.*) She's tough, cracker. You're in a rotten situation, I know.

GERTRUDE: (*Disgusted.*) Jesus. There ain't nothin' slower than a worthless white nigger. Shut up, Updike.

JUNIOR: (*A cat.*) Hey, man. I'm carrying a piece of States' Rights. Right here in my hand. I didn't even know it either. Want me to kill him, Mama?

GERTRUDE: (*Surprised.*) Huh?

JUNIOR: (*A killer.*) You heard me. Want me to blow Cracker's brains out?

SISSY: (*An accomplice.*) I told you he ain't got no brains.

TILLICH: (*Feels the threat completely.*) Please don't. I got kids. I got a family. Please. I'll do anything for you. Honest to God. Don't shoot me.

GERTRUDE: (*Taunting, to Tillich.*) You're very scared now, ain't you, boy?

TILLICH: (*A plea.*) Yes. Wouldn't you be?

GERTRUDE: (*Flip.*) Yep. I'd be scared all right.

JUNIOR: (*Presses for permission.*) Shit. Mama. We got one. We'll pretend he's all of them. (*Pauses, then he pleads viciously.*) Let me kill him, Mama?

GERTRUDE: (*Stunned.*) I don't know. I don't know.

SISSY: (*Slowly, clearly.*) Mama. I'm sick to my stomach, Mama. I feel like I'm gonna throw it all up.

GERTRUDE: (*Watches.*) Wait a minute, honey. I'll think of somethin'.

JUNIOR: (*Means it.*) I feel sick to my stomach, Mama.

GERTRUDE: (*Confused.*) I'll think of something, honey. I'll think of something.

UPDIKE: (*Retching.*) I'm sick too. Christ! It's comin' up on me. I'm sick too!

GERTRUDE: (*Reeling, pained.*) Christ! I'm sick to my stomach now too. It's comin' up! (*As she walks to the window.*) Updike. Damn it. Updike. (*Gertrude walks to the window and stares outside.*)

UPDIKE: (*Ill.*) What you up to woman?

GERTRUDE: (*A matriarch.*) The sun's almost straight above us, Updike. The morning's almost gone. We been white one morning, darling. (*Pauses, then softly.*) Remember what you did this morning?

UPDIKE: (*Slowly.*) The lipstick-kiss?

GERTRUDE: (*With enormous pride.*) Uh-huh. I don't want it, darlin'. Not that I don't love you. I love you more now than when I met you. More this morning than ever before. Even though you're a stupid shit, darlin'. You are, too. But I'm stupid, too, huh? (*She rubs her dress against her belly.*) Do as I'm doing, Sissy. Rub your lipstick-kiss off. Off! Off! (*Sissy does.*) That's my little girl.

(*Gertrude begins to weep. Then she cries. Sobbing. Tillich stares. Sissy begins to weep. Then Junior too. Finally Updike.*)

UPDIKE: (*Weeping openly. He hugs her.*) Darlin'. My black beautiful darlin'. Oh shit, honey. Honey, I love you.

(*They kiss a long, loving kiss. A tape recording of the Creation of Man begins to play and they all pause, listening to their own voices.*)

GERTRUDE: (*On tape.*) In the beginning, there was only God on Earth. And the sunshine.

JUNIOR: (*On tape.*) At first, man was ravaged by scratchy rash and itchy skin blisters.

UPDIKE: (*On tape.*) When God turned a bronze and beautiful brown, He created man in the image of Himself.

SISSY: (*On tape.*) In his journey from Heaven to 126th Street, two of the pills spilled from his pocket and were lost forever.

GERTRUDE: (*Screams to the tape-recorded voice.*) Say that again!

SISSY: (*On tape.*) In his journey from Heaven to 126th Street, two of the pills spilled from his pocket and were lost forever.

GERTRUDE: (*Screams violently to Sissy.*) Say that again.

SISSY: (*Simply. Explaining.*) Two of the pills spilled from his pocket and were lost forever. (*She begins to realize. She stares at Tillich.*)

TILLICH: (*Explaining, desperately.*) Please, brothers. Let me explain. Please. I'm black too. Brothers. Please. Let me explain. I'm black too, I'm black too.

SISSY: (*Reeling backwards.*) A pill.

JUNIOR: (*The same.*) One of the missing pills!

TILLICH: (*Weeping.*) After all this time. My Alice. A black baby. Please . . . My wife. My kids. They don't know. They don't know. They never knew. They never knew.

GERTRUDE: (*After a huge ugly silence in which they all freeze and stare at Tillich begging. Violently.*) MAKE HIM BLACK! MAKE HIM

BLACK! PAINT THE BASTARD AND MAKE HIM BLACK! (*Music, very loud, is heard. There are buckets of black paint and brushes under the bed. Gertrude dives after them and passes out brushes to all. Updike brings out three buckets also. They grab Tillich, throw him down and dance around him, chanting and painting him with the black paint. Tillich tries to flick the paint from his body as though he were being covered with stinging insects. Spoken mechanically.*) Black is beautiful.

SISSY: (*A sound.*) Black is beautiful.

JUNIOR: (*A sound.*) Black is beautiful.

UPDIKE: (*A sound.*) Black is beautiful.

GERTRUDE: (*A sound.*) Black is Jesus.

SISSY: (*A sound.*) Black is Jesus.

JUNIOR: (*A sound.*) Black is Jesus.

UPDIKE: (*A sound.*) Black is Jesus.

GERTRUDE: (*A sound.*) Black is love.

SISSY:: (*A sound.*) Black is love.

JUNIOR: (*A sound.*) Black is love.

UPDIKE: (*A sound.*) Black is love.

(*They continue blackening Tillich. They blacken themselves as well. They dance as they scream, laugh and cry – all at the same time. Tillich is frozen with horror. He tries to escape the paint. He can't.*)

GERTRUDE: (*Spitting fire.*) Black is black is black is black

ALL: (*Chanting and crying, they repeat the phrase in turn, not in unison.*) BLACK IS BLACK IS BLACK. BLACK IS BLACK IS BLACK. BLACK IS BLACK IS BLACK. (*The chanting becomes a frenzied fugue.*)

GERTRUDE: Kill the white man!

ALL: KILL THE WHITE MAN. KILL THE WHITE MAN. KILL THE WHITE MAN.

GERTRUDE: BLACK IS BEAUTIFUL.

ALL: (*Overlapping.*) BLACK IS BEAUTIFUL.

GERTRUDE: Kill the white man.

ALL: (*Overlapping.*) Kill the white man.

GERTRUDE: Black is love.

ALL: (*Overlapping.*) Black is love.

GERTRUDE: BLACK IS BLACK IS BLACK. BLACK IS BLACK IS BLACK. BLACK IS BLACK IS BLACK.

ALL: BLACK IS BLACK IS BLACK. BLACK IS BLACK IS BLACK.

BLACK IS BLACK IS BLACK.

GERTRUDE: KILL THE WHITE MAN. KILL THE BLACK MAN.

ALL: KILL THE WHITE MAN. KILL THE BLACK MAN.

GERTRUDE: KILL. KILL. KILL. KILL. KILL. KILL.

ALL: KILL. KILL. KILL. KILL. KILL. KILL.

TILLICH: (*Screams in frantic horror.*) NO!

(*The chanting and music stop.*)

GERTRUDE: (*Simply.*) Yes.

(*In the three buckets previously brought out from under the bed by Updike are catsup and bits of black fabric cut into squares. All the buckets look exactly the same. Music comes on in the beginning of the chant. The stage manager cues as follows: On Tillich's scream "No!", the music bumps out. On Gertrude's "Yes," all flip brushes at Tillich, giving him final black streaks on his clothing. At the flip of the brushes, the lights switch from the stage to special lights focused on the audience. The stage is in blackness now, as the pistol is fired. Blam! Blam! A second shot. Blam! The final shot. During the shots Sissy sets the catsup bucket near Tillich, who, during the BLACKOUT on stage, scoops catsup into his mouth. LIGHTS switch from the audience to the stage. Gertrude and Updike throw buckets of black fabric at the audience. Precisely when the fabric leaves the buckets, the lights switch from the stage into the audience's eyes again. During this blackout on the stage, Tillich turns on his back, dead, with his head over the lip of the stage, his face, upside-down, facing the audience with a hideous stare. The lights quickly switch from the audience to a special on Tillich's face. Blood slowly trickles from his mouth. Junior walks calmly to Tillich and photographs him with a flash camera. Then the family poses over Tillich's body as hunters with a slain lion. They are photographed. Then they all photograph the audience. There is a pin spot on Tillich. The lights fade.*)

CURTAIN.

THE HONEST-TO-GOD SCHNOZZOLA

THE HONEST-TO-GOD SCHNOZZOLA gave its first performance for the press (after three weeks of public previews) on April 21, 1969, at the Gramercy Arts Theatre, 138 East 27th St., in New York City. Prior to its New York premiere, this play was given workshop performances at The Act IV Theatre, Provincetown, Massachusetts, and the Actors' Studio, New York City.

The company for the New York production of this play was as follows:

THE MUSICIAN .... John Hall
COFFEE .... Hervé Villéchaize
HONEY .... Ann Wedgeworth
ATHENIA .... David Edgell
JIMMY .... Lane Smith
JOHNNY .... Salem Ludwig
THE OWNER .... Julie Garfield

The scenery was designed by Charles Brandon, lighting by Roger Morgan. Music was composed by John Hall, lyrics by Israel Horovitz. The associate director was Timmy Everett. The production was directed by Rip Torn.

Mr. Horovitz won the 1969 OBIE Award and the 1969 Show Business Award – Best American Playwright for THE HONEST-TO-GOD SCHNOZZOLA .

Introduction

When I first started writing for a living, full-time, I would answer the question "Where do you work?" with a proud "I don't work—not any more!" ... I still feel that way, sort of. It still rather amazes me that I can be paid so well to do something I love so much. It's been a lucky 27 years!

The Honest-to-God Schnozzola was the first play produced in my 2nd season as "A New York Playwright". It had its roots in Berlin, where it is set. One of the last times I worked for a living, I worked for an advertising agency in NYC. They sent me to Germany, to Berlin, to shoot televison commercials I'd written for a new mens cologne called Dante. ("The glory of Rome in a classic cologne!") *The Indian Wants The Bronx* and *It's Called The Sugar Plum* had already been performed at the Eugene O'Neill Memorial Theatre Center's National Playwright's Conference ... and seemed to be heading for a production in NYC. *Line* was set for November production at Café LaMama. I saw myself as a playwright, first and foremost. In my mind, writing and directing television commercials gave me a chance to feed my kids ... and to learn camera ... just in case Hollywood beckoned. And Dante gave me the chance to see Berlin.

A side-note, about me and Dante: Some years before my cologne-trip to Berlin, I nearly drowned. It happened in Boston. I'd fallen asleep in my bathtub, during a middle-of-the-night scrup-up. I'd spent that day, and the night before, working as a stagehand, loading scenery into a theatre ... for 26 consecutive hours! As soon as my exhausted body relaxed in the warm water of my bathtub, I fell asleep. I remember, quite vividly, that I was dreaming about drowning, and it was not at all unpleasant. In Time's penultimate nick, however, I was spared. A plaster death-mask of Dante I'd bought for $0.25 in a thrift-shop, fell from itssticky-tape mooring on the wall above the bathtub, and smashed against my feet, waking me up ... saving my life.

And now, Dante was beckoning me to follow him to Berlin. (Perhaps, to keep his name—his celebrity—alive?) Without the slightest hesitation, I followed the man. It was the least I could do. I owed him my life.

The first shock for me in Berlin was the German language. Growing up Jewish in the 1940's did not prepare me well for hearing Deutch sprechen, all around. As an 8-year-old, I was certain that the Nazis would find their way to Wakefield, Mass., and into my bedroom. Twenty years later, that particular dream had yet to evaporate.

The second shock for me in Berlin was the food. Vegetarianism in c.1967 Berlin was not a popular sport. I could not believe how many different ways the German nation had found to prepare pig-meat. In those days, I weighed in at 128 lbs., and a month without food was not a good idea.

But, the real shock for me in Berlin, in the 1960's, was the prevailing German attitude toward young American Jews, *comme moi-même*, who wanted so much to talk about the War and The Six Million. I brought both of those subjects up, endlessly. Needless to say, during my month in Berlin, I failed to make a lot of new friends.

But, I did find a new play.

My hang-out was a late-night hooker-bar, not far from my hotel. I watched the action, nightly, and I took copious notes. (Even then, I played playwright to the hilt.) As soon as I found this place, I'd felt it was a perfect stage-setting for my new play ... But, I had no idea whatsoever what my new play would be about. For several consecutive nights, I sat at the bar talking with a tall, thin, long-haired hooker (not a great beauty, but, not bad), in between her tricks. She gave me everything I wanted: for hours and hours, she spoke with me in halting English about the War and about The Six Million. The manager of the bar, a youngish homuncle of nearly circus proportions, would interrupt our chat, once or twice, every hour or so, in a sort of commando voice, sending the other half of my conversation into the back room, and business. She would return to the bar, twenty minutes later, poker-faced, often picking up our conversation, mid-sentence, where she'd left off.

One night, about three weeks into our relationship, I heard her screams from the back room ... followed by the sound of hands-on slapping ... And then, I heard the sound of a male voice, enraged, yelling something (presumably nasty) in still another language I didn't speak. The enraged man appeared from the back room, alone. He was a businessman, small and mean-featured. His face was aglow with off-the-charts primal rage. In a flash, the enraged man had the tiny manager by the throat. He punched the little fellow, fiercely, five or six times, all the while yelling some explanation of his rude behavior in a language I'd simply never heard before. And then, the enraged man let loose of the tiny manager and, quickly, made an exit into the post-modern German night. There was a pause, and then, the sound of my hooker-friend, sobbing,. She staggered into sight, from the back room, holding her long, blonde hair carelessly in her hands. A wig. She was a man. Not a great beauty, but, not bad.

Rather than facing twenty more years of psychoanalysis, let me leave it at this: I hadn't a clue, not a clue! But, I certainly did have a new play. I imagined two American businessmen in Berlin ... one Jewish, a Jimmy Durante wannabe ... Anyway, you've come this far. You'll read the play.

I wrote the first draft of *The Honest-to-God Schnozzola* while still in Berlin, in my hotel, middle of the remaining nights. When I got back to NYC (a/k/a "home"), I had to spend all my waking time editing my Berlin cologne commercials ... and then selling them to The Client. Soon-after, my first plays opened in NYC, and, with $100-a-week in royalties promised, I quit my job. I stopped working. I got over-busy, doing everything you've been reading about in the introductions to my other plays printed in this edition. For several months, *The Honest-to-God Schnozzola* was set aside; forgotten.

I'd somehow given a copy of *The Honest-to-God Schnozzola* to my actress-friend Ann Wedgeworth, who, in turn gave the script to her ex-husband-friend, Rip Torn. Rip loved the play, and put together a small production at the Act IV Café Theatre in Provincetown, Massachusetts, in Summer (which I didn't see). But, then, in the Fall,

Rip's production of *The Honest-to-God Schnozzola* made it to the tiny stage at the Actor's Studio (which I did see). I was, frankly, shocked by what Rip had achieved with my little play. He'd captured every nuance of the Berlin bar ... its seediness, its sadness, its anti-humanity ... its absolute decay. Somehow, seeing it all at arm's length, on stage, quadrupled the intensity of the actual place ... spotlighted its cold theatricality, its chilling cruelty. In the end, I suppose I am quite pleased to have written a play like *The Honest-to-God Schnozzola*, when I did ... if only to say I seemed to be finding some enlightenment on my own, at a time when the world was (like the Nazis) totally homophobic. I think that characters of the Jews, homosexuals and Germans are treated fairly in the play. Perhaps *The Honest-to-God Schnozzola* is a bit obvious, today. But, it is certainly an accurate record of what people thought and felt, back then, on that particular dot on the planet Earth.

The Honest-to-God Schnozzola opened in NYC in the Spring of 1969, at the Gramercy Arts theatre, in a commercial (off-Broadway production). My play was once again graced by Rip Torn's stunning direction, and by excellent performances from Ann Wedgeworth, Lane Smith and Salem Ludwig. Best of all, however, was the then-unknown (but already-brilliant) Hervé Villechaise as the homunclear bar-manager. Hervé was mezmerizing ... huge. There was no doubt that he would soon be a star.

The Honest-to-God Schnozzola failed to find a wide audience, but, managed to win the OBIE as Best Play of that particular year. *The Honest-to-God Schnozzola* has rarely been performed since its NYC premiere.

Characters

THE MUSICIAN A musician.
COFFEE A midget.
JIMMY A little man with a large nose.
JOHNNY A large man with a little nose.
HONEY A small hooker with large breasts.
ATHENIA A large hooker with small breasts.
THE OWNER A tough lady who also steps in and out of the play as MOLLY and SWEETIE, the wives.

NOTE: The Musician is optional. Music can be taped or played live by a band on stage. The author prefers the latter, whenever possible.

Setting

The interior of Cafe Society, a tourists' bar in West Berlin, Germany. Just before closing. Early morning. This morning.

NOTE: The ideal stage for this play is no stage at all. Instead, an actual cabaret serves the play best of all, with the audience "on stage", with the play taking place in and around its observers. In this environment, Jimmy and Johnny should be members of the audience.

THE HONEST-TO-GOD SCHNOZZOLA

PROLOGUE

The stage is not yet visible. The house lights fade out. There is a glow of light on the back wall, which is white. Several television commercials are projected onto the wallat the same time. Each one is perverse. When they are over, the play begins.

COFFEE: (*Wanders through the audience, stopping to talk directly to the people. Softly.*) Are you happy? Do you tell lies? Do you love your wife? Do you hate dirt? Do you want to kiss me? Do I frighten you? (*He wanders through the audience slowly, carefully. He caresses women in the audience – their faces, gently. Sometimes he merely smiles quietly, standing silently, staring at people until they turn away. When he "stares someone down": forces them to turn away from his stare, he laughs. Giggles.*) Do you believe what you see? Everything·you see? Always? (*Finally.*) I am Jesus Christ and I am telling you that I am lying to you. Do you believe me? Do *I* believe *you?* (*He laughs and exits. The lights slowly fade up, revealing the setting.*)

(*The setting is an abstraction of the interior of a nightclub. There is a piano downstage. Chairs and tables scattered. A bench and table are upstage right. A curtain that opens and closes on a rod hangs in front on the bench and table. Dressed in garish Hollywood stuff, Jimmy and Johnny stand frozen, facing the audience, as the lights fade up. Jimmy is 30-ish; Johnny, 45-ish. When the lights are full, music, Germanic-jazz, blares at full blast, played by The Musician. The owner (optional) sits stage right. The men remain frozen. Two strippers appear upstage, dead center. They each do one obscene terrific bump and the music switches off. The women freeze and the men come to life.*)

JIMMY: (*Slowly. Intensely.*) She's the one, Johnny-boy. The one you've been dreaming about. Thinking about. Living about. Wanting about. (*Drearily.*) Talking about. Dreaming about. Talking about.

Talking about.

JOHNNY: (*Excited.*) Which one, huh? Which one, Jimmy-baby?

JIMMY: (*Flatly. To the audience.*) We're Americans. Married. Families. Great kids. Great jobs. We're here in Germany on expense accounts. If I were Jewish, I'd hate this place. I'm not Jewish. I'm nothing.

JOHNNY: (*About to burst.*) Which one, Jimmy-baby? Huh?

JIMMY: (*Back to Johnny. A put-on.*) The one you been dreaming about. Talking about. Living about. The one on the left.

JOHNNY: (*A child.*) Oh, wow! Oh, she's a terrific one. Jimmy-kid. Oh, wow, Jimmy-baby. Are you sure?

JOHNNY: (*A con-man's sincerity.*) Where was I until twenty minutes ago? Was I walking down Koo-fen-stem-damn or whatever the Christ they call that damn street . . . was I walking that street staring at nothing, or was I where I told you I was? Getting what I told you I'd get? What you've been talking about.

JOHNNY: (*A sound.*) Living about.

JIMMY: (*A sound.*) Talking about.

JOHNNY: (*A sound.*) Dreaming about.

JIMMY: (*Disgust.*) Talking about.

JOHNNY: (*A sound.*) Thinking about.

JIMMY: (*Disgust.*) Talking about.

JOHNNY: (*A sound.*) Oh, wow! Dreaming about.

JIMMY: (*Slowly. Reasonably. To the audience.*) You see. I really hate this guy. We're both Americans, but you think all Americans are just the same, don't you? Well, let me tell you a terrific piece of news: there's one hell of a hell of a difference between your average American and I, myself, for example. I, myself, have been to Europe before. I've done all the things that tourists do . . . you know how those tourists act with their loud noise and their expecting all the French to speak English and *everybody* to speak English. Although I, myself, have never been to Germany before, you can tell that I've at least been to Europe before. And I'll probably come back a third time after this trip. There'll be another trip for me. Maybe with my wife and my kids, when they get older.

My wife is one in a million and I had to get stuck with her. But she's a peach, a peach, next to this typical American tourist, who, on his first trip away from his wife just talks about getting laid. Talks about getting laid so much I can't stand to be with the foul-mouthed son of a bitch. I can't stand his shitty, lousy-assed, foul mouth. (*One of the girls does another bump as the music snaps on and off instantly.*) Would you look at those knockers? Why couldn't I have picked her instead of the other one? Huh? Why couldn't the lousy German bastards have tipped me off as to what their game is here? In New York, they'd go to jail . . . go to jail if they pulled the kind of crap they pull here. If I were a Jew, I'd hate these German bastards for what they did. Hate them. (*To Johnny.*) The one on the left. She's the one, Johnny-boy. She's yours for the asking. And the tab's on me.

JOHNNY: (*Quickly.*) What tab?

JIMMY: (*Laughing. Kidding. Stroking.*) The price. The tab. The price, Johnny-baby. You pay a price, right?

JOHNNY: Oh, wow! She looks just like Trixie. You did that on purpose, didn't you, ya' sly son-of-a-bitch? Sneaky bastard. Does that mean you ain't mad any more?

JIMMY: (*A sound.*) You pay a price.

JOHNNY: (*Walks directly to the audience, trying not to take his eyes away from the girls. He smiles at the audience, rather embarrassed. Then he speaks, directly to the audience. An excited explanation. Reasonably.*) It's incredible. Trixie's not my wife. She's Peter's wife. Peter's a Kraut. Nice guy, but a spook. Trixie's his wife. She came on strong to me. Like gangbusters. I mean, I almost couldn't believe how strong she came on to me. It was really something. Really something.

JIMMY: (*Calls to Johnny. Viciously.*) That's a lie.

JOHNNY: (*A defense. Quickly. Never taking his eyes from the audience.*) He thinks I'm lying, ladies and gentlemen. He doesn't believe a word I tell him. Trixie came on so strong to me, she almost turned me off. Honest to God.

JIMMY: (*As a sword slash.*) You raped her!

JOHNNY: (*Quickly now. Desperate. Without turning, he continues talking to the audience as though Jimmy's calls were not real. Thoughts. Guilt. The excuses follow.*) I was pretty horny. I'll admit *that!* (*Smiling. A salesman. Pushing. Straining. Without turning.*) When I finally got her into the hotel room . . . well, I don't have to tell you the details. I was like a Marine back from the front.

JIMMY: (*A soft scream. A killer's warning.*) You almost killed her. She almost died.

JOHNNY: (*Turning on Jimmy venomously.*) How did I know she was pregnant? She was skinny!

JIMMY: (*Slowly now. A snake sees his enemy. Moving slowly towards Johnny.*) She came to pick you up. To take you to dinner. So you wouldn't be lonely. You raped her.

JOHNNY: (*Hurt. An explosion.*) We've had this out and we agree to forget it, right? Every time I tell you the truth, you call me a liar. I'm not a liar, pal. Not me! I may be a tough son-of-a-bitch, but I don't tell lies, pal. Not me.

JIMMY: (*The sound of a judge.*) You raped that girl. You beat her and you almost killed her.

JOHNNY: (*Fighting for his life.*) That's a Goddam rotten lie and you know it. I've never hit a woman in my life. Never. I'd kill myself first. What is this? This fight was finished, Jimmy. Finished. I didn't come in here . . . I didn't agree to meet you here . . . to start all this up again.

JIMMY: (*The final verdict.*) You beat her and you raped her and you almost killed her.

JOHNNY: (*A child.*) How was I supposed to know she was pregnant? Huh? Just tell me how?

JIMMY: (*An angry child.*) You got eyes. She's Peter's *wife!*

JOHNNY: (*A sound.*) He's a Kraut!

JIMMY: (*Screams.*) You almost killed her!

JOHNNY: (*The sound repeated. Empty.*) She's a Kraut.

JIMMY: (*A switch. A button is pushed.*) Jesus Christ! Jesus Christ! (*Jimmy laughs a strange laugh.*)

JOHNNY: (*Almost sweetly.*) They killed six million Jews. Six million. She's only one.

JIMMY: (*A sound.*) One at a time.

JOHNNY: (*A sound.*) She's only one.

JIMMY: (*A sound.*) One at a time. Six million times.

JOHNNY: (*A sound.*) They killed our boys.

JIMMY: (*A whiskey-laugh.*) That's right, Johnny. They killed our boys.

JOHNNY: (*A child watching his hat in a tree. Trapped. Makes a false exit.*) I wanna' get out of here. I don't want to kill another Goddam night with you. (*Pauses.*) I got to tell you something, kid. I got to get something off my chest. You're getting to be a big pain in the ass. A real big pain in the ass. Now I am just sick and tired of this fight we're having over a Goddam stupid mistake. I don't give a shit about Peter or his Kraut wife or your insults or your lies. I know who I am and what I'm doing. I am sick and God *damned* tired of this trip . . . of you . . . of all of it. If I had one bit of courage left in me, I'd quit this God *damned* job right here and just get my ass home where I can make some sense.

JIMMY: (*Laughing.*) Courage?

JOHNNY: (*A man, again. Self-pitying, but a man.*) Courage. Right. Courage. Plain and simple courage. I am not what you call a young man, pal. And you only got a couple of good years left yourself, so don't you laugh your God *damned* laugh at me. I'll wait it out for a couple of years and see who gets the last laugh out of this, believe me.

JIMMY: (*Flatly. A defense.*) Only a couple of years, huh? That's the way you see it?

JOHNNY: (*An announcement.*) I wanna' get out of here. I've had enough. (*Starts to exit again. Jimmy stops him.*)

JIMMY: (*Sugar-free sugar.*) Hold on, pal. Come on, Johnny-baby. We're getting off the track. This is a night out, Johnny. This is a celebration.

JOHNNY: (*Bitchy. Arch. Wiry.*) Yeah? Well, I don't feel in a celebrating mood, somehow. You got me going back at the hotel, but to tell you the truth, I don't believe you. I don't think I'm gonna' get laid. I don't even think I'm gonna' get happy.

JIMMY: (*Selling a stolen watch.*) Would I lie to you, Johnny-baby? Would I lie?

JOHNNY: (*A sound. Disgust.*) Come off the shit!

JIMMY: (*A friendly cobra.*) Just look at those two, Johnny. Look at those knockers. You think that's a lie? (*He laughs.*) It's on me.

JOHNNY: (*Slightly confused. Quickly. A look.*) What's on you?

JIMMY: (*Flatly.*) The tab.

JOHNNY: (*Honestly confused.*) What tab?

JIMMY: (*While he strokes and strikes.*) The tab. You think the kind of woman who does what that kind of woman does does that kind of thing for nothing? You think she does that kind of thing for the hell of it? The fun of it? The love of it?

JOHNNY: (*An attempt.*) Back in school . . .

JIMMY: (*A laugh of superiority.*) Back in school! That was America, baby. This is Germany. You know what they did to those Jews? They slaughtered them.

JOHNNY: (*The philosopher speaks.*) If I were Jewish, I'd hate these bastards.

JIMMY: (*Delighted.*) With good cause.

JOHNNY: (*Angry.*) If I were Jewish, I'd kill these bastards.

JIMMY: (*Mock seriousness.*) Rightly so.

JOHNNY: (*Disgusted.*) If I were Jewish, I don't know if I would have come here.

JIMMY: (*Softly. Flatly.*) That's interesting. (*To the audience.*) He is Jewish. But you knew that, right?

JOHNNY: (*Proud.*) Thank God I'm not Jewish.

JIMMY: (*Laughing. Agreeing.*) We've got a lot to be thankful for, Johnny-boy. A lot.

JOHNNY: (*A sound.*) Great wives.

JIMMY: (*A sound.*) One in a million.

JOHNNY: (*A sound.*) Great kids.

JIMMY: (*A sound.*) Two in a million.

JOHNNY: (*A sound.*) We must be the luckiest guys alive.

JIMMY: (*A sound.*) Two hundred million.

(*Coffee, a midget, appears from a curtain. He wears a black tailored suit and has a whistle on a gold chain around his neck. He blows the whistle.*)

COFFEE: (*A showman's enthusiasm.*) Good evening, ladies and gentlemen. Welcome to Cafe Society. My name is Coffee. I am little but . . . (*He gives a "high sign."*) Oh, my!

JIMMY: (*A sound.*) Two hundred million.

JOHNNY: (*A thought. A look.*) He's kinda' weird, huh?

JIMMY: (*Calling Coffee.*) Coffee's my little buddy. Right, Coffee?

COFFEE: (*With the good cheer of a happy eel.*) You are all my buddies. And Coffee wants all his buddies to be happy. Coffee wants all his buddies to be warm. Coffee wants all his buddies' money. Oh, boy!

JOHNNY: (*Scared. Defensively. Loud. Confident.*) Oh, wow! What a weird place. Fucking little pervert, huh?

COFFEE: (*An announcement from the stage.*) Coffee wants to introduce you to his two lumps of sugar. Athenia and Miss Honey Bee.

(*Blows the whistle. The lights switch color. The men freeze, the music blares. The women do a strip. Athenia on the left, strips to her underwear, lots of garters, braces, straps, stuff. Honey, on the right, gets down to her skin, all pink and wonderful. The musician and the owner sings.*)

"A Bit of Night Life"

Was spielt man heute abend?
Geben Sie mir zwei Karten.
Sind diese Platze gut?
Amusieren Sir sich?

CHORUS:

Fahren Sie mich zum Cafe Society.
Fahren Sie mich zum Cafe Society.
Lassen Sie Kappelle "Schraube, Schraube" spielen.
Kommen Sie wieder, bitte.
Kommen Sie wieder, bitte.
Rufen Sie mir ein ander taxi.

CHORUS: (*Speaks.*)

Darf ich um diesen Tanz bitten? Die Vorstellung
beginnt in ein paar Minuten. Entschuldigen Sie,
Eintritt nur in Abendleidern. Das ist letze
Vortellung heute aben. Ist alles in Ordnung?
Was speilt man heute abend?
Geben Sie mir zwei Karten.
Sind diese Platze gut?
Amusieren Sir sich?

(*As soon as the dance is over, the Actors freeze. It is silent. The owner speaks as Molly. She calls out to Johnny.*)

MOLLY: (*Haltingly.*) Johnny?

JOHNNY: (*Looks up absently. Plays straight out front as if a soap opera character.*) Uh?

MOLLY: (*Urgently.*) Do you *have* to go? I mean, is it essential?

JOHNNY: (*He crosses to Molly.*) What? I didn't hear you.

MOLLY: (*Annoyed.*) I said, do you have to go? On the trip. Is the trip essential?

JOHNNY: (*Angry.*) For Chrissakes, Molly! For Chrissakes!

MOLLY: (*Bitchy.*) Don't jump at me! I just asked a simple enough question. Do you have to go? That's all. That's a reasonable question.

JOHNNY: (*Quickly.*) 'Course I have to go. For Chrissakes! I got my passport. Got my tickets. Got my advance. Kissed the kids goodnight. What a hell of a time to ask.

MOLLY: (*Softly.*) I know. I'm gonna miss you, that's all.

JOHNNY: (*Softly.*) I'm gonna miss you too, you know. It ain't like we're chasin' off to Germany for the *fun* of it. Can you imagine me going to Germany for a *vacation?* (*He embraces her. They kiss. He pulls back.*) I love you, Molly. Honest-to-God, I love you. I'm gonna write every day. I'll even call you. It ain't like I'm goin' in the army. I'll be back in a couple of weeks.

MOLLY: I know. I love you. I do, you know. That's why I'm scared. Because I love. (*Johnny swings back into the scene. As he turns, the lights restore on the strippers. They do a "bump".*)

JOHNNY: (*A child's delight.*) Holy Mother of God! Will you look at those knockers! (*Amazed. Instant erection.*) Oh, wow! (*The music switches off and Honey puts on a robe. Athenia walks into the back room, draws the curtain. Honey walks to the men, who have been standing, frozen. Staring.*)

HONEY: (*Without surprise. To Jimmy.*) You're back?

JIMMY: (*Quietly.*) Yeah.

JOHNNY: (*To Honey, his trousers bursting.*) Oh, wow! He told me he was here before but I didn't believe him. I mean, I just didn't believe it was real.

HONEY: (*Sexy.*) You want to dance?

JOHNNY: (*Can't believe it.*) Oh, wow! (*Soft chicken-soup music plays and they dance. Jimmy stands and watches.*)

HONEY: (*A well-rehearsed question.*) You're German?

JOHNNY: (*An unrehearsed reply.*) No. I'm American.

HONEY: (*Acting. Over-acting.*) You fooled me.

JOHNNY: (*Smug. Happy, almost thrilled.*) Well, I try to . . . you know.

HONEY: (*Sexy.*) Are you here on business?

JOHNNY: (*Strutting.*) Hell no! Business? Me? Why would I be here on business?

HONEY: (*Moving in on him.*) Then, why are you here?

JOHNNY: (*A rooster.*) Oh, hell. Me and my friend, Jimmy, there. We're just hacking around. Two bachelors. Roaming around. We make movies.

HONEY: (*Stroking his face.*) Movies?

JOHNNY: (*Sweaty.*) Oh, yeah. Sure. Movies. For television. Commercial movies.

HONEY: (*Without thinking. Still stroking.*) Television commercials?

JOHNNY: (*Shocked.*) Did he tell you?

HONEY: (*Surprised.*) Who?

JOHNNY: (*Angry.*) Jimmy?

HONEY: (*Soothing. Commences stroking.*) No. I only talked to him for a minute. He's Athenia's friend.

JOHNNY: (*Slyly.*) Do you do what Athenia does?

HONEY: (*Coy bitch.*) What do you mean?

JOHNNY: (*Coyer still.*) Well, hell. You know. Do you do what she did to Jimmy?

HONEY: (*Cat and mouse.*) I just work here. I dance, if that's what you mean?

JOHNNY: (*The cat. Cautiously.*) What's the matter? Is somebody listening? I mean, is it illegal here in Germany too, huh?

HONEY: (*The mouse. The music stops.*) The music stopped.

JOHNNY: (*Very hip. Cool. Inside talk.*) Oh, yeah. I get it. Okay. I'll play it cool so you won't get into trouble. Who is it? Who's listening?

HONEY: (*Wounded explanation.*) The owner. She's mean to us. If she catches us paying too much attention to one man, we get in trouble. Like you said. You have to buy drinks, too. If you want me to dance with you, you have to buy me a drink. Otherwise, I'll have to go to one of the other men. Would you buy me a drink?

JOHNNY: (*A quiz-kid's pride.*) You don't really get booze in your drink. Your drink is just colored water, right? I know the game. I don't blame you, don't get me wrong. I know that you kids have to play it by the rules and all, but I'm on to the game. I just want that understood right off the bat. I know the game. You just get colored water right? Does she split the take with you? After you drink that colored water, does she give you any of the money?

HONEY: (*Flatly. Self-pitying.*) That's how we get paid.

JOHNNY: (*Sincere.*) That's awful. I mean, that's just a terrible thing. I don't think anything like that could ever happen in America. You probably ought to come to America. Would you like to come to America?

HONEY: (*Eyes closed. Savors the moment.*) I dream of America every night.

JOHNNY: (*A psychiatrist's understanding.*) It's a crime the way they degenerate you kids. A crime. You ought to save your money from your colored water and come to America. You really ought to. (*The music plays again.*) We can dance again, if you'd like.

HONEY: (*Hates to say it.*) You really should buy me a drink.

JOHNNY: (*Very hip again.*) I don't mind. I mean, I know what the game is and I know that you have to play by the rules. I understand all that so don't think it bothers me to buy you that colored water. (*Pauses.*) Do I get colored water too?

HONEY: (*Flatly.*) You get a real drink.

JOHNNY: (*Excited.*) I wouldn't mind giving you my drink and you could give me your colored water. I'd get a hell of a kick out of breaking the rules that way and knowing that you drank my drink and I drank your colored water.

HONEY: (*Explaining. A bit amazed.*) I can't have any liquor on my breath. It's very bad for the customers and the owner would smell it and I'd get into trouble.

JOHNNY: (*Thinks he's in a movie.*) Oh, wow! It's that bad, huh? I mean, the Germans are that sneaky. (*Pauses.*) Are you German?

HONEY: (*Flatly. Too certain.*) No.

JOHNNY: (*The camera's rolling.*) What are you then, huh? What are you??

HONEY: (*All true.*) I come from a little town with a long name, nothing special. I hate the Germans.

JOHNNY: (*Hides from the camera.*) Oh, yeah. Me too. I really hate the Germans too. I think that's terrific that you work in here and take money away from the Germans. I mean, you sort of steal money from those German bastards with your colored water and then you're using that money to come to America. That's a terrific thing. (*Cross-fade lights to Jimmy and Athenia, who has appeared from behind the curtain. Johnny and Honey freeze.*)

ATHENIA: (*Hesitantly.*) Hello, Jimmy.

JIMMY: (*Quietly. Intensely.*) Don't "Hello" me. Don't even talk to me.

ATHENIA: (*Quietly.*) I thought you knew. I'm sorry.

JIMMY: (*Too loud.*) *You're* sorry. That's a laugh. That's a terrific laugh. You're sorry. How the Christ do you think I feel?

ATHENIA: (*Quickly. Softly.*) I am what I am. A whore.

JIMMY: (*Contains his anger. We see the struggle.*) A whore? (*He laughs.*) A whore! That's even better than "I'm sorry."

ATHENIA: (*Looking around. Softly. Quickly.*) Please, Jimmy. You'll make a scene. The owner. Please. I thought you knew. I thought you could tell. (*The lights cross-face.*)

JIMMY: (*Crossing to the Owner: Sweetie.*) I could have made you a dress by the time you got into that one. For Christ's sakes, Sweetie. This is ridiculous. (*As Jimmy reaches for the zipper on her dress, she turns around quickly and tries to kiss him. He pulls back quickly.*)

SWEETIE: Jimmy?!

JIMMY: What the hell are you doin'?

SWEETIE: Trying to kiss you. Is that so awful?

JIMMY: No. 'Course not. You turned so quick, you scared the hell out of me. You shouldn't turn so quick. That's all.

SWEETIE: Well?

JIMMY: Well, what?

SWEETIE: Kiss me.

JIMMY: Why?

SWEETIE: What do you mean "why"?

JIMMY: What do you mean "what do you mean"?

SWEETIE: Jimmy? What's the matter? What's going on? Please kiss me?

JIMMY: Yeah, sure. (*He kisses her as a child kissing an ancient aunt on the cheek: a peck.*)

SWEETIE: Jimmy, I said "kiss me"! (*She turns him about and kisses him passionately on the lips. He slaps her face, violently. The noise is awful. Sweetie recoils, shocked.*)

JIMMY: Oh, Christ. Oh, Jesus Christ. Here, Sweetie. Get up. Oh, Jesus.

SWEETIE: Why? Why? Why? Jimmy, why? (*She tries to kiss him again. This time he violently pushes her away, repulsed.*)

JIMMY: Damn you, don't touch me! Just don't touch me! How dare you? How dare you? (*Jimmy turns on Honey fiercely. The lights cross-fade back on to the stage proper. The lights to full.*)

ATHENIA: (*Looking around. Softly. Quickly.*) Please Jimmy. You'll make a scene. The owner. Please . . . I thought you knew. I thought you could tell. You'll cause a scene – you'll cause a scene –

JIMMY: (*Whispers.*) A scene? I'll make a scene? That was the deal, wasn't it? Wasn't that the deal?

ATHENIA: (*Sincerely.*) Please, Jimmy.

JIMMY: (*Angry.*) I paid you, didn't I? You took the money, right? I paid the full price?

ATHENIA: (*Quickly. Sincerely.*) I would have given you a discount.

JIMMY: (*A flash of fear.*) I paid the full price. Now you ain't gonna' back out of our little deal, are you?

ATHENIA: (*As explanation.*) I don't want trouble.

JIMMY: (*Struts. Contains his anxiety.*) No trouble at all, Athenia. Believe me. It's no trouble at all. You're just going to give a man what he's been talking about. The man's lonely, Athenia. You're going to give a lonely man what he's been talking about. Just exactly what he's been asking for. You're not going to back out of a chance like that, are you?

ATHENIA: (*Flatly. Checking.*) Are you sure?

JIMMY: (*Firmly.*) I'm sure. I'm sure. (*Points to Johnny.*) That's him. That's the lonely man I told you about.

ATHENIA: (*Unhappy.*) He's not very pretty.

JIMMY: (*Imitates her.*) No, he's not very pretty. (*He laughs maniacally.*) No, Athenia. He's not very pretty at all. Not at all

ATHENIA: (*Sexy.*) You're pretty, Jimmy. You're very pretty.

JIMMY: (*At first, rage. Then open disgust. Laughing again.*) Yes. Yes, I am. Very pretty. I'm pretty. I'm lovely. I'm beautiful. I'm as pretty as a fucking picture, Athenia. Pretty as a fucking flower. (*Pauses, laughing.*) And smart as a whip, too. Huh? (*Moves to Johnny. Full stage lights.*) Johnny? Johnny-baby. She's ready.

JOHNNY: (*Confused.*) Who?

JIMMY: (*Moving in.*) She's here.

JOHNNY: (*Triple-takes it.*) I'm okay here with . . . what's your name?

HONEY: (*Simply.*) Honey.

JOHNNY: (*Distracted. A bit wounded.*) That's your real name? Honey? C'mon. Don't kid an old kidder.

HONEY: (*"Acts" angry.*) That's my name. My mother and father wanted to give me a cute name. Don't you think it's a cute name?

JOHNNY: (*Plays it cool.*) Oh, yeah. Honey is a terrific name. Very cute. Cuter than hell. Huh? I'm okay here, Jimmy-baby. Very okay.

JIMMY: (*Moving closer.*) I want you to meet Athenia.

JOHNNY: (*Angry.*) Why?

JIMMY: (Coming on strong.) Athenia! *She's* the one. You've got things mixed up a little, Johnny-boy.

JOHNNY: (*Furiously.*) Don't try to cut in. I appreciate everything you've done for me, Jimmy. Honest-to-God I do. I'll always be grateful for what you've done to me tonight, but don't cut in. I mean, don't push your way in. I've got Honey here and we're hitting it off just fine. (*The women move to one side and freeze in position.*)

JIMMY: (*Quiet, whispered ferocity.*) Honey is a fake, pal. I didn't steer you wrong here, did I? I tried them both. Honey's a sweet kid and all that but Athenia's the one. They don't all do it. Honey don't do it. Athenia does it. If you want to spend all your time feeling her up and filling her up with colored water, then go right ahead, but you're wasting valuable time. I didn't steer you wrong here and I'm telling you that Athenia's the one. You saw me talking to her, didn't you?

JOHNNY: (*Taken.*) Yeah. I did. Out of the corner of my eye, I saw you talking to her.

JIMMY: (*Selling the watch again.*) I was setting you up, Johnny-boy. Setting you up for the little room with the curtain. See it back there, kid? That's the dressing room, Johnny-boy. That's where she does it, and she loves it, Johnny-boy.

JOHNNY: (*A last try.*) But me and Honey have been hitting it off real good. I mean, I got real feelings for this kid, Jim. She wants to come to America.

ATHENIA: (*Makes it sound like "Let's fuck."*) Hello, Johnny.

JOHNNY: (*Startled and pleased.*) Holy Christ. She's a beautiful thing, Jimmy. How do these kids get mixed up so young? They're such young kids. She's a big one, huh?

ATHENIA: (*Pours it on.*) Hello, Johnny. Jimmy's been telling me everything about you.

JOHNNY: (*Desperately.*) Did he tell you about the television commercials too? I mean did he tell you all about that?

ATHENIA: (*Laying it out, gushing sexuality.*) He told me you were wounded.

JOHNNY: (*Completely confused.*) The war? Oh, yeah. (*To Jimmy.*) What war? You told her about the commercials, right?

ATHENIA: (*A bad novel.*) Your love left you. Your heart is broken.

JOHNNY: What the hell's going on here?

ATHENIA: (*The camera's rolling for her now.*) Poor Johnny. My poor Johnny. Your heart is broken and Athenia will try to help you. I know all about love, Johnny. All about love.

JOHNNY: (*Moves into frame.*) Oh, yeah! That was a terrible thing that happened to me. I'll never get over it.

ATHENIA: (*Wants an Oscar. Really starts to work him over like crazy.*) I know secret things about love, Johnny. (*Everybody freezes. Athenia talks.*) Did Jimmy tell you about me?

JOHNNY: (*The innocent speaks.*) Tell me about you? I don't know what you mean. Hell, he told me he met a pretty girl and you talked, if that's what you mean.

ATHENIA: (*Wants to know.*) That's all he told you?

JOHNNY: (*Wants to change the subject.*) Nothing else. Why would he tell me anything else? We're not what you'd call the best of friends, you know. I mean, just 'cause we're traveling together. We get paid to. (*They unfreeze.*)

JIMMY: (*An announcement.*) Drinks. Drinks around and I'm paying. Honey?

HONEY: (*Sweetly.*) That's very kind. (*They sit at the center table.*)

JOHNNY: (*Calling.*) Coffee? C'mon, little buddy. We want to warm our cockles.

COFFEE: (*Running in, smiling.*) On the house, buddy.

JIMMY: (*Tough. Sweet.*) No sir, little Kraut. I pay the price.

COFFEE: (*In German. As commands.*)

Mogen Sie amerikanishce Musik?

(Do you like American music?)

Darf ich um den Tanz bitten?

(Do you want to dance?)

Spielen Sie gern Golf?

(Want to play some golf?)

JIMMY: (*Thrown.*) Hey. Say it in English, buddy.

COFFEE: (*Confidentially.*) Call me "Herr Ober." Okay?

JIMMY: (*Really thrown. A bit angry.*) What's that?

COFFEE: (*Grinning.*) It means nothing. I like it. That's all.

HONEY: (*Laughing.*) It means "waiter." He's playing with you.

JIMMY: (*Knows he's angry.*) Let's leave it at "Coffee," okay, buddy?

COFFEE: (*Mystically. Scary.*) I am Jesus Christ. Do you believe me?

JIMMY: (*Keeps his confidence.*) Anything you say, little buddy.

COFFEE: (*Moving in.*) I am Jesus Christ and I am lying to you. Do you believe me?

JIMMY: (*Laughing nervously.*) Sure I do, champ.

COFFEE: (*Terrifingly intense.*) I am Jesus Christ and I am telling you that I am lying to you. Do you believe me?

JIMMY: (*A sound of confidence.*) Yep.

COFFEE: (*A slow-motion slash.*) Do *I* believe *you?*

JIMMY: (*Doesn't like it at all.*) Watch your ass, Coffee. Just watch your ass. I've had enough games for one night. (*Pauses, laughs.*) Almost enough. You're all right. Coffee. God damned all right.

COFFEE: (*Knows he went too far.*) Drinks for everybody?

JIMMY: (*Simply. Smugly.*) For everybody.

COFFEE: (*A favor.*) You want something special to smoke?

JIMMY: (*Misunderstands.*) I don't like your cigarettes. No offense.

COFFEE: (*Tries to explain. Slowly.*) I mean something special. You know what I mean?

JIMMY: (*Smugly.*) No offense.

HONEY: (*Hates the game.*) He means marijuana. That's very special.

Very dangerous here. Coffee likes you.

JIMMY: (*Embarrassed. Covers.*) Hell. I like Coffee. Mary Jane, huh? No, thank you, Coffee. That's for my kids. I'll stick to my booze.

COFFEE: (*Screams.*) ANGELN VERBOTEN! (*No fishing!*)

JIMMY: (*Jumps up. Frightened.*) What's he screaming? (*The lights cross-fade to Sweetie.*)

SWEETIE: (*Shocked.*) Jimmy, for God's sakes!

JIMMY: (*Loudly. Defensively.*) Look, I don't make those decisions. How the hell did I know it would end up like this? Huh? Who the hell would have guessed?

SWEETIE: (*Slightly angry.*) But he hired you. He gave you the job to begin with. You even admitted it. You told everybody we know.

JIMMY: (*As angry.*) But it ain't an old man's game, Sweetie. It just ain't. The same thing's gonna happen to me. You know it.

SWEETIE: It's wrong. I hate it. Can you imagine how humiliated he is? Johnny's not an old man, for God's sake. He's forty.

JIMMY: (*A sound.*) Forty-five.

SWEETIE: (*Amazed.*) That's old?

JIMMY: (*Softly ferocious.*) Yeah. I guess it is.

SWEETIE: (*Reasonably.*) But couldn't he work in another group? Does he have to work for you?

JIMMY: (*Furious now.*) I told you that I don't make those decisions. Look. I'll give it to you straight. When they asked me if I wanted him, if I'da said "no," they probably would have canned him. Now how do you like that?

HONEY: (*Laughing.*) He's funny. I love Coffee. He's funny.

JIMMY: (*Furious. He sits.*) Get the booze, Coffee. And keep it in English. I want to know exactly what's happening. You get me?

COFFEE: (*Laughs. Exiting.*) I get you.

JIMMY: (*Quickly. Angry.*) What did he yell for?

HONEY: (*Still laughing.*) He's funny.

JIMMY: (*Not happy at all.*) I guess I just ain't in a funny mood. I want a drink. I'm getting a headache. I need a drink. Shit! I'm confused. No, I'm not sure. Not me. I got a couple of good years left and this is not one of them. (*He laughs.*)

HONEY: (*Confused.*) What's funny?

JIMMY: (*Happy again.*) Nothing, baby. Nothing. (*Yells.*) Coffee!!! Booze!!! (*Coffee serves the drinks.*)

ATHENIA: (*Camera rolling.*) I wouldn't take a drink from you, Johnny, but the owner.

JOHNNY: (*A friend.*) I know all about the colored water and, hell, I don't mind, especially since Jimmy here's paying the tab.

ATHENIA: (*A friend in need.*) There are certain men you take drinks from . . . lots of drinks. And then there are men you hate yourself for taking drinks from.

JOHNNY: (*Terribly pleased.*) Well, Christ, Athenia. If I didn't understand that, I wouldn't be a man.

ATHENIA: (*Really moving in on him now.*) You're a man, aren't you, Johnny?

JOHNNY: (*Swaggering.*) Man. Boy. Call it what you will.

ATHENIA: (*Moving in. Wants to know.*) Did Jimmy tell you about the back room?

JOHNNY: (*Overacts like crazy.*) What back room?

ATHENIA: (*She knows.*) Are you sure he didn't tell you?

JOHNNY: (*He knows she knows.*) Well, come to think of it, he did make mention a bit about a back dressing room. The room over there, I guess. But it didn't sound like anything important. He didn't make any big deal out of it, you know what I mean?

ATHENIA: (*The rules of the game aren't yet established.*) Did he tell you everything?

JOHNNY: (*Thinks she's playing.*) He told me that you went back there and . . . well . . . you know.

ATHENIA: (*Frightened.*) Did he tell you about the bottle?

JOHNNY: (*Honest.*) What bottle?

ATHENIA: (*Dismayed.*) You have to buy a bottle. A special champagne. It's not very good, but it's a rule.

JOHNNY: (*Honest.*) Do they know you do that sort of thing back there?

ATHENIA: (*Frightened.*) Shhh. The owner might hear you.

JOHNNY: (*In the movie again.*) They don't know?

ATHENIA: (*Deciding.*) If they knew, I'd be fired at once.

JOHNNY: (*A friend.*) Dirty bastards.

ATHENIA: (*Still deciding.*) You have to pay for a special bottle of champagne. It's not very good, but it's terribly expensive.

JOHNNY: (*Curious.*) How much?

ATHENIA: (*She's decided. A friend in need.*) I don't know. The owner puts the price on the bill. They never shown me.

JOHNNY: (*A friend indeed.*) Dirty rotten bastards!!!

ATHENIA: (*Last chance, baby.*) You don't have to do it if you don't want to.

JOHNNY: (*Won't stop now.*) Athenia . . . (*Pronounces it Athe-a-nee-*

ah.)

ATHENIA: (*The rules are set. Corrects him.*) Athenia.

JOHNNY: (*He goes. Quickly.*) Athenia. Right. Athenia, of course. I'll buy the bottle. What the hell's money for, anyway? (*Coffee steps down and holds out his hand.*)

COFFEE: (*A simple truth.*) Four thousand marks.

JOHNNY: (*Shocked.*) Hey. Whoa, man! That's a lot of marks!

COFFEE: (*Sexy. Motions to Athenia.*) That's a lot, too, buddy.

JOHNNY: (*Deciding.*) Four thousand marks? That's too much, pal.

ATHENIA: (*Placing her heart in his hand.*) Please, Johnny, please. I love you, Johnny. Please.

COFFEE: (*Placing his other hand on her other breast.*) How could you turn away from love, Johnny?

JOHNNY: (*Doesn't move his hands away. Angrily.*) Is he the owner, Athenia? Huh? Is he the owner? Just tell me and I'll break his little dwarf head. No shit. Just tell me.

JIMMY: (*From nowhere. Handing the money to Coffee, stepping in.*) The price, Johnny-baby. I told you I'd pick up the tab. Here ya' go, Coffee. Go on Johnny. Go get what you've been talking about. (*He laughs, madly. Coffee blows the whistle.*) Get me a drink, Coffee. Get me ten drinks. And when it's over, Coffee . . . when it's over . . . you get me home, Coffee. You get me home where it makes some sense. (*He laughs. The lights cross-face.*)

JOHNNY: I've taken guys twice his size. Five hundred times before. Little Goddam shrimp got me confused, more than anything else. All I had to do was hit him once. He was a shrimp. One punch. One Goddam punch. I just don't understand. My credit cards. My license. Everything. Christ! I even had a blank check. I got credit cards from here to Miami. From Miami to Las Vegas. From Las Vegas to Los Angeles. Every Holiday Inn. Every Texaco station. Every store on the Miracle Mile. They all know me. Carte Blanche. Diners. American Express. They all know me. I'm a Charter Member of Carte Blanche, for Christ's sakes, I just don't understand what came over me. One punch and I could have nailed him.

MOLLY: (*THE OWNER.*) It's over.

JOHNNY: (*A scream.*) It isn't!! It isn't!! I want him I want him here in front of me. Don't you understand??? I want another chance!!! I'll kill him!!! I'll squash his little shrimp head. I want another chance! (*Athenia touches Johnny.*) Don't you put your hands on me!

Don't you put your Goddam filthy hands on me. You've bled me for fifteen years. Fifteen years. There's almost nothing left. I had a punch . . . a left . . . that's what I had. I had a fake with my right and a low straight left that would cripple Louis. I could hold my own with the best of them, baby, and don't you ever forget it. Just don't put your filthy God damn hands on me ever again. Do you understand? Do you understand? (*Athenia steps in, touches Johnny's arm. He slaps her, instinctively, sharply.*) Did I hurt you? Molly? Did I hurt you? (*She looks up quietly.*)

ATHENIA: No. I love you, Johnny. Honest-to-God. (*The lights cross-face back to the stage proper. Coffee blows the whistle again. Music blares back into Germanic-jazz. Athenia and Johnny rush into the back room. They can be seen drinking and talking as Honey does a terrific number, a berserk Nazi tune: "Back from the Front." Jimmy watches.*)

HONEY: (*Back from the Front.*)

When I think of the boys
Back from the front,
How my heart bleeds. (*Repeat.*)

I love all the boys
Back from the front,
I am the mother of the Fatherland,
To every wounded arm and wounded hand
That reaches to hold my heart.

I will bend over backwards
So they can see
The love in me. (*Repeat.*)

I love all the boys
Back from the front,
I am the mother of the Fatherland,
To every wounded arm and wounded hand
That reaches to hold my heart.

(*She dances.*)

I will bend over backwards
So they can see
The love in me. (*Repeat.*)

(*Big finish here.*) I love all the boys
Back from the front,
I am the mother of the Fatherland.
To every wounded arm and wounded hand
That reaches to hold my heart.
When I think of the boys
Back from the front,
How my heart bleeds.

When I think of the boys
Back from the front.
How my heart bleeds.
My heart bleeds. (*Cross-dissolve to back room.*)

ATHENIA: (*Breathy, Closing the curtain, so only fragments of their bodies can be seen.*) You don't mind it like this?

JOHNNY: (*A child whining.*) Can't we do it the regular way?

ATHENIA: (*Quickly.*) I'll get caught. They can see through the crack in the curtain. If I see or hear them coming, we can sit up and just talk and drink until they pass. The owner, Johnny. I'm afraid.

JOHNNY: (*Dismayed.*) Will you meet me after you close so we can do it in bed?

ATHENIA: (*Quickly. Excitedly.*) We don't close until five in the morning.

JOHNNY: (*Babbling now.*) I'll wait for you, darling. Honey, I had a bad marriage. If I had met someone like you . . . it would have been different. Very different. (*They disappear in a tangle of Johnny's legs, Athenia's arms and other parts. Until, finally, the lights dissolve down to fill Johnny's face and a slight area about him. The music is all chicken soupy. Athenia and Johnny freeze. Cross-dissolve to Jimmy and Coffee.*)

JIMMY: (*Seriously. Then considers what he says.*) You remind me of my boy, Coffee. He's five. (*Jimmy laughs.*)

COFFEE: (*Flirting.*) I'm everybody's little boy. I'm old enough to smoke. I like American cigarettes.

JIMMY: (*Mock seriousness. A cancer warning.*) I'd give you one, buddy, but smoking's no good. It stunts your growth. (*He laughs.*)

COFFEE: (*Pissed off. Bitchy. Arch. Cute. Cool.*) You like to laugh. That's good. Laughing is good. Coffee likes to laugh. Coffee likes to fuck, too. You like Honey? Miss Honey Bee? You like her?

JIMMY: (*Contained rage.*) I'm being civil, Coffee, buddy. Honest-to-God. Don't push me. I'll squash your little dwarf head flatter than a pancake. Don't start up again, buddy. You got a good thing going now. Don't push me over the edge, buddy. You know what I mean?

COFFEE: (*Laughing maniacally.*) Laughing is good. You agree?

JIMMY: (*Laughing.*) I agree. You're okay, okay. Very okay. Did you lock the door? No more in, right?

COFFEE: (*Moves in again.*) Right. Just as you said. Now you give me a cigarette and I'll send my favorite lump of sugar to you. Miss Honey Bee is very nice. You agree?

JIMMY: (*Furious.*) Don't push it too far.

COFFEE: (*Goes too far. Way too far.*) I promise you that you'll love Miss Honey Bee. Would Coffee lie to his buddy?

JIMMY: (*Laughing.*) No. Coffee doesn't lie. Send her out, Coffee. (*He picks Coffee up by the neck strangling him.*) Send her out, Coffee. And so help me Christ, you stunted-little-dwarf-midget-Kraut-Pervert, so help me Christ – it better be right this time.

COFFEE: (*Scared. Enraged. Hitler. Screams.*) FRISHCH GESTRICHEN! (Wet paint!) RECHTS FAHREN! (Keep to the right!) BETRETEN DES RASENS VERBOTTEN! (Keep off the grass!)

JIMMY: (*Laughing hysterically. Thrilled.*) In English, Coffee. In English!!

COFFEE: (*Screaming.*) ICH HABE HUSTEN! ICH HABE HIER SCHMERZEN! ICH HABE MAGENSCHMERZEN! MEINE BEINE SCHMERZEN! MEIN RUCKEN SCHMERTZ! MEIN ARM SCHMERTZ! MEIN OHR SCHMERTZ! ICH HABE SCHUTTELFROST! ICH HABE FIEBER! (I have a cough! I have a pain *here!* I have a stomach ache! My legs hurt! My back hurts! My arm hurts! My ear hurts! I have chills! I've got a fever!) (*In English.*) For Christ's sakes! PUT ME DOWN!

JIMMY: (*Laughing, he puts Coffee on the floor.*) You're okay, Coffee. God damned okay.

COFFEE: (*Showing his neck to Jimmy.*) Ist es gebrochen? Es IST gebrochen! (Is it broken? It IS broken!)

JIMMY: (*Laughing.*) What's your problem, buddy?

COFFEE: (*Absolutely enraged. The ultimate bitch.*) You broke my neck, you fucking *Waschfrau* (laundress)! For crying out loud.

JIMMY: (*Laughing.*) Bring her out, Coffee. Bring her out.

COFFEE: (*Bitterly, softly.*) Sie mussen eine Gebuhr zahlen. (You'll pay for that! – Literally: "You'll pay a tax!") (*He calls.*) HONIG!! MEIN SCHATZ!! BITTE!! DIE BATTERIE IST LEER. KOMMEN LADEN DIE BATTERIE!! HONIG. MEIN SCHATZ!! (Honey. My Honey. Please! His battery is dead. Come charge his battery! Honey! Honey!) (*She does appear.*) Give me a cigarette. Give me one. Not for me, for Honey. She must be wanting one. I'll entice her with a cigarette.

JIMMY: (*Laughing.*) Take six, little buddy.

COFFEE: (*Three beats: friend, dictator, lover.*) Just one. (*Pauses.*) Light it! (*With a sinister laugh.*) Sie sind so schoen. ("You are so beautiful.") (*He takes the lit cigarette and walks to Honey's dressing-room.*) HONIG!! HONIG!! HONIG!! MOCHTEN SIE EINE ZIGARETTE? (Honey! Honey! Honey! You want a cigarette?) (*Coffee holds the lit cigarette in front of him and walks into the dressing-room. There is a pause, then we hear Honey's terrifying scream of pain. Torture. Then, a pause. Then, she appears and walks to Jimmy, smiling. Honey and Jimmy freeze. Cross-fade into Athenia's dressing-room.*)

JOHNNY: (*Breathing hard.*) Your hair is fantastic. I love it.

ATHENIA: (*Quickly.*) Thank you.

JOHNNY: (*Reasonably.*) Your breasts are terrific, too.

ATHENIA: (*Impatiently.*) Don't be silly.

JOHNNY: (*Gleefully.*) I'm glad I came here.

ATHENIA: (*Flatly.*) I'm glad you're glad.

JOHNNY: (*Breathing normally.*) Maybe I could meet you later, huh?

ATHENIA: (*Impatiently.*) Shhh. Be quiet. Close your eyes.

JOHNNY: (*A plea.*) Would you meet me at my hotel?

ATHENIA: (*Quickly. Disgusted.*) Close your eyes.

JOHNNY: (*Desperately.*) Please?

ATHENIA: (*Imploringly.*) Close your eyes.

JOHNNY: (*Simply.*) They're closed.

ATHENIA: (*Pleased.*) Good. (*Cross-fade to Jimmy and Honey. They unfreeze.*)

JIMMY: (*Placing his hand into her robe.*) Are yours real?

HONEY: (*Sexy.*) Touch them.

JIMMY: (*Flatly.*) The rest of you?

HONEY: (*Sexy.*) Touch it.

JIMMY: (*A bad joke.*) I'm almost afraid to.

HONEY: (*Taking his hand and guiding it.*) Here, silly. Feel. Oh. That's nice.

JIMMY: (*Thrilled. Lusty.*) That *is* nice.

HONEY: (*Throaty.*) You want to meet me?

JIMMY: (*Confused.*) The room's taken up now. They're in there.

HONEY: (*Quickly.*) No, not here. You can't do it here. I have a place.

JIMMY: (*Softly.*) I don't think so.

HONEY: (*Working.*) Are you sure, darling? Jimmy, darling.

JIMMY: (*Angry.*) Don't give me your "darling" crap.

HONEY: (*Quickly.*) Don't be bitter. We thought you knew.

JIMMY: (*Slowly.*) I almost feel sorry. About him. Not about me. I'd like to kill myself, that's how I feel about me.

HONEY: (*Slow. Working hard.*) You meet me at your hotel if you want. Or my flat. My flat is really quite fantastic. And it's quiet. I have a wonderful transistorized stereo that heats up as soon as you turn it on. (*She really goes to work now.*) It heats up. You know?

JIMMY: (*Considers it.*) Maybe it would do me good.

HONEY: (*Pouring it on.*) It would be wonderful. I could leave early, if you paid here. Through the owner. We could leave right away.

JIMMY: (*Curious.*) How much?

HONEY: (*Without changing gears.*) It's usually four hundred marks. But you've paid so much already, I could get it for half.

JIMMY: (*Considering. Deciding.*) Two hundred marks.

HONEY: (*Goes too far.*) Just for you.

JIMMY: (*The answer is "No." A beat.*) One hundred marks for each of my kids. I'm married.

HONEY: (*She knows it's over.*) Of course.

JIMMY: (*Angry. Kidding.*) What do you mean, "Of course"? Do I look like some kind of married man?

HONEY: (*Angry as well.*) Who else would come in here?

JIMMY: (*Angry. Not kidding.*) I've been to Europe before. There's a hell of a difference between Americans, you know. I'm not your average American. Not the kind you see in here. I'm different. *I've* been to Europe before. I'll probably come a third time. With my wife. (*Pauses.*) I wish my wife could have your way with me. Just for one night.

HONEY: (*A bad joke.*) Are you proposing marriage?

JIMMY: (*Sincerely.*) I wish my wife could be free for a while. A whore. Like you.

HONEY: (*A bitch.*) Maybe she is.

JIMMY: (*Furious. Slowly.*) Don't you insult my wife. Not my wife. She's no whore. Don't start that game. Not with my wife. A whore. Hah! That dumb bitch wouldn't have the imagination.

HONEY: (*Circling.*) You're so sure?

JIMMY: (*A sound.*) I'm sure.

HONEY: (*Slowly. Laughing.*) Is she sure of you?

JIMMY: (*Anger is sustained.*) What's that supposed to mean?

HONEY: (*Takes his hand.*) Does she think you're with me now, huh? With Honey at Cafe Society? You like my breasts, don't you?

JIMMY: (*Playing. Toying. Enjoying.*) I like your breasts. I like your breasts very much.

HONEY: (*Coyly.*) Is she as sure of you as you are of her?

JIMMY: (*A machine. Breaking.*) She knows I don't mess around. You think I'm the average American bastard like that foul-mouth, lousy-assed, son of a bitch in there? Six weeks on this trip! Six weeks of his talking about sex. And sex and sex. You'd think he never had it before, the way he talks. You think I'm like that foul-mouthed shithead in there?

HONEY: (*Ruefully.*) No. I don't think you're like that foul-mouthed shithead in there. (*Pauses.*) You like both of my breasts?

JIMMY: (*Hugging. Clinging. Fondling.*) I like both of your breasts. And I like your thing too. (*Cross-fade to:*)

JOHNNY: Athenia? Athenia? Athenia?

ATHENIA: What? What? What?

JOHNNY: I love you. I really love you. I've never been in love before. Not really. Never like this.

ATHENIA: Hurry up. Close your eyes.

JOHNNY: Do you love me, Athenia? I mean, has it ever been the same for you?? Has it?

ATHENIA: Don't be silly.

JOHNNY: It has. It has. I'm just another guy, right? Just another job, right?

ATHENIA: (*Almost disgusted. Flatly.*) Of course not. You're special. You're fantastic. I never knew I could love anybody the way I love you. Close your eyes.

JOHNNY: Have you ever done this before?

ATHENIA: Huh?

JOHNNY: Do you do this often? Do they make you do this? The lousy German bastards? Do they make you do this?

ATHENIA: Close your eyes. I love you. The Germans don't make me do anything I don't want to do. I swear to you. I love you. Just you.

JOHNNY: Oh, I love you too, Athenia. I really do.

ATHENIA: Close your eyes.

JOHNNY: Why did you do it with Jimmy?

ATHENIA: They made me.

JOHNNY: Who? Who made you?

ATHENIA: The Germans. They made me do it. I didn't want to.

JOHNNY: Dirty bastards.

ATHENIA: Please Johnny. Close your eyes. If you really love me, you'll close your eyes.

JOHNNY: I will. I will.

ATHENIA: Good. Good. (*Cross-fade to:*)

HONEY: (*Quickly.*) There are six million of you. Is that what you said?

JIMMY: (*Involved then shocked.*) Six million? Are you crazy? You said two hundred!

HONEY: (*Introspectively.*) In Petrozavodsk, there were only one hundred and thirty-five thousand.

JIMMY: (*Thrown.*) Petro . . . What?

HONEY: (*Sincerely. But quickly.*) When I was a little girl. A little town in Russia. No, not a town. A city. But a little city. Petrozavodsk. Peh. Treh. Zeh. Vahtsk.

JIMMY: (*Curious.*) You're Russian?

HONEY: (*A sound.*) Finnish.

JIMMY: (*Amazed.*) Finnish?

HONEY: (*Sweetly. Simply.*) Finnish. Finland. A little country. We moved to Petrozavodsk when I was five or six. I can't remember. We had a little house overlooking the lake. Lake Oneaga. It was pretty close.

JIMMY: (*Surprised anger.*) We're in the middle of a deal and you're making talk about Petro – what?

HONEY: (Simply.) I was thinking about your friend.

JIMMY: (*Furious.*) He's not my friend.

HONEY: (*Suddenly weeping. Then laughing.*) All right, I was thinking of that man in there with Athenia. I was thinking of you. I was thinking of me. I was thinking. I shouldn't do that.

JIMMY: (*Flatly.*) You're a nice kid, Honey, That's not your name. What's your real name?

HONEY: (*Composed. Sexy.*) Honey. Honey's the name I like best.

JIMMY: (*As though sucking a cigar.*) You're a nice kid, Honey. Why'd you become a whore? I'm sorry to put it bluntly, but it's more honest, huh?

HONEY: (*Flatly. Coyly.*) It's much more honest.

JIMMY: (*Pressing.*) Why'd you become a whore?

HONEY: (*Laughing.*) I like to make love. I love to make love.

JIMMY: (*Strutting.*) So do I. I got a real reputation for it. A real reputation. It's a wonder my wife doesn't know.

HONEY: (*A set-up.*) It's a wonder. (*Cross-fade into Athenia's dressing-room.*)

ATHENIA: (*Flat, quick, impatience.*) Hurry up, Johnny.

JOHNNY: (*Not with it.*) Why'd you become a whore, Athenia? A young kid like you? You must be lonely.

ATHENIA: (*Flatly. Disgusted. Anxiously.*) I'm not lonely.

JOHNNY: (*A regular priest.*) You must be. It must be awful. Loneliness. I understand.

ATHENIA: (*Sounds of impatience: quick, flat.*) I'm not lonely. I'm not lonely.

JOHNNY: (*Protesting.*) Yes, you are. You are.

ATHENIA: (*Can't believe what's being said.*) But I'm not. I'm not.

JOHNNY: (*Sounds.*) I understand. I understand. I really do. (*Cross-fade back to Honey and Jimmy.*)

JIMMY: (*The same sounds.*) I understand. I really do.

HONEY: (*Impatient. Quick.*) But I'm not. Why do you think it's so simple?

JIMMY: (*Protesting.*) Listen, if you think this trip has been a PICNIC, well, I've got a piece of news for you. I understand loneliness. Oh, boy, do I! You think my wife knows? That's a laugh. A whore named Honey. Terrific.

HONEY: (*Slow. Pure awful disgust.*) Ich finde Ihre Frau ist sehr schoen. (I think your wife is beautiful.)

JIMMY: (*Senses the intonation.*) What?

HONEY: (*Moving in now.*) What's your name? Is it Jimmy?

JIMMY: (*Startled.*) Sure. Jimmy. You've probably heard of me. I'm famous.

HONEY: (*Setting him up. Disgusted.*) You are? You're famous?

JIMMY: (*Checking – goes slowly.*) Sure. I'm Jimmy Durante. The comedian. Bet that surprises you.

HONEY: (*Playing.*) Dur-an-dee?

JIMMY: (*Amazed.*) Durante. Jimmy Durante. For Christ's sakes. I'm the most famous comedian in the world. The old Schnozzola. Jimmy

Durante! Don't you know me?

HONEY: (*Simply. Bored, rather.*) I've heard of you. Jimmy Durante.

JIMMY: (*Still checking.*) You believe me, huh?

HONEY: (*Groping him. Very, very sexy.*) I think you should pay the owner her money. Two hundred marks. It's usually four.

JIMMY: (*Angry.*) Wait a minute. I'm telling you who I am. I'm Jimmy Durante.

HONEY: (*Moving in. Thinks she's winning.*) I know. It's just that it's getting late and once it gets close to closing, you fall into the four hundred mark category. I can't help it, Jimmy. Those are the rules. The owner.

JIMMY: (*To the world, first. Then to Honey.*) When I was a little kid I used to tell jokes. No fooling. Maybe three years old and I could make anybody laugh. Then I got famous. You know what I mean?

HONEY: (*Impatiently.*) The owner is very sticky about closing time. The price doubles. She's got a tick about closing time. It makes her nervous.

JIMMY: (*Shocked.*) But you're going to sleep with Jimmy Durante tonight!

HONEY: (*Simply.*) I know. I'm very happy, Jimmy. I love the way you feel. I'm nervous about the time, Jimmy.

JIMMY: (*A child. No, a childish man.*) All my life I wanted to be special. Make people laugh. Be famous. Go on television. Stoneham.

HONEY: (*Thrown. A beat.*) Stoneham?

JIMMY: (*Thinks she's involved.*) No, no. Stone-um. Stone-um. It's a little town in Massachusetts. That's where I was born. We had a little house near the lake. Spot Pond. It was a reservoir, but we used to swim in it anyway.

HONEY: (*Tries to get him back.*) She'll charge at least three hundred marks now. I'm sure of it. We really should leave.

JIMMY: (*Strong now.*) Don't you believe I'm Jimmy Durante?

HONEY: (*Impatiently.*) Yes. I've heard of you.

JIMMY: (*In a pathetic Durante imitation.*) But don't you care?

HONEY: (*Sweating.*) I care very much, Jimmy. I want to go with you now.

JIMMY: (*Babbling.*) See, he's the most famous of them all. He's everything I ever wanted to be. He's the best, Schnozzola. The old Schnozzola. (*Cross-fade to Johnny and Athenia in booth.*)

JOHNNY: This is weird, Athenia. This is weird.

ATHENIA: Close your eyes.

JOHNNY: It ain't right, Athenia. It ain't right.

ATHENIA: Close your eyes.

JOHNNY: It's a sin, Athenia. It's a sin.

ATHENIA: Close your eyes.

JOHNNY: I shouldn't be doing this, Athenia. I shouldn't be doing this.

ATHENIA: Close your eyes.

JOHNNY: I hate myself, Athenia. I hate myself.

ATHENIA: Close your eyes. Close your eyes. Good.

HONEY: (*Angry.*) You'll probably have to pay the full price now. Four hundred marks. I wanted you to be special. Because you've paid so much already. I thought I could work it out for you. But it's too late now, Jimmy.

JIMMY: (*Helpless. Compelled. Floating. Does a Durante imitation.*) Jimmy. They call me Jimmy. The old Schnozzola. I can make you laugh. I can make you cry. (*Moves to the audience.*) I can make you love me. Don't you love me? I can sing a little "rink-ah-dick-ah-dink. Ah-dink-ah-dink-ah-doo." Oh, yes. (*Confidentially, to the audience, choosing specific people to talk to.*) I'm a legend in my lifetime, folks. A legend. A little tip of my hat. A little smile. And you smile with me. Smile. Smile. Smile. I bring a little ray of sunshine right into your homes. A little truth. A little love. Because I love you, folks. God, I really love you. And you've been good to me, folks. Good to the old Schnozzola. You made me rich. You made me happy. You made a man with a nose like this happy. And that takes a lot of happy, I want to tell you. A lot of happy.

(*Sings.*)

When you're smiling.
When you're smiling.
The whole world smiles with you.
When you're laughing.
Yes, when you're laughing.
The sun comes shining through.

(*Speaks. He's almost weeping now. He quickly slides a hand to his eyes, then laughs.*) But when you're frowning. God, when you're frowning. The old Schnozzola just crumbles up and cries like a baby. Because if there's anything the old Schnozzola wants at all, he wants you folks to be smiling.

HONEY: (*Slowly. Mystically with him. Calling him back to her.*) I wanted you to be special. I wanted to make you happy. Be special. You paid so much already. I thought I could work it out for you. But it's too late now, Jimmy. Jimmy? Jimmy? Jimmy? (*Fading.*) Jimmy? Jimmy? Jimmy?

JIMMY: (*A sob.*) That's right. Jimmy. Jimmy Durante. (*They all freeze. The Germanic-jazz music fades up to a fraction of what it was before and mixes with the chicken-soup music. Jimmy talks to the audience.*) It's funny. All my life I wanted to be something special. You can understand that. I wanted to be something special. I just became Jimmy Durante and she doesn't give a shit. She doesn't give a shit. (*Pauses in disgust and self-pity.*) Celebrities really lead rotten lonely lives. (*Cross-dissolve to Johnny and Athenia. The are still in an eerie soft light. The music continues. It's really awful music.*)

JOHNNY: (*Breathy. Throaty. Choking.*) You'll meet me later so we can do it right?

ATHENIA: (*Exploding impatience.*) Please. Don't talk. Close your eyes. Tell me when you're ready.

JOHNNY: (*Try to stay rational.*) I can't understand it. I keep feeling like I'm going to explode. But then it's so beautiful, Athenia. It's so much better for me this way than the regular way. It's just nice and soft and easy.

ATHENIA: (*Quickly. Flatly. Desperately.*) Don't talk. Close your eyes.

JOHNNY: (*Gasping with excitement.*) I was getting sleepy but I'm waking up again. It's crazy, 'cause usually I have so much trouble sleeping. This trip has been a nightmare with that bastard beside me all the time. I hate him. I really hate him.

ATHENIA: (*Gasping with impatience.*) There's just us. Please, Johnny. Close your eyes. Hurry up. The owner's going to come in here. Hurry up! (*Cross-dissolve back to Jimmy and Honey. They are pressed together.*)

HONEY: (*Throaty. Impatient.*) Hurry up, Jimmy.

JIMMY: (*Throaty. Breathy. Gasping.*) Don't stop. That's nice.

HONEY: (*She works her body and his into one. They are, of course, fully clothed.*) Hurry up, Jimmy. Hurry up. (*Jimmy stiffens and jerks forward, clinging to Honey.*)

JIMMY: (*A sound.*) Marie!

HONEY: (*Amazed.*) What happened? What happened?

JIMMY: (*Shocked at where he is.*) Oh. Honey. I finished. I finished.

HONEY: (*Shocked at what he's achieved.*) You did?

JIMMY: (*Gasping his words. He sits.*) It's been weeks. You don't understand. I've been about to explode for weeks. I got tired of doing it myself in my room. (*From the back room.*)

JOHNNY: (*A sound.*) Marie! (*He stiffens and jerks forward, clinging o Athenia.*)

ATHENIA: (*Gasping.*) Johnny. Johnny?

JOHNNY: (*Shocked at where he is.*) Huh?

ATHENIA: (*Curious.*) Who's Marie?

JOHNNY: (*Amazed.*) What? What the hell? Marie?

ATHENIA: (*Loudly.*) Marie? Your wife? Is Marie your wife?

JOHNNY: (*Controlling his panic.*) Oh, Jesus. I forgot where I was. That was beautiful, Athenia. Nicer in its own way than it's ever been. Beautiful.

ATHENIA: (*Angry. Jealous, perhaps.*) Who's Marie? You yelled "Marie!"

JOHNNY: (*Flatly. He starts to dress.*) A girl. Nobody. A girl in the typing pool.

ATHENIA: (*Confused.*) The typing pool?

JOHNNY: (*Rubber-kneed.*) You wouldn't understand.

ATHENIA: (*Softly.*) Will you meet me later, Johnny?

JOHNNY: (*Absently.*) Oh, yeah. Sure thing. Sure. Later. (*Full stage lights now.*)

HONEY: (*Softly.*) Please, Jimmy. Can we go? Let's leave now.

JIMMY: (*Absently.*) Leave? Oh, sure. We'll leave. I mean, I got to talk to my friend, Johnny. We've got a rough day tomorrow. You know, meetings . . . with the newspapers and magazines. Interviews. (*Pauses, then pained.*) I got a headache. (*Holds his neck.*)

JOHNNY: (*Pained. Holds his neck.*) I got a headache. (*As he walks from the curtained room, Jimmy meets him stage right. They stagger confused down stage center for a moment, then stare at each other, quietly.*) You finished?

JIMMY: (*Curiously nonchalant.*) Me? I didn't do anything. I was just talking with Honey here.

JOHNNY: (*Flatly.*) I got a headache.

JIMMY: (*Smiling. Nervous laugh.*) You like it?

JOHNNY: (*Babbles.*) Well, you know. It ain't the same, is it? But she's terrific. I think I'll ask her to split the room with me for the rest of the trip. Until we go home. (*Pauses.*) Did you write home? (*Jimmy laughs; roars.*)

HONEY: (*A sound.*) Four hundred marks.

JIMMY: (*Proud. Angry.*) Four Hundred? That's for tourists!

HONEY: (*Quickly.*) Maybe I could talk the owner into two hundred. A special price.

JIMMY: (*Laughing.*) Two hundred. A hundred for each kid.

JOHNNY: (*Finishes dressing. Straightens his tie.*) Did you buy presents for your kids? The presents. The puppets. For your boy's puppet show.

JIMMY: (*His laugh is maniacal.*) A hundred for each kid.

JOHNNY: (*Sincerely.*) Did you buy the presents?

JIMMY: (*Gasping with laughter. Hugs Johnny.*) Any kid that's dumb enough to have a father like me can go without presents.

JOHNNY: (*Returns the hug. Shower-room love.*) It was terrific, Jim-baby. The best. I've had 'em all different ways. Maybe a little better. Sure, I've had better. But this was damned good.

HONEY: (*Softly.*) Two hundred.

ATHENIA: (*Softly.*) Meet me later, Johnny. We'll have breakfast. I can spend the whole day with you.

JOHNNY: (*Strutting.*) I've had Spades. Jews. Yellows and High-Yellows. Where you from, Athenia?

ATHENIA: (*Quietly.*) Prague.

JOHNNY: (*A pig. He laughs.*) Now I've had me a Prague.

HONEY: (*Quietly.*) Two hundred, Jimmy. A special price.

JIMMY: (*His laughter is false. A snake.*) Schnozzola. The old Schnozzola. He was the greatest!

JOHNNY: (*A winner.*) It was the greatest, Athenia. Don't you worry. I'm gonna be in town awhile and probably I'll be back in Germany before you can say "Peter, Peter Pumpkin Eater." I got to thank you, Jim-baby. I got to really thank you. (*The chicken-soup music goes away and the Germanic-jazz blares to full.*)

JIMMY: (*Fiercely.*) Take it off, Athenia.

JOHNNY: (*Confused.*) Hang on, Jimmy-boy. Athenia's my girl this trip. Don't push in.

JIMMY: (*As a whip-snap.*) Take if off, Athenia.

JOHNNY: (*Reasonable anger.*) Come on, Jim-boy. Fair's fair. Besides, the kid's tired. You know what I mean?

JIMMY: (*A sound. Fierce. Hitler.*) Take it off, Athenia.

ATHENIA: (*A plea. Panic.*) He doesn't know! He doesn't know!

JIMMY: (*A shot – an explosion.*) Take it off Athenia! (*Full stage lights.*)

THE OWNER: (*A sound. Terrifying.*) He doesn't know, Jimmy.

JIMMY: Take it off, Athenia.

ATHENIA: He doesn't know, Jimmy. He doesn't know! !

JOHNNY: What the hell is this anyway?

THE OWNER: (*A command.*) Stop it, Jimmy. Stop it!

ATHENIA: (*A final plea.*) Please, Jimmy. Please? (*Jimmy turns fiercely to the wives.*)

JIMMY: You two just shut the fuck up! You hear me? (*He turns back into the scene. The wives watch the rest of the play, weeping.*) You hear me, Athenia. Take it off. Now! (*Jimmy walks to Athenia and rips off her wig, exposing that she's a transvestite. Obviously, a man. They all freeze. The music goes back to a mixture of the chicken-soup and Germanic-jazz. Johnny stares dumbly at Athenia.*)

JOHNNY: (*Slowly. Disbelief. Numb. Awful.*) For Christ's sakes. What is this, a joke? Is this supposed to be joke? Is this your idea of what's funny? (*Athenia begins to sob. She reaches out to Johnny who punches her in the mouth, viciously. She falls to the ground.*) For Christ's sakes. For Christ's sakes. (*Honey goes back into her dance, singing her insane song.*)

ATHENIA: (*Sobs, over and over again.*) I'm a woman. I'm a woman. Ich heisse (my name is) Athenia. Ich heisse Athenia. Ich heisse Athenia. Etc.

HONEY: (*As a machine. Singing and dancing.*) When I think of the boys, etc.

JIMMY: (*Flatly. Controlled, at rest. He stands staring and laughing.*) I'm going back to the hotel. Back to the room. I'm going back to the hotel room. Are you coming or staying, Johnny-boy? Are you coming or staying? (*Jimmy begins to weep, sob.*) My God. My God. My God. My God. (*Then he stops and laughs. Then he sobs again. Then laughs again. Then both at the same time.*) Oh my God. My God. My God, my God. Oh my God. My God. (*Johnny staggers frantically about the stage. First to Athenia. He stares at her, laughing, weeping. Then he walks to Honey, who begins her song and dance again. The music is full now. Johnny kicks Athenia who rolls over, anguished with pain. Johnny walks forward to the audience. He tries to speak, but vomits instead. The sound of his retching is awful. Coffee slithers to the audience screaming.*)

COFFEE: (*Slowly, carefully, He caresses and spits his words.*) Don't watch. Don't look at that. It isn't real. I am real. I am Jesus Christ. I am Jesus Christ and I am lying to you. Do you believe me? I am

Jesus Christ and I am telling you that I am lying to you. Do you believe me? (*Pauses.*) Do *I* believe *you?* Do *I* believe *you?* (*Simply.*) I do. (*Everything – every sound, every image – grows and swells and melds together. And then the stage snaps to blackness.*)

THE PLAY IS OVER.

PLAY FOR GERMS

PLAY FOR GERMS was first written for television, in May, 1972. It was adapted for the stage by Mr. Horovitz, in August of the same year.

PLAY FOR GERMS was first presented by National Education Television (WNET/TV) on October 8, 1972, as part of a special program entitled VD BLUES, with the following cast:

SOCRATES .... James Coco
ARISTOTLE .... Robert Drivas

Written and directed for television by Israel Horovitz

Introduction

From time to time, I get loony phone-calls from people saying they/their fathers/mothers/uncles/aunts are/were fascinating, clearly stageworthy. Would I care to know the story? One lady asked, as I'd created stage-rats in *Rats*, and a stage-bear in *Shooting Gallery*, had I thought about writing a family dog? So, when I got the first phone-call asking if I would create stage-germs for a TV play about VD, I smiled.

The caller was from National Public Television. WNET-TV was about to create a program called *VD Blues*. It was the 1970's, and pre-AIDS America was being ravaged by venereal disease. In the end, obviously, I agreed to join the project and write a play—*Play for Germs*—but, with a condition that I, only I, direct it. I'd directed TV commercials, some years before, and I had been toying with the idea of directing feature films. Later that same year, M-G-M actually agreed to let me direct my first feature, but, when faced with the reality of a two-year film-project, with no time for writing plays, I withdrew my fantasy. But, *Play for Germs* would only be a two month commitment. I signed on the dotted line.

James Coco, Robert Drivas and I were close friends. We'd had been playing poker together for several years. I have never known more talented, nicer, funnier men. I cast them both in *Play for Germs*: Coco played Syphilis, and Drivas played Gonorrhea. But, trying to actually direct Coco and Drivas was like trying to direct the Hudson and Patomic Rivers. I said "Stand". They sat. When I proposed a serious meaning for the play, they rolled their eyes and laughed at me. After a few days of no work, I insisted we sit and talk about the play's inner life. They walked out of the room.

We rehearsed for six days at the Sullivan St. Playhouse, on the set of *The Fantasticks*. Jimmy and Bobby spent most of the week, singing and dancing the entire Jones/Schmidt score ... plus, scenes from many of their favorite plays. Let me say this: If you missed Drivas playing Blanche to Coco's Stanley, you missed Greatness.

Rehearsal-week passed without work or incident. We were driven in a long funereal limo to Philadelphia, mid-summer, 100+ degrees. The day before the shoot, I'd arranged for Coco and Drivas to visit a Philadelphia hospital with me, to talk with diseased patients. They refused, of course. They told me they'd found a better research project. Instead of the hospital ward, Coco and Drivas took me to see *Deep Throat.* They knew I would be horrified. They spent the movie watching me watch the screen.

The night before our shoot, our hotel was evacuated at 3 a.m. The central air-conditioning system had broken down and heating had come on. We got to the *Play for Germs* set at 7 a.m., sleepless. In my mind, disaster were a sure thing. Once in front of the camera, Coco and Drivas were consummate professionals. They had somehow heard every word I'd said in rehearsal. Every detail, every nuance, was attended to. I sort of stood by in amazement and watched it happen. They were wonderful.

Play for Germs and I shared the EMMY that *VD Blues* won, that year. I also won a Christopher Award for *Play for Germs.* In fact, I did very little to deserve either honor. The real credit goes to Bobby Drivas and Jimmy Coco, two brilliant actors ... both dead, now. If someone calls, asking me to write an AIDS play, I won't smile.

Characters

SOCRATES
ARISTOTLE

Setting

A warm, pink place.

PLAY FOR GERMS

A warm, moist, pinkish place. Shaped round, cavernous, yet puffy and safe. All soft pastel lights.

A fat, old germ, Socrates, lying back on the floor-lump throne. Admiring the large photos in the top album of a stack of six.

An old potbellied stove to his left. Coffee perking happily. Trash overspills baskets all around. Newspapers on floor, rising up edges of walls.

He laughs and turns a page. Laughs again. Sips coffee. Turns another page.

Cave full-shaped. Empty stage all around. Lights only in cave. Outside is unknown.

He speaks, identifying images in album.

SOCRATES: King of France, King of England . . . (*Pauses, sips coffee.*) Keats, Casanova, Napoleon, Boswell. (*A noise. Scratching. Outside. Getting louder. Socrates frightened. Closes album. Movement nervous. Looks about cave.*) Who's there? Who is it? (*Absolute silence.*) Who's there? I hear you scratching! You're making a big noise! This is my uterus! Private property! Can't you read the sign??? (*Another scratching noise. Louder than before. Closer now.*) You made another big noise. (*Pauses.*) Are you near the cervix? If you are, you can be heard! (*Aristotle into cave, from hole in back wall. Slides in spinning. Young germ, sleek. Once at floor, instantly to his feet. They circle each other.*)

ARISTOTLE: Don't.

SOCRATES: I know who you are: Syphilis. Out!

ARISTOTLE: Don't.

SOCRATES: Out! Outta' my uterus. These genito-urinary organs are mine! You gave 'em up. I took over! This whole pelvic region is mine! Out!

ARISTOTLE: Don't! Don't make sudden moves. I've been swimming up that cervix for minutes . . . hours . . . just trying to reach you . . . to talk with you.

SOCRATES: Outta' my uterus, syphilis punk. Outta' here. This is my place now! You gave it up! Mine now! All mine! Gonorrhea here. No syph. Out! Outta' here!!! (*Aristotle reaches into his carpet bag and offers an unpeeled banana to Socrates. After a moment, he peels it. Socrates stares.)*

ARISTOTLE: Socrates . . .

SOCRATES: (*Grabs and eats banana.*) You know my name?

ARISTOTLE: Doesn't everybody? Socrates the Gonorrhea germ.

SOCRATES: Wrong. Dead wrong. I'm Socrates, the Greatest Germ of Them All . . .

ARISTOTLE: Germ backwards . . . merg. Us. Merge. You and me. (*Silence.*) Now let me back in? Fair's fair. I was here first.

SOCRATES: Never. Back out the cervix and down the vagina! This is private property. Private. You get me? You follow me so far? You moved out and I moved in!

ARISTOTLE: Syphilis *belongs* here, not Gonorrhea.

SOCRATES: Oh yeah?

ARISTOTLE: Oh yeah.

SOCRATES: You prove to me that there was ever a Syphilis punk could hold a candle to Gonorrhea.

ARISTOTLE: I did well in the bible . . . my family, I mean. Abraham and Sarah, the Pharaoh of Genesis, King Abimelech of Gerar, their wives, Miriam, David, Bath-Sheba and Job. All first-born! All syphilis.

SOCRATES: All biblical. All hard to prove. Probably all mine. You think I can't name names? You think I'm chicken? Caesar. Cleopatra. That's right, Cleopatra.

ARISTOTLE: Wow!

SOCRATES: That's nothin' . . . Herod, king of Judea. Charlemagne, King of the Franks and Emperor of the West. Weston, Dean of Windsor. Charles the 5th of France . . . .

ARISTOTLE: I got kings too, ya know. King Ladislaus of Poland. Wancelaus, king of Bohemia . . . .Henry the 8th . . .

SOCRATES: I got Henry the 4th and Henry the 3rd.

ARISTOTLE: I got popes! Sixtus the 4th. He was pope from 1471 to 1484. Three in a row with Alexander the 6th, Leo the 10th and Julius the 2nd. And don't forget Francis the First. (*Aristotle laughs. Stops. Smiles.*) Pretty impressive, huh?

SOCRATES: Big deal. Big names. Beat Boswell!

ARISTOTLE: Oh yeah? Well, I got Cellini the sculptor, and Louis the 14th . . .

SOCRATES: (*A long deep laugh.*) Louis the 14th??? Louis the 14th???

ARISTOTLE: What's so funny?

SOCRATES: He had fourteen kids. Lived to be 77! Some big deal. Some dangerous dose you are!

ARISTOTLE: Ever hear of the English playwright, Sir William Davenant?

SOCRATES: If he's famous, he's had clap.

ARISTOTLE: I gave him a dose so outrageous, his nose fell off. Big goodlooking WASP with no nose . . . and I also got Molière, the French playwright.

SOCRATES: Oh yeah? I got Casanova . . . beat that! . . . I got NAPOLEON!!! . . . Beat THAT!!!

ARISTOTLE: I had plenty of big ones. Don't worry, I got Beethoven. Catherine the Great . . . Goya, the artist. Yuh, got him. Franz Schubert at 24. Heinrich Heine, same age . . .

SOCRATES: I got John Keats. Same age. 24.

ARISTOTLE: I got Friedrich Nietzsche. Syphilitic meningitis, Goethe: drove him bananas. Oscar Wilde. Vincent Van Gogh. Guy de Maupassant. Strindberg. (*Aristotle circles Socrates now. Light, happy.*) Winston Churchill's father, Randolph. King Edward the 7th . . . Jack the Ripper! Gaugin the painter. Frederick the Great of Prussia used to sing:

> J'es l'honneur
> De recevoir par mon malheur
> D'une certaine imperatrice
> Une bouillante chaud pisse.

SOCRATES: In English, kid. In English.

ARISTOTLE: I had the honor/ Of a dreadful kiss/ From a certain empress/A bolting hot piss.

SOCRATES: KNOCK IT OFF!

ARISTOTLE: Well?

SOCRATES: You still gotta' beat my Napoleon.

ARISTOTLE: You don't know?

SOCRATES: What?

ARISTOTLE: You really don't know?

SOCRATES: What? I don't know what?

ARISTOTLE: Mussolini and Hitler.

SOCRATES: Both of them?

ARISTOTLE: Yep.

SOCRATES: You kidding?

ARISTOTLE: Nope.

SOCRATES: Okay. You can stay. (*Upstage hands raised, palms open. Germ handshake follows. Spit in each other's palm, rub hands, dance around, clapping a lot.*)

ARISTOTLE: A sore botch to you!

SOCRATES: A sore botch and a blaine to you and yours! Nice to have you back.

ARISTOTLE: Nice to *be* back. Haven't been here in ages. (*Aristotle now can look around the cave.*) Nice womb.

SOCRATES: Sure, yeah, well, yeah. I fixed the place up kinda' comfy, ya' know?

ARISTOTLE: Oh yeah. Sure is comfy.

SOCRATES: Syphilis, huh? I know your family. What's your first name?

ARISTOTLE: Aristotle.

SOCRATES: Oh well, that's okay. Where you from? Columbus?

ARISTOTLE: Ohio?

SOCRATES: No, Columbus the Italian.

ARISTOTLE: Oh, no. Nobody knows. Nobody knows for sure.

SOCRATES: Me neither. Nobody knows nothing about me neither. Couple of New York sharpies figured out I got hair, but that's about it. (*Pauses.*) How's the family?

ARISTOTLE: Oh. Very well. Very well. Spreading like hotcakes. Getting older all the time. I got a brother who's already fourth stage.

SOCRATES: No kidding. I'm impressed. Truly impressed. (*Pauses.*) How're you doing cardio-vascularwise?

ARISTOTLE: Oh very well, very well, thank you. We got 500 last year alone. I myself have done a little brain damage. Young kid . . . real lover – you know the type. I nailed him third stage.

SOCRATES: Paralysis?

ARISTOTLE: Worse.

SOCRATES: Stroke?

ARISTOTLE: Don't think about it. It was fast. (*Laughs.*) Slow at first, though. Saddlenose and gumma of the lips. What a case . . . What a case! (*Silence.*) Nice place you got here. Very nice. How long you been here?

SOCRATES: Oh, this place? It's not much. You know. I been here maybe 8 or 10 days.

ARISTOTLE: You gonna' bleed her?

SOCRATES: Bleed her? Oh yeah sure sure. I'll bleed her.

ARISTOTLE: When?

SOCRATES: When?

ARISTOTLE: This isn't a lip-reading exercise: I asked you when.

SOCRATES: Soon. Soon. When I find a new place. You know. I got this place fixed up kinda' . . . well . . . it's kinda' comfy. (*Pauses.*)

How'd you find me? My litter, huh? Always gives me away. I'm a born slob. A natural.

ARISTOTLE: I know your brother.

SOCRATES: Which one? I got millions.

ARISTOTLE: Mario.

SOCRATES: Mario?

ARISTOTLE: Mario. Mario. Your brother. Mario Gonococci. You don't know your own brother?

SOCRATES: It's just that I got so many, you know.

ARISTOTLE: (*Looking around.*) Is she a pro?

SOCRATES: Who?

ARISTOTLE: Your patroness. Is she a pro?

SOCRATES: A pro? Her? That's a laugh. She's just a kid. Fifteen. Picked me up off her boyfriend, Eddie.

ARISTOTLE: You got any kids?

SOCRATES: Yeah. A few. Had millions but most of 'em . . . You know ... (*They slap their necks, eyes bulging, they then continue normally.*)

ARISTOTLE: Penicillin?

SOCRATES: Most of 'em. Couple were tougher. Didn't matter. Got 'em with streptomycin. Those wonder-boys are mean. You know.

ARISTOTLE: I had one kid, he was fantastic. Made it into a preggy's 7-month fetus.

SOCRATES: Congenital?

ARISTOTLE: How'd you guess? One in 46. What a kid!

SOCRATES: Terrific. That's really terrific.

ARISTOTLE: That's the way you gotta' fight. You gotta' get them before they get you!

SOCRATES: Ah, I don't believe all that talk. When I was a kid, everybody said the same thing: *world's coming to an end.* Look at us! Look at us! Nothin' changes!

ARISTOTLE: That why you're so slow?

SOCRATES: Huh?

ARISTOTLE: You're slow. Too slow. Slowest clap germ in the world. Any clap should be weeks faster than my kind. You're a disgrace to all VD. I would have had her screaming by now. I was busy up and around. Wasn't paying attention.

SOCRATES: What's that supposed to mean?

ARISTOTLE: I heard you moved in on me, down here. I could see your garbage. Everybody's seen your garbage, you know? You're a slob. Really a slob. You're gonna' get the whistle blown on us.

SOCRATES: Don't talk crazy . . .

ARISTOTLE: Who do you think you're talking to???

SOCRATES: Who do *you* think *you're* talking to???

ARISTOTLE: You gonna' destroy her?

SOCRATES: I destroy. I destroy. Just not the way you do it. I make myself all nice and warm and comfy first. You understand? Nice and warm and comfy . . .

ARISTOTLE: I'll be damned.

SOCRATES: What's the matter? (*Aristotle laughing now.*)

ARISTOTLE: I'll be damned!

SOCRATES: What's so funny? What the hell's so funny???

ARISTOTLE: I heard you were really hot stuff, King Germ. The oldest known germ: King. King Germ. What a laugh.

SOCRATES: What's that s'posed to mean?

ARISTOTLE: Nice place. Very nice.

SOCRATES: Hey look . . . you ain't thinkin' of . . .

ARISTOTLE: Moving back in with you? Taking over from you? Finishing her off? What?

SOCRATES: She's already got me. The both of us together too much . . . I told you she's just a kid!

ARISTOTLE: She asked for it, Socrates. What the hell, she asked for it. We're supposed to be able to live together in *any* body. Hey, Socrates, this ain't a social call – this is a social *disease* – I'm on official business. Don't you know who sent me?

SOCRATES: Them?

ARISTOTLE: They took a vote.

SOCRATES: I thought you said it was my brother, Mario. I thought you said it was Mario.

ARISTOTLE: I was swimming right beside him when he died.

SOCRATES: Mario . . . died . . . Mario is dead?

ARISTOTLE: C'mon, Socrates. Don't play it so cute and dumb. You're a little old for that game.

SOCRATES: Sink or swim. Dog eat dog. Rat-race all the way. You work and you work and then you finally find the urethral orifice you can call your own. Maybe you're tired. You know. Maybe you wanna' rest awhile. You're gonna' destroy her, but not right off. That's me: I wanted to rest.

ARISTOTLE: How tall's her posterior wall? Six inches? I could filter through her placenta wall, I s'pose. How tall's the wall????

SOCRATES: Five and a half. Average. I told you, she's just a kid. Honest-to-God, she don't deserve nothing bad. (*Aristotle strutting now. Nervous. Eyes dart to each niche in the warm, moist pink cave.*)

ARISTOTLE: Oh, wow! You're goin' soft. Soft in the head. "Don't deserve nothin' bad . . . " (*Aristotle places his hand around a nubby-shaped bump on the ceiling.*)

SOCRATES: What are you doin'? (*Sees Aristotle's crazed eyes.*) WHAT THE HELL DO YOU THINK YOU'RE DOIN'???

ARISTOTLE: I'm going for her heart! (*He rips the bump from the ceiling and runs to another, on the opposite side of the tiny cave.*)

SOCRATES: Please, Aristotle, please. Don't. It's been good for me in here. Warm, safe, nice.

ARISTOTLE: I'm going for her eyes! (*He rips another bump from the wall.*)

SOCRATES: (*Screaming, terrified.*) Please, Aristotle, please . . . please don't. You'll only pull the meds down on us. I almost got hit my last case. Can't you tell? Please, Aristotle . . .

ARISTOTLE: (*At another nubby-shaped bump.*) I think I'll make her bleed a little. (*The sound of a female voice from above the cave. A big booming voice, yet at a level of whisper in tonal quality.*)

FEMALE VOICE: Eddie? Why? Please, Eddie . . . please . . . please . . . (*Aristotle running about the tiny cave now, pulling off nubby-shaped bumps, in a mad attack.*)

SOCRATES: Aristotle . . . stop . . . you're gonna' pull the meds down on us . . . Penny, Aristotle. Penny. You never seen it, but I have. It burns you inside-out, Aristotle. You claw your hands into your shoulders and roll and scream and wish you were dead. You'll wish you were never born, Aristotle. It burns at your eyes, pulls the flesh like claws. Your eyes, your eyes . . .

FEMALE VOICE: My eyes, Eddie. Eddie, my eyes. Help me, Eddie. Help me . . .

ARISTOTLE: This is terrific, really terrific.

SOCRATES: Please, Aristotle, please, please . . . (*Aristotle stands near the back wall of the cave. Eyes darting. Tongue hanging over his bottom lip. His pose is evil. He cannot stop this mad attack of his.*)

ARISTOTLE: (*An almost unbelievable confession.*) I've never had a woman before . . . I hate to admit it, Socrates, but I never had a woman. I like it, Socrates, I really do . . . (*He flashes a desperate smile.*) I'm going for her brain! (*From above, there is a horrible shriek.*)

FEMALE VOICE: NOOOOOOOOO!!!!!!

SOCRATES: NO! NO! NO! NO! NO! NO! NO! NO! (*Socrates leaps at Aristotle and chops at him, striking the back of his neck. Aristotle slams against the wall and slides to the floor. He whips around and stares up at Socrates incredulously.*)

ARISTOTLE: My God. My God. You crazy bastard. My God! You hit me. You hurt me. (*From above, the sound of a female voice sobbing...*)

SOCRATES: Stop. It's okay now! Stop! I won't hurt you! He's finished. Just me again! I'm old and slow. Don't cry. Stop crying. (*Aristotle rises; to Socrates.*)

ARISTOTLE: I'll kill you!!! . . . I'll kill you.

SOCRATES: No. Please don't. (*An incredibly loud scraping sound. Smoke pours into the tiny cave. Both germs jerk and convulse with pain. Both terrified. Near the end now.*)

ARISTOTLE: What? What's that?

SOCRATES: In . . . ject . . . shun . . .

ARISTOTLE: Huh?

SOCRATES: Penny . . . can't you smell it? Penny, I told you. I told you, you fool . . . you fool. It's over. (*Another awful scraping sound. More smoke.*)

ARISTOTLE: You did this. You did this. Your fault. Your fault. Over . . . all over . . . it's over . . . (*Aristotle is dead.*)

SOCRATES: Aristotle. Hey, kid. C'mon, kid. Don't play dead. That's not funny . . . (*Reeling. He yells above.*) What the hell did you do that for? Why? Why? He ain't all bad, you know!!! I know his family . . . they ain't all bad . . . drove Hitler crazy . . . Mussolini? Ruined him altogether . . . MY EYES. Get Eddie . . . don't get *me* . . . MY STOMACH . . . (*The scraping sound again. Socrates to his knees. The smoke is awful.*) Bitch! Bitch! You bitch! You're too late. I been in your blood stream six months now. In your heart. Arthritis, baby. Arthritis! MY EYES . . . PLEASE, NO! MY EYES! MY EYES! You bitch! . . . PLEASE STOP. NO MORE PENNY . . . . (*The final scraping sound. More smoke. Socrates drops to the floor.*) Penny kill me. Penny kill me . . . no more. No more . . . (*Silence, but for the sound of breathing. More breathing. Over. Lights to black.*)

THE PLAY HAS ENDED.

SHOOTING GALLERY

For Gill.
If I go for the bear, shoot me.

SHOOTING GALLERY was first presented by Workshop of the Players Art (WPA), in New York City, on June 8, 1972. It was directed by Peter Schneider, the sound was by George Jacobs, the stage manager was Melanie Ray. The cast was as follows:

WOMAN .... Faith Stanfield
MAN .... Harold Oringer
BEAR .... Gabriel Oshen

Introduction

I have had very little experience with *Shooting Gallery*, until now: 1994, twenty-two years after writing the play.

Shooting Gallery was first performed in NYC, at the WPA Theatre, in June, 1972. I was in Italy, at the time, and didn't actually get to see my play performed until three years later, when Lynn Meadow directed a production at the Manhattan Theatre Club, starring Lenny Baker and Gretchen Cryer. I'd written the play to be a companion-piece to *Rats*, but, at MTC, *Shooting Gallery* was used as the curtain-raiser to *Spared*.

I have, just now in Paris, directed *Des Rats et des Hommes* (*Of Mice and Men*), a triptych containing *Rats* (*Des Rats*), *Acrobats* (*Pas de Tango*) and *Shooting Gallery* (*Stand-de-Tir*), and I have, finally, discovered why I wrote *Shooting Gallery* in the first place. It is not a happy discovery.

Shooting Gallery is a ferociously cruel, deeply sad play. It offers little hope. Like *Acrobats, Shooting Gallery* is a marriage play. But, unlike *Acrobats, Shooting Gallery* is, first and foremost, a woman's play...spotlighting a woman who has had enough of domineering men for a lifetime. In NYC, c.1974, *Shooting Gallery* ended with a woman saying "I'm sorry." In Paris, c.1994, *Shooting Gallery* ends with a woman holding a smoking rifle trained on the audience...There are two dead men at her feet.

Shooting Gallery bubbles with a burgeoning awareness of women's rights...and an appropriate dose of self-hatred for the rat-husband I had been. My first wife died before I ever had a chance to fully apologize to her. Writing *Shooting Gallery* was as close as I got.

I absolutely loved directing *Shooting Gallery*. It is a complicated, highly-inventive play that demands truly talented actors...and a skillful director. *Shooting Gallery* has the same youthfulness that I find so annoying in most of my early plays, but, at the same time, it has a wide-eyed energy that I find to be ever so...*enviable.* It may seem an odd comment for an author to make, but, I am really so glad that I wrote this play. I only have the vaguest memory of actually doing so...but, I vividly remember the impulse...the thing that drove me to it. And I am lucky that I, somehow, found the courage to get it all down on paper...to write a deeply self-critical work without concern for public image, without fear of exposure. I wonder if I could weather such a self-inflicted storm at my age, now?

Surprisingly, given its history (or lack of history), *Shooting Gallery* is produced quite often, in the USA, but, almost exclusively in non-professional, student-acted productions. Because the play has never actually been reviewed in NYC, it never had the springboard leap...it has never had the buzz. *Shooting Gallery* has, over the years, remained a little-known play. I suspect that *Shooting Gallery* will now have a long, large life in Europe, post its highly-successful Paris outing in *Des Rats et des Hommes.* and I will try to find the time to direct *Shooting Gallery,* in English, at Gloucester Stage, perhaps this coming summer.

A confession here. Mostly, I look back at my early plays with embarrassed smiles. I find myself looking at *Shooting Gallery* with rare (for me) admiration and self-esteem. It is still a mystery to me: how I began, at age 17, to think of myself as a playwright? At age 54, I am certain, more than ever, that Creativity is God's gift to the suffering child.

I've said enough on this matter...for now.

Characters

YOUNG WOMAN
YOUNG MAN
BEAR

Setting

A shooting gallery. Winter.

SHOOTING GALLERY

Unpleasant amusement park music in the auditorium. Auditorium lights fade out. The stage is set to seem barren, but for columns or a broken wall, Upstage, the Bear's alley. Perhaps there is a small counter, Downstage. Perhaps, there is a bench on the opposite side of the stage. Neither is essential. The stage lights and the auditorium lights are out: there is blackness. The music swells. It is increasingly unpleasant. The music fades under and out. There is blackness and silence. It is broken by the Young Man's voice.

YOUNG MAN'S VOICE: Blam! (*There is silence. There is a count of five and then we will hear the sound of the Mechanical Bear.*)

BEAR: Oooo-Eeeee. Oooo-Eeeee.

(*There is silence again. The lights will fade up on the stage after another count of five. As it does, the music will fade back in at a low level. We will see Young Man standing, as a man firing a rifle. He is in his thirties, he wears expensive, trendy clothes, now in tatters. His rifle could be a stick. He wears tie, sports jacket. As he fires the rifle, he yells shooting sounds such as* Blam! *or* Cschuuukkk! *The target is the Bear, an ageless fluffy thing, played by a chubby man, black or white. A bear costume should be used. If not possible, it is essential that fur be indicated in some way. The Bear moves and makes sounds throughout the entire play. He moves precisely as a mechanical shooting-gallery bear: in jerky, ritualistic marching steps, arms pounding, from side to side of the playing area in front of the Young Man. He makes constant "ooooo-eeeeee" sounds as he struts. When he is hit by a bullet, he jerks around face-front, raises his arms over his head, stands tiptoe, bumps forward, screams an awful "oooo-eeee-oooo-eeee-oooo-arggh," then reverses directions and struts again, the target. The Young Woman is the same age as the Young Man, as contemporary of dress. She is, however, at once wistful and sad-eyed. She sniffles into a lace handkerchief. She sits on the stage, exhausted, watching the Young Man fire away at the Bear. After the lights are full, there is a full count of thirty seconds, during which the Young Man and Young Woman are frozen. The Bear moves and sounds as he will throughout the play. When the pause has past, the Young Man fires and misses. He does again three times, before he speaks. The music will soon fade under. The play has begun.)*

YOUNG MAN: Blam! I missed, dammit! I missed.

YOUNG WOMAN: (*Absently.*) I'm hungry.

YOUNG MAN: (*Quite angry.*) Blam! This game is rigged. Fixed. Blam! Missed. Blam! Missed again.

YOUNG WOMAN: (*Absently.*) I'm sleepy.

YOUNG MAN: (*Without looking away from his target, the Bear.*) Blam! Blam! Please knock off the idle chatter. You made me miss six times straight. You're babbling. Blam! Blam!

YOUNG WOMAN: But you've been shooting at the bear for nearly eight months now. Maybe longer. Maybe it's a year and eight months. I've lost track. I can't remember. It's enough, really. It's Winter again. I'm hungry. I'm cold. I'm bored. I'm sleepy. I'm hot. I'm nervous . . .

YOUNG MAN: (*Still not really turning to her.*) You're making me nervous. Blam! Blam! And you're making me miss. Blam! There. See? Missed again! (*Pauses.*) I don't think you're fair. (*Silence.*)

YOUNG WOMAN: I'll be quiet.

YOUNG MAN: Blam! Blam! (*Hit. The Bear reverses direction. The Young Man is giggling.*) Jesus. Jesus. Jesus, did you see that? Was that beautiful, or what? Huh? Huh?

YOUNG WOMAN: Very nice. You shot the bear. Very good. I'm proud. Now can we please go home?

YOUNG MAN: (*Young Man shoots at Bear.*) Click. (*Bear freezes. Game has ended.*) Gimme another quarter!

YOUNG WOMAN: You have our carfare. You spent it shooting the bear. You spent our food money and our babysitter money and our movie money and our Cerebral Palsy Donation money and our mortgage money and our car-payment money and our . . . It's our last quarter. It's all we have . . . please . . .

YOUNG MAN: (*He screams.*) GIMME THE QUARTER!

YOUNG WOMAN: Here.

YOUNG MAN: (*Turns and aims.*) Zzzt. Click. Okay, watch this. (*The Bear now moves again.*) Blam! Blam! (*Two hits. The Bear reverses direction twice.*) Sonofabitch! Ain't that a fantastic thing? Huh? HUH?

YOUNG WOMAN: Yes. It's wonderful! I'm awfully cold . . .

YOUNG MAN: (*Aiming.*) Knock it off. Hold the chatter. I promised I'd win you a goldfish, and, dammit, I'm gonna win you a goldfish.

YOUNG WOMAN: I don't want a goldfish. I want to go home. The children are getting old. We haven't seen them since they were babies. Please . . .

YOUNG MAN: Boy, you just don't understand me, do you? Blam! Blam! (*Two more hits. The Bear reverses direction twice.*) Holy jumping Christ! Four for four! Best yet! Just hold the chatter now. Hold the chatter . . . BLAM!

YOUNG WOMAN: (*At the same instant, overlapping his shot.*) I'm cold.

YOUNG MAN: You made me blow it! I missed by ten feet! You crazy bitch. You crazy slut. You crazy housewife! You made me miss!

YOUNG WOMAN: I'm sorry. I'm sorry. It's just that I haven't eaten for almost a week. I like to watch you shoot, but I'm hungry.

YOUNG MAN: I'm hungry too, you know.

YOUNG WOMAN: At least you've had the hot dogs. I haven't eaten for almost a week.

YOUNG MAN: (*Still aiming carefully.*) For Christ's sakes. You don't understand me at all. I promised I'd win you a goldfish and I'm going to win you a goldfish. You don't seem to appreciate the way I work for you. Food. All you think about. You think I enjoy standing here like a goddamn cowboy with a rifle in my hand? Wow! You just don't understand! Blam! Blam! See? I missed again. By twenty feet. Why? Because you chatter about meaningless drivel. On and on. Boy-oh-boy. You know something? I'm lonely. You know why? Because I'm with you and you don't understand me. Kee-rist, am I lonely. BLAM! (*Hit. The Bear continues his "ooo-eee" sound, raises arms and reverses.*)

YOUNG WOMAN: You hit it.

YOUNG MAN: (*Turns proudly to her.*) God damn right, I hit it.

YOUNG WOMAN: Five more for a win?

YOUNG MAN: (*Aims at the Bear again.*) Oh, I see. Greedy now, huh? Now that I'm close to it. Can't wait, can ya'? Ha ha! Just stand back, honey. That old goldfish is so close, I can smell it. Blam!

YOUNG WOMAN: You missed.

YOUNG MAN: Sure I missed. Certainly I missed. What's to win for? For you? God! That's no incentive. I need to know I'm winning for somebody who cares. Somebody who *really* cares . . .

YOUNG WOMAN: But I've given you all my money? Our carfare. Our charity money. Our mortgage money. Our Club Med money, our health club money, our Land's End catalogue money . . . I haven't seen our children since they were babies. I've brought you hot dogs and Orange Juliuses. All you wanted, all week. All month. All year. I care. I care.

YOUNG MAN: Say it then.

YOUNG WOMAN: (*Softly.*) I love you.

YOUNG MAN: Louder. You say it like you were ashamed or something.

YOUNG WOMAN: I love you. I love you. I really love you.

YOUNG MAN: Shhh. Blam! (*Hit. The Bear "ooo-eee's" and raises his arms and reverses direction.*) Neatly done, eh? Four more to goldfish. What do you have to say? Huh? What do you have to say?

YOUNG WOMAN: (*Smiling.*) Neatly done.

YOUNG MAN: (*He turns, fiercely.*) Huh?

YOUNG WOMAN: (*Quickly, apologetically.*) Neatly done. Neatly done.

YOUNG MAN: (*Turning away from her in disgust.*) Sometimes you worry me, I swear to God. You don't have an original thought. Not one original thought. "Neatly done"? That's what *I* said, "Neatly done"? Christ! Doesn't it worry you that you're so . . . so . . . non-verbal???

YOUNG WOMAN: (*Whining.*) I'm cold. I'm hungry. I'm lonely.

YOUNG MAN: (*Spits his words: aims.*) Non-verbal. Inarticulate. Almost retarded. A mental deficient.

YOUNG WOMAN: I want to see the children. The little girl . . . what's-her-name . . . she had her birthday this month. She must be eight.

YOUNG MAN: (*Leaning in to the Bear.*) Strange marriage. (*He walks in circles behind Bear.*)

YOUNG WOMAN: (*She calls out.*) You say you're working for the children, but we never SEE them! I want to go home!

Young Man: Lucky for you I'm constant. Loyal. I overlook the worst. That's a lesson for you, you know. You should think about it. Blam! (*Hit. The Bear makes his sound and ritualistic movement.*) Seven. Boy-oh-boy, seven and eightnineten to go! I knew I could. I knew I could, if I stuck to it . . . constant and loyal. Ambitious too. The average guy would have left this months ago. Rigged. Odds way against. Not me. I know what's mine. And what's mine is mine! Boy-oh-boy.

YOUNG WOMAN: (*Not paying attention.*) The little boy . . . what's-his-name . . . the oldest. He's probably six. He had a birthday weeks ago. I remember the weather was like this when I went into labor.

YOUNG MAN: (*Really annoyed.*) Now just hold it. Hold it. That's not my fault. God made women to have babies. That's the way He wanted it. If I had 'em, I'd just have 'em. You'd never hear me bitch the pain of it. It's God's sexual will.

YOUNG WOMAN: I'm very cold and hot. My stomach hurts.

YOUNG MAN: (*Puts his gun down, turns angrily.*) I really can't take your complaining. It really isn't fair. God knows I'd prefer to have you up here . . . gun in hand . . . and me down there . . . with no more responsibility than watching you work. But that wasn't God's sexual will. So here I am. Firing away. But not complaining. Shit and piss, no! Uh uh.

YOUNG WOMAN: (*Frightened, beaten.*) I'll be quiet.

YOUNG MAN: (*Screams.*) JUST SHUT UP!!! (*Pauses.*) Kee-rist, you're getting my nerves edgy. I gotta aim. This could be eight. Steady, boy. Blam! (*Hit. The Bear moves.*) I did it! I hit the bastard where it scores. Lookit that, huh? Eight! Say something!

YOUNG WOMAN: (*Mock sincerity.*) That's eight.

YOUNG MAN: (*Straight to her, furiously.*) Jesus, you dumb bitch. You dumb slut. You dumb housewife. I said it was eight and all you can say is "That's eight."? What kind of help is that? Huh? What kind of help is that?

YOUNG WOMAN: I'm just worried about the children. If they take the house and car away . . . and the babysitter . . . we haven't been home for so many months . . . she's a college girl. She must have missed classes waiting for us. She was supposed to graduate, last Spring. She told me that before we went out. She must have left and if she didn't, she must be angry. I'm really worried about the children. The baby had a birthday, you know. He's got to be at least four by now. We should have sent him a card.

YOUNG MAN: This chatter could do me in. Could ruin me. Just shut it up. Okay? Okay? Shhhh. Shhhh. Shhhhhhhh. And . . . BLAM! (*Hit. The Bear "ooo-eee's," raises his arms and reverses direction.*) Nine! My God, NINE! I can. I know I can. I really know I can. (*They hug.*) Say something to me. Say something!

YOUNG WOMAN: That's nine.

YOUNG MAN: Oh, God . . .

YOUNG WOMAN: Don't look at me that way.

YOUNG MAN: What way?

YOUNG WOMAN: Like you hate me.

YOUNG MAN: How else can I look at you?

YOUNG WOMAN: Do you?

YOUNG MAN: What?

YOUNG WOMAN: Hate me?

YOUNG MAN: Of course I do.

YOUNG WOMAN: Then why am I here? Why am I waiting with you here in the middle of the Winter? Why did I give you all my money . . . all our money . . . a quarter at a time? All those hot dogs and Orange Juliuses? Why? You must love me. Why else would you be trying so hard? You want to win for me. That's it, right? I understand. I really do. I know how much you love me. Why else would I have let our children grow old without my noticing? You must love me or I wouldn't have done that, right? (*She smiles, sweetly.*) Oh, I love you. I really do. And mostly because you love me so much. That's what keeps me here. Keeps me running back and forth with your hot dogs and Orange Juliuses. And it's not easy for me. Not at all. The hot dog man went away three months ago and the *Orange Julius* stand closed sometime last Fall. I have to walk ten or fifteen miles every time. The Orange Julius man . . . oh I hate him. I really do.

YOUNG MAN: What about him?

YOUNG WOMAN: Who?

YOUNG MAN: The Orange Julius man?

YOUNG WOMAN: Oh. *Him.* He's so . . . cruel. Cruel, that's it. He can't keep his hands to himself, either. I'm going to write a letter to the Orange Julius Company someday and turn him in. I swear to God. If you can't trust an Orange Julius man, who can you trust? He's terrible. But he's not as bad as the new hot dog man. (*Silence.*)

YOUNG MAN: (*After a long hold.*) Is this your idea of a *joke?*

YOUNG WOMAN: Oh, I wouldn't joke like *that.* I don't like jokes like that! You know *me.*

YOUNG MAN: (*Almost alarmed, softly.*) What does the . . . new hot dog man . . . do?

YOUNG WOMAN: Do?

YOUNG MAN: (*Staring at her.*) Do! Do! To you! What does he do to you????

YOUNG WOMAN: (*Squirming.*) Things . . . with his hot dogs. It's abominable.

YOUNG MAN: (*To the world.*) I'm losing my mind.

YOUNG WOMAN: It's all right. You shouldn't worry. I don't love him. I love *you.*

YOUNG MAN: With *hot dogs?*

YOUNG WOMAN: I just close my eyes and pretend it isn't happening.

YOUNG MAN: You goddamn dumb bitch. You goddamn dumb slut. You goddamn dumb housewife!

YOUNG WOMAN: Please don't call me those things.

YOUNG MAN: I have been slaving away here for God knows how long . . . SLAVING! . . . FOR WHAT? For a dumb bitch slut housewife who's putting out for hot dog and Orange Julius men. You're a pervert!

YOUNG WOMAN: You're angry.

YOUNG MAN: (*Bear begins to smile and flirt with Young Woman, who smiles back at the Bear; responds. Young Man sees flirtation.*) My God! Oh, my God! What am I working for? What is this??? I must be crazy! Really crazy! I'm shooting a gun at a goddamn stuffed bear . . . for what? For WHO??? For YOU??? Oh, boy. Oh, boy-oh-boy! I'll tell you what! You just turn around so I don't have to stare at your face. You just turn around and let me get a bead on this bear, see? . . . You turn around and let me get a bead on this bear and end it once and for all. I can win this. *With* you or *without* you. I can beat this son of a bitch. I'm ready. Really ready.

YOUNG WOMAN: I'd like to watch. I've given you all my money. I've been with you here all these years now. I don't even remember the children's names, anymore. I have an investment. I would like to watch.

YOUNG MAN: Okay.

YOUNG WOMAN: I can?

YOUNG MAN: Yup.

YOUNG WOMAN: You don't mind?

YOUNG MAN: Nope.

YOUNG WOMAN: I'll stay really still. Really quiet. Okay? (*He stares at her with the hatred of a lifetime. She senses it and recoils.*)

YOUNG MAN: Yup.

YOUNG WOMAN: Why did you look at me that way?

YOUNG MAN: Which way?

YOUNG WOMAN: Like you hate me.

YOUNG MAN: Because I do.

YOUNG WOMAN: You do?

YOUNG MAN: Yup.

YOUNG WOMAN: You do?

YOUNG MAN: Yup.

YOUNG WOMAN: You don't. I know you don't.

YOUNG MAN: Quiet! I'm going to shoot. I'm doing my work! Quiet! This could be it. This could be goldfish. Look at him. Big black and delicious. The win. (*Pauses.*) Click. (*The Bear says "click", in unison with the Young Man. Long pause. The Bear freezes, the game is over.*) Hey, I don't get it. Empty. Over. I don't understand . . .

YOUNG WOMAN: You don't . . .

YOUNG MAN: This is a fraud. THIS IS A FRAUD! This is terrible. Awful. It's empty. Over. It's gone. We wasted our time!

YOUNG WOMAN: Don't say that. Please.

YOUNG MAN: It's true. It's true.

YOUNG WOMAN: (*Weeping.*) Please. Please.

YOUNG MAN: It's over. Over. Empty. Fixed. Cheated. All lies. No goldfish.

YOUNG WOMAN: Please.

YOUNG MAN: Admit it!

YOUNG WOMAN: No.

YOUNG MAN: ADMIT IT! (*He slaps her face.*)

YOUNG WOMAN: Please. Don't. Don't. Please. (*He slaps her face. Again and again against her face, his fists and hands. The bear screams.*)

BEAR: oooo-eeee. ooooo-eeeee. (*The Young Man and Young Woman stop and stare, stunned.*)

YOUNG MAN: No. No. No. Please. Please don't hurt me. Please. No. No. No. (*The Bear continues to move toward the Young Man, who backs away, frightened. The Bear is enraged.*)

BEAR: oooo-eeee. ooooo-eeeee.

YOUNG MAN: Don't. Don't hurt me! (*To the Young Woman.*) Don't let him hurt me. Please. Stop him. I love you. I really do. Stop him....

YOUNG WOMAN: Oh. Don't. He loves me! Stop. Don't hurt him. Stop.

BEAR: (*Bear prances and flirts with Young Woman.*) ooooo-eeeee. ooooo-eeeee. (*The Bear moves close to Young Woman, lovingly, prancing, flirtatiously. The Young Woman grabs rifle; aims at Bear.*)

YOUNG WOMAN: I warned you. I warned you. Blam! Blam! (*The Bear *looks at her, helplessly. His voice fading. Kneels. Dying.)*

BEAR: ooooo-eeeee. ooooo-eeeee. oooooo-eeeeee. eeeeee. eeeeee. (*Dies. Silence.*)

YOUNG WOMAN: (*Kneels beside Bear.*) I'm sorry. I really am. I'm sorry. I really am. (*Stroking the Bear's furry back.*) I really am . . .

YOUNG MAN: (*Holding Bear's furry caps and ears.*) Look at this. You killed the Bear.

YOUNG WOMAN: (*Proudly; smiles.*) I did. I did.

YOUNG MAN: You killed the Bear. You dumb bitch! You dumb slut! You dumb housewife! You killed the goddamned Bear! (*The Young Woman shoots and kills the Young Man.*)

YOUNG WOMAN: Blam! (*Shoots him again.*) Blam! (*Shoots Bear, again.*) Blam! (*Young Man, again. Turns to audience; aims. She will kill every man in the audience, if this play doesn't soon end. Reprise of amusement park music. As the lights fade, we hear a large, distant explosion. Blackout.*)

THE PLAY IS OVER.

ACROBATS

For Doris, who carried me.

ACROBATS was first presented in the USA by The New Comedy Theatre (Jerry Schlossberg, James Hammerstein, Israel Horovitz, Albert Poland) at the Theatre de Lys, in New York City, on February 15, 1971. They were directed by James Hammerstein; the production was designed by Neil Peter Jampolis; additional staging was by Grover Dale, and the production stage manager was Robert Vandergriff. The cast of ACROBATS, in order of appearance, was as follows:

MAN .... Danny duVal
EDNA .... Trina duVal

ACROBATS had its world premiere at the Mickery Theatre, in Amsterdam, Netherlands, on October 20, 1970.

Introduction

I have such a strong memory of the moment in which *Acrobats* was first imagined.

I was watching Johnny Carson's monologue, as was my perverse wont in the early, sleepless '70's. My then-young son Matthew was, like me, a confirmed insomniac. (Midnight was, quite possibly, the only time that Matt could get my attention.) We would lie on the sofa, together, a typically-American father-son couplet, and pepper Johnny's monologue with "That's not funny"..."That's funny"...

On this particular night, Ed had promised us a husband-wife acrobatic team: The duVals. Why this prospect so intrigued me, I'll never know. I stuck with the Tonight Show, through Hollywood puff after Hollywood puff, waiting for the promised duVals' appearance ... and appear they did. Danny and Trina duVal must have been well into their fifties when they did Johnny's show: their big break. How or why they hit the tube is a mystery. But, as soon as they were on camera, a chill went through my body. They were so clearly husband and wife. The pressure on them—on their *marriage*—was incredibly obvious. Danny was an acrobat; Trina was not. She'd probably been a dancer. I can't remember. In their act, Trina would lock her joints in this position or that, and Danny would do hand-stands on her body. All variations were strictly on that theme. No more, no less. In between their moves, they would argue ... not with words, but, with stares, with astonishingly clear body-language.

As soon as their act concluded, I ran to the phone and called NBC. Of course, I got a recording, telling me to call back in daylight. I spent the entire night sketching out the opening moments of *Acrobats: an empty stage...a fanfare...acrobats—husband and wife, not young—enter, face front: all professional smiles. She reaches Him, slowly, with both hands, never breaking her smile. He leaps upward, and is now, suddenly, high above her, upside down, in a hand-stand on her hands. They both face front, smile. He speaks, never breaking his smile:*

MAN: (*Simply, sternly, flatly.*) I want a divorce.
WOMAN: (*An arch whisper.*) My hand. Let it go.

The next day, through Johnny's office, I tracked down the duVals. They lived near the Pennsylvania-New Jersey border. I told them that I was writing a play for a husband and wife acrobatic team and asked for a meeting. A week later, we had a coffee, together, in Greenwich Village, where I lived. I loved them, instantly. I seriously doubt that I will ever know sweeter, dearer people than Danny and Trina duVal. They were the opposite end of the world from my play: their marriage was (not much of a pun intended) totally supportive. And they were indeed perfect for my play.

I wasn't ever sure how I'd get *Acrobats* into production. It's a short play—twenty minutes long—not cheap to produce, and absurdly difficult to perform. In fact, the only offer I could muster up for several months after writing the play was from *Show Magazine* ... to publish the play.

But, then, in the Winter of 1971, *Line* was announced production at Theatre de Lys (of late the Lucille Lortel theatre) on Christopher Street in the Village. When it was determined that *Line* was too short (65 minutes) to fill an evening on its own, *Acrobats* was added, as the evening's curtain-raiser ... And that's how Danny and Trina duVal broke into Legit.

The critical reception to *Acrobats* was less than brilliant. It wasn't so much that the critics disliked *Acrobats*. It was more that they liked *Line* a lot ... In a word, *Line* overwhelmed *Acrobats*. Double-bills—two short plays in one evening—almost always suffer from critics tending to like one play, and, by default, not the other. Simply put, critics, lumbered with the task of describing the theatrical event, usually feel they must compare the two plays they've just seen, pit them one against the other. Anyway ... *Line* got great reviews; *Acrobats* didn't.

The filmmaker, Walker Stewart, made a short feature-film of

Acrobats, starring the duVals. But, there was little interest in a film of such an odd running-time, and, beyond a few short-film festivals in the boondocks, the film-version of *Acrobats* quietly went to live out the rest of its days in the great movie-pasture.

Once *Acrobats* and *Line* had closed at Theatre De Lys, I figured *Acrobats*, out there on its own, with all of its implicit and explicit production problems, would soon find its way to the great play-pasture. In fact, I was wrong. Almost immediately, Acrobats began to find a life among young actors, often transposing acrobatics to dance—to Apache, or Ballet...or to wholesome gymnastics, or balancing acts. I began to hear of productions of USA and European productions of *Acrobats* that used all sorts of illusions and stunts: husband and wife magic acts, knife-throwers, whatever.

To my surprise and delight, *Acrobats* seemed to have a life.

In fact, I am, at the moment, directing *Acrobats* in Paris, in a triptych called *Des Rats et des Hommes* (*Of Rats and Men*), composed of *Acrobats* (*Des Rats*), *Shooting Gallery* (*Stand de Tir*), and *Acrobats* (*Pas de Tango*). Jean Moussy, the French choreographer, has created a Tango for *Acrobats*.

Acrobats is a much sadder play than I'd ever thought it was. If it were an old photograph, I would want it to be well-hidden in an obscure album, looked at once or twice in a decade ... pasted down on a quickly-turned page. But it is not a photograph. It is a play...to be rediscovered and redefined...and rededicated to my late wife, Doris, with my never-ending love.

Characters

MAN A nameless, middle-aged acrobat
WOMAN His wife, Edna

Setting

Where it actually is happening: on a theatre stage.
When it actually is happening: now.

ACROBATS

The stage is absolutely empty, dark. There is silence for a count of five. Bright white light snaps on. The silence continues for another count of five. Half a fanfare sounds but is instantly switched off.
Note: The action of the play should be punctuated with appropriate music and fanfare, building in rhythm as the play builds, ending in crescendo as does the play.
A man enters. He is an acrobat: all rippling muscles and a professional smile. He will hold his smile throughout the play, until he can no longer smile. His costume is tight white cotton. He walks to the center of the stage and neatly, professionally, proceeds to lie on his back on the stage floor, his feet facing the audience.
There is silence for a count of five.
A woman enters. She is his wife: as muscular in the way that women are muscular. Her breasts are small, her arms and legs thick and strong. She wears a tight white cotton acrobat's costume and a solid professional smile. She walks to a position just above her husband's head, facing the audience straight-on, neatly. She reaches down to her husband with both arms. His hands reach up to her. He takes her hands in his, never really looking up nor moving his body at all. Suddenly, She seems to dive at his head with hers. In an instant, he stiffens his arms and she is in a handstand position, locked on his hands. Slowly, stiffly, carefully, He rises until He is standing erect. They are now in a full handstand position. She carefully maneuvers a turn, so both their faces are to the audience. Their smiles are quite fantastic.
There is silence as they hold their position. If there is applause from the audience, the silence must be doubled. When the applause has ended, he speaks, never breaking his smile.

MAN: (*Simply, sternly, flatly.*) I want a divorce.
WOMAN: (*An arch whisper.*) My hand. Let it go.
MAN: Can you do it? Are you sure you can do it?
WOMAN: Don't be ridiculous.
MAN: I'm here. Don't be frightened.
WOMAN: I'm all right.
MAN: Tell me when.
WOMAN: Okay. (*After a long hold.*) Now! (*He pauses, smiling.*)

MAN: Which? Which hand? You didn't tell me. Which hand?

WOMAN: This one. (*She wiggles her left arm. He slowly, carefully, takes his right arm down. The movement is almost indiscernible at first, then he snaps his arm away from her. She now stands on one hand, resetting her weight on him to maintain the balance. They hold in that position for a count of five. As before, if there is applause, the silence is doubled. When the applause has ended, He speaks.*)

MAN: (*Slowly, sternly.*) I hate your guts, Edna. I swear to God. I really hate your guts.

WOMAN: Your hand.

MAN: Here. (*He takes her hand back in his again, and she descends to the stage floor. They step neatly beside each other, holding hands, smiling.*)

WOMAN: (*Facing absolutely front.*) Who is it?

MAN: Nobody. Don't be ridiculous. There's no one else. You'd like that, wouldn't you? If there were someone else. Sorry, Edna. There's nobody else.

WOMAN: (*After a silent hold.*) Ready?

MAN: (*A military reply.*) Ready. (*He bends forward and she leaps so that she is standing on the base of his spine. Bitchy.*) I want you off my ass, Edna. I've got to have a life of my own. You wouldn't understand that. (*Pauses.*) Ready? (*They change positions in an amazing move, so that he is now standing on her back.*)

WOMAN: Lower. (*He steps down lower on her back.*)

MAN: Sorry.

WOMAN: It's all right.

MAN: (*Walking tiptoe up her back until he stands triumphantly on her shoulders.*) Dependency, Edna. Pushing, pulling. I can't fill my life this way . . . so little time alone – so little time with you demanding, pushing, pulling. It's gone way beyond. Way beyond. I'm a laughing stock. I'm a jerk. I can't decide who I hate more, me or you. I hate both of us. Say something, Edna, something.

WOMAN: Ready?

MAN: Ready. (*He leaps to the floor. They stand and face the audience again, hand in hand, smiling completely.*)

WOMAN: Just tell me when.

MAN: Why not tonight? Right now.

WOMAN: Ready?

MAN: Lead.

WOMAN: Now! (*He falls onto his back again and she dives into a handstand on his shoulders. His hands are on her shoulders. He wriggles in a circle as she does a split in the air.*)

MAN: Watch your nails.

WOMAN: Sorry:

MAN: It's all right.

WOMAN: What about the twins? What will I tell them? Huh? What words?

MAN: Split up. They're better off with us split up. I swear to God. How do you think they feel? Us fighting all day, all night? Huh? How do you think they feel?

WOMAN: I know how *they* feel, believe me! I've talked to them.

MAN: (*Amazed, rather angry.*) You've had words with the twins?

WOMAN: You think they're blind? You think they can't see? They know. They see. Ready?

MAN: Ready. (*He leaps precisely as she jumps backwards. He falls forward and she leaps on his back. She quickly does a handstand on his back as he bends forward.*)

WOMAN: Okay?

MAN: Perfect. Okay for you?

WOMAN: Perfect. Down a little. (*He wriggles up a bit.*)

MAN: Who is he?

WOMAN: We've had that out.

MAN: Well it ain't out of me, believe me. I'm a laughing stock, a clown, a freak.

WOMAN: I won't get into that with you again.

MAN: The truth. You wouldn't know the truth if you fell on it.

WOMAN: On dead ears. Your lies are falling on dead ears!

MAN: Ready?

WOMAN: Ready. (*They both leap at the same time and stand facing the audience again. They smile, holding hands.*)

MAN: What did you tell them?

WOMAN: That you might be moving. Alone.

MAN: Lies!

WOMAN: They asked. Twice. I had to tell the truth.

MAN: They're too young. Too young to know. There's time. They'll know in time. I really hate your ass, Edna.

WOMAN: Now! (*They both dive at the stage floor beside each other. They stand on their hands and walk the stage, from side to side, in a comic handstand stroll.*)

MAN: I can't walk anywhere . . . do anything . . . without people laughing. I'm funny to people. Funny. A laughing stock, a clown, a freak. Everybody knows. (*They spring to their feet and stand side by side, holding hands, facing the audience.*)

WOMAN: I can't go into that with you. You want to leave, leave. You want to stay, stay. But I can't go into that with you. You understand? (*Pauses.*) Ready?

MAN: Ready. (*She lies back on the stage floor and he does a headstand on her knees.*) I don't need you.

WOMAN: I don't need you. (*They continuously, rhythmically exchange positions. They speak and move in point and counterpoint.*)

MAN: I hate you.

WOMAN: I hate you more.

MAN: I wish I could drop you, Edna. I could you know. Just like that. (*Snaps his fingers.*) I just might, Edna. I just might.

WOMAN: Bullshit. Pure, plain and simple bullshit.

MAN: You've got a rotten mouth.

WOMAN: I never did. Never did, 'til I got stuck with you. I'll tell you that.

MAN: Really? Oh really. You know what I wish? You know what I wish? I wish you were dead. I swear to God. That's what I wish. I wish I could drop you, that's what I wish. (*She leaps onto his back.*) I wish I had the guts to leave, that's what I really wish.

WOMAN: Ready?

MAN: Ready. (*She leaps from his back onto the stage floor. She stands on her hands and he walks her around, holding her feet, so they form a berserk wheelbarrow.*) I really want you off my back.

WOMAN: You wanna leave, leave. You wanna stay, stay. I personally couldn't care less.

MAN: I hate you, Edna. I hate you.

WOMAN: You said it already. You said it.

MAN: And I meant it. I meant it. You'll see after I'm gone. You'll see. Who's gonna tell you when to move? When to think?

WOMAN: Now! (*He leaps into the air and she does a roll under his legs. He falls forward into a handstand and she walks him around now as the wheelbarrow.*)

MAN: When to move? When to think?

WOMAN: Now! (*They leap into their forward position, holding hands and smiling.*)

MAN: Who I want *when* I want.

WOMAN: Now! (*He leaps into a handstand and she dives through his legs. They're both walking on their hands again in a reprise of their comic stroll.*)

MAN: "That I was moving. Alone" How could you?

WOMAN: What should I have said? That you want a divorce?

MAN: Who said that? I didn't say "divorce"! Not me. I hinted maybe, but I never said that. Not divorce. Not me.

WOMAN: (*Showing emotion now.*) *I* said . . . I said . . . divorce.

MAN: When?

WOMAN: In my mind. In my *mind.* I said I want out. I said I want away from you.

MAN: You're crazy, you know that? How are you gonna manage the twins? Without me? Huh? What are you gonna do? Tell me *that*!

WOMAN: I don't care, that's what. That's what I got to tell you is that I don't care. I slave for *what?* To put your supper on the table? You don't eat it. You eat it and you don't like it. If I didn't put your supper on the table, you'd starve. Why? – because you're too dumb to get your own supper.

MAN: Up your ass, Edna.

WOMAN: Ready?

MAN: Ready. (*She leaps forward and he leaps onto her back.*)

WOMAN: Get out. Just get out. But don't tell anybody you left *me,* because I'll tell 'em all the truth.

MAN: And what's that?

WOMAN: That I threw you out. Threw you right out.

MAN: The hell you threw me out. *I left.*

WOMAN: No chance.

MAN: I left. I walked right out. I'm free. Me. I walked out.

WOMAN: Right out!

MAN: No chance. Right out. I *walked* right out in the . . . into the . . .

WOMAN: Garbage.

MAN: Street!

WOMAN: Words!

MAN: Words!

WOMAN: Ready?

MAN: Ready. (*They leap forward and face the audience. Strained smiles. They don't move.*) My back. It hurts.

WOMAN: Age.

MAN: Don't be ridiculous.

WOMAN: Age.

MAN: I'm young, Edna. Bitch. Rotten bitch. Rotten-bitch-Edna, I'm young.

WOMAN: Smile, face-front. Bend slow. Touch your toes. It'll unlock. Smile . . .

MAN: (*Following her instructions.*) Unghhh.

WOMAN: It unlocked.

MAN: Pull up your tits. They're sagging.

WOMAN: Don't be ridiculous.

MAN: Pull them up. They're sagging. Sagging way the hell down, too. Awful to look at, those two sagging glands. M'am – short for mammary. (*Considers it.*) Not bad at all. It's a sad, sad sag, Edna-m'am.

WOMAN: Bastard! (*She rushes at him, fist clenched, trying to punch him. He grabs her fist and they wrestle. The advantage shifts back and forth . . . the fight is fierce . . . but neither seems to be winning, ever, really.*)

MAN: Saggy.

WOMAN: Bad-back!

MAN: Sad saggy sacks!

WOMAN: Crack-back. Crack-back. Out of whack.

MAN: Whack this, Edna. You're wrestling a man! A man!

WOMAN: Old. Old. An *old* man!

MAN: The same age, Edna. Precisely and exactly the same goddam age.

WOMAN: Perform.

MAN: Well as ever.

WOMAN: Back locks.

MAN: Sacks sag.

WOMAN: There's still time.

MAN: Goddam right!

WOMAN: There's still time!

MAN: Goddam, goddam right!

WOMAN: For what?

MAN: "For what?" What?

WOMAN: For what? Time? For what?

MAN: Can we stop?

WOMAN: What? Stop what?

MAN: The wrestling.

WOMAN: (*After a long, long silence.*) Yes. Tonight. Tonight we can stop.

MAN: Are you . . . sure? Are you sure you don't just say "tonight" and not really mean "tonight"?

WOMAN: (*With quiet dignity, resignation.*) I'm sure. I mean tonight. That's clear enough. Tonight.

MAN: Never to wrestle again, then? Tonight then? *Never?*

WOMAN: Never.

MAN: You're not frightened to . . . to . . . end it?

WOMAN: The wrestling?

MAN: The wrestling. The balance. That too.

WOMAN: Frightened? No. No, I'm not frightened.

MAN: I wouldn't mind living a bit more. If only it could be . . .

WOMAN: Pleasant?

MAN: Yes. That too.

WOMAN: I'd like to . . .

MAN: End it?

WOMAN: End it. Finish. Yes. That too.

MAN: You're sure, then. You're absolutely . . .

WOMAN: Certain?

MAN: Yes. I'm certain.

WOMAN: Yes.

MAN: Ready?

WOMAN: Ready. (*They begin to do cartwheels, slowly and controlled at first. The dialogue is spaced between the acrobatic movements.*) Tonight then?

MAN: Why not?

WOMAN: This is the last time?

MAN: The last time.

WOMAN: Make it good then. If this is the last time, make it good. (*Their cartwheels increase furiously.*)

MAN: I don't need you.

WOMAN: I don't need you.

MAN: I hate you.

WOMAN: I hate you. (*Now the cartwheels have lost form. The Man and Woman are in a berserk dance of death. They lift themselves up from the stage floor and flog themselves down again. The thumping and crashing against the stage floor is awful to watch. They gasp and groan in pain.*)

MAN: Please . . .

WOMAN: Stop . . .

MAN: God! Oh, God!

WOMAN: Oh my God!

MAN: Please . . .

WOMAN: Please . . .

MAN: Edna? (*He stops and lies as an animal on his haunches, watching her slam herself against the floor, screaming in agony.*) Edna! Edna!

WOMAN: Arghhhh! Arrrr! Arghhhh! (*She moves slowly now as her weight becomes heavier and heavier and the sound of her body hitting the floor more awesome.*)

MAN: (*A scream in terror as he realizes.*) Ednaaaaaaaa! (*She lies still. He bangs his body against the floor in a short definite rhythm to his short stabbing cries.*) Edna. Edna. Edna. Edna. Edna. Edna. Edna. Edna. Edna. Edna. Edna. Edna. Edna. Edna. Edna. Edna. (*Slowly, as He beats himself against the floor, heaving his body higher each time and heavier with each blow. There is a silence. She raises her head slightly. He raises his head slightly. He stares at her.*) You're not dead.

WOMAN: (*Softly.*) No.

MAN: You're still alive?

WOMAN: Yes.

MAN: I love you.

WOMAN: I love you.

LIGHTS FADE.
THE PLAY IS OVER.

THE GREAT LABOR DAY CLASSIC

This play is dedicated to my teammates of
The Winaercheek Runners Club,
Gloucester–Rockport, Massachusetts;
and to all my friends who have completed the race,
from start to finish, again and again and again.

THE GREAT LABOR DAY CLASSIC was first produced by the Actors Theatre of Louisville, in Louisville, Kentucky, in the winter of 1979.

Introduction

Sometime in the early 1970's, I knew I had to change my life, or lose it. I was smoking, drinking, overdoing recreational drugs, never sleeping. I was having daily attacks of free-floating panic, that almost always ended in agonizing, blinding, migraine headaches. I weighed in at under 130 lbs., dressed up.

It happened while I was staying in L.A., for movie-meetings ... Whilst driving through Malibu canyon, enroute to dinner at Oliver Hailey's house in Studio City, a pain shot through my head that was the color red. My wife and kids were happily singing along with Neil Young (on the radio). My vision blurred, then, faded to black. Somehow, I managed to stop the car, inches from a 500ft drop into an unthinkable California earth-crease. The last thing I remember is my children's laughter. Then, the hospital, vaguely ... and, finally, vividly, a Sigmund Freud-bearded psychiatrist named Dr Millstein asking "Have you ever done any exertion exercise?". I told him I'd been a high school and college sprinter of some significance. I was not—by any stretch of imagination, not even mine—one the of the greats, but, I'd managed to win a fair share of my races. Dr Millstein told me to get up in the morning and do some running. Told me. Thank you, Dr Millstein.

I got up, the next morning, and attempted a morning run along the Pacific Coast Highway's bike-path. An entire family—motherfatherlittlechildren—jogged past me, effortlessly. I remember a similar incident, a few months later, on a Fire Island beach: a 12-year-old girl challenged me to a race, said "go". She went forwards, I went backwards. I seemed to be giving new definition to "slow". But, as is the condition of my nature, I stuck with it. In no time, the frequency and intensity of my headaches lessened, smoking seemed disgusting. My appetite returned ... I bloated up to 135lbs.

Every morning, I tried to run a bit farther, a bit quicker. Every next morning, I tried again.

For years and years, after writing Dr. Millstein's brilliant piece of direction into my particular life-script, I played the same character ... and well. I learned to balance my time at the typewriter with time running ... on the roads ... in the woods ... through Paris parkland, along the Seine, along Gloucester's rocky coastline ... in the hills above Nice ... at the gym. (I won't proselytize, further. If you want the full pitch, read any of George Sheehan's inspirational books.) I ran three hours for the marathon, and broke 40 minutes for 10kms, not easily, but frequently ... Not great, but, not nothing. Simply said, I'd found sanity in sport. I became a reasonable club-runner, competing for Warren Street, when in NYC, and for the Wingaersheek Runners and The Greater Boston Track Club, when in Gloucester.

In my mind, I was as much a runner as a writer. I worked on my plays, daily. I also wrote numerous articles on running. Almost nobody in the running world knew I was a playwright. And almost no one in the theatre knew I was a runner. *The Great Labor Day Classic* is the play that blew my cover.

Jon Jory asked me to write a short play for his annual new play festival in Louisville. He was planning a show with 8-to-10 one-acts. I'd long wanted to write a play about runners and road-running ... about the sport's wondrous crisscrossing of what we Americans call "socio-economic lines". (Brits call it "class".) I wanted to write about the sport's brotherhood-sisterhood ... about Competition (my very favorite subject) ... about small-scale heroism ... about Health. I knew that I wanted to have a race on stage, but, I also knew I'd need a cast of ten actors for such a play. I couldn't figure out how a large-cast play would ever get produced in the USA., so, I'd stopped myself from ever starting. When Jory told me that a large-cast play would in fact be preferable for his project, I blurted out my idea for *The Great Labor Day Classic* . Obviously, he said "go" ... and, in no time, I sketched out a draft of *The Great Labor Day Classic* . This play is, clearly, the blueprint for the enormously complicated play I would write for Joseph Papp, two years later ... *Sunday Runners In The Rain.*

I hadn't seen any of the rehearsals for the premiere of *The Great*

Labor Day Classic. I flew to Kentucky, the night before my play's final matinee performance, with my (Beastie-Boy) son Adam, and Adam's best friend Josh. Both were 7 years old. I spent most of the next morning in a blizzard, competing in a 10kms road-race (18th place, overall). Just before the matinee began, Josh, ill with the flu, threw up on Ted Kalem, then the drama critic for Time Magazine. I'll never forget Kalem flying out of the mens room, screaming "*Who's kid is that? Who's kid is that?*" It was, for me, a low-point. Nonetheless, *The Great Labor Day Classic* brought the Louisville audience—critics, Kalem, included—to its feet. It was, for me, not a low-point.

Mel Gussow was there and reviewed the play for the New York Times. He liked it.

ADDENDUM: A few years after *The Great Labor Day Classic* was first produced, around the time I met my wife Gillian (also known as #1 in the Marathon de Paris, #2 in the NYC Marathon, #3 in the Boston Marathon, former British Womens Marathon Record Holder, currently English National Marathon Champion, etc, etc). It was also around the time *Sunday Runners In The Rain* was at the Public. I bumped into Billy Squires at a party in Boston, the night after the Boston Marathon. Squires is a living legend in the running-world. He coached Bill Rodgers and Alberto Salazar through their great running-careers. By some odd quirk of Fate, Squires had also coached track, many years before that night, at my old high school in Wakefield, Mass., not long after I'd graduated and fled Wakefield, my father's favorite town.

On this particular night, Squires was celebrating Rodgers' 4th B.A.A. Marathon win (not my 3:11: 51). He'd celebrated a tad overmuch, and was both giddy and gregarious. We made eye-contact as I was leaving the party, Coach Squires was holding court with a couple of dozen top top top runners, among them, Rodgers, Salazar, Ron Hill, and many of my other heroes. (If only Beckett and Ionesco had run the Boston Marathon, that year!) Squires squinted at me, focused, and screamed: "Horovitz! Hey, Horovitz! ... If you'd been just a couple of years younger, I would have coached you in high school and you probably never would have been a playwright!" Everybody turned to hear his next line. I held my breath, waiting for what I assumed would be a pronouncement of unthinkable praise from an indescribably great man. In front of everybody, Coach Billy Squires finished his thought. "You probably wouldn't have been a playwright, Horovitz! You would have been a mediocre sprinter!"

Humility, like fine wine, is something acquired.

Characters

AUGUST DAY 19-20 years old, extremely thin, quick, nervous. He speaks with a strong New England accent. Smiles a lot. Class runner.

DOREEN DUFFY 19-20 years old, quite intelligent, beautiful, strong Irish looks, New England accent. Also smiles a lot. Class runner.

MARY PEAS in her 30's, thin, athletic, severe, hair tied back, mannish. Louisiana speech. She is a champion runner.

SPIKE COFFIN 35-40 years old, athletic, muscular, handsome, suntanned, confident. California looks and accent. Champion runner.

EBEN COON in his 70's, white-haired, distinguished Yankee looks, Yankee humour; he is a famous runner, a champion.

REBECCA COON in her 50's, daughter to Eben Coon. Rebecca is thin, graceful, long-haired, lovely, strongly intelligent manner, Yankee accent is slightly less pronounced than father's. She is a class runner.

Setting

A road somewhere on Cape Ann,
on the North Shore of Massachusetts.
Labor Day, morning.

THE GREAT LABOR DAY CLASSIC

Darkness in auditorium.
The sound of anxious breathing, amplified.
Music in, under breathing, low volume. The music is classical, perhaps Bach or Vivaldi.
We hear a voice over loudspeaker in auditorium.

VOICE ON LOUDSPEAKER: Runners on the line, please. We welcome you to The Great Labor Day Classic . . . the 29th Annual Around Cape Ann 25-kilometer . . . 15-point-5 mile event . . . this is an official A.A.U. event in both the Open and Seniors fields, male and female . . . Silver Championship for New England . . . so's you'll hav'ta' cross the line in a shirt . . .

FEMALE VOICE: (*Calls out.*) I'm not wearin' a shirt! It's too hot! (*Laughter and cat calls and whistles.*)

AUGUST'S VOICE: (*In darkness. Broad-A'ed Boston accent.*) If ya' don't hurry up and start this race, I'm gonna' be too old for the Opens...

VOICE ON LOUDSPEAKER: . . . This year's race is the 3rd Annual Chicken Frank event . . .

SPIKE'S VOICE: (*In darkness. California speech.*) Hey, Frank, you hear that? He's calling you "chicken"!

VOICE ON LOUDSPEAKER: . . . sponsored by The Hammond Chicken Frank Company, who gave us the race t-shirts again this year and your post-race luncheon . . .

DOREEN'S VOICE: (*In darkness. Boston speech.*) Hot dogs with feathers!

VOICE ON LOUDSPEAKER: The sun is hot, so we'll get started . . . (*We hear hundreds of people cheering . . . in distance. The music swells. The sound of the breathing swells as well.*) Runners, on your marks . . . set . . . (*A gunshot is heard. The lights snap on: bright white light. Six runners are at the starting line, a broad white line across the downstage center of the stage. They will race U., straight away from the audience. They wear brightly colored satin shorts and racing singlets and absurdly sloganed t-shirts. They will run in place, only moving slightly through actual space: enough to cover a figure-8 pattern once throughout the alloted time for the play. Thus, they will alter the angle in which they move from time to time to indicate a change in the race's route. Actual progress, however, from start to finish, must occupy and expire only the alloted time of play: no more. Thus, the race is danced in rhythm to the sound of the breathing and the musical underscore. The runners are: August Day, 19-20 years old, in 1st place; Spike Coffin, 35-40, 2nd place; Mary Peas, 30's and Doreen Duffy, 19-20, are tied for 3rd place; Eden Coon, 70's, 4th; his daughter, Rebecca Coon, 50's, just behind him. The music should be full now and its texture should be like the breathing: anxious and quick. The music and breathing should be taped and played throughout the play, rising and falling in volume as best underscores the action and the dialogue. The banner, mile markers, and water stop tables, will "float" past the runners, on black rods, or ropes, or moving platforms, in a direction opposite to the runners, at a speed and motion to better indicate to the audience that the runners are progressing along the course. The conclusion – the finish – to the race will be at the same white line, but will, of course, be approached by the front pack from the opposite direction to the start: the runners will move from upstage to downstage, Doreen now moves forward and is next to August. They will talk and run. Their breathing is strained; conversation difficult. The banner, THE GREAT LABOR DAY CLASSIC, floats away and is replaced by an arrow-shaped marker on which is written the words, 15 miles to go. That marker, as will all markers, doesn't stop, but floats immediately offstage.*)

DOREEN: Hi, August . . .

AUGUST: Hey . . . Doreen. We're goin' out wicked fast . . . (*They run a moment. Another marker floats past: 14 miles to go.*) You're lookin' great, Doreen . . . (*Another marker: 13 miles to go.*)

DOREEN: Paper said it was the biggest field, ever. More'n a thousand . . . from all over . . . California and Alaska, even . . . (*Another marker: 12 miles to go.*)

AUGUST: How ya' feelin'? (*Another marker: 11 miles to go.*)

DOREEN: I'm good, good. I think we overdid it with the carbo loading.

AUGUST: Yuh, I think ya' shoulda' left off the tomato sauce and cheese . . . (*Doreen laughs.*) How're yo'r legs feelin'? Okay?

DOREEN: (*Gasping.*) Strong, strong. You?

AUGUST: My foot's givin' me a little trouble . . .

SPIKE: (*Interjecting.*) You haven't heard from my foot, yet . . .

AUGUST: Hey . . . got about ten more miles for that . . .

DOREEN: How many've we done?

AUGUST: I figure about 5, maybe 6 . . . (*A marker floats by, U. It is an arrow-shaped sign, on which is printed the words: 10 miles to go.*) Look!

SPIKE: Ten ahead . . .

DOREEN: Six-point-five behind . . . My God! What's the time?

AUGUST: What's the time?

SPIKE: 32.

DOREEN: 32?

AUGUST: We went out pretty fast . . .

DOREEN: Too fast for me! I've never done this kinda' time in my life!

SPIKE: Always a first time for anything . . .

AUGUST: First time for first.

DOREEN: (*To Spike.*) August came in 2nd last year . . .

SPIKE: Good man. Maybe I can push you up a notch this year . . .

AUGUST: Let's hope . . .

DOREEN: (*Looking behind her.*) I don't see anybody else . . .

AUGUST: There are about 900 others back there . . .

DOREEN: I just see our pack of six . . . that's it . . .

SPIKE: 954 started . . . in this heat, too . . .

AUGUST: This is nothing compared to last year . . .

DOREEN: I just see the 6 of us, that's all . . .

SPIKE: Hot?

AUGUST: Nearly a hundred. 750 started; 450 finished –

SPIKE: And you took 2nd?

AUGUST: Well, yuh . . .

DOREEN: I wonder if there was a false start or som'pin?

SPIKE: What was your time?

AUGUST: I dunno . . . don't really remember . . . 73:29.5 . . .

SPIKE: Good man! That's class time . . . *for sure!*

DOREEN: I think there was a false start! There's nobody behind the six of us!

SPIKE: That's 'cause we're the front pack . . .

AUGUST: Doreen's runnin' distance for the first time this year. She's a natural, huh?

DOREEN: We're the what?

AUGUST: My name's August Day, this here's Doreen Duffy . . . (*The men shake hands.*) Pleased . . .

DOREEN: (*Amazed; shocked.*) *We're the front pack???* You mean we're winnin' this race???

AUGUST: This here's Doreen's first big distance event ever . . .

SPIKE: I'm Spike Coffin. My real name's John, but everybody calls me Spike . . .

DOREEN: (*Slaps her forehead.*) *OH . . . MY . . . GOD!!!* (*She immediately drops back into last place; stunned. August whips his head around, looking for her. He calls to her, over his shoulder.*)

AUGUST: *Doreen! Dooorrreeeeennnnnn!!!* (*The entire pack of runners shifts the angle of their run, indicating that they have turned a corner, altered their course. Another marker floats by: 9 miles to go.*)

EBEN: How ya' holdin' up. Rebecca?

REBECCA: Wicked awful fast pace . . .

EBEN: You wanna' slow it down?

REBECCA: We're in the front pack! I'm fine, really . . .

EBEN: We could lay back a bit, make it up later . . .

REBECCA: I'd rather run with the leaders . . . are you okay?

EBEN: Whatever you want. I'll stay with you . . .

REBECCA: Thanks, Pa. How are *you* feelin'?

EBEN: Strong, strong . . . it's *you* I worry about. You're in the cardiac stage. I'm too old for disease . . . A man my age only dies in bed. As long as I keep runnin', I can't die . . . Right, Becca?

REBECCA: Right, Pa.

MARY: (*To Rebecca.*) How old's your dad?

EBEN: (*Pretending to think it is he to whom the question's been directed.*) He's 200 . . .

MARY: *What?*

EBEN: He's won every possible record in his age group . . .

MARY: *What?*

REBECCA: He's kidding, he's kidding . . .

EBEN: I am like hell!

REBECCA: Tell her how old you are, Pa . . .

EBEN: Why? You don't know?

REBECCA: He's 76 . . .

MARY: That's great.

EBEN: What's great about it? How old are you? 20?

MARY: 36 . . . I'm Mary Peas . . .

REBECCA: I'm Rebecca Coon and this is my father, Eben Coon . . .

MARY: I've certainly heard a lot about you, Mr. Coon . . . it's an honor to run next to you . . .

EBEN: How would you feel runnin' *behind* me?

MARY: Oh, I'm afraid I just couldn't allow *that*, Mr. Coon . . . (*Mary pulls ahead of Eben, slightly.*)

EBEN: Oh, well . . . (*He pulls up even.*) I'm afraid I just couldn't allow *that*, girlie-girl . . . (*He pulls ahead; slightly.*) Sorry. (*He smiles.*)

REBECCA: (*Pulling up even.*) Me, neither . . . (*Smiles at Mary.*) Happy Labor Day . . . (*They all race a while, silently. Each shows pain and exertion. Each is at work. Another marker floats by: 8 miles to go. A table, upon which is placed 200-300 paper cups of water, floats by, just U. of this front pack of runners. Each grabs a cup of water on the run. Most drink some of the water, dumping the rest over their heads. The cups are thrown down on to the ground, quickly, and float off with the table. The stage is clear once again, but for the runners.*)

AUGUST: My goddam nipples!

SPIKE: You tape 'em? That's what I had'da' do in the Jersey race: tape.

AUGUST: *Vaseline* . . .

SPIKE: Next time, tape 'em . . .

AUGUST: Next time, sure . . . if I live . . . (*They all race a while, as the music continues. Nota Bene: It might be possible to control the level of the music so that it fades under the dialogue, and fades up again for the dance/race. The breathing-sound level can function in the same manner as the music. Another marker floats by: 7 miles to go.*)

DOREEN: (*Alongside Mary.*) Seven, huh?

MARY: Yup. Put it on automatic pilot and coast home . . .

DOREEN: Where ya' from?

MARY: New York.

DOREEN: (*Thick Boston accent.*) Noo Yawk, huh? Born there?

MARY: Nope. Born in New Orleans . . . right on the corner of Bourbon and Saint Charles. You?

DOREEN: Right here: Cape Ann . . . Gloucester . . . born right over in the Addison Gilbert Hospital . . . about a mile from the starting line . . .

MARY: Nice around here . . .

DOREEN: Yup. We like it . . .

MARY: Must be a good place to take a vacation . . .

DOREEN: So they tell me . . .

MARY: Lot of summer people here?

DOREEN: Everybody in the race with a tan is a summer resident. All the pastey lookin' runners are local . . . August Day, the frontrunner, he's my boyfriend. He got me into runnin' . . . This is my first distance race. I've run five milers and ten k's, and a couple of eight or nine milers, but, this is my first real distance . . . Labor Day Classic 'n all . . . I'm very pleased to be doin' it . . .

MARY: You're doing very well . . .

DOREEN: Oh, well, yuh, I know. That's 'cause I train with August, ya' know what I mean?

MARY: He's good, huh?

DOREEN: August? Yuh, he's great, really. He's the best runner around these parts, and that's a well-known fact . . .

MARY: I see . . .

DOREEN: Yuh, well, and, you know, I train with him every day . . . I mean, I run at his pace 'n all, so's that's probably why I'm up here in the front pack 'n all . . . with you guys . . . (*Laughs.*) I nearly *died* when I saw where I was . . . in the race . . . that's August's doin' . . .

MARY: Well, yuh, but you're runnin' your own race now. Pretty good, too, Doreen . . .

DOREEN: What'd you say your name was?

MARY: Mary. Mary Peas.

DOREEN: Right. Well, yuh, but that's August's doin' . . . teachin' me his pace n' all . . .

AUGUST: (*To Spike.*) My foot's hurtin' wicked awful . . .

SPIKE: You could drop out, if you wanted.

AUGUST: Well, naw, maybe I won't. My other foot's still okay.

SPIKE: This might be an opportune time to drop, though, August. Think about it . . .

AUGUST: Is that what they call a "Psychological Tactic" in the *Runner Magazine*?

SPIKE: Nawwwww . . . a psychological tactic is when I tell you that you've got a funny kinda' white foam comin' out'ta' your armpits . . .

AUGUST: I do?

SPIKE: Nawwww . . . that's just an example of a psychological tactic . . .

AUGUST: Oh, yuh? *Really* . . . (*Smiles.*) You run pretty good . . . for a man of your years . . .

SPIKE: My *ears*?

AUGUST: Years.

SPIKE: Oh, yuh, *really* . . . (*They each smile and nod at one another.*)

DOREEN: (*To Mary.*) You race a lot?

MARY: Not too much. Just weekends . . . two a week. Yuh. I do. A lot.

DOREEN: You win a lot?

MARY: Oh, well, no, not really, yuh, yuh, yes, I do . . . (*Smiles.*) I've got best womens' national ten and fifteen thousand meter times . . . yuh. I win a lot.

DOREEN: I thought so.

MARY: First race, huh?

DOREEN: At this distance, yuh. I've run 10-K's, ya' know, but mostly local . . . and in training . . . I've run some pretty quick times.

MARY: With August . . .

DOREEN: With August . . . (*Pauses; smiles.*) I've come close to your best ten thousand meter times . . . maybe twice now . . .

MARY: I thought so . . . (*Smiles.*) Let's hope you can go the 25-K's, huh?

DOREEN: Oh, well, yuh, let's hope, huh? I've done it in training . . . with August. He says I'm the best woman runner in the country . . .

MARY: (*Looks at her watch.*) According to my watch, I'd say that's just about true . . . (*She fakes a move into a position ahead of Doreen, who leaps forward.*) One of us is, Doreen: either you or me. (*There is a short silence.*)

REBECCA: How ya' doin', Pa?

EBEN: My legs were hurtin' about two miles back. Lucky for me, they've gone numb. Can't feel nothin' . . . (*Another marker floats by: 6 miles to go.*)

SPIKE: Ever hear about the guy in the New York Marathon who lost his shorts right near the finish line?

AUGUST: What's that? Some sort'a psychological thing again, where I'm s'pose'ta' think my shorts are fallin'?

SPIKE: Naw, I'm just tryin' ta' tell you about the time my shorts fell down ta' my ankles . . . end of a big race.

AUGUST: *You?* (*Spike nods; suddenly pulls into 1st place. Another marker floats by: 5 miles to go.*)

EBEN: (*To Rebecca.*) I think your socks are slippin' into your shoes. Better check yo'r left one. The little ball's almost out'ta' sight . . . (*Rebecca hops in air, brings foot up into position for quick probe with hand. Eben, her father, passes her.)*

REBECCA: My sock's fine . . . (*She looks for Eben behind her.*) Hey . . . (*She sees that he has tricked her.*) Nice. Really nice . . . (*Another marker floats by: 4 miles to go.*)

DOREEN: Gettin' a little thirsty from this heat. You?

MARY: Oh, yuh, som'pin awful . . .

DOREEN: Wicked awful . . .

MARY: Ya' lose too much of your electrolytes, you can get delirious . . . this kinda' heat . . .

DOREEN: No lie there . . .

MARY: Water stop should be comin' up soon . . .

DOREEN: Just around this bend, I think . . . fronta' Don and Betty Spittle's house . . .

MARY: I'm gonna' stop and drink this time. I can make the time up after . . .

DOREEN: Me, too. I'm gonna' drink two and use three on my head . . .

MARY: Good idea. Nothin' lowers the body temp faster than ice water over the head . . .

DOREEN: There it is . . .

MARY: There it is . . . (*A water station floats by: 200-300 paper cups of water on a table top. August, Spike, Eben and Rebecca all slow down and take cups of water. Both Mary and Doreen streak by without stopping to take in any water, neither do they slow down, nor do they even reach in an attempt to grab a cup of water. Mary and Doreen are now tied for 1st place. All look up amazed.*)

SPIKE: Hey!

AUGUST: Hey!

EBEN: Hey!

REBECCA: Hey! (*Another marker floats by: 3 miles to go.*)

AUGUST: (*To Spike.*) We got some work here.

(*A race-within-a-race is on. Spike and August work their way back to the head of the race, overtaking Mary and Doreen. They are now in 1st position, tied. The women are tied in 2nd position. The Coons are in third position.*)

DOREEN: Goddamned men!

MARY: (*After a pause; she smiles.*) You learn *that* from August, too? (*All alter their angle of direction again and the pack has taken another turn in the course. Music and breathing, full. Another marker floats by: 2 miles to go.*)

AUGUST: S'hat where you're from? New Jersey?
SPIKE: California . . . up near San Francisco . . .
AUGUST: Oh, yuh? I thought you said Jersey?
SPIKE: Naw, uh uh . . . California. I *ran* Jersey . . . they've got a cold weather marathon . . . out and back . . . it's new. 1st year . . .
AUGUST: How'd ya' do?
SPIKE: Me? Okay? Second . . . It was real hilly . . .
AUGUST: Oh, yuh? That's great . . .
SPIKE: Thanks . . .
AUGUST: What was your time?
SPIKE: Two-twelve-twenty-six . . .
AUGUST: My God, that's great!
SPIKE: Yuh. I was pleased.
AUGUST: Who beat ya'?
SPIKE: Huh? Oh, local guy, I guess . . . Tom Fleming . . . two twelve-twenty . . . talked him inta' comin' . . .
AUGUST: Oh, yuh, good runner: Fleming . . .
SPIKE: Yuh, one of the best kicks I ever saw . . . from behind.
AUGUST: I ran against him up year last winter . . . we had a middle distance he come up for. Visiting some of his friends, I guess. Rogers, Thomas, that group . . .
SPIKE: How'd you do?
AUGUST: Me? Oh, well, ya' know, good, good. I won it . . . (*Spike nods. Another marker floats by: 2 miles to go.*)
MARY: (*To Rebecca.*) Do much racin'?
REBECCA: Why? Does it look like I don't?
MARY: Your father was a legend . . .
REBECCA: That legend is my father . . .
MARY: Are you the same Rebecca Coon who ran the Toronto Police Marathon last year? . . .
REBECCA: Yuh, I ran it . . .
MARY: Set the Seniors record?
REBECCA: Well, yuh, I did, yuh . . .
MARY: My God! What a family, huh?
REBECCA: Oh, yuh, we're a bunch'a winners in my house . . .
MARY: Any brothers and sisters?
REBECCA: Yuh, couple'a each . . .
MARY: Mother still living?
REBECCA: My mother? Living? Yuh, yuh, she is . . .

MARY: Anybody else run?

REBECCA: In my family?

MARY: Yuh.

REBECCA: Only if they're bein' chased.

MARY: You be'n runnin' all your life?

REBECCA: Yuh. I have. Started runnin' with my father when I was seven or eight . . . never stopped . . .

MARY: You married?

REBECCA: Oh, yuh.

MARY: Kids?

REBECCA: Four kids, yuh. You?

MARY: Two. Two boys . . . you?

REBECCA: Me, too. All boys.

MARY: Shame.

REBECCA: Yuh, 'tis. You can't control the sexes, though, can you?

MARY: Not yet, anyhow . . .

REBECCA: You a reporter or som'pin'?

MARY: Me? (*Laughs.*) Uh uh. Key punch operator . . . I.B.M.

REBECCA: They a good company?

MARY: Huh?

REBECCA: I.B.M.

MARY: Oh, no, I don't work for I.B.M. That's the make of the key-punch machine. I work for a local knitting mill . . . in the office . . . in my town . . .

REBECCA: Sounds nice.

MARY: It's awful. But . . . (*Pauses.*) I'm divorced . . . (*Pauses.*) On my own . . .

REBECCA: They give you time for running, though, huh?

MARY: Time? Well, yuh. They do. If I make it up, nights. It's worth it, though. My kids are both in high school . . . (*Pauses.*) They're movin' in with their dad . . .

REBECCA: That must hurt.

MARY: Yuh, well . . . it's better for them. Boys should be around men, don't you think?

REBECCA: My husband's dead. My boys grew up with my father and my brothers around, but, mostly, they were with me. Didn't hurt 'em any. (*Pauses.*) I guess the votes aren't in yet . . .

MARY: You brought up four boys . . . on your own?

REBECCA: Yuh, well, yuh, I did that, yuh . . . (*Pauses.*) You get no choice, do ya'?

MARY: We're comin' on ta' the last mile here. How you feelin'?

REBECCA: I feel . . . strong.

MARY: What kind of work do you do?

REBECCA: Local. Down at Gorton's. I pack fish. On the line . . .

MARY: *Really?*

REBECCA: Be'n doin' it since after high school. Started when I was sixteen. Only stopped at the end of each pregnancy . . . ya' know . . . until I could get them on a bottle . . . (*Pause.*) It's be'n a livin', ya' know? Not bad . . . (*Pauses.*) The time passes. (*The front pack shifts its angle. Eben eases up beside Doreen.*)

EBEN: You're runnin' strong, Doreen . . .

DOREEN: Yuh, I've be'n trainin' . . . yo're lookin' wicked strong yo'rself, Mr. Coon . . .

EBEN: I do it with mirrors . . . it's a trick . . .

DOREEN: My mother said to say "Hello" . . .

EBEN: Hello back to your mother . . .

DOREEN: They miss you down at the school, she says . . . she said to tell you that . . .

EBEN: If they miss me all that much, Doreen, they could have me back . . .

DOREEN: I hear you're workin' down State Wharf . . . for Mifisi Brothers . . .

EBEN: Oh, yuh, yuh, I am . . .

DOREEN: August told me . . .

EBEN: Oh, yuh, seen him lumpin' . . .

DOREEN: He's only gonna' do that for another six months or so . . . then he's gonna try ta' get inta' school . . . so's he can be a teacher . . . maybe get inta' Salem or Boston State. Lumpin's no life . . .

EBEN: Nope. No life . . .

DOREEN: Yo're the night watchman, huh?

EBEN: Oh, well, yuh, I am. The night watchman . . . (*Pauses.*) Their old dog died, I guess, so's they hired me in his place . . . (*Smiles.*) I come cheaper, I guess. That musta' be'n it . . . (*August is beside Spike.*)

AUGUST: Maybe I'll see ya' after, huh?

SPIKE: For a quick beer, maybe, but I gotta' head right into Boston. I got work tomorrow. How're your nipples?

AUGUST: My nipples? Don't ask. You gotta' get to work, huh? In California?

SPIKE: For sure. 9 a.m . . . .

AUGUST: You be'n on vacation?

SPIKE: For sure. Ain't doin' *this* for money . . . not yet . . .

AUGUST: Money runners: the wave of the future . . .

SPIKE: For sure.

AUGUST: What kinda' work you do?

SPIKE: Oh, nothin' special. I'm a machinist . . .

AUGUST: Oh, yuh. Indoors, huh?

SPIKE: For sure, for sure. I used'ta' work outdoors . . . farms and stuff. I'm gettin' older.

AUGUST: Don't show in yo'r runnin' none . . .

SPIKE: We still got a little kickin' ahead . . .

AUGUST: I've be'n workin' as a lumper* . . . down the State Wharf . . . unloadin' the fleet. (**Pronounced "lum-pah".*)

SPIKE: That sounds good. Physical work . . .

AUGUST: Oh, yuh, it's physical all right . . .

SPIKE: That kinda' work'll keep ya' goin' forever . . . like old Eben Coon back there . . . the man's a miracle of science, huh? He musta' done outdoor work all his life, huh? It shows . . . that's the advantage of livin' around the ocean . . . in a seaport . . . outdoor work . . .

AUGUST: Mr. Coon? Lumpin'? Uh *uh . . . hell no!* Eben Coon was the English teacher down the high school for nearly fifty years. They just dumped him. Federal law, I guess. They kept him on way past his 65th birthday, but they finally had'da' dump 'im, I guess. He taught English ta' almost everybody in this race, 'ceptin' you out'ta towners . . . Eben Coon: the man's a legend . . .

SPIKE: I've been following his career since I was a little kid. Won the Boston Marathon how many times? Four?

AUGUST: I guess, yuh. They'll never be another Eben Coon, that's for sure . . . the man is my ideal. He truly is . . . (*The final marker floats by: 1 mile to go.*)

SPIKE: This is it. (*Breath heavily amplified again.*)

AUGUST: C'mon, legs, kick for me!

MARY: Lungs too . . . full . . . hurting . . .

EBEN: Still . . . kicking . . . I . . . am . . . still . . . kicking . . .

REBECCA: Chest . . . on . . . fire . . .

DOREEN: Head . . . neck . . . pain . . . I'm hurtin' . . . hurtin' . . .

AUGUST: Legs . . . achin' . . . quads . . . gone . . . kick . . . kick . . . KICK!!!

SPIKE: I'll get ya', kid . . . legs . . . kick! Legs . . . kick!

AUGUST: Kick! Kick!

SPIKE: Kick! Kick! (*Spike and August pull away from pack. They shift angle and are arm-in-arm, heading straight the way D., toward the line and the audience. We hear a voice over loudspeaker in auditorium.*)

VOICE ON LOUDSPEAKER: One half mile to go, ladies and gentlemen. After the crest of the hill, you can coast on in. It's been a tremendous effort and you are to be congratulated . . . (*The voice trails off, under, lowering in volume and changing source to backstage speaker; softly, fading into distance and out. Banner floats into position: THE GREAT LABOR DAY CLASSIC. Voice continues.*) You are to be congratulated . . . You are to be congratulated . . . You are to be congratulated . . . You are to be congratulated . . . (*Spike edges August out and Spike crosses the finish line in first place. Mary will place 3rd. Doreen will place 4th. Rebecca slows to stay with Eben, who is fading to the rear. She looks at him; worried.*)

REBECCA: Papa?

EBEN: Finish!

REBECCA: Papa?

EBEN: Finish! (*Rebecca crosses the finish line, in 5th place, under the banner, facing the audience. Music and breathing amplified, heavily. Eben walks to the finish line with his final shard of strength. August, Spike, Mary and Doreen are each bent over forward, singular. Each gasps for air. Each will walk in birdlike steps, stretching out leg muscles a moment, before seeing Eben standing at the line.*)

AUGUST: Mr. Coon . . .

DOREEN: Mr. Coon . . .

REBECCA: Papa . . .

MARY: Mr. Coon . . .

SPIKE: Eben Coon . . . Do it, Mr. Coon . . . finish . . . cross over. You *gotta'!*

(*Eben steps over the finish line. He smiles. All applaud him. Suddenly, all is still; frozen, silent. Tableau: Eben, at line. Mary, Rebecca, Spike, Doreen, and August, staring at Eben; smiling, exhausted. The banner overhead: THE GREAT LABOR DAY CLASSIC. The lights fade out. The music returns.*)

THE PLAY IS OVER.

THE FORMER ONE-ON-ONE BASKETBALL CHAMPION

THE FORMER ONE-ON-ONE BASKETBALL CHAMPION had its first public reading in May, 1978, at The Actors Studio, New York City, directed by J. Ranelli. The cast included:

KATZ ....Matthew Horovitz
ALLEN ....Paul Gleason

The play's first public performance (world premiere) took place in August, 1980, at The Gloucester Stage Company, Gloucester, Massachusetts; Artistic Director, Israel Horovitz; stage director, Denny Blodgett. The cast featured:

KATZ ....Adam Horovitz
ALLEN ....Jay Blitzman

Subsequently, the play was adapted by its author and taped for National Public Radio/EARPLAY, directed by Tony Giordano, featuring:

KATZ ....Scott Jacobi
ALLEN ....David Birney

The first broadcast was in 1981. Subsequently, the play was translated and produced by WDR radio in Cologne, Germany. That production won the Prix Italia, 1983. In 1987, a stage production in Seattle, Washington, starred former Boston Celtic great, Bill Russell.

Introduction

Here's a small subject, rarely discussed. How many American playwrights are actively raising children whilst earning their livings writing plays? We have a few, romantic, book-jacket images of women breast-feeding suckling infants, while, at the same time, typing their novels. But, by and large, the unspoken truth is that family life is not the normal state of being for American artists. Most artists in America are childless, or, worse, have children they never seem to see ... children that are out there, somewhere.

For better or worse, I have tried, throughout my career, to balance an artistic life with a family life. Sometimes, especially early on, it seemed impossible. Children would need money I didn't have ... or they would need time I selfishly withheld for non-money work: writing plays. No one around me seemed to understand my struggle. And yet, I knew, somehow, that my family was my reason why ... without my family around me, I would be totally, utterly lost.

When my older sons, Matthew and Adam, were just about teenaged, they were basketball fanatics. I was desperate to find both time and money to take them to their beloved basketball games. The year was around 1975-6, and I was earning a large portion of my living commuting between NYC and Boston, where I was teaching playwriting, once-weekly, at Brandeis University. I had taken the job at Brandeis in order to earn money, of course, but, also, to be close to my daughter, Rachael, who was living away at school at Phillips Academy, in Andover, Massachusetts. During Rachael's first year at Andover, we had dinner together every Friday night, no misses. Not bad for a dad who lived in NYC.

To solve a major family money/time problem, I created a television assignment for myself, by selling CBS an idea for a mini-series about a basketball player. I organized press-passes for me and my sons, and two or three nights a week, we took ourselves to either Madison

Square Garden for Knicks games, or to Boston Garden for the Celts. My daughter Rachael loathed basketball. She was too busy riding her unicycle to stop and watch anybody play *anything*. I worked, and my sons watched the games. Throughout the season, Matt and Adam and I were regulars, both at courtside and in the changing-rooms, at half-time, as well as before and after the games. We were as close and close could be ... to the game and to each other. Matthew put together an autograph collection that he would later sell for a small fortune. Adam collected images that would salt and pepper Beastie Boy songs for years to come. And Matt's first novel, written 18 years later, *Jon's Harmony*, is a beautifully-observed chronicle of an autograph-collector's best and worst season.

I was paid $80,000 for writing the mini-series, which was never filmed. In the end, I sat down at my typewriter with fresh paper and a year of extraordinary, first-hand experience, and I wrote the first draft of *The Former One-On-One Basketball Champion* ... a one-hour, two character drama about a washed-up pro on his way to commit suicide. The former champ plays a one-on-one game with a little Jewish kid, who...

The Former One-On-One Basketball Champion had its first public showing at the Actor's Studio, NYC, starring Matthew Horovitz as the kid. A few years later, after Matt had grown a tad old for the role, *The Former One-On-One Basketball Champion* had its first full production ... the first play ever produced by The Gloucester Stage Company ... starring Matthew Horovitz's kid brother, Adam. Adam stole the reviews. I remember one Boston critic writing "11-year-old Adam Horovitz is an acting-dynamo. The kid's career will be as big as his dad's!" She was wrong, of course. Adam's career is much, much bigger than his dad's.

In any case, my kids and I had gotten through still another year ... and I had solved still another major family money/time crisis. And I had, also, managed to create a work of art that belonged as much to my sons as to me. And, in the doing, I'd fed my sons much-needed food and affection.

But, somehow, in my struggle to earn a living during the following year, *The Former One-On-One Basketball Champion* was a play I overlooked ... I didn't "push" it. I was deeply involved with premiere productions of my seven-play cycle, *The Wakefield Plays*, which were being done in regional theatres all over the country. By contrast, *The Former One-On-One Basketball Champion* was a one-hour, one-act play, not particularly commercial.

I got a call from Linda Hartzell, Artistic Director of the Seattle Children's Theatre, in Washington, asking me for the right to produce *The Former One-On-One Basketball Champion.* Seattle Children's Theatre specializes in plays not for young people, but, about young people. It's really a wonderful theatre. Hartzell stunned me by saying that a former basketball player named Bill Russell was living in Seattle, and had agreed to play the lead in *The Former One-On-One Basketball Champion.* Russell was a great Boston Celtics star in the 1950's, precisely when I was going to basketball games and collecting autographs.

I flew to Seattle, and I saw Bill Russell, at age 55, step out on stage for the first time in his life, and give a great, great, great performance. At first, it was a shock to see Russell as an aging actor ... gray-bearded, slightly stooped. But, then, the basketball was in his hands, and, on stage, the one-on-one game began. The Bill Russell I remembered from my youth suddenly reappeared ... tough as iron, and graceful as a gazelle. When we talked, after the performance, Mr. Russell confessed to me that he was suffering from indescribable stage-fright. What courage! What a champion.

The Former One-On-One Basketball Champion is best played with an actor of color. Although any old pro will do. I'd love to do this play, one day, with my old pal Phil Jackson. *The Former One-On-One Basketball Champion* is a tough, gritty, upsetting play. Clearly, I'd studied a lot of Greek tragedy before writing *The Former One-On-One Basketball Champion*, yet, the play is best approached like an Arthur Miller drama. It's obvious to me, looking back to when I wrote the play, that the main influences on me, then, were Euripides and Lee Strasberg..

About family. I've married, again. Gill and I have twins, Hannah and Oliver, eight years old. Matthew is writing novels, full-time. Adam is a Beastie Boy and a film-actor. Rachael is a film producer. I went to the world premiere of a new Horovitz play, in Paris, last week, at Mrs Lennen's Bi-lingual School in the Eglise Amèricain. The play was called *The British Army.* I didn't write it. Oliver did. *The British Army* is Oliver's third play. Hannah starred in *The British Army.* Her work, as always, was excellent.

Characters

IRVING "KID" KATZ 14 years old, small, slightly chubby, athletic, intelligent looks.

IRVING ALLEN 40–60 years old, tall, stringy, obvious athlete; can be played by black or white actor.

Setting

A New York City playground basketball court, metal backboards, netless rims; asphalt. A sunny afternoon, the present.

THE FORMER ONE-ON-ONE BASKETBALL CHAMPION

Music.
Lights fade up to bright white.
Morning.
City playground basketball court, asphalt. A netless hoop, regulation height. Backboard is battered aluminum, stanchion is thick aluminum pipe. Chain-link fencing defines playing area: front open to auditorium. A 14-year-old boy, Irving Katz, shooting baskets: some from way outside, some inside: all in rhythm with the music. Katz wears jeans, leather sneakers, a t-shirt and sweatband around his forehead. Irving "Sonny" Allen enters, watches Katz a moment, sits by the side of the court. Allen is enormous, just under 7' tall. He wears a powder blue gabardine suit with a white short-sleeved shirt, open at the collar, with the collar of this shirt spread over the collar of his suitjacket. Katz continues to shoot, not acknowledging the entrance of the older man. The music fades out, as the lights reach their ultimate brightness. We now hear the sound of Katz's movement and the basketball hitting the ground and backboard. Otherwise, silence. Katz is first to speak.

KATZ: You a pervert?

ALLEN: Why? You lookin' for one? (*Katz continues to play. When he sinks an exceptional shot, he turns to Allen and smiles.*)

KATZ: I sunk ten of those in a row yesterday . . .

ALLEN: I picked the wrong day, huh?

KATZ: Never can tell. Maybe I'll do twelve, today . . . (*Shoots: misses.*)

ALLEN: That's one in a row . .

KATZ: Gotta' start *some*where . . . right? (*Shoots; hits.*) *Right!*

ALLEN: Too much wrist.

KATZ: Huh?

ALLEN: Too much wrist. You're shooting like a girl.

KATZ: If you're a pervert, mister, I got some bad news: my father's due back here about five minutes ago. He's a cop. With a gun . . .

ALLEN: Gimme. (*Allen stands: Holds out hands for ball. Katz throws it to him.*) There. (*He shoots a long straight shot: hits.*) See how my hand came down . . . sharp . . . but very little wrist. Straight lines . . . automatic.

KATZ: (*Rebounds, drives, shoots lay-up. He looks at Allen.*) You got one in a row. Wanna' try for two? (*Throws ball to Allen, who shoots: hits.*) Two-in-a-row. Three? (*Nota Bene: Adjust dialogue to hits and misses. i.e. "Ya' missed two in a row. Wanna' try for three?"*) (*Throws ball to Allen, who now moves from sidelines on to court, jumps: shoots one-hand push shot from above his head. Katz bounds, dribbles out to center court.*) Check my wrist, okay? (*Katz shoots.*) That better?

ALLEN: Still too much. Try none.

KATZ: How can I shoot with no wrist? My hand's attached to my arm by my wrist. I've *gotta'* use wrist . . . (*Set to shoot again.*) Watch. (*Shoots.*) Better?

ALLEN: Sure. Now add in a *little* wrist.

KATZ: What are you? A coach or som'pin? (*Katz sets, shoots, looks at Allen.*) Better?

ALLEN: Didn't it *feel* better?

KATZ: (*After a pause.*) Yuh. Did. (*Looks at Allen.*) You wanna' play a little one-on-one?

ALLEN: For real?

KATZ: Well, you'll hav'ta' spot me some, right? I mean, how tall are you? Six-seven?

ALLEN: Six-six.

KATZ: You ever play pro?

ALLEN: Me? (*Shoots.*) Don't talk crazy.

KATZ: (*Rebounds: lays ball up and in.*) Play to twenty-one, spot me ten.

ALLEN: Ten?

KATZ: Ten.

ALLEN: That's *all?*

KATZ: Nickel a point?

ALLEN: How old are you, anyway?

KATZ: Sixteen.

ALLEN: Fourteen?

KATZ: Yuh. You?

ALLEN: Oh, I dunno' . . . fifty, sixty . . .

KATZ: Thirty-five?

ALLEN: Forty.

KATZ: My father's thirty-eight. You gotta' *see* it to believe it!

ALLEN: Good shape?

KATZ: Like an avocado.

ALLEN: Green?

KATZ: That, too . . .

ALLEN: Big seed in the middle?

KATZ: Probably . . .

ALLEN: He never shoots with you?

KATZ: My father? (*Shoots: hits.*) You got kids?

ALLEN: Me? (*Shoots: hits.*) How come you're not in school?

KATZ: Me? (*Shoots: hits.*) You on unemployment?

ALLEN: You cut the day or what?

KATZ: (*Shoots: hits.*) We keepin' score here?

ALLEN: Who goes first? Throw fingers . . . okay?

KATZ: You crazy? I started three shots back. I'm leading, thirteen-zip.

ALLEN: I hit one!

KATZ: Wasn't your turn. I didn't miss yet. (*Shoots a short shot: hits.*) Fourteen.

ALLEN: Time!

KATZ: (*Stops.*) What'sa' matter here?

ALLEN: (*Takes off his jacket.*) I got a rep I gotta' protect here.

KATZ: You got keys? . . . A wallet? . . . Better watch your stuff, huh? Put it in your pants pocket.

ALLEN: It's just you and me . . .

KATZ: You never know . . .

ALLEN: I'll risk it . . .

KATZ: I wouldn't . . .

ALLEN: It's *my* stuff, huh?

KATZ: Okay, you rather be sorry than safe . . . that's your business. You ready?

ALLEN: Go. (*Katz dribbles towards basket, but Allen guards him. The difference in their height is comic. Each time Katz shoots the ball, Allen simply takes his hand and pushes it back into Katz's hands. Each time Katz leaps into the air, Allen simply shoves the basketball, thereby shoving Katz as well, to the ground. Possible to revive music and choreograph this section, fading music and dance in and out. At end of wordless section, Katz speaks.*)

KATZ: Hold it.

ALLEN: Som'pin' wrong?

KATZ: Just hold it!

ALLEN: You callin' time?

KATZ: *Time!*

ALLEN: What's'a'matter here? (*No reply.*) Something wrong?

KATZ: You've got a eighteen inch advantage. I'm five-even.

ALLEN: But you're leading, fourteen-zip.

KATZ: I've got a pain in my chest.

ALLEN: You're too young for that.

KATZ: I've gotta' talk to my boys. (*Katz holds his fingers to his temples, play-acting deep thought.*)

ALLEN: What are you doing?

KATZ: *Shhhh!* (*Pauses: talks to himself, smiling.*) Right. Got it! (*Looks at Allen.*) You ready?

ALLEN: (*Nods.*) Mmmm.

KATZ: (*Yells.*) Skywriting! (*Allen looks up. Katz bounds in for the lay-up; hits.*) Fifteen! (*Whoops with laughter.*) *Whoaaaa!* (*Dribbles back out to center line.*) Six to go. (*Grabs his chest.*) Oh, wow!

ALLEN: What is it?

KATZ: I got some kinda' weird pain in my chest . . .

ALLEN: You kidding?

KATZ: Wow! It really hurts . . . (*Katz kneels down on ground.*)

ALLEN: You kidding me?

KATZ: I've never had this before!

ALLEN: Are you kidding me or what?

KATZ: Ohh . . . wow! This is very scary!

ALLEN: Just relax, now. Go easy . . . (*Allen moves to Katz, takes ball, turns, dribbles in for lay-up, scores, turns to Katz again: smiles. Katz looks up slowly. He drops hand from chest.*)

KATZ: Nice.

ALLEN: Fifteen-one. My outs.

KATZ: (*Standing.*) Really nice.

ALLEN: How's your chest?

KATZ: I called time, ya' know . . .

ALLEN: Not true.

KATZ: I did!

ALLEN: Didn't hear it.

KATZ: Maybe som'body else did! (*Looks around.*) Just us . . .

ALLEN: You're just gonna' hav'ta take my word.

KATZ: No way! We'll throw fingers.

ALLEN: Uh uh.

KATZ: C'monnnn!

ALLEN: Fifteen-one.

KATZ: I'm five-even, you're six-six – eighteen inches over me – and you're playing shady.

ALLEN: *Me* playing shady? *Me* playing shady? *You're* the one's calling "Planes! Planes!" *You're* the one in coronary arrest! You ready or what?

KATZ: (*Stands; moves into position to guard Allen.*) Go!

ALLEN: (*Nods.*) 'kay . . . (*Allen dribbles forward, bounding, driving on Katz, who flies backwards on contact, skidding backwards in sitting position to point beyond the audience's sightline: offstage. Allen sinks a lay-up. There is a long pause. Allen stands, center-court, frozen, watching point at which Katz skidded off-stage. Katz enters quietly. he walks to Allen, looks at him.*)

KATZ: We need a rule.

ALLEN: What kind of rule?

KATZ: Like "no driving" . . .

ALLEN: No driving?

KATZ: No driving.

ALLEN: What kind of game are we playing if there's no driving?

KATZ: A no-driving game. We shoot from outside.

ALLEN: You kidding me?

KATZ: Mister, I've got my whole life ahead of me. I have no plan to end it here, with you driving up one side of my head and down the other . . . (*Pauses.*) No driving.

ALLEN: What's your name?

KATZ: Irving.

ALLEN: Irving?

KATZ: Yuh. Irving. Som'pin' the matter with Irving?

ALLEN: How'd you get stuck with a name like Irving?

KATZ: What do you mean?

ALLEN: You *named* for somebody? Is that how?

KATZ: My uncle. He was named Issac. He died and they named me for him.

ALLEN: I thought your name was Irving?

KATZ: It is. I don't understand it either . . .

ALLEN: You're Jewish, huh?

KATZ: Som'pin' the matter with Jewish?

ALLEN: 'Course not. You just don't see too many basketball players who're Jewish.

KATZ: That's true.

ALLEN: There was a guy played for the Celts, name of Finkel. He was a Catholic, but everybody figured, with a name like Finkel, he was Jewish. He had a big Jewish following . . . up in Boston. He never played much . . . more of a warmup center . . . third-line. Nice guy, everybody liked him. The Celts were in a series and Heinsohn put him in towards the end of the game . . . Cowens and Havlicek were both out with injuries, Jo-Jo White was down with the flu. Somebody else was sick, too . . . I forget. Anyway, Heinsohn put Finkel in near the end of the game, tie score, about four minutes to go. First thing Finkel does is get fouled. They were playing the Knicks and Phil Jackson was still playing—not coaching—and Jackson jumped on Finkel's back. (*Smiles.*) Finkel was a big guy . . . Maybe six-eleven . . . (*Pauses.*) My father said there was this huge roar when the announcer called his name. Every Jew ten towns around was cheerin' . . . it was funny . . . (*Smiles, remembering.*) Anyway. Finkel goes up to the foul line and what does he do? He genuflects . . . (*Allen laughs.*) You should'a' heard the groan from the Jews in the crowd! It's hilarious, huh? (*Allen laughs: Katz does not.*) Don't ya' get it?

KATZ: Not really, no.

ALLEN: They all thought he was Jewish until they saw him genuflect.

KATZ: 'S'that dirty?

ALLEN: Is what dirty?

KATZ: That word.

ALLEN: "Genuflect" means to cross yourself. Like this. (*He genuflects.*)

KATZ: Oh, right.

ALLEN: You never heard the word?

KATZ: I must have heard it and forgot.

ALLEN: You ever hear of Finkel?

KATZ: Sure. He signed four times for me when I was little.

ALLEN: You have a big collection?

KATZ: Yuh, I guess.

ALLEN: Have you got any old timers?

KATZ: Sure.

ALLEN: Like who?

KATZ: Cousey?

ALLEN: You've got Cousey?

KATZ: Yuh, I've got him on a series card from the '50's and I've got him twice on index cards.

ALLEN: How'd you do that? He never signs.

KATZ: I sent away.

ALLEN: With a letter?

KATZ: Sure. They never sign, if you don't send a letter. (*Pauses.*) You were a pro, right?

ALLEN: Me? Naw. I just followed the game, closely . . .

KATZ: You ever meet any players?

ALLEN: A few.

KATZ: You from Boston?

ALLEN: How so?

KATZ: You follow the Celts?

ALLEN: Sure. I did.

KATZ: Who's your all-time favorite Celt?

ALLEN: My all-time favorite? (*Pauses, smiles.*) Cousey. Yours?

KATZ: Yuh. I guess. (*Pauses.*) What's your name?

ALLEN: Same as your's.

KATZ: Irving?

ALLEN: Irving.

KATZ: You Jewish?

ALLEN: Uh uh. Baptist.

KATZ: Is that a Protestant?

ALLEN: Very much so, yuh.

KATZ: A Protestant Irving?

ALLEN: It's a fact.

KATZ: How the hell did you get stuck with a name like Irving?

ALLEN: I got screwed.

KATZ: Me, too.

ALLEN: If you could pick any name under the sun, what would you pick?

KATZ: Instead of Irving?

ALLEN: Mmmm.

KATZ: Instead of Irving . . . I would . . . pick . . . Irwin.

ALLEN: You're kidding!

KATZ: Yuh, I am. Lemme' think . . . I would pick . . . "Kid."

ALLEN: Kid?

KATZ: Yuh, ya' know how in movies, there's always somebody who's just called "Kid" . . . like "Who the hell could ever lift a Buick, barehanded?" and they answer "Let Kid try . . . " And then some really serious guy kinda' slithers over and lifts up the car ... and his name is "Kid."

ALLEN: What's your last name?

KATZ: Oh, right. I see what you mean.

ALLEN: Huh?

KATZ: Katz. Kid Katz. No good.

ALLEN: Sounds like a middleweight contender.

KATZ: Sure, in 1936. Kid Katz . . . knocked out in eleven seconds in the first round . . . (*Pauses.*) Maybe it's best that a name just gets picked for you in the first place.

ALLEN: Sure it's best. you could spend your whole life just looking for a better name . . .

KATZ: What's your last name?

ALLEN: Mine? Allen.

KATZ: Irving Allen?

ALLEN: Yuh. Ridiculous, huh?

KATZ: Irving Allen's a good name . . . Sounds like a president. Or a pro.

ALLEN: Sounds like a *butler.*

KATZ: You never signed, did you?

ALLEN: (*After a long pause.*) No. (*Stands: smiles.*) What'a'we got goin' for a score here? Fifteen-one?

KATZ: Yuh.

ALLEN: No driving?

KATZ: No driving.

ALLEN: My outs?

KATZ: We'll throw fingers for it.

ALLEN: You kidding me? You think I'm a dope or som'pin'? It was definitely my outs!

KATZ: We've been stopped for about an hour now . . . right? It's not like a time-out. It's like a new half, with a tip-off.

ALLEN: You wanna' do a jump?

KATZ: Yuh, sure. Wait'll I get my brother.

ALLEN: Why? He tall?

KATZ: Naw, he's a shrimp like me, but he's got a car. (*Pauses.*) I'll stand on the car. (*Pauses.*) For the tip-off.

ALLEN: Okay, we'll throw fingers. Once?

KATZ: Two out'ta' three.

ALLEN: Call it: ev's or odds?

KATZ: Uhh, odds. (*They throw fingers.*)

ALLEN: Once, twice, three . . . shoot! Yours! Once, twice, three, shoot! Mine. Once, twice, three, shoot! (*Pauses. Katz laughs. Allen throws ball to him to take out from behind half-court line.*) That should show you what a great guy I am. It was definitely my outs . . .

KATZ: You ready?

ALLEN: No more Mr. Niceguy.

KATZ: What's that s'pose'ta mean?

ALLEN: Just what you think. I've been laying back, watching your game. The way I figure it, you don't score another point on me . . . (*Pauses.*) You've got nothin' from the left . . .

KATZ: Oh, yuh?

ALLEN: Everything you've hit is from the right . . . typical for a right-handed kid.

KATZ: Oh, yuh?

ALLEN: All I have to do is keep you down left, there's nothing to worry about.

KATZ: Uh huh . . . (*Suddenly, Katz bolts D. L. of the basket, dribbling the ball with his left hand. He leaps in the air and takes a left-handed jump shot. He hits. Nota Bene If he misses, Allen allows him to continue to take shots until he hits.*) *Right!* (*Katz turns to Allen and smiles.*) Sixteen-sip, I believe.

ALLEN: One.

KATZ: Sixteen-one. (*Smiles.*) I took it up, left-handed; I dropped it, left-handed.

ALLEN: Once.

KATZ: Whoaaaa . . .

ALLEN: *Once!* (*Katz bolts toward basket. Allen steals the ball from him, easily. He leaps into the air and swishes a clean one-handed jump shot.*) Sixteen-two, I believe? My outs . . .

KATZ: Hold it.

ALLEN: What's the matter?

KATZ: Just hold it.

ALLEN: What's the matter?

KATZ: Time.

ALLEN: Chest pains again? (*Katz runs his hand through his hair, pulling it up from in front of his eyes and tucks it behind his ear.*)

KATZ: Okay.

ALLEN: Ready?

KATZ: Yuh. Ready. I said I was. (*Allen dribbles the ball forward five feet, lunges to the left, stops suddenly, fakes to the right. Katz fades to the right and Allen moves easily in on the right, stops, sets, shoots, hits. Nota Bene: If he misses, he rebounds and hits a lay-up. There is a pause. The ball rolls to a stop. Allen walks back to the half-court line and waits.*) What are you waiting for?

ALLEN: The ball.

KATZ: I'm supposed to get the ball for you?

ALLEN: Yuh. I hit, you get. When you hit, *I* got. Remember?

KATZ: That's a new one on *me.*

ALLEN: You want me to walk all the way back for the ball, I'll do it, okay?

KATZ: I'll get it. (*He does.*) No problem. (*He aims the ball at Allen.*) No sweat. (*He tosses ball to Allen.*) Let's go.

ALLEN: Ready?

KATZ: Ah, come on, will ya?

ALLEN: Sixteen-three?

KATZ: Right, right.

ALLEN: You nervous?

KATZ: I don't get psyched out like that easily, ya' know?

ALLEN: You look nervous.

KATZ: Why? Just 'cause my pantleg's wet?

ALLEN: You're really ready, huh?

KATZ: Go. (*Allen shoots from where he stands. Swish.*)

ALLEN: Four. (*Smiles.*) Ready? (*Katz nods.*) Me, too. (*Allen shoots again from where he stands. Swish again.*) Five.

KATZ: Okay. Time.

ALLEN: What for?

KATZ: Makes no sense to call this a game if you're gonna' just stand there and swish 'em through.

ALLEN: Well, hell, man. If I can't drive and I can't shoot from outside, what's left? You don't want to play basketball . . . you want to play a game called "I Win."

KATZ: It just doesn't make any sense for me to just stand here and watch you just throw 'em through from there! Maybe you figure I should let you *STUFF?*

ALLEN: No wonder you were playing by yourself.

KATZ: What's *that* supposed to mean?

ALLEN: A guaranteed win: you against you. You win. No wonder.

KATZ: I was M.V.P. on my team last year, ya' know.

ALLEN: I can imagine. Just *you* on the team . . . who else *could'a* been M.V.P.?

KATZ: We had twenty men on the squad.

ALLEN: Twenty?

KATZ: Twenty.

ALLEN: What was your scoring average.

KATZ: Same as your's: eighteen.

ALLEN: You know who I am, huh?

KATZ: Eighteen-a-game lifetime average . . . M.V.P. two series years in a row with Boston . . . pulled a hamstring in your rookie year that put you on options from Milwaukee . . . that's when Boston picked you up . . . pulled the same hamstring the last three years you played . . . your last season was about . . . let's see . . . ten years ago. As far as I know, you never signed for anybody, not even your own kids.

ALLEN: I don't have kids.

KATZ: Yes, you do. Two. A boy and a girl.

ALLEN: You got a computer up there instead of a brain?

KATZ: I remember things.

ALLEN: Their stepfather adopted them. I haven't seen either one of them in six years now . . . (*Smiles.*) They live up in Canada . . . last I heard.

KATZ: (*After a long pause.*) You're walkin' fine *now.* You plannin' a comeback?

ALLEN: I'm forty.

KATZ: Look at Havlicek.

ALLEN: There's only one of them every hundred years or so.

KATZ: If that's what you think, then it's true. I guess.. I personally believe I could be playing still at forty . . .

ALLEN: What's your secret.

KATZ: Desire.

ALLEN: Oh.

KATZ: I don't plan to give it up.

ALLEN: Aren't you kinda small? Not that I want to cramp your style, but you are kinda' small . . . for sixteen.

KATZ: Fourteen.

ALLEN: Oh.

KATZ: Yuh. I'm the smallest kid in my class.

ALLEN: Look at Calvin Murphy.

KATZ: Exactly.

ALLEN: I'm sorry I brought that up . . . about your being small. I don't know why I did that.

KATZ: How come you never signed autographs?

ALLEN: I never liked the whole thing, ya' know? Kids down around my knees with pens and pictures. I never liked it. (*Pauses.*) It used to make me think of death. (*There is no response. Katz waits for Allen to continue. He does.*) I figured I could just drop dead, ya' know . . . and the kids would just want a *picture* of it . . . (*Pauses.*) I didn't like them selling my autograph . . . you know . . . for money . . . at the card conventions and all –

KATZ: Nobody ever *had* yours to sell, 'cause you never signed.

ALLEN: How much do you figure it was worth?

KATZ: Your autograph?

ALLEN: Mmm.

KATZ: On an index card or a picture?

ALLEN: Either. Both.

KATZ: Now or then?

ALLEN: (*Pauses, thinks: laughs.*) Then.

KATZ: Hmm. Let's'ee . . . I would have to say, given the fact that you never signed, fifteen, *definitely*, for a picture and probably ten for an index card. 'course, if you signed a lot, that would bring it way down . . .

ALLEN: Fifteen? Times how many?

KATZ: Huh?

ALLEN: How many times before I brought the value down?

KATZ: . . . Let's see . . . a thousand maybe . . .

ALLEN: Fifteen thousand . . . you know how much I've got in my wallet now?

KATZ: I've got a buck-fifty.

ALLEN: Me, too. Hmmm. Same name, same bank account.

KATZ: That's all you've got?

ALLEN: Yup.

KATZ. How about your restaurant in Rhode Island?

ALLEN: For crying out loud, Katz, you know everything!

KATZ: I read about it. Fried clams. I like fried clams a lot.

ALLEN: They're not kosher.

KATZ: You got something against Jews, or what?

ALLEN: It went pretty good, while I was still playing . . . and for a couple of years after. But then, you know how things are, I sort of lost my name . . . (*Pauses.*) I lost my name and . . . well . . . people sort of took it out on my clams: stopped eating them.

KATZ: You go bankrupt?

ALLEN: Worse. It was like a poker game when you don't know how to quit losing . . . and you start signing I.O.U.'s . . . that's what I did . . . with everybody I knew . . . all my friends . . . I signed I.O.U.'s. (*Pauses.*) I was pretty dumb.

KATZ: You borrow from players, too?

ALLEN: Sure.

KATZ: Anybody big?

ALLEN: That's the nature of my business, Katz . . .

KATZ: I mean big names.

ALLEN: Sure. Everybody.

KATZ: You pay 'em back?

ALLEN: (*After a pause.*) No.

KATZ: Who runs the restaurant?

ALLEN: Some people. A family. They bought it for taxes. I had to give it over to the town. Portsmouth, Rhode Island. Near the bridge to Newport. (*Pauses.*) Pretty.

KATZ: Jews?

ALLEN: Huh?

KATZ: The family who got it?

ALLEN: Naw, I don't . . . (*Smiles.*) Yuh. I guess they were . . . are.

KATZ: (*After a pause.*) My father used to own a restaurant. Cuban.

ALLEN: Your father's Cuban?

KATZ: The restaurant was Cuban. Havana Take-Out . . . that was the name of it . . . Havana Take-Out.

ALLEN: Sounds awful.

KATZ: Awful? Awful's nothin'! This place was guaranteed death. The black beans were so old they were green. The plantains were so old, they were black. You know what we used to call the hot diced beef? (*Pauses.*) Chili-Cats. You know why?

ALLEN: You kidding me?

KATZ: Hey, listen, if I had eaten at my father's restaurant, I wouldn't be here to be leading you sixteen-four, and that's a fact.

ALLEN: Sixteen-*five.*

KATZ: Whatever.

ALLEN: What happened to the restaurant? Does he still have it?

KATZ: My father? Naw. Long gone. There's a Dunkin' Doughnuts there now . . .

ALLEN: Business no good?

KATZ: In what sense?

ALLEN: Did he fold up the restaurant . . . your father . . . 'cause business was slow?

KATZ: Nothin' like that. My father folded up, *personally*, because he was shot six times in the face and neck by a kid I went to school with . . . he robbed the register of a hundred and sixty-five dollars. There was a thousand more in the cigar box under the counter.

ALLEN: (*After a pause.*) He . . . died?

KATZ: Beyond any question of a doubt.

ALLEN: (*Quietly.*) What happened to the kid?

KATZ: That was sixth grade. Seventh grade, he spent up in upper state somewhere . . . in a correction school. They say he learned printing. He's back down here now for eighth grade.

ALLEN: Are you kidding?

KATZ: How come you always think I'm kidding? I'm not kidding.

ALLEN: Do you ever . . . see him?

KATZ: Naw. Never felt like it. No point.

ALLEN: My God! That's ridiculous. (*Pauses.*) Don't you . . . you know . . . wanna' *get even?*

KATZ: Do I want to kill him? Is that what you mean?

ALLEN: Well, yuh.

KATZ: I don't know. (*Looks up at Allen.*) Let's play ball, huh?

ALLEN: Sure. You take it.

KATZ: You're just doing that 'counta' my father, right?

ALLEN: Naw . . . right. (*Nods.*) That's the reason: 'counta' your father.

KATZ: I accept. There isn't too much I can do about my father, but maybe I can still pull this game out . . . (*Pauses.*) You ready?

ALLEN: Sure. (*Katz dribbles downcourt, fakes to his right, rolls left, lays the ball up and in.*) Seventeen.

KATZ: You just let me have that?

ALLEN: Nope.

KATZ: It wouldn't'a matter, anyhow. I would'a taken it . . . (*He dribbles to halfcourt line, looks at Allen, smiles: nods. He dribbles to position four steps in from halfcourt mark, jumps, shoots, hits. NB: If he misses, he goes in for rebound and lay-up.*) Eighteen. Three to go.

ALLEN: How long ago?

KATZ: I told you. Couple'a years now . . .

ALLEN: That's a rough break.

KATZ: Pulling a hamstring and sitting out three season's a rough break, too, huh?

ALLEN: I guess.

KATZ: Basketball Digest picked you as number one rookie, twice, right? Counta' you didn't finish your first year.

ALLEN: I don't remember.

KATZ: Twice, I think . . .

ALLEN: Just once. You can only be a rookie once. They didn't count my first year, 'cause'a my injury. They counted my second year as my rookie year and named me number one.

KATZ: But they said you *would've* made number one, first year, if you didn't get injured, right?

ALLEN: You weren't even born then . . .

KATZ: I collect back issues.

ALLEN: That's amazing!

KATZ: I remember the video of the game against the Knicks, when you scored forty-one . . . best one-on-one player in the game . . . "The One-on-One Champion" . . . right? None better . . .

ALLEN: Twenty years ago, now . . .

KATZ: The thing that was amazing about your game was the number of assists you had . . .

ALLEN: I was lucky –

KATZ: More n' fifty assists . . . in one game . . . *and* . . .

ALLEN: Lucky –

KATZ: . . . forty-one points . . .

ALLEN: I got hot.

KATZ: You were *great!* Why don't you say it? You were great . . .

ALLEN: Don't talk dumb . . . (*There is a pause.*) I played a good game . . . (*A second pause.*) I worked hard at it. (*Smiles.*) You couldn't have seen the game. You weren't born.

KATZ: I've got all your clippings . . . I saw that game, maybe twenty times, on a training film . . .

ALLEN: You go to basketball camp?

KATZ: At the "Y" . . .

ALLEN: They used the film, huh?

KATZ: I borrowed it and played it over and over at home . . .

ALLEN: Sixteen millimeter?

KATZ: Uh uh. Video. I borrowed a VCR from my Sunday school . . . (*Pauses.*) I was just a kid. (*Pauses.*) Maybe it's 'cause we've got the same name. Maybe that's it. (*There is a long, hard stare between the two men. Neither smiles. Neither speaks. Katz throws the ball to Allen for a "touch," before he takes it out to resume wordlessly. Katz shoots from mid-court, hits.)*

ALLEN: Nineteen. I'm gonna' give you one more, Irving, then I'm going to play hard, left-handed.

KATZ: Hey, listen. You play your game the way you wanna' play your game. No skin off my teeth, right? (*Throws ball to Allen.*) Check. (*Allen throws it back to Katz.*) Ready? (*Allen nods. Katz dribbles past him, stops beneath the basket, looks at Allen, shrugs; shoots an easy lay-up, in.*) No skin off my teeth.

ALLEN: Five, right?

KATZ: Right.

ALLEN: Let's go.

KATZ: Check. (*Katz throws the ball to Allen for a touch and Allen returns it. Katz dribbles out, Allen steals the ball from him, turns, leaps, and drops a one-hand jump-shot. Allen takes his own rebound and moves quickly back to the half-court line, bounding gracefully. It is at this point that we first see his grace and confidence: he is a professional player, clearly so. He throws the ball to Katz.*)

ALLEN: Check. (*Katz looks at him, but Allen interrupts.*) Don't talk to me! Play! (*Katz returns the ball to Allen and gets himself set for Allen's attack. Here, Allen should make an impressive head fake fade and hook shot, in.*)

KATZ: Hey!

ALLEN: Seven. (*He moves to half-court line.*) Check. (*The ball goes to Katz and back to Allen, who bounds in half-way, leaps, sinks shot.*) Ball! (*Katz breaks into a smile. He tosses the ball back to Allen, thoroughly enjoying Allen's expertise.*)

KATZ: Ready.

ALLEN: You sure? (*Allen drives straight at Katz, who is terrified. Allen stops, suddenly. Katz falls over, backwards. Katz looks up from the ground to see Allen slowly set, shoot, and drop another basket.*) Eight. (*He throws the ball to Katz, who has risen from the ground.*) Check. (*Katz does.*)

KATZ: (*Returning the ball.*) I thought that you were going to let me win?

ALLEN: *Any*body can let you win. It takes me to score sixteen straight.

KATZ: You and what army? (*Allen dribbles out, Katz comes forward. Allen headfakes, rolls left, Katz rolls right, Allen dribbles in for an easy shot.*)

ALLEN: Nine.

KATZ: Time.

ALLEN: You really want to play it chicken, Katz, play it chicken. No skin off *my* teeth.

KATZ: I just have to fix my hair. (*He brushes hair out of his eyes.*) Okay. Ready.

ALLEN: (*Standing at half-court line: smiles.*) Lefty. (*He takes one step, stops, shoots, hits.*) Rebound. (*Katz goes for the ball, but kicks it. The ball rolls to Allen's jacket. Katz gets the ball, sits on ground next to jacket.*)

KATZ: Time. I've gotta' sit down. (*He leans on Allen's jacket.*) What the hell is this?

ALLEN: Nothing. (*Both Katz and Allen are shaken.*)

KATZ: C'mon, will ya'! What're'ya' doin' with this? Huh?

ALLEN: I'm just carrying it . . . for a friend.

KATZ: You've got great friends . . . (*Katz takes a pistol, .32 caliber, from Allen's jacket pocket.*) It's loaded?

ALLEN: (*Nods.*) Careful with that.

KATZ: Why? You 'fraid I'll hurt'cha'?

ALLEN: No, I'm afraid you'll hurt yourself. (*Katz aims the pistol in opposite direction from Allen and fires a shot.*)

KATZ: Wow!

ALLEN: WHAT THE HELL ARE YOU DOIN!? (*Allen takes a step toward Katz, who turns and aims the pistol at him.*)

KATZ: Back up! . . .

ALLEN: Irving, what are you doing?

KATZ: What are *you* doing?

ALLEN: I was just walking up to the bridge . . .

KATZ: You planned to shoot the bridge? How come?

ALLEN: I was giving myself a choice.

KATZ: Oh. Right. A choice. Jump or . . . (*Puts gun back in Allen's coat pocket. The two face one another. There is a long pause.*)

ALLEN: You don't know what it feels like to owe money all around . . . I owe more money than I'll make in ten lifetimes . . .

KATZ: Money, huh? That's it?

ALLEN: I'm finished, Irving. I'm walking around dead. The day the game threw me out, I was dead. I've just been walking around since then . . . making a fool of myself to everybody. No family left . . . no friends . . . just me inside my skin. Maybe a circus would have me, huh?

KATZ: So, it's not the money? It's the walking around dead?

ALLEN: You're a kid. You wouldn't understand . . .

KATZ: Boy, it's all through your family, isn't it?

ALLEN: What'd'ya mean?

KATZ: What do ya' mean "What do ya' mean?" (*Smiles; pauses.*) Supposing we just stop lying now, huh?

ALLEN: I wasn't sure you knew.

KATZ: What did you think? I was a dope or something? You think I never looked at'm? You think I'd really let'm walk around *my* streets . . . *my* neighborhood . . . and I was never even gonna' take a little peek?

ALLEN: I shouldn't have come here.

KATZ: Canada? What kinda' crap is *that?*

ALLEN: When they first got married . . . his mother and her new husband . . . that's where they lived.

KATZ: You see him?

ALLEN: Bobby? Yuh. I saw him.

KATZ: When?

ALLEN: 'bout an hour ago now . . .

KATZ: And before that.

ALLEN: Six years.

KATZ: You like him?

ALLEN: I hate him, Irving. I've never met a kid I hated so much in all my life. The worst is, I see my mother-and-father's faces on'm . . . and that's the truth of it: that's the worst.

KATZ: He looks just like you. Spitting image.

ALLEN: What I came to do is to offer you the chance to get even.

KATZ: (*Flashes gun.*) With this?

ALLEN: (*Nods.*) Mmmm.

KATZ: You want me to kill your son?

ALLEN: Me.

KATZ: Huh?

ALLEN: I want you to kill *me.* Father for father.

KATZ: (*After a pause.*) Too late. (*Smiles.*) You're already dead. (*Pauses.*) I got a different plan . . .

ALLEN: Give it to me, then . . .

KATZ: Stay back. (*Aims gun at Allen, who pauses.*) What the hell am I doing? That's what you're after! (*Points gun at himself.*) Stay back or I'll shoot myself. (*Looks up at Allen.*) I don't *want* to shoot myself! (*Aims gun at sky; fires six rounds.*) Empty. (*Drops gun.*) You ready to play?

ALLEN: I . . .

KATZ: That was a question.

ALLEN: I . . .

KATZ: (*Screams.*) *That . . . was . . . a . . . question!!!*

ALLEN: (*Nods.*) Mmmm.

KATZ: Then, let's go, old man. Let's hit it. (*Katz moves to the halfcourt line and faces Allen.*) I've been holding back on you a little, Mr. Allen, 'count'a I didn't actually know if you knew. You knew. No reason to hold back any more, is there?

ALLEN: Irving, you've got to understand why I looked you up . . .

KATZ: You playin' ball, or what?

ALLEN: If I had money, I would give it to you . . . all of it . . .

KATZ: (*Throws ball to Allen.*) Touch!

ALLEN: You got'ta' understand that when I saw Bobby last, he was eight. That's all: eight!

KATZ: Nineteen. Two to go . . . gimme the ball!

ALLEN: His mother let us both down . . . I was on the road . . . I don't blame her, but . . .

KATZ: You're pathetic . . . (*Allen looks at him.*) Gimme the Goddam ball! (*Allen holds the ball.*) I use'ta' have *dreams* about you . . . I use'ta' see you playin' in my dreams. I'd be down in the front seats . . . on the press row, or sittin' bottom of the stand to the backboard with the *special* kids . . . ya' know . . . kids like Bobby . . . that kind of thing. May I please have the ball? Please? (*Motions for ball: Allen throws it to him, reflexively.*) I once paid ten dollars for one of your cancelled checks, you know that?

ALLEN: Once I knew I was going to . . . you know . . . end it . . . I wanted to offer you the chance . . . to even things up.

KATZ: I sold it two years later for fifteen. It wouldn't be worth a dime now, you know that? Not a dime . . .

ALLEN: I wanted to bring him here with me . . . Bobby . . . so that he could look at you, face to face, man to man, and tell you he was sorry . . .

KATZ: (*Screams.*) But he's *not* sorry, you asshole! *He's not sorry!* Do *you* think he is??? Huh??? HUH??? Do you? Do you??? *DO . . . YOU???*

ALLEN: (*After a pause.*) No.

KATZ: I want to play now. I want to finish this game now. I don't want any more talk now. Do you get me?

ALLEN: Irving, you're fourteen . . .

KATZ: I'm *nine*teen! Nineteen, and two to go! Are you ready?

ALLEN: No!

KATZ: Well, *get* ready!

ALLEN: All my life, they treated me like a sideshow freak . . .

KATZ: I bought your old check for ten bucks . . . what does that make *me?*

ALLEN: Then they toss you out like ashes . . . you scatter . . . you blow around . . . you disappear. I don't want to disappear.

KATZ: Too late for that, Mr. Allen . . . I couldn't get a nickel for your autograph now. Nobody would know who you were . . . too late . . . (*Katz dribbles ball up-court. Allen screams.*)

ALLEN: No! (*Katz fakes to the left and dribbles right. Allen dives after the ball and falls. Katz looks at the fallen older man and smiles. He stops and watches a moment as Allen weeps, then he drives in to the basket, up and in: scores. Allen stops weeping and faces him.*)

KATZ: (*Cooly walking to half-court line.*) One to go, Mr. Allen. Just one. (*Throws ball to Allen.*) Touch. (*Allen catches the ball and stands: his attitude changed, icy. He throws the ball back to Katz, fast and hard.*)

ALLEN: Come on.

KATZ: I'm comin', Pop . . . (*Katz dribbles out; Allen moves in to guard him. Katz fights bravely, but Allen steals the ball, turns, drives, scores.*)

ALLEN: Nine?

KATZ: Yuh. Twenty to nine . . .

ALLEN: (*Moves to half-court. He throws ball to Katz.*) Touch. (*Katz throws it back to Allen: nods. Allen drives, scores. Katz is perspiring.*) Ten. (*Throws ball to Katz.*) Touch. (*Katz returns ball. Allen moves out, drives, scores.*) Eleven . . . Touch . . . (*Allen lopes back to half-court and waits for Katz to throw ball to him. As soon as Katz does, Allen takes it out, leaps, scores.*) Twelve . . . (*Allen dribbles to half-court, smiles; throws ball to Katz, who throws it back and nods. Allen dribbles out to Katz, who dives in hard for ball. Allen lifts ball, Katz flies on to his stomach on the ground. Allen waits for Katz to rise and dive for ball again. Katz does. Allen again raises ball, allowing Katz to fall again. Allen walks to basket, dribbling ball slowly in front of him, scores. Katz is weeping. Allen moves to half-court line, Katz rises, faces Allen.*)

KATZ: Thirteen . . .

ALLEN: Touch. (*Throws ball to Katz, who whips it straight back to*

Allen, who takes one step forward, leaps up, shoots a one-hand push shot, scores. Allen then steps back one step to half court line and waits for Katz to retrieve the ball.) Ball. (*Katz turns, walks to ball, picks it up, tosses it to Allen, who tosses it straight back, wordlessly. Katz, in turn, tosses it back to Allen, who drives straight past Katz and scores again.*) Twenty-fifteen.

KATZ: Let's go . . . (*Allen and Katz face each other, as Katz fights for the ball. He succeeds in stopping Allen's drive, but Allen turns suddenly and shoots a smooth hook shot, bouncing the ball not near the basket, but instead violently off the backboard proper, causing the ball to bounce straight back to Allen, who turns quickly around, catches the ball and shoots an easy one hand push shot. A startled Katz watches, mouth dropped open, eyes wide.*)

ALLEN: Sixteen. (*Allen retrieves ball, jogs back to halfcourt line, smiles. He tosses ball to Katz, who touches it with a slap and tosses it back to Allen.*)

KATZ: Go!

ALLEN: Nervous?

KATZ: Yuh. Sure. You bet. Let's go, okay?

ALLEN: Yuh. Sure. You bet. Okay . . . (*Allen dribbles ball out, slowly. Katz moves in front of him, cautiously. Katz suddenly lunges and steals the ball. Allen rolls between Katz and the basket. Katz leaps to make a jump shot. Allen leaps to guard the shot. Katz does not shoot, but instead holds the ball, committing a "traveling" penalty. Wordlessly, Katz tosses the ball back to Allen and play resumes. Allen moves back to the halfcourt line, tosses the ball to Katz, who touches same and tosses it back to Allen, who nods and begins his move forward again, toward the basket. Katz tries the identical lunge and fake that worked before. This time, Allen lifts the ball, Katz stumbles through and Allen rolls to his left, drives in to the basket, shoots: scores.*)

KATZ: DAMMIT!

ALLEN: (*Smiles.*) Nice try.

KATZ: Thanks.

ALLEN: Good move.

KATZ: Right. Thanks.

ALLEN: Just shouldn't try it twice in a row . . .

KATZ: Yuh. Right.

ALLEN: Seventeen. Four to go . . . (*Tosses ball to Katz.*) Touch. (*Katz returns ball.*) Thanks. (*Allen nods, steps forward, shoots, scores, nods, tosses ball to Katz.*) Touch. (*Katz bows his head, weeps. Allen looks at him.*) You want to stop?

KATZ: *God damn you! God . . . damn . . . you!!!*

ALLEN: You didn't answer me, Katz. Do you want to stop?

KATZ: What for?

ALLEN: Call it a draw?

KATZ: (*Throws ball violently to Allen.*) Eighteen, you: twenty, me. Play!

ALLEN: Okay . . . (*He steps forward and shoots an easy long one-hand push shot that swishes in for a score.*) Nineteen. Ball, please? (*Katz turns and retrieves ball. He bounces it to Allen.*)

KATZ: You ever play with your son?

ALLEN: With Bobby? (*Pauses.*) Not too much, no.

KATZ: He's not too much, sportswise, is he?

ALLEN: I don't know. I haven't seen him much . . . He was smoking cigarettes, I guess. Drugs, probably . . . (*Pauses.*) Naw, he's not too much, sportswise. I guess that's true . . .

KATZ: Kinda' strange, isn't it? His father being who he is: you . . . all that . . . you'd figure he'd be more than he is . . . sportswise.

ALLEN: Maybe that's the way it is, with fathers and sons . . . maybe that's just natural.

KATZ: What did *your* father do? For a living, I mean . . .

ALLEN: Yuh. I see what you mean.

KATZ: You didn't answer me.

ALLEN: What he did?

KATZ: Yuh.

ALLEN: I figured you knew.

KATZ: Why would I ask then?

ALLEN: He coached junior high basketball.

KATZ: Yuh. You were right. I knew.

ALLEN: He wasn't *my* coach.

KATZ: How come?

ALLEN: He wasn't alive . . . when I started playing . . . seriously.

KATZ: How'd he die?

ALLEN: You know something, Irving? The relationship of father and son isn't exactly *planned.* I mean, I didn't *pick* Bobby. He was what *came along.*

KATZ: You believe that?

ALLEN: Yuh, I believe that. I know guys I've played with . . . pro players . . . their sons are decent . . . some of them play ball . . . some of them don't . . . but they're not all ashamed of their fathers, ya' know. And plenty of them are divorced, too!

KATZ: The sons? Divorced? Early isn't it? Little kids getting divorced? Sounds strange. Weird.

ALLEN: I always heard Jews had the brains . . .

KATZ: Yuh. You got it. Brains, money and big noses: that's what we've got . . .

ALLEN: I've never met a kid as smart as you are. That's a fact.

KATZ: How's my game?

ALLEN: Pro-level potential.

KATZ: How do I rate against you at age fourteen?

ALLEN: Even.

KATZ: I'll have to work harder . . .

ALLEN: It must have been something for you, huh? When your father . . . died. It must really taken the wind out of your sails.

KATZ: I don't have sails.

ALLEN: Three years now, right?

KATZ: Four years, four months, six days . . . (*Looks at watch.*) . . . six hours. (*Looks at Allen.*) I don't think about it much. What the hell, right? The worms crawl in, the worms crawl out. What's to think about?

ALLEN: What's your mother like?

KATZ: Nice. What's your's like? (*Pauses.*) You lookin' to set up a trade or somethin'?

ALLEN: Were you real close with your father?

KATZ: You gonna' play, or you losing your nerve?

ALLEN: Were you?

KATZ: What's goin' on here, huh? Is this a game, or what?

ALLEN: Were you?

KATZ: He was thirty-eight; fat; never even watched sports on television, let alone play them. He went to work at seven in the morning and he came home around ten at night. I'd wait up every night just to hear him say "What's'a matter with you, Irving? It's ten'a'clock and you got school t'morrow? You wanna' end up sellin' black bean soup like your father? You wanna' end up cryin' day and night like your mother?" (*Looks at Allen: smiles.*) My mother has emotional problems. She cries a lot. Since my father got shot in the neck, she only cries from seven in the morning 'til ten at night. She use'ta go 'round the clock. She's getting better. (*Pauses.*) I don't wanna' end up with the black bean soup and I don't wanna' end up cryin' round the clock . . . and I don't wanna' end up like you. I don't like any of the choices here . . . (*Pauses.*) I use'ta' wanna' end up like you. That's a fact.

ALLEN: You're your own man, Irving.

KATZ: (*Interrupting sharply.*) I'm my own birdturd. Irving! *OOOooooo!!!* How come you turned out ta' be such a nothing, huh? How come you turned out ta' be such a *whining nothin'? OOOOOoooooo-Ooooooo!!!* You got all the yah-tah-duh yah-tah-duh *sincere* crap look in your eyes, like I'm s'pose'ta' feel *sorry for you!* Bad break, huh? Your game just sort'a fell to nothin', right? I'm s'pose'ta' feel sorry for that! Your lunatic son empties a gun into my father's neck and gets to walk around the neighborhood like he's a hero and I'm some sorta' jerk for havin' no father and *you* want *me* to feel sorry that *it hurts you!* (*Screams.*) *I'M SORRYYYYYYYeeeeeee!!!* (*Softer.*) You bet your ass Jews are smarter. I just wish we were *taller,* that's the truth. Then we'd have it all! *ALL!* (*There is a short silence during which the two men look at one another. Katz breaks the silence, softly. His attitude changes.*) I wanna' finish this game now, okay? (*Throws ball to Allen.*) Your move. (*Allen nods. He starts out with the ball, fades to his left and intentionally knocks ball toward Katz, who catches it and tosses it back to Allen, fiercely.*) Don't you ever – *ever!* – boot a ball in my direction, pal. I got my points on you *straight* and I'm gonna' beat you straight. *You . . . hear . . . me???* Shoot! (*Allen pauses, aims, shoots, hits.*)

ALLEN: Even up.

KATZ: (*Softly.*) Yuh.

ALLEN: You wanna' throw fingers 'ta see who takes it out? (*Pauses.*) Counta' it's tied and my height advantage and all . . .

KATZ: (*Softly.*) I wouldn't mind.

ALLEN: Throw two out'ta' three?

KATZ: (*Nods.*) Call it.

ALLEN: Odds.

KATZ: Once, twice, three, shoot! (*They do.*) Mine. Once, twice, three, shoot! (*They do.*) I'll take it out. (*Katz dribbles the ball to the halfcourt line. He offers the ball to Allen.*) Touch.

ALLEN: Ready. (*Allen tosses the ball back to Katz, one bounce. Katz holds the ball in one hand, wipes his other hand on his pant leg;*

then switches hands and wipes the hold hand; then his brow; then he places his hair behind his ears: he nods. Katz dribbles the ball out and fakes left. Allen rolls with him. Katz rolls quickly right; Allen drifts off-balance. Katz charges around and straight to a point underneath the basket. he could easily sink a basket, but he doesn't. Instead, he faces Allen.)

KATZ: (*He tosses the ball to Allen; starts to exit. Stops.*) I changed my mind. I don't wanna' win this way. I wanna' win it straight. I don't want you spottin' me no 15 points . . . no 5, or nothin' really. I wanna' win it straight . . . start it even. (*Pause.*) I'll give you a rematch exactly ten years from now, okay? (*Pauses.*) I'll be taller. You'll be fifty (*Nota Bene: adjust to correct age of Allen.*) . . . (*Allen tosses the ball to him. He tosses it straight back at Allen.*) Keep it. Practice. The more you practice, the better you get. (*Two steps backwards, closer to exit.*) I'll be twenty-four. Right here. June 5th. (*Nota Bene: insert date of performance here in place of June 5th, except on June 5th.*) . . . 2 o'clock . . . (*Pauses.*) You ought to wear better shoes. you won't slip so much . . . (*Two more steps backwards: edge of stage.*) You won't forget, okay? . . . (*Allen stares at Katz.*) You'll be here, right? (*Allen nods agreement.*) You got it. (*Katz turns and exits the play. Allen bows his head a moment. Silence. Allen looks at basketball in his hand. He moves to a position under the net. He tosses in a lay-up. He looks at the ball in his hands. He tosses in another lay-up, catches the ball as it passes out of the net, and tosses in another lay-up. Slowly, at first; the rhythm of Allen's hops, shots, catches and hops increases until it is machinelike: perfect. He moans a long low moan, softly at first, growing increasingly sonorous. All sound stops: the shots continue. he hops, lays the ball in the basket – one bounce off the backboard each time – catches the ball as it passes through the net, hops; starts it all again. Except for the sound of the ball against the backboard and its passing through the hoop and net, and the sound of Allen's movement and breathing, there is silence. The lights fade out.*)

THE PLAY IS OVER.

HOPSCOTCH

For Paul Simon

HOPSCOTCH had its first public performance in April 1974, at the Théâtre du Centre Culturel Américain, Paris, France, by invitation of the United States State Department, in an English-language production that was directed by the author, with the following cast:

ELSA (a/k/a Lorali) .... Swoosie Kurtz
WILL (a/k/a Earl).. Lenny Baker

Rehearsals for the French premiere of HOPSCOTCH were located at the Manhattan Theatre Club, New York City, where staged readings of the play were offered to MTC subscribers.

In March 1978, the New York premiere of HOPSCOTCH was produced by the New York Shakespeare Festival, New York City, produced by Joseph Papp. Woods Mackintosh designed the sets; Jennifer von Mayrhauser designed the costumes; the director was Jack Hofsiss; and the cast was as follows:

ELSA (a/k/a Lorali) .... Mary Beth Hurt
WILL (a/k/a Earl).. John Heard

Introduction

Hopscotch was written almost immediately after Thornton Wilder's cryptic comment to me in reaction to my 7-play cycle, *The Wakefield Plays*: "Of course, there isn't very much Wakefield in those plays."

More than anything else, I wanted to write a play that would capture the spirit and sound of Wakefield, Massachusetts. I drove from NYC to my parents' house in Wakefield, set my typewriter up in my father's office, and began my work. Instead of delving into Greek myth, as I had with my *Alfred Trilogy*, I delved into my own particular history.

I decided to write a group of short plays to frame the long-winded *Alfred* plays. I, thus, began with *Hopscotch*, and with details of my own life in Wakefield, Massachusetts.

Let me pause for a moment to state, simply and clearly, that *nobody's* life—certainly not mine—is ipso-facto, word for word, stageworthy. In the end, we must improve almost everything we live, before opening the curtain. What we call Realism has very little to do with what we call Reality. Recently, I wrote a film for Warner Brothers, based on the action-packed life of the actor James Dean. It was quite striking to me to realize that, even when dealing with a life as compressed and as passionate as James Dean's life, large amounts of passion and compression had to be created to make the story coherent and dramatic...to make the thing work.

Back to *Hopscotch*, Wakefield, and Real Life...When I was 17, my 16-year-old girlfriend got pregnant. We asked our parents for advice. They organized a Rabbi and wedding service (in my parents' living room) within a week. Six months later, the child was born—a boy—with hopelessly malformed lungs. The child struggled and gasped for eleven days, and then, he died. Our parents bought a small, concrete casket, and arranged to have the boy buried in an unmarked grave.

I sensed that many adults around my wife and me were somehow relieved that the Sin was erased.

We stayed married for a few months, but, neither of us seemed to know why. One night, we slept apart...I, with friends; she, with her parents. I don't recall having an argument. When I went back to our apartment, the next day, her parents had emptied it of anything that could have possibly been called "hers." She and all evidence of her ever being there was, in a word, gone.

My father, a new and enthusiastic lawyer, arranged for our marriage to be annulled. "What does that mean?" I asked. My father explained that annulment was a way of legally wiping the marriage from the record books...as though it never happened. The marriage disappeared...simply, swiftly, legally. I don't recall ever discussing the matter with my father, prior to his magic trick.

My writing *Hopscotch* was a way of bringing the marriage back into the books. It was only fitting (and dramatic) that I would travel hundreds of miles to my parents' home, to sit and write this painful play.

Hopscotch is full of imagined detail. I won't attempt to make a list of what's true and what's false in the play, as I am no doubt unqualified, except to say that I did and do clearly recall my legally-non-ex-non-wife saying to me "I wish you were dead!". The circumstance surrounding her wish was her telephone call to me, several weeks after we'd been annulled, to tell me that she was once again pregnant. She told me that she was certain the child was mine. I answered, quickly, saying that I would send money to her, but, that I did not want to be married to her, again. She then said "I wish you were dead!" ...which I now realize was a generous, liberating act on her part...a gift of freedom. Had she instead said "Don't give up on me" or, "I'll call you in a couple of weeks to see if you've changed your mind", *Hopscotch* would be quite a different play. (For the record books, she married a law student, shortly after her child was born. I was asked to sign adoption papers, which I did, obviously, do. From all reports, 35 years later, mother, father, child are all doing well.)

Thus, *Hopscotch* rings of something terrible and true. And yes, I know, it is really awful how we artists take events from our lives, launder them, reshape them, and hang them, flagrantly, on a most public clothes-line. For what it's worth, I do apologize.

Hopscotch is dedicated to my old pal Paul Simon. Paul's song "Was A Sunny Day" was as much an inspiration for *Hopscotch* as was all of the above. "Her name was Lorali...She was his only girl...She called him Speedoo, but, his Christian name was Mr. Earl!" ...If you're anything close to my age, and you're still, like, cool, you know all the hidden references. Popular music is so incredibly important in our lives. It locates us in a time, in a place. I remember so many sweet and sour teenage kisses in vivid images from whatever song was playing on the radio, or in my head, at the moment of contact. And I do also remember, ever so happily, Paul's thrill when he first saw *Hopscotch* on stage...when he first saw a song of his come to life through my particular kind of magic act. He told me, recently, that he and our friend Derek Walcott are writing a musical, together. I'm sure it will be great. And I'm also sure that *Hopscotch* in no small way inspired Paul to write for the theatre.

The production Paul saw was courtesy of the late and great Joseph Papp. Papp produced *Hopscotch* at the New York Shakespeare Festival in 1978, during a time when I was not allowing critics to review my plays. Mary Beth Hurt and John Heard starred in a sublime production, directed by Jack Hoffsiss. The word got around NYC, quickly, that Hurt and Heard were *magnifique*, and our theatre was packed, every night. Without benefit of reviews or hype, *Hopscotch* quietly took its place among those American plays that get done and done and done. *Hopscotch* has been translated and played in some twenty languages, around the world. I directed a French-language production, in Paris, last season, and I've been told of upcoming productions in Rome, Stockholm, and Munich...as well as countless productions at home.

For better or worse, til death do us part, we are in the books.

Characters

ELSA Calls herself Lorali, thirtyish, youthful body, blonde hair, fair.

WILL Calls himself Earl, thirtyish, tall, dark-haired, dark-complexioned, thin.

Setting

Park playground, overlooking Lake Quannapowitt, Wakefield, Mass. September, sunny afternoon.

AUTHOR'S NOTE

There are four related plays of which *Hopscotch* and *The 75th* are two, that are designed to be performed in a rotating repertory of two double-bills, under the umbrella-title *The Quannapowitt Quartet.* The title refers to Lake Quannapowitt in Wakefield, Massachusetts, the shared setting of all four plays.

The other two quartet plays are *Stage Directions* and *Spared*, which should be performed in their own evening or bill, in that order. *Stage Directions* is meant to precede *Spared* on the alternate evening or bill.

A company of just three performers may be sufficient to play the entire quartet. I am especially interested in the possibility of the performers who play *Hopscotch* also playing *The 75th.*

Scenic elements designed for all four plays should be in themselves minimal with maximum attention given over instead to the design of lighting and sound effects.

Finally, the entire quartet is related to the trilogy, *The Wakefield Plays:* part one, *Alfred the Great*; part two, *Our Father's Failing*, and part three, *Alfred Dies.* If the seven plays were ever to be played in cycle, they would occupy five evenings: the first, *Hopscotch* and *The 75th*; the second, *Alfred the Great*; the third, *Our Father's Failing*; the fourth, *Alfred Dies*, and the fifth, *Stage Directions* and *Spared.*

HOPSCOTCH

Lights out in auditorium.
Music fades in.
Lights fade up.
Asphalt patch, small park playground.
Small traditional green park bench, baby-carriage set at bench's outermost corner, facing Upstage.
Elsa is discovered, drawing hopscotch grid on asphalt with yellow chalk. She marks the work "HOME."
She throws a pebble into the first square and hops to it, picks it up, continues hopping to end of grid, turns, returns to starting position: her game has begun.
Music plays to completion.
As Elsa plays, we sense she is bothered by something or someone Offstage, beyond auditorium.
As music fades out, Elsa calls out into and above auditorium.

ELSA: You like what you're seein'? (*No response. She returns to her game. When she reaches the end of the grid, she turns, stops, calls out again.*) Hey, c'mon now, will ya'! If yo're gonna' gawk, gawk from where I can gawk back! Fair's fair! (*No response.*) I'll turn my back, I won't watch. You can either come out and show yourself . . . or go away . . . (*Pause, calls louder.*) Either's way okay with me! You gotta' do one or the other, okay? (*She turns her back to auditorium. A moment of silence passes. A young man, Will, appears in auditorium. He will stop a moment and then walk swiftly and directly on to stage, directly to Elsa. He will never alter his course, once he begins to move to her. She turns, sees him. She is obviously frightened.*) I'm not frightened, you know . . . (*Will continues his move to her.*) This place is crawling with people, you know that? (*Elsa is frozen in fear. Will continues to move to her.*) You better just back down, huh? This place is crawling with people . . . I mean there's no danger here, right? . . . (*Will reaches Elsa. He takes her in his arms and kisses her on the lips. She is overwhelmed by his size and acquiesces, at first, to his embrace and kiss. She then responds with noticeable strength and emotion. They hold their kiss a while. They break apart, holding a fixed stare between them.*) That was a good one . . . (*She smiles.*)

Strong silent type, huh?

WILL: (*Looking at baby carriage.*) Where's the baby?

ELSA: (*After a substantial pause.*) Playing. Why?

WILL: Yours?

ELSA: Sure. (*She throws the pebble and begins her hopscotch game again.*)

WILL: Where's your husband? Working?

ELSA: It's daytime, isn't it? (*Points to sky.*) That big round bright thing up there's the sun. When you can see it, you can pretty much figure it's daytime. And when it's daytime, people are working . . . (*Smiles.*) *Most* people.

WILL: This what you do for a living?

ELSA: (*Smiles.*) Naw. Not yet. I'm not turning pro 'til after the next Olympics . . . (*She throws pebble again and plays. Will sits and watches a moment.*) You married?

WILL: Me? Naw.

ELSA: Ever close?

WILL: To being married? (*Pauses.*) Naw. Not even close.

ELSA: How come?

WILL: I looked around me. All my married friends were spending their weekends playin' softball. Their wives were home spending their weekends complaining about bein' left alone . . . while their husbands were playin' softball.

ELSA: That's why?

WILL: Sure. I hate softball. All's I needed was to get married and hav'ta' start bullshit like *that!* You know what I mean? (*He smiles.*)

ELSA: You've got a lot a charm and a wonderful sense of humor.

WILL: You noticed?

ELSA: MMMmmm. I never miss a trick. (*She begins to play again.*)

WILL: I see you waited . . .

ELSA: For what?

WILL: Babies. (*She looks at him, suddenly. He nods to carriage.*) I could tell from the age. Still in a carriage and all.

ELSA: Oh, yuh. I waited. (*She smiles.*)

WILL: Boy or girl?

ELSA: Well, now. It's gotta' be one or the other, right?

WILL: Nine chances out'ta' ten, yuh.

ELSA: Girl.

WILL: Name?

ELSA: Lorali.

WILL: How's that again?

ELSA: Lorali.

WILL: That's pretty. Yours? (*He is staring into carriage, lost in a memory.*)

ELSA: (*Stops, looks at him.*) My name? (*He smiles.*) The same: Lorali. (*She resumes play.*) I'm Lorali the 2nd, she's Lorali the 3rd. My grandmother was Lorali and my mother was Lorali, Junior . . . (*Smiles.*) Very common name around these parts.

WILL: No kidding. I never heard it in my life before, now I hear of four of them . . . And in a jerk town like Wakefield, too . . .

ELSA: Very well-known and very well-respected name, too . . .

WILL: Around these parts, huh? (*Stands.*) Wakefield, Massachusetts, United States of America, North America, Western Hemisphere, Earth, Universe, Infinity . . . (*Smiles.*) I'm very deep.

ELSA: Oh yuh. So's the lake.

WILL: What da'ya' call it?

ELSA: The lake?

WILL: Yuh. The lake.

ELSA: Janet. I call it Janet. See these shoes? (*Points to her shoes.*) These are the twins. (*Nods to bench.*) The bench is Nanny Mary Poppins and you are what we see of Silver as he rides off into the sunset: a horse's ass! (*Stops, controls her anger by turning away from him.*) *Unbelievable!* (*Faces him again.*) Lake Quannapowitt. Named for the local Indians . . . a tribe that vanished.

WILL: Oh, right . . . I forgot . . . (*Silence. Ten count.*)

ELSA: You wanna' know about my husband?

WILL: Sure. What does he do for a living? Break backs?

ELSA: Naw. Not for a living; he just breaks backs as a weekend hobby kind of thing . . .

WILL: He sounds nice . . .

ELSA: He's a minister.

WILL: No kidding?

ELSA: No kidding.

WILL: What kind of minister?

ELSA: Protestant.

WILL: A Protestant minister. You don't say? What denomination?

ELSA: Baptist. (*Pauses.*) Blonde. (*Pauses.*) Blue eyes. Both of them . . . (*Pauses.*) Six-five-and-a-half . . . (*Pauses.*) Square jaw, thick neck . . . (*Pauses.*) He's a hunk.

WILL: He is?

ELSA: Mmmm . . .

WILL: Of what?

ELSA: Huh?

WILL: A hunk of what?

ELSA: (*Resumes her game.*) You just passing through . . . or are you planning to set up a business here? (*Smiles.*) Hey! Maybe pizza. Wakefieldians eat a hell of a lot of pizza. Santoro hit it big with subs. Maybe you could be pizza! A pizza-place with a real gimmick could be a real hot-shit success!

WILL: Anybody ever tell you you've got a mouth like a toilet?

ELSA: Oh, yuh. Couple'a'guys. They didn't get too far with me, though . . . not with an obvious line like that. (*Smiles.*) You know . . . maybe a quick feel, but nowhere solid. (*Pauses.*) I've never been a sucker for an obvious come-on line. I like something more subtle . . .

WILL: A gun, a knife? That sort of thing?

ELSA: No. Uh uh. (*Smiles.*) Money's more what I had in mind.

WILL: (*After pretending to fish in his pockets.*) Jees, . . . what a shame! (*Smiles.*) I used all my spare change on the train from North Station. . .

ELSA: Hey, well, listen! You can't win 'em all! I had a guy here just the other afta'noon . . . a real blowah' . . . real bullshit ah'tist-type, ya' know . . . he tried to pay me with magic beans . . .

WILL: No kidding?

ELSA: No kidding.

WILL: Was he youngish?

ELSA: Yuh, youngish . . .

WILL: Sho't?

ELSA: Yuh. Wicked sho't. Nearly teensy . . .

WILL: Was he leading a cow on a rope?

ELSA: That's him!

WILL: Never heard of 'im!

ELSA: You do night work, huh?

WILL: Huh?

ELSA: You work anywhere?

WILL: Yuh. I work.

ELSA: What kind:

WILL: I work for a big company . . . construction.

ELSA: Oh, really? You construct things?

WILL: Me, personally? Nope. Opposite. I tear things down. I'm in the destruction end . . . wrecking.

ELSA: Gee, it, well, sounds like you've done really well with yourself . . . very successful. (*Pauses.*) Wrecking, huh? (*Pauses.*) They pay you a lot of money to do that?

WILL: Money? Sure, well . . .

ELSA: Sounds like it took a lot of schooling . . .

WILL: Schooling? Well, I . . .

ELSA: You have a big desk? . . .

WILL: C'mon . . .

ELSA: . . . a big *position?*

WILL: You s'posed'ta' be *cute* now or somethin'?

ELSA: Me? Cute? Uh-uh.

WILL: (*Forces a calm pitch to his voice.*) I have a middle-sized position . . . middle management, they call us. (*Smiles.*) It's a middle-sized position.

ELSA: Do you like it?

WILL: (*Yells.*) *My position? Do I like my middle-sized position???* (*There is an embarrassed pause.*) I'm still wicked awful tired from traveling. My nerves are all edgy . . .

ELSA: Don't sweat it. (*Hops.*) I can understand that . . . (*Pauses.*) I meant "the town."

WILL: Huh?

ELSA: When I asked "Do you like it?": I meant "Do you like the town?" (*Smiles.*) Being here.

WILL: Oh, I get'cha'. You wanted to know if I liked being here. (*Smiles.*) I love it.

ELSA: I figured you did. (*Stops.*) Most everybody here was born here . . .

WILL: Really? . . .

ELSA: . . . And stayed! (*Pauses.*) You know what I mean?

WILL: Your parents? Are they still . . .?

ELSA: My parents, are they still? Sure. Still as they come. (*Smiles.*) Two days apart. (*Pauses.*) Happens.

WILL: I was gonna' ask about their house and all . . . I never even guessed . . .

ELSA: *That* happens, too . . .

WILL: How long ago?

ELSA: How long ago what?

WILL: How long ago did you lose them?

ELSA: Lose them? (*Pauses.*) You mean, like in Filene's Basement . . . You make it sound as though I were careless! (*Pretends to be talking to third person.*) Excuse me, but I seem to have lost my parents . . . (*To Will again, timbre of voice suddenly changed.*) Last month. Four weeks ago. You just missed the excitement . . . the hustle and the bustle . . .

WILL: I'm sorry . . .

ELSA: Don't be.

WILL: I am . . . I really am.

ELSA: Long time comin'. Just as well . . .

WILL: I'm really very sorry to find out . . .

ELSA: Yuh, I was, too . . . (*Looks directly at Will.*) I'm not scared of you at all anymore, not at all. So just don't get that into your head, okay? (*Resumes playing hopscotch.*) I used to hate boys . . . (*Pauses, throws pebble.*) I grew up . . . (*Hops, stops.*) Things changed. (*Hops, stops.*) Now I hate men. (*She smiles.*)

WILL: His heart?

ELSA: Huh?

WILL: Your father. Was it his heart?

ELSA: What do *you* think?

WILL: And your mother? She was sick long, too?

ELSA: Take a wild guess . . .

WILL: (*Angrily.*) *Aren't you getting tired of this???*

ELSA: *Where . . . have . . . you . . . been???*

WILL: I . . . dunno' . . .

ELSA: That out'a state? (*Pauses.*) I don't hear an answer!

WILL: Newport News.

ELSA: Where's that?

WILL: Virginia.

ELSA: What'd'ya wreck there? Men? Women? Bunch'a kids?

WILL: Navy yard. Tore it down.

ELSA: (*After a pause, she stops the game.*) He had his heart attack, finally. Waited long enough, worryin' . . .(*Pauses.*) Shot out'ta' his chair like he'd be'n kicked by a mule . . . watching Miss America.

WILL: Were you there?

ELSA: Sure.

WILL: That must'a frightened you.

ELSA: I don't know. I s'pose . . .

WILL: Your husband?

ELSA: What about him?

WILL: Was he . . . with you? . . . then?

ELSA: Then? No. Just me.

WILL: And your mother?

ELSA: On display. Being waked. In the living room.

WILL: Oh . . . I see. (*Walks to her.*) And you were . . . alone, huh?

ELSA: That's what I said, right? You've got yourself a sho't-memory problem, don'tcha? (*Throws the pebble, hops to it.*) You know who won? You maybe know her. (*Pauses, no reply.*) Miss Virginia. A brunette with mushy big brown eyes, a wicked dumb drawl, mouth always open real slutty-like, and a pair of tits shot, no doubt about it, full of sand . . .

WILL: C'mon . . .

ELSA: Your type . . .

WILL: Don't be vulgar!

ELSA: But I am! Born vulgar, grow up vulgar, die vulgar; it's kinda' a tradition around here . . . among those who stay and miss out on the sophistication of world travel . . . (*Pauses, then quietly.*) Must be nice. (*No reply.*) Your life.

WILL: (*Smiles.*) It's the greatest.

ELSA: You speak any languages?

WILL: Je's, I thought' I'd be'n doin' it since I got here . . . fact is, I thought we'd both be'n!

ELSA: (*Flat, childish reading.*) Ho. Ho ho. Ho ho ho. Some rapid fire slashing wit, ya' got there! (*Pauses, throws pebble.*) Foreign tongues is what I meant.

WILL: Nope. You?

ELSA: What'da' *you* care?

WILL: I don't. I really don't.

ELSA: I know. I really know.

WILL: You ever be'n out'ta'here? Out'ta' Wakefield?

ELSA: Too happy ta' wanna' leave! Everything I'll ever want is right here . . . right in Wakefield . . . squashed in between Reading, Stoneham, Greenwood and Lynnfield . . . (*Smiles.*) Everything I'll ever need is right here. Always be'n, too . . . (*Pauses.*) Everythin' else is bullshit. That's the way I see it.

WILL: You finish college?

ELSA: (*After a long pause, quietly.*) Nope . . . never started.

WILL: How come?

ELSA: I was busy!

WILL: Oh, yeah? Doin' what?

ELSA: You own anything?

WILL: You always answer questions with questions?

ELSA: I try to. Okay with you?

WILL: Fine with me. Sure.

ELSA: You own anything special?

WILL: What, exactly?

ELSA: How about weird belts? I always notice that men who travel around, like you do, get to wearin' a lot of weird belts . . . you know . . . hand-carved stuff . . . sometimes with studs . . . the kind quee-ahs sometimes wear . . . (*She smiles.*) You know what I mean? (*There is a long pause. Will slowly lifts his shirt and displays his waist to her. There is no belt around his waist.*) You've lost weight. You're skinny.

WILL: I'm not skinny. I'm thin. You get tired of airport food. You don't eat. You get thin. . .

ELSA: I used'ta'be skinny, 'til high school. I got a big stomach in high school. (*Pauses.*) Sometimes I used to wake up worrying, in the middle of the night. Sometimes I used to wake up maybe two or even three times a night. (*Pauses.*) I used to have to go into the bathroom. We had a full-length mirror on the door. I use'ta' stand in front of it and hoist up my nightgown, about to my chin, and stare at my stomach. (*Pauses.*) It really worried me a hell of a lot! It sort'a . . . well . . . it sort of ruined me, you might say. My twirling. (*Pauses.*) I used to twirl. I was very good at it. Some people used to think I could twirl wicked . . . I still could . . . if I had to. (*Pauses.*) You're pretty weird, you know that?

WILL: Do we *have* to???

ELSA: I'm gonna' be thirty soon. Next month . . .

WILL: You look younger . . .

ELSA: Yuh, that's what they tell me . . . (*Stops, looks at him.*) You ever be'n anywhere that you actually thought was . . . you know . . . exciting" Worth stayin' at, maybe?

WILL: I guess . . .

ELSA: Someplace where you might send somebody like me?

WILL: You might like cities . . .

ELSA: I've seen cities!

WILL: It's indigenous.

ELSA: What's that supposed to mean?

WILL: Indigenous? "Peculiar to."

ELSA: I'm not stupid!

WILL: I never said you were!

ELSA: You travel a lot, huh?

WILL: Sure, wherever they have a big demolition job, I have to go there first and estimate the costs . . .

ELSA: Sounds really crappy.

WILL: It's pretty bad. (*Pauses.*) Do you think I'm dull?

ELSA: Yes. I really do.

WILL: I don't talk to people much.

ELSA: It does show a little, yuh. (*She throws pebble, plays a while, stops. She turns to him.*) Here's a fact about me you probably missed: did you know that I was very nearly Miss America?

WILL: C'm'off it, will ya'?

ELSA: It's true! (*Pauses.*) I came really close. I did! (*Pauses.*) I twirled for my specialty.

WILL: How close?

ELSA: Very. (*Pauses.*) Fourth. (Pauses.) State runoffs . . .

WILL: You get any money? (*No reply.*) What did you get?

ELSA: (*Suddenly angry again.*) You've got no right to just come around and stare at people and start up all sorts of bullshit, ya' know!!! (*Pauses.*) What the hell do you think ya' get for fourth in the goddamn state runoffs!??? (*More softly now.*) I got nothing.

WILL: I bet you were cute.

ELSA: (*Carefully.*) *The things . . . they . . . promise . . . you.* (*Silence.*)

WILL: I've personally always found twirlers to be . . . you know . . . a little *stupid*, but . . . you know . . . stimulating. (*She looks up. He smiles.*) It's true! It always turned me on. Maybe it's the way you fingered the aluminum stick . . .

ELSA: Thanks a lot.

WILL: But it's true! You are! (*She looks at him, tight-lipped.*) Cute. (*He smiles.*) You're more than that. You're really pretty . . . beautiful.

ELSA: (*Looks at him, directly.*) You got feelings like the side of a hill, you know that?

WILL: I keep hearin' that. Yuh.

ELSA: Did it ever occur to you that I might be special?

WILL: Special? (*Smiles.*) Never. (*Pauses.*) Not at all.

ELSA: I do a lot of special things . . . I have special talents . . .

WILL: Like what? Acrobatic dancing? Musical saw: (*Looks at hopscotch grid.*) Oh, *this* you mean . . .

ELSA: I'm good at voices. Especially on the telephone. (*Smiles.*) You ever make any dirty phone calls?

WILL: A few. Maybe twenty, thirty. That's about it.

ELSA: I mean really *filthy* phone calls. The kind you don't even read about . . . The kind you just sort of muse over . . . Really *filthy* phone calls . . .

WILL: Oh, I thought you just meant *dirty* phone calls. Filthies? Oh, sure I guess I've done several hundred filthies . . . (*Pauses, adds quickly.*) This month!

ELSA: I did thirty-one straight days in a row.

WILL: I think I read about it.

ELSA: I called the butcher.

WILL: What the hell are you talkin' about anyway?

ELSA: I called the butcher. (*Pauses.*) Every time I used'ta walk by his butcher shop, he used'ta call out'ta me . . . usual things like "Hey blondie, you want some of my meat?" or "How about some nice loins, cutie?" That kind of thing. (*Smiles.*) I called him every night from the 1st of July right through til the 31st, inclusive. Gave *him* something to think about!

WILL: You like it?

ELSA: I loved it! (*Pauses, smiles.*) At first he was really made nervous, you know, by my language and all . . . but by the middle of the month . . . even earlier . . . by the 10th, or so, he'd calmed down really quite a lot. By the 20th, he'd worked it out to get his wife and family to stop picking up the phone. He worked it out most of the time to get them right out'ta the room! (*Pauses.*) He started whole conversations! (*Pauses; excited.*) You know what he said on July 28th?

WILL: If I knew, it's somehow slipped my mind!

ELSA: I love you.

WILL: What?

ELSA: (*After a pause.*) That's what he said: "Miss, I want you to know that I really love you." That's what he told me. I asked him if he wanted to meet me, but, all he wanted was my telephone number.

(*Nota Bene Following section to be played quickly.*)

WILL: C'mon, will you . . .

ELSA: It's true! He kept avoiding the question. He just kept asking for my number . . .

WILL: What time of day did you call him?

ELSA: What the hell kind of weird question is that?

WILL: I just wondered . . .

ELSA: Time of *night*. Five minutes to eleven . . . just before the news.

WILL: Every night?

ELSA: Religiously.

WILL: How could be get his family out of the room, every night, five to eleven?

ELSA: (*Smugly.*) *He was dedicated!*

WILL: *You're* the weird one here!

ELSA: How come you're all jittery?

WILL: Me?

ELSA: On the 31st, I walked into his shop and asked him if he liked my halter top . . . it was hot and I had a halter that was kinda' loose-fitting, wicked thin . . . no bra or anything . . . and shorts that were kinda' wrecked from bein' washed so much . . .you know . . . holey. (*Smiles.*) Nothin' underneath them, either . . . (*Pauses.*) He pretended he didn't know me. Even when I did the same sentences I did on the phone, over and over again to his face, he pretended he didn't know me. He said he'd have to call the cops if I didn't stop my dirty talk. Can you imagine? We were all alone in the shop . . . me, just talkin' the sentences over and over to his face. Him, standing there with his bloody hands and apron. A look of honest-to-God shock on his face!

WILL: (*Suddenly.*) This is an awful thing, but it's on my mind . . . I've forgotten your name!

ELSA: What?

WILL: I know it was pretty, but I can't remember it exactly . . . (*Pauses.*) I'm sorry.

ELSA: (*Furiously.*) What the hell do you want from me, anyway?

WILL: I don't want anything from you. It was a sunny day, I was walking, I saw you, I thought it might be interesting . . .

ELSA: Bullshit! You've be'n following me for a week now!

WILL: I saw you over here by yourself . . . hopping around like some kind of weird kind of retarded hooker, you know . . . and I estimated that it might be interesting . . .

ELSA: (*Interrupts.*) Drop dead!

WILL: (*Yells.*) . . . *to pick you up!*

ELSA: *Was it???*

WILL: *Was it what???*

ELSA: *WAS . . . IT . . . INTERESTING???*

WILL: (*After a long pause, softly.*) No. Not very. (*Pauses.*) Not *bad*. (*Pauses.*) You're not stupid. Just not very . . . (*Smiles.*) interesting.

(*She throws pebble and misses mark.*) You missed.

ELSA: I wasn't concentrating. (*She picks up pebble, throws it into square, hopping to it. Again and again, in succeeding squares. Will picks up her yellow chalk, writes "Elsa" quite visible on top slat of bench. Adds heart with arrow through it.*) It's Lorali. (*Spells the name aloud.*) L-O-R-A-L-I is the way we spell it.

WILL: I don't think that's correct. (*Smiles.*) Okay. I'm . . . Earl. Earl the Third. My grandfather and father were both Earls. (*Will writes "Earl" in large letters scrawled over her hopscotch grid. He suddenly grabs her and pulls her down on to the hopscotch field with him, pinning her arms behind her, holding her down to the ground with him. He yells angrily.*) I'm Earl the Third! (*Pauses.*) Maybe even Earl the Fourth! Who's keepin' score, huh? (*Screams.*) How about *Mister* Earl??? (*He forces her to kiss him.*) Is that any better?

ELSA: Let me up!

WILL: When I decide to!

ELSA: *YOU LET ME UP!!!* (*He kisses her again, roughly, forcing her into a somewhat docile state. Elsa is quite visibly shaken, frightened. Their difference in size is unquestionable. Will breaks the kiss.*)

WILL: Is that any better:

ELSA: Yuh. (*Quietly.*) Just what I've be'n waiting for. Must take a lot of courage to throw around somebody who's half your size.

WILL: I'm ready to hear about this frocked and collared husband of yours . . . (*Pauses.*) Do you two enjoy each other? (*No reply.*) I expect an answer here *please* . . .

ELSA: Yes, we do.

WILL: How? I'd really like to know how. Speak to me. Tell me . . . some of the good things you do together.

ELSA: You're hurting me!

WILL: Good . . .

ELSA: Son of a bitch!

WILL: C'mon, Lor-ah-*liar!* Let's hear what you and the Reverend do for your jollies! (*Leans even closer, bending over her.*) I'm really curious. (*Lets loose of her arm now.*) You're free. (*Sits back, watches, as she weeps.*) You gonna' tell us?

ELSA: (*Weeping.*) You've got no right . . . (*Pauses.*) Rides . . .

WILL: You say "rides?"

ELSA: We . . . take rides . . . together . . .

WILL: Horses?

ELSA: In our car. We take rides. That's what we do around here. We ride up one-twenty-eight to the shopping centers . . . up in Burlington . . . down in Peabody . . . usually after they're closed . . . we sit in our car and look at the outsides of the stores . . . (*Pauses.*) Everybody does it. (*She sobs a moment.*) We don't talk much. Hardly at all. If he died during the rides, we'd crash. If I died, nothing much would happen . . . (*She regains her composure.*) You've really got no right . . . no more . . . (*Pauses, then deep-throated, carefully.*) I . . . am . . . so . . . unhappy. (*There is a long pause.*)

WILL: (*Smiles.*) Is he a good driver?

ELSA: Who?

WILL: Your husband. Does he like trying new roads? Branching out . . . being . . . inquisitive?

ELSA: This isn't fair . . .

WILL: What is it? I'd really like to give it a try . . .

ELSA: What are you talking about?

WILL: Your number. What is it? I'll give you a ring, huh? Here. Write it down . . . (*He throws a piece of chalk at her. She takes it and writes her number in huge letters on the asphalt. She stands, her attitude changed, composed.*)

ELSA: I should call a cop!

WILL: (*Pauses.*) You invited it. (*Pauses.*) You forget so soon? A week ago, Park Street, outside the Greyhound Station. (*Smiles.*) I couldn't believe my goddamn eyes! (*Pauses, attitude changed now.*) You forget? Ahhhh, that's too bad. (*Leans in, he is quite angry.*) I just got off the bus. Still carrying my suitcases. You were leaning against the building . . . with the others . . . a real pro, huh? Wicked tough!

ELSA: You're crazy!

WILL: Oh, yuh, really crazy. (*Pauses.*) You smiled, I smiled.

ELSA: I never saw you outside of any bus station! What the hell are you talking about?

WILL: Who was he? (*No reply.*) *Who was he?*

ELSA: Who was who?

WILL: Answer me! Who were you waiting for?

ELSA: You're making all this up!

WILL: (*Yells.*) *Come off the shit!*

ELSA: Okay, fine. That's what you need. That's what you get! I don't know who he was! Just somebody passing through! Okay.

WILL: "Somebody passing through?" What the hell is that s'posed'ta' mean?

ELSA: It just means . . . somebody. (*Turns to him, suddenly.*) *I have to have somebody!*

WILL: You could leave.

ELSA: I can't.

WILL: *I* did.

ELSA: But you're back! How come?

WILL: Just passing through, believe me. Nothing here that interests me enough to stay around this jerk town.

ELSA: I loathe you.

WILL: You're really a tramp, aren't you? I mean, when you get right down to the bottom of things, you just whore around, don't you? Isn't that right? (*No reply.*) How many?

ELSA: (*Yells.*) How many what?

WILL: (*Same volume.*) How many men? How many men do you have to have?

ELSA: (*Spits her words.*) AS MANY AS I CAN GET! (*Silence.*) My husband . . . he went to Baptist clergy council meeting in Worcester to give a speech on family planning. That's his specialty: family planning. He likes to use Gray Line buses instead of driving . . . gives him time to study his notes. He likes his speeches to be perfect.

WILL: You're mother? How'd she die?

ELSA: She just did.

WILL: That's no answer . . .

ELSA: What's the goddamn difference to you, huh?

WILL: I'd like to know . . .

ELSA: She's *my* mother, not yours!

WILL: I'd like to know.

ELSA: You should'a' stuck around! You would'a' known!

WILL: Elsa . . .

ELSA: Fourteen years! Nothing! Not a word! Not a call not even a pigeon with a note, not even a bottle floating in the lake with a message. Fourteen years and not a word. *Nothing! What do you want?*

WILL: Want?

ELSA: Here? Now? What do you want?

WILL: A look.

ELSA: A look? Okay, fine: look! (*She spins once around, faces him again.*) You had your look. Now, leave!

WILL: I don't know anybody around here any more, just you . . .

ELSA: (*Screams.*) *Join a club!*

WILL: Elsa, please . . . (*He reaches for her. She pulls away, slapping his face, sharply.*)

ELSA: Don't you *for-Jesus-Christ's-sake! ever* put your hands on me again!

WILL: I was seventeen!

ELSA: I was sixteen!

WILL: I'm sorry.

ELSA: You've got no *right* to be sorry. (*Faces him.*) Sixteen years old and pregnant and terrified and you run away and just fucking leave me here to . . . to *what?* To die? To what? What did you figure I was gonna' do? Run the Bank? Drink the lake? I'm really curious, Wilbur. I really am!

WILL: I was seventeen. I was scared.

ELSA: How about when you were nineteen? How about when you were twenty-five? How about when you were twenty-seven? (*Pauses.*) I'll tell you what's really on my mind right now, Wilbur . . . what's really right on the tip of my tongue as I stand here lookin' at you face-to-face . . . (*Clearly.*) I wasted so much of my time worrying about you and you're nothing! I've had dozens more interesting boys than you right here in town. Practically *all* of them!

WILL: Shut it up, now, okay?

ELSA: Can't take it huh?

WILL: I don't give a fat shit about you *or* your boys . . .

ELSA: I gave yours away.

WILL: What's *that* tidbit s'pose'ta' mean?

ELSA: I was pregnant, remember? (*Pauses.*) Did you forget? I gave it away.

WILL: Boy or girl?

ELSA: Which da'ya' want it'ta' be?

WILL: Don't be stupid!

ELSA: But I am!

WILL: Elsa!

ELSA: Boy?

WILL: Boy?

ELSA: Girl!

WILL: Which?

ELSA: Both. Twins. Triplets. A litter! I had a litter! You shoulda' stuck around. It was quite a show . . .

WILL: Listen to me!

ELSA: Nope.

WILL: *Listen to me!* If you had a son . . .

ELSA: (*Quickly, correcting him.*) Daughter!

WILL: If you had a son . . . and he were seventeen . . . and he got a local girl knocked up . . . and he could either stay here and . . . be married to her . . . or he could get the hell out'ta' Wakefield . . . once and for all . . . which would you want him to do?

ELSA: (*She lunges at him. He throws her down on to the hopscotch grid.*) You filthy rotten son-of-a-bitch!

WILL: Elsa, listen!

ELSA: You filthy rotten bastard!

WILL: Elsa!

ELSA: There's no son! I killed it! I killed your son! It's true. I couldn't take his crying. I couldn't take his noise. (*Pauses.*) He had your face. That's what I *really* couldn't stand . . . That's what I *really* couldn't take. He was you! (*Pauses.*) It's true.

WILL: I didn't make a mistake at all did I? I did just the right thing, didn't I? (*Pauses, then suddenly.*) I think you're a *monster!*

ELSA: Swell. Great. That's just great. Is that what you came back here for? To tell me that?

WILL: (*Touches baby carriage.*) Whose is this?

ELSA: It's not mine. You said that, not me. It probably belongs to somebody young. Town's full of young families. The town's crawling with young families . . .

WILL: I'm sorry about your mother and father. I really am . . .

ELSA: Save it, okay?

WILL: I'd hoped to see them . . . to talk to them . . .

ELSA: To what? To get them to forgive you? They didn't. They never would've, believe-you-me. (*Pauses.*) That's a fact.

WILL: I would've liked to have tried to explain . . .

ELSA: Hey, listen, be my guest. Try. Explain. They're buried right over there in Lakeside. You know the spot, don't your? Right next to yours . . .

WILL: I never guessed you'd still be so . . . involved.

ELSA: Now what's that s'posed'ta' mean, hmmm?

WILL: You just seem so . . . involved . . . with me. Still so passionate.

ELSA: You're really unbelievable, Will. You were an unbelievable kid and you ran away and saw the world and grew up and now you're back here and I can see you've become just an unbelievable middle-aged adult. It's all just unbelievable. (*Pauses.*) I'm really happy to see the way you've turned out . . to see what a stupid little asshole you turned out to be . . . (*Pauses.*) I can see exactly what you are I . . . am . . . so . . .lucky. (*Suddenly.*) *I WISH YOU WERE DEAD!* (*There is a substantial silence. Will moves to her, faces her, but cannot touch her. She stands, facing him. He is suddenly eloquent, precise. He is somewhat aloof.*)

WILL: I'm getting married. (*Pauses.*) I've met a girl. She's very nice. I think you'll like her. (*Pauses.*) I've decided to stop . . . you know . . . moving around. (*Pauses.*) I'm coming back. (*Suddenly angry.*) We're settling here . . . home. (*Pauses. Yells.*) *Aren't you going to say anything?* (*Pauses. No reply.*) We'll talk. I'll call you. (*Moves away from her, stops, turns and faces her from new distant position.*) I'm sorry it's so . . . awkward . . .so awkward between us . . . still. (*Pauses.*) I was sure you'd . . . well . . . you'd understand. (*He moves away from her, to edge of stage, at point from which he entered play. He stops there a moment, silently. He then speaks, angrily.*) I never played hopscotch with you! I don't know what the hell you think you're doing! (*He exits the play. The music fades in. [Nota Bene Simon song used from specific lyric "Her name was Lorelei," through end of song.] Elsa sits on bench, alone, in front of her name and the heart with an arrow through it. Graffiti written with her yellow chalk, all around, her telephone number, his name. She looks at the marks on her hopscotch grid; she is weeping. She punches her own thigh – punishing herself – once, twice, again, again . . . Music plays to completion. Lights fade with music.*)

THE PLAY IS OVER.

NOTE TO THE DIRECTOR OF "HOPSCOTCH"

Hopscotch is a first view of Wakefield, Massachusetts, the setting of all four plays of *The Quannapowitt Quartet* and the 9-act trilogy, *The Wakefield Plays*. Thus, this play is really a first view of the entire cycle of Wakefield-based plays. As such, *Hopscotch* presents a reasonably realistic view of a real place. The language and rhythms of Hopscotch are intentionally straightforward and simple. It would not be in the best interest of the play to stylize the presentation at all, but, instead to find recognizable behavior patterns for the playing. Thus the pauses indicated in the text should not be made noticeable to the audience, nor should the game of hopscotch that is played throughout the piece.

The hopscotch game should be played easily, under the dialogue. The only references to the game that I desire are indicated in the dialogue of the play. Otherwise, the audience should be more intent on the relationship between Elsa and Will.

Hopscotch is a mystery play; small, but complete. The mystery elements of the play are already in the text and need not be underscored in the playing at all. In this play, the mystery is born not of information missing to the characters, but of information missing to the audience. Thus, the play can be played realistically, with faith in the dialogue, and faith that the text will bring the missing information to the audience in a pattern that is compelling and theatrical.

Careful attention must be paid to the orchestrating of the build of anger and rage in this play. The lighter, more humorous and more simple the start of the play, the more easily room will be found to accommodate the enormous rage that is this play's conclusion.

Israel Horovitz

New York, November, 1977

THE 75th

For Mary Dolan

THE 75TH was first presented in a staged reading by The Aleph Company, Milwaukee, Wisconsin, in November 1976, directed by Sharon Ott and the author, with the following cast:

AMY CHAMBERLAIN .... Bonnie Dillingham
ARTHUR "COOKIE" SILVERSTEIN .... Ollie Nash

THE 75TH had its New York premiere in April–May 1978 at the New York Shakespeare Festival, New York. Joseph Papp was producer; Woods Mackintosh designed the scenery; Jennifer von Mayrhauser designed the costumes; Jack Hofsiss was the director; and the cast was as follows:

AMY CHAMBERLAIN .... Elizabeth Wilson
ARTHUR "COOKIE" SILVERSTEIN .... Tom Aldredge

In June 1978, THE 75TH was adapted by its author and was taped for *Earplay*, National Educational Radio, for broadcast over five hundred affiliate stations in the United States and Canada. The producer was Howard Gelman; the director was Jack Hofsiss; and the cast was as follows:

AMY CHAMBERLAIN .... Rosemary Harris
ARTHUR "COOKIE" SILVERSTEIN .... Fritz Weaver

Introduction

The 75th is, I think, the sweetest of all my plays. It is a *hommage* to my high school English teacher, Bernice Caswell. It is Miss Caswell, bless her, who made a playwright of me.

I had an awful time in high school. I was shorter than every girl I loved (which is saying quite a lot), and I was bored silly by my course-work. I went from being a straight-A student, from First Grade straight the way through Junior High, to not caring at all about study or grades. During my first few years of high school, I put most of my interest and energy into a boys club in a neighboring town: The AZA. I became president of my chapter...and was ultimately elected to office in AZA's District #1 (which was territorially defined as "Everything East of the Mississippi, and Canada"). I competed and won AZA's Oratory Contest, locally...then, I competed and won AZA's New England contest...and the, the AZA's District #1 contest...

But then, the curtain fell. As punishment for my low school-grades, my father prevented me from competing in AZA's International Oratory Contest. As parental decisions go, my father made one of the very worst. Low as my grades had been prior to my father's decision, I allowed my grades to plummet even further...to no doubt punish my parents.

It was Miss Caswell, and only Miss Caswell, who saw my depression. She also saw my name in a Boston paper. She asked me about my preparation for the AZA International Oratory Contest. I told her the truth. The next day, she handed me an entry form for The Red Feather Oratory Contest. I cannot for the life of me recall what "Red Feather" symbolizes, exactly. To my shock and amazement, Miss Caswell reported my forensic triumph to my entire English class, and invited me to stop to the front of the classroom and perform my winning speech. There was a small silence. And then, the class applauded. I went to the front of the room, and with more courage than I ever thought I had, I performed my speech. And, again, the class applauded, peer-thumbs, in a word, up.

I soon wrote my Red Feather speech (which I've recently chronicled in my newest play, *Unexpected Tenderness*). Under Bernice Caswell's guidance, I competed and won the Red Feather Oratory Contest...And then, I competed and won a bunch of other public-speaking contests. and then, at age 17, wrote my first play, with the wickedly clever and ironical title, *The Comeback*.

For sure, for sure, for sure, Miss Caswell gets The Big Assist.

The 75th is, like the other plays of *Quannapowitt Quartet*, set in Wakefield, Massachusetts...in a restaurant, head of Lake Quannapowitt. The situation is this: Wakefield High School Class of Godonlyknowswhat is having its 75th Reunion. Only two people from the graduating class are still alive. A man—a wise-cracking, Yankee-Jew; and a woman—a Jew-hating WASP. They are obliged to get along.

Once again, popular music proved to be an inspiration in my writing. For *The 75th*, I borrowed "Still The One", a hit song from the 1970's , written by my friends John and Johanna Hall, and performed by John's band Orleans.

Jack Hoffsiss, once again, created the quintessential production of one of my *Quannapowitt Quartet* plays. As he'd done with *Hopscotch*, Hoffsiss found two stunning actors for *The 75th*: Tom Aldridge and Elizabeth Wilson. Elizabeth's performance was particularly detailed. I'll never forget her gluing blue-rubber veins to her beautiful face. Elizabeth called me, recently, to suggest a London production of *The 75th*. Her friend Paul Schofield had expressed interest in playing the other role. Would I agree? I did.

The 75th opened in NYC, without critics or reviews, as was my wont at that time. The play has found productions and audiences, continuously, since its premiere. *The 75th* has also been played with success, on radio (with Fritz Weaver and Rosemary Harris), and on television (with Barnard Hughes and Mildred Natwick).

The 75th is an unusually hopeful and positive play for me to have written. Of course, one must remember that *The 75th* was inspired by an unusually hopeful and positive woman...Bernice Caswell...who is, for me, forever, a memory to cherish.

Characters

AMY CHAMBERLAIN Thin, well-groomed, attractive, ninety-three.

ARTHUR "COOKIE" SILVERSTEIN Tall, thin, well-groomed, handsome, ninety-three.

Setting

Small private dining room in restaurant overlooking Lake Quannapowitt, Wakefield, Mass. September, evening.

THE 75th

Darkness in the auditorium.
Uptempo popular music is heard at substantial volume.
Garish lights of coin-operated juke box switch on, revealing juke box on stage.
A human figure, back to audience, leans over front of machine, thumping same with her hands.
It should appear that figure is beating time to rhythm of music.
Lights to soft glow, revealing section of small-town, small restaurant. Figure is woman, Amy Chamberlain. She is extremely old, thin. She wears a long overcoat. Her back is still to auditorium, but it has become evident that she is trying to stop juke box from playing. She is now kicking the machine, as well as beating same with her hands.

AMY: (*Yells.*) HOW D'YA' STOP THIS ABOMINABLE RACKET??? (*She kicks machine again, music continues loudly. She moves to table, chooses chair, removes coat, folds same over back of chair, sits. She looks about for a waiter. There is none. The record continues to play on juke box, even more loudly and more raucously than before. Amy is amazed.*) ANYBODY HERE???? (*No response.*) THIS MUSIC IS A BIT SONOROUS! (*She stands and moves to juke box, kicks and whacks same several times.*) HELLO! (*She exits, leaving her coat on chair. The music continues. Arthur "Cookie" Silverstein enters. He is, like Amy, nearly ancient. He, too, wears a long overcoat. He carries brown bag. He looks about the room and, seeing no one, moves to juke box and tries to stop same from playing loud music. Unable to stop same, he kicks machine and soon begins to whack same with hands and brown bag. Music continues. Silverstein goes to second table and removes coat, sets down brown paper bag, folds coat over back of chair and sits in chair next to coat. He searches through brown bag and removes rolled banner. He stands, goes to juke box, carrying rolled banner. He kicks juke box several times. He yells.*)

COOKIE: ANYBODY HERE??? (*No response, he continues to kick juke box.*) ANYBODY KNOW HOW TO SHUT THIS GODDAMN THING OFF??? (*He screams now.*) *THIS IS OFFENSIVE!!!* . . . (*Music ends abruptly, as song is completed. Cookie's scream is now in the clear.) I SAID THIS IS OFFENSIVE! . . . (Realizes his screams have not been covered by music.)* . . . Thank you very much. Thank you. (*Looks about room. Sees he is still alone. He fastens banner to wall, after unrolling same. Lettering on banner reads: WELCOME 75th. He stands back and looks at banner. Amy's coat catches his eye. He walks to same and touches it, then lifts it to look at it closely. Amy pokes her head on to stage again. Watches a moment.*)

AMY: Alan Roberto? (*Cookie turns and faces her.*)

COOKIE: Eleanor Fritz!

AMY: No.

COOKIE: Me, neither . . .

AMY: Frank Lazzaro?

COOKIE: I'm not Italian . . .

AMY: Oh, my goodness! Jimmy Kiley!

COOKIE: Nope! (*Pauses.*) Annie MacGlennon!

AMY: Not at all . . . Edgar Lancing?

COOKIE: Nope.

AMY: Philly Drinkwater?

COOKIE: Nope.

AMY: Wilbur Lynch?

COOKIE: He's dead.

AMY: I thought not. (*Pauses.*) Are you Wakefield High?

COOKIE: Yup.

AMY: Don't tell me. Let me guess. (*Smiles.*) You wouldn't be Hannah's cousin Adrian?

COOKIE: Right. I wouldn't be.

AMY: Everybody else is . . . well . . . accounted for, in terms of men.

COOKIE: Silverstein.

AMY: A what?

COOKIE: Silverstein. Arthur Silverstein.

AMY: I'm sorry . . .

COOKIE: *Cookie* Silverstein . . .

AMY: Oh, of course, *Cookie* Silverstein! That's you!

COOKIE: (*Smiling.*) Yup.

AMY: Cookie!

COOKIE: And you're . . . ?

AMY: Amy.

COOKIE: Amy?

AMY: Chamberlain . . .

COOKIE: Amy *Chamb*erlain! (*There is a pause in which they both smile at one another.*)

AMY: I don't think I remember you at all.

COOKIE: Nor I you.

AMY: Where did you live?

COOKIE: In high school? Elm Street.

AMY: Elm Street? West Side?

COOKIE: Elm Street. Runs up from the tracks on North Avenue all the way to Reading . . .

AMY: Well, I know that. It's just that . . . well . . . I know everybody on Elm Street and . . . Silverstein?

COOKIE: Cookie!

AMY: I beg your pardon?

COOKIE: Me. Cookie. That's my name.

AMY: Well, listen, at my age, why do I doubt *any*thing? (*Pauses.*) Silverstein, you say?

COOKIE: Silverstein. My father was Samuel Silverstein . . . the mover . . . he had his shop in Medford and another one later in Stoneham. Silverstein the Mover. You remember?

AMY: Well, listen. At my age. (*After pause.*) How have you been?

COOKIE: Oh, very well, very well.

AMY: Cookie?

COOKIE: Cookie.

AMY: What an odd name for a boy!

COOKIE: You were up Lynnfield way, right?

AMY: When?

COOKIE: High School.

AMY: No. We were up the Park. West Side. Parker Road, in fact . . .

COOKIE: Parker Road?

AMY: Number twenty-seven . . .

COOKIE: White house with green trim.

AMY: Yellow. Bright yellow.

COOKIE: There's no yellow house I can remember on Parker . . .

AMY: There was a Taffy.

COOKIE: A taffy *house?*

AMY: Taffy *Turner.* But never a Cookie . . . (*Pause.*) Tuffy, I mean. Tuffy Puddle! You remember?

COOKIE: Do I remember Tuffy Puddle? Do I remember Tuffy Puddle? Didn't we play together every day on the West Ward hill?

AMY: You did?

COOKIE: Every day.

AMY: Tuffy.

COOKIE: Tuffy.

AMY: Wonderfully good-natured boy . . .

COOKIE: Salt of the Earth . . .

AMY: Never wanted much . . .

COOKIE: Never got much . . .

AMY: What became of Tuffy?

COOKIE: Tuffy? (*Pauses.*) Dunno' . . . (*Pauses.*) Probably quite successful.

AMY: No doubt. (*She pauses; sits. Leans back.*) Just us?

COOKIE: I suspect so.

AMY: How many were we?

COOKIE: Then? Eighty-one.

AMY: Eighty-one?

COOKIE: *If* we count the Reilly girl . . .

AMY: Carol?

COOKIE: Her sister: Helen.

AMY: Why wouldn't we count Helen?

COOKIE: She never actually graduated with us – with our class. She had . . . trouble.

AMY: Ah, yes. (*Pauses.*) What sort of trouble?

COOKIE: Family.

AMY: With her family?

COOKIE: Excuse me?

AMY: She had trouble with her family?

COOKIE: Who?

AMY: Helen Reilly? Family trouble?

COOKIE: Family *way:* she was in it.

AMY: Ah, yes. Did we know the father?

COOKIE: There was none.

AMY: There *had* to be one. There always is . . .

COOKIE: Not from us: from our graduating class. (*Pauses.*) She always turned her affection away from our year. Either above us or beneath us. (*Pauses.*) She was fond of my brother.

AMY: Was she?

COOKIE: Very fond. You might even say she was *keen* on him.

AMY: Was she?

COOKIE: *He* said so . . . (*Pauses.*) I suppose she was. (*Pauses.*) He was a full head taller than me.

AMY: Was he?

COOKIE: I can vouch for that myself. A full head. Two years younger, too. One of those flukes of genetics . . .

AMY: I'm sure.

COOKIE: My entire family was flukish, genetically speaking.

AMY: Were they?

COOKIE: Not my mother and father. They were normal. I mean, who *knows* if they were? It's just that the genetic fluke I'm speaking of was found out in their children: me and my brothers and sister.

AMY: Bald?

COOKIE: Short.

AMY: Really?

COOKIE: I was nearly a foot shorter than my younger brother . . .

AMY: Helen Reilly's friend?

COOKIE: Right. Him. And he was nearly a head taller than me, but a foot shorter than my father.

AMY: That would make you a head and a foot shorter than your father . . .

COOKIE: At the minimum.

AMY: That is strange!

COOKIE: Oh, yes. A fluke. My sister, poor thing, she was incredibly short.

AMY: Was she?

COOKIE: Nearly a legal midget.

AMY: *Was* she?

COOKIE: Becky! – poor Becky . . . incredibly short, really . . .

AMY: Little Becky Roberto?

COOKIE: Excuse me?

AMY: Was that the way we knew your sister?

COOKIE: Little Becky Silverstein.

AMY: I don't think so.

COOKIE: *I know so!*

AMY: I don't think I remember her . . .

COOKIE: Couldn'ta' forget her, once you saw her. Tiny little thing, but very well formed, for her size and all. Very attractive to the multitude of men here in town . . .

AMY: Was she?

COOKIE: Oh, very much so. The Lazzaro boys couldn't keep their hands off her . . . (*Pauses, embarrassed.*) . . . I hope you pardon my bein' so blunt.

AMY: Oh, well. Times have changed, haven't they?

COOKIE: And for the better, too, I'd have to say!

AMY: I knew the Lazzaro family quite well. Funny, you should mention them in relation to your poor stunted sister.

COOKIE: They lived closeby. On Eustis Avenue . . .

AMY: They did indeed. And I on Parker. Number twenty-seven . . .

COOKIE: And we were thirty-three Elm. (*Smiles.*) You place us now, do you?

AMY: I suppose.

COOKIE: It was an enormous gray house with a Dutch-shaped roof. My uncle built it for my grandfather . . . (*Smiles.*) Very wealthy.

AMY: Your grandfather?

COOKIE: My uncle.

AMY: Your *grandfather* lived in Wakefield?

COOKIE: Born here. Same house as me.

AMY: Native Wakefieldians?

COOKIE: We were very nearly Yankees . . . *Puritans*, almost.

AMY: Goldstein?

COOKIE: Silverstein.

AMY: And your sister married a Lazzaro?

COOKIE: Excuse me?

AMY: Your sister married a Lazzaro. You said that. Am I getting it bollixed up? I do that . . .

COOKIE: Oh, not bollixed badly. You're very close to what I said. (*Smiles.*) I said my sister Becky was tremendously bothered by the Lazzaro brothers' sexual advances to her body . . .

AMY: Was she?

COOKIE: Something terrible!

AMY: I am simply amazed! Simply amazed! *Sexual?*

COOKIE: With their hands.

AMY: I don't completely understand . . .

COOKIE: While walking . . . on the street . . . their hands!

AMY: In an acrobatic fashion, you mean?

COOKIE: No, you've made a major bollix of it now. Now you have. (*Pauses.*) My sister, the stunted one, was tremendously bothered by the Lazzaro boys fondling her breasts when she took walks . . .

AMY: Are you *serious?*

COOKIE: Deadly so.

AMY: I am simply amazed!

COOKIE: Italians.

AMY: I am simply amazed.

COOKIE: So was she, the first dozen or so gropes . . .

AMY: I can well imagine!

COOKIE: It made her a bit frightened to take walks . . .

AMY: Which brother in particular?

COOKIE: All of them.

AMY: There were five or six . . .

COOKIE: Six. And we suspected the father as well . . .

AMY: You *can't* be serious???

COOKIE: Is the Pope Catholic?

AMY: He certainly is!

COOKIE: Then there you are.

AMY: I would have to say shocked and amazed. I am simply shocked and amazed . . .

COOKIE: Sorry to have brought it up . . .

AMY: Not at all. These things are good to know . . .(*Pauses.*) Which brother, in particular? Did she say?

COOKIE: It was always difficult for her to be sure . . . she bein' so short . . .

AMY: . . . and they bein' so tall!

COOKIE: Exactly.

AMY: Poor little thing.

COOKIE: It was horrible . . . for her . . . first dozen or so times . . . until she learned.

AMY: To stop them?

COOKIE: Opposite. To just let them do it (*Pauses, tight-lipped.*) It was the only way. (*Pauses.*) Get it over with, quickly.

AMY: I am simply beside myself.

COOKIE: As were we all.

AMY: Why, do you suppose, am I hearing this for the first time?

COOKIE: Oh, well, you can understand *that* . . .

AMY: I suppose I can . . .

COOKIE: You knew the Lazzaro family well then, did you?

AMY: Well, my Lord! Not *that* well!

COOKIE: I wasn't insinuating.

AMY: Of course not. I'm just a bit shaken from the news.

COOKIE: Oh, Christ, it was more than sixty years ago . . .

AMY: I suppose, but the sting's still there . . . (*Pauses, smiles.*) I had quite a crush on a Lazzaro. You might even say I was . . . you know . . .

COOKIE: Keen?

AMY: Oh, that too . . .

COOKIE: Which one of them?

AMY: Alan.

COOKIE: Alan?

AMY: He pitched a no-hitter against Reading . . . and a one-hitter against Melrose . . .

COOKIE: Of course, Alan . . . the pitcher. (*Pauses*) I remember him well . . . leftie . . . left-handed, right? (*Pauses.*) Oh, I don't think Alan hardly groped her at all . . . maybe once or twice, just to keep up the family image, but that's all.

AMY: I shouldn't think so. Alan wasn't very happy in that family.

COOKIE: You don't say?

AMY: Couldn't wait to leave town.

COOKIE: Did he?

AMY: For the War.

COOKIE: Of course.

AMY: Came back very well decorated, too.

COOKIE: I think I'd heard that . . .

AMY: But never really happy again . . .

COOKIE: Did you see him?

AMY: Excuse me?

COOKIE: *Date* him, I suppose you'd say?

AMY: Oh, no. (*Pauses.*) An occasional dance. A walk . . . (*There is a pause.*) He was quite tall. A six footer, I think.

COOKIE: Oh, I don't think so. Not Alan Lazzaro. Maybe, Angelo . . .

AMY: Really, Mr. Silverstein, I should know . . .

COOKIE: Cookie.

AMY: Oh, no thank you . . . stuffed.

COOKIE: My name. My name is Cookie.

AMY: Your given name?

COOKIE: Nick.

AMY: This is very confusing.

COOKIE: My given name is Arthur. My nickname is Cookie. (*Smiles.*) I prefer Cookie. I don't know why. It suits me . . .

AMY: I wish I could remember you. I don't.

COOKIE: May I be truthful?

AMY: I wish you would.

COOKIE: I don't remember you, either.

AMY: But that's just ridiculous!

COOKIE: But it's the truth!

AMY: I was a cheerleader, for goodness sake!

COOKIE: You were?

AMY: K.

COOKIE: You were K.

AMY: Senior year. I was L, junior year . . .

COOKIE: (*Trying to remember.*) L, junior year . . . K, senior year . . . (*Squinting now.*) K, K, K . . .

AMY: Martha Beebe was W . . .

COOKIE: Carol what'shername was A . . .

AMY: And I was K!

COOKIE: I can do no more than draw a blank on K . . . (*Pauses.*) Christ! (*Squints. He visualizes and points to each imagined cheerleader in line, on the air between he and Amy.*) W . . . A . . . a blank . . . E . . . F . . . I . . . E . . . L . . .(*Remembers.*) Let's just wait a minute! L! Junior year! (*Sings to melody of "My Old Kentucky Home."*) "Oh, the moon shines bright . . . (*Points to Amy, who completes the song by singing the final line.*)

AMY: "O'er my Quannapowitt home . . ." (*She laughs.*) You remember!

COOKIE: (*Laughing as well.*) Ah, yes. You were L . . .

AMY: Between E and D . . . (*They both laugh.*)

COOKIE: Elaine Hawkins was E, and Maud what'sher name was D . . .

AMY: (*Stops laughing.*) Not at all . . .

COOKIE: Huh?

AMY: Not at all! It was Maud Anderson and she was a majorette, not a cheerleader. Elaine Hawkins was neither a cheerleader, nor a majorette. She was quite hefty, if I recall correctly.

COOKIE: (*Stunned.*) Christ! She was more than hefty! She was a battleship . . .

AMY: Could you please not use that expletive?

COOKIE: What?

AMY: I've never taken to people just saying "Christ!" like Christ was just a word. I'm sorry.

COOKIE: Oh, God! I'm really sorry.

AMY: No, *I'm* sorry. I don't mean to embarrass you . . .

COOKIE: I'm embarrassed . . .

AMY: There, you see? (*Pauses.*) I'm sorry. I apologize. (*Looks about the room.*) Where are the others?

COOKIE: The others?

AMY: There are supposed to be twelve of us. Alice and Rosemary Simon . . .

COOKIE: Oh, no . . .

AMY: What?

COOKIE: There's just us, I think . . .

AMY: No there are twelve of us. (*Looks for her coat and pocketbook.*) There's a letter with the ticket . . .

COOKIE: It's from me.

AMY: There's a list in with the ticket: those lost, those . . . well . . . gone . . . and those found. There are twelve of us.

COOKIE: I sent the letter.

AMY: Rosemary . . . (*Hears.*) You what? You sent the letter:

COOKIE: I did.

AMY: Oh. (*Pauses.*) Did you? (*Finds letter by now and looks at it.*) Arthur "Cookie" . . . (*Looks at Cookie.*) You?

COOKIE: Me.

AMY: Then you should know. About the others . . .

COOKIE: I do.

AMY: *All* of them?

COOKIE: Our class had a bad year. (*There is silence.*) One of the worst.

AMY: Rosemary?

COOKIE: Car wreck. Horrible.

AMY: A car wreck? At her age?

COOKIE: Ironical.

AMY: I should say. Rosemary?

COOKIE: Route One-Twenty-Eight, down near the Manchester exit, in North Beverly. (*Smiles.*) Read it in the *Globe*. A very nice sized notice.

AMY: Large:

COOKIE: Oh, very large. Excellently thought out, too. At least I thought so.

AMY: Well, then. I can just stop waiting for the others, can't I?

COOKIE: I was quite relieved to find you here. I didn't get your form back.

AMY: I don't understand.

COOKIE: There was a personal history form. I didn't get yours back.

AMY: Were you a class officer?

COOKIE: Me? (*Laughs.*) No.

AMY: I should think not. (*Pauses.*) Oh. Not to cast any insinuendos, but I do remember our class officers . . .

COOKIE: John and Janette?

AMY: Lovely couple . . .

COOKIE: Did they date?

AMY: John and Janette? Oh, more than that. They married.

COOKIE: Did they?

AMY: They reunited at our own reunion. It was a beautiful thing to see.

COOKIE: I can imagine . . .

AMY: Dancing, cheek to cheek and all . . . it was our thirty-fifth . . .

COOKIE: I missed that one.

AMY: His first marriage, her fourth, I believe . . .

COOKIE: They must have been fifty . . .

AMY: Fifty-three.

COOKIE: Must have been.

AMY: Precisely.

COOKIE: I was off fighting. . .

AMY: For whom?

COOKIE: For us! For whom? Whom did you think? There was no time for me to be dancing cheek to cheek, I'll tell you that!

AMY: That old and still fighting?

COOKIE: I re-enlisted after the Second War . . .

AMY: Did you?

COOKIE: I was piss and vinegar . . . Ex*cuse* me!

AMY: Ah, well . . .

COOKIE: I missed our thirty-fifth . . . couldn't get the weekend. I remember it well . . .

AMY: You would have won "Traveled Longest Distance" . . .

COOKIE: Oh, no. I was just up at Devens . . .

AMY: England?

COOKIE: Fitchburg. Just up here. Fort Devens.

AMY: Oh. were you? Fitchburg?

COOKIE: Not much of a town.

AMY: Never was.

COOKIE: I tried for the weekend, but I couldn't get it. Paid for my tickets, too. . .

AMY: Tickets, were they? In the plural?

COOKIE: Married, no children. Married late for children. She was sixty.

AMY: Local girl?

COOKIE: No, Fitchburg. A spinster, but very nice. Taught English in the O'Malley School; the junior high . . . a Gloucester spinster . . .

AMY: I taught English. . .

COOKIE: Oh, I didn't mean . . . (*Pauses, embarrassed.*) Nothing wrong with not marrying. I think not marrying is a fine institution! (*He laughs, pleased by his small joke. No response at all from Amy.*) That was a play on words.

AMY: I married twice.

COOKIE: Did you?

AMY: Once to a Frenchman and once to a Californian.

COOKIE: You seen the world, then, haven't you?

AMY: I have some memories.

COOKIE: Sounds like it. Sounds like it. (*Smiles.*) In France then, with the Frenchman?

AMY: Providence.

COOKIE: Ah, yes. Rhode Island French. Quite a few of them in Providence, aren't there?

AMY: Oh, thousands. Even still . . .

COOKIE: Children?

AMY: No.

COOKIE: Neither time?

AMY: No.

COOKIE: *There's* something in common then . . . between us, I mean.

AMY: Yes. (*There is a silence.*)

[*Nota Bene Following section to be spoken rapidly, until the next silence.*]

COOKIE: Do you remember Evelyn whosis?

AMY: Who could forget?

COOKIE: She won the award for "The Most Children" every reunion...nobody could catch up. . .

AMY: Catholics.

COOKIE: Insanely so, I'd say . . .

AMY: She stayed in town, didn't she?

COOKIE: Married a Lynch . . .

AMY: Never moved from town, did they?

COOKIE: They couldn't, could they? Fourteen screaming children all around them all the time . . .

AMY: Shocking way to waste your time!

COOKIE: I agree.

AMY: Cleaning noses . . .

COOKIE: Wiping up spilled milk . . .

AMY: Packing lunches . . .

COOKIE: Sunday meals . . .

AMY: Telephone calls from long distances . . .

COOKIE: Tragedy befalling . . .

AMY: (*After a pause.*) Yes. That would've be'n the worst. (*There is a silence.*) Who wins the award for "Distance Traveled" then? You or me?

COOKIE: I'm down from Burlington. . .

AMY: Vermont?

COOKIE: No, Burlington . . .

AMY: Just up here? (*He nods.*) Burlington's only four miles from here.

COOKIE: As the crow . . . you know . . .

AMY: . . . flies?

COOKIE: Flies. (*Looks down, embarrassed.*) I did live once, for a month, in D. C.. . . . (*Pauses.*) But that was a hotel. Hotels don't really count. (*Pauses.*) Very little traveling alone. I guess I never wanted to, because, I . . . well . . . I didn't. (*Looks up.*) You?

AMY: What:

COOKIE: In from the Coast?

AMY: Oh, no. He passed on almost immediately after we married. (*Pauses.*) Very soon after. (*Pauses.*) Within the week, in fact.

COOKIE: Did he?

AMY: Very sudden.

COOKIE: Tragic business. Heart?

AMY: Lungs. They both collapsed . . .

COOKIE: Simultaneously?

AMY: Spontaneously, as well.

COOKIE: Tragic business. No warning?

AMY: He coughed.

COOKIE: Not much warning in a cough . . .

AMY: One never knows.

COOKIE: That's the truth.

AMY: I had a great deal of trouble locating his family. (*Pauses.*) I'd not yet actually met them. (*Pauses.*) Californians.

COOKIE: You mentioned that.

AMY: We were living up Stoneham way . . .

COOKIE: Were you?

AMY: Do you know Gould Street?

COOKIE: Near the junk shop?

AMY: Scrap yard.

COOKIE: Oh, yes, I do. I'm very interested in that . . .

AMY: In junk?

COOKIE: In the phenomenon . . .

AMY: I don't completely understand . . .

COOKIE: Those of us who move away . . . far away . . . from birthplaces . . . and those of us who . . . you know . . . don't.

AMY: Ah, yes, I see. (*Smiles.*) I've always quite liked it here . . .

COOKIE: As do I.

AMY: Never saw the need to move about . . .

COOKIE: Nor I . . .

AMY: I've had my work . . .

COOKIE: Teaching English?

AMY: Precisely.

COOKIE: In Stoneham?

AMY: Not for a while. Not since my retirement.

COOKIE: (*Smiles.*) Well, it looks as though I win. I must say, this is a surprising victory . . .

AMY: I would call it a tie myself . . .

COOKIE: Nonsense. In order to reach Burlington, you have to pass through Stoneham *and* Woburn . . . (*Smiles, shrugs.*) No question who wins "Longest Distance Traveled" . . .

AMY: Long*er* distance traveled.

COOKIE: I see. Yes.

AMY: If there were three of us, it could be long*est* . . .

COOKIE: I remember that, now that you bring it up. (*Smiles.*) Do you remember Miss Caswell?

AMY: Remember her? She started me out!

COOKIE: All of us! Wonderful teacher, wonderful woman as well . . .

AMY: On my career, I mean! I actually taught English!

COOKIE: Oh, yes. I see what you mean.

AMY: I remember the day she took me aside. (*Smiles. Imitates still older woman.*) "Amy Chamberlain, you have a talent." (*Pauses.*) "For what?" I asked. I was young. (*Pauses, smiles. Changes vocal pitch to older woman's timbre.*) "For teaching the language, its rules and usage's." And she was right . . .

COOKIE: Nearly always.

AMY: I do have talent . . .

COOKIE: A way with words . . .

AMY: Do you think so?

COOKIE: Very certainly so.

AMY: Thank you . . . Cookie.

COOKIE: It's something I notice in an English-speaking person . . .

AMY: You're very kind.

COOKIE: Would you have any interest in dancing?

AMY: The ballet?

COOKIE: With me.

AMY: Oh, I see. (*Smiles.*) It's been a while. (*Pauses.*) I would. Yes. I think we should. It's an occasion, after all . . .

COOKIE: We're the seventy-fifth . . .

AMY: Together again . . .

COOKIE: We're the lucky ones . . .

AMY: I should say!

COOKIE: (*Fishing in his pockets.*) Do you have a favorite? (*She stares at him blankly. He nods to juke box.*) Song?

AMY: I doubt if it's there.

COOKIE: You might be surprised.

AMY: "Don't Fence Me In."

COOKIE: Is it?

AMY: It is. Never known why. (*She hums a melody, smiling happily.*)

COOKIE: Let me have a look . . . "Don't Fence Me In," huh? (*He stands and moves to juke box. She continues to hum smiling.*)

AMY: (*Her smile fades, suddenly.*) I can't seem to remember the words to the song.

COOKIE: It's be'n years since I've played one of these things . . . (*Jiggling coins, reading price.*) My Christ! It's certainly risen from two-for-a-nickel, I'll tell you that!

AMY: (*She hums again, this time worried.*) I've lost it! (*She hums again. To Cookie.*) Do you remember what comes in between *fences* and *commences?* (Cookie drops coin in slot and lights on machine flash signal for him to choose a song.)

COOKIE: Let's just have a peek here . . . (*Puts on his eyeglasses.*) Right!

AMY: I've lost it completely. . . right between *commences* and *fences* . . . a perfect rhyme. (*Pauses, hums.*) Like a sieve! (*She hums again, a while, stops.*) Well, that's gone now. All gone.

COOKIE: I don't see the song here. I'm afraid it's not on the machine . . .

AMY: It doesn't matter . . .

COOKIE· It was so popular, too . . .

AMY: Play anything you like . . . Play one of *your* favorites. . .

COOKIE: Mine? Oh, well, I never knew too much about music . . . (*Looks over selection list.*) I always admired "Those Wedding Bells Are Breaking Up That Old Gang Of Mine."

AMY: Oh, good, then. Play that.

COOKIE: I don't see it.

AMY: (*She hums "Don't Fence Me In" again, this time clearly panicked.*) It fits perfectly between *fences* and *commences*. I don't know *how* I could have forgotten! I sang that song a hundred times a day! (*She hums again.*) Gone!

COOKIE: I don't think it's here!

AMY: Surprise us, then!

COOKIE: You mean just pick any number that comes to mind?

AMY: Certainly.

COOKIE: Oh, well, then . . . (*Smiles.*) Fifty cents.

AMY: For a song?

COOKIE: That's what it costs now.

AMY: It's all relative, isn't it?

COOKIE: Relative to what you've got, you mean . . .

AMY: (*Smiles.*) That's very good, yes. (*Pauses.*) I've got my pension. I foxed them on that one, didn't I? Worked thirty years, pensioned for twenty-eight. . .

COOKIE: So far . . .

AMY: Right! So far! They'll change the retirement dates one day, when they smarten up, won't they?

COOKIE: I've been pensioned nearly forty-seven years now.

AMY: You're not serious?

COOKIE: Imagine if I'd'a quit at forty, like they wanted?

AMY: You went straight in after high school, did you?

COOKIE: Many of us did. Things were different then.

AMY: Never any thought of college?

COOKIE: College of Life and Hard Knocks. That's me. (*He smiles, she doesn't.*) College of Life and Hard Knocks.

AMY: I suppose.

COOKIE: And you? Radcliffe, I suppose.

AMY: Smith.

COOKIE: (*Amazed.*) Did you? I was making a joke there. I really thought you'd come back with "Salem Normal." I never dreamed you'd be comin' back with "Smith." (*Pauses.*) You've been beautifully educated, haven't you?

AMY: Miss Caswell's the wonder behind all that.

COOKIE: I'm sure she is. Wonderful woman. Wonderful teacher, and a wonderful human being to boot. (*Pauses, suddenly upset.*) Oh, God!

AMY: What's the matter?

COOKIE: You remember old Mrs. Nicker . . . Warren School?

AMY: Fourth grade?

COOKIE: That's her.

AMY: Died when we were in fifth . . .

COOKIE: *You* were Warren School, too?

AMY: Parker Road . . .

COOKIE: Do you remember old Nicker then?

AMY: Certainly.

COOKIE: She had a problem with flatulency, so to speak . . . (*Amy looks down.*) Sorry. Anyway, you remember her?

AMY: Yes, of course. She died when I . . . we . . . were in the fifth grade . . .

COOKIE: My fault.

AMY: What?

COOKIE: My fault. In fourth grade, I kicked her. Her leg never healed and she died from it. My fault. It was my fault.

AMY: You're not serious?

COOKIE: She took us out for recess. We were playing kickball, when the bell rang. I was up. I'd been waiting for my up about ten minutes, about half the recess. The pitcher pitched . . . I kicked... Mrs. Nicker stepped in to stop me from kicking and end the game . . .

AMY: And you kicked her?

COOKIE: Kicked her? Damn near flew her into the trees!

AMY: You can't be serious?

COOKIE: Deadly so. She was in her grave within the year. Her leg never healed. I think they took it off before she finally went, nothing could've saved her . . .

AMY: You've got it all wrong!

COOKIE: Would that I did!

AMY: But you do! She lived right next to us . . .

COOKIE: Parker Road . . .

AMY: Right next to us. Twenty-nine!

COOKIE: That's a fact!

AMY: It was her stomach that killed her. Some sort of tumor . . . they were Christian Scientists. I heard the screams for weeks. Terrible thing. I'll never forget.

COOKIE: Emily Nicker, fourth grade, H. M. Warren School?

AMY: Twenty-nine Parker Road. Flatulency problem . . . so to speak . . .

COOKIE: My God!

AMY: I remember it like yesterday . . .

COOKIE: All these years . . .

AMY: Poor old thing . . .

COOKIE: What a relief!

AMY: I can imagine! . . .

COOKIE: You can't. You really can't . . . (*Pauses.*) I . . . am . . . so . . . relieved!

AMY: I'm very happy for you . . .

COOKIE: I'd like very much to dance. Would you?

AMY: I wouldn't mind.

COOKIE: I say number 6. How's that sound?

AMY: Fine.

COOKIE: (*Inspecting machine.*) That doesn't seem to be the way this works. Would you choose 6-A, 6-B, 6-C, 6-D, E, or F?

AMY: F.

COOKIE: (*Pushes buttons.*) Here goes. (*Machine clicks into action. He goes to her. She rises. They assume ballroom dance position in each other's arms. Uptempo music, same as earlier, begins. They stare awhile at one another. They attempt a few steps of a waltz. Amy sits. Cookie goes to machine and pushes all buttons then kicks and whacks same. Amy stands, goes to machine, removes plug. Music and lights on machine fade out together.*) I thought I would lose my senses! (*Cookie is exhausted from whacking machine. He leans against chair.*)

AMY: (*Suddenly screams.*) *That's it!*

COOKIE: (*Amazed, he sits at other table.*) What's it?

AMY: *Lose my senses!* (*Laughs.*) Isn't that ironical? Lose my senses!

COOKIE: I've missed the context, I think . . .

AMY: It fits . . . between *commences* and *fences* . . .

COOKIE: It does?

AMY: It rhymes. With *commences* and *fences. Commences, fences, lose my senses.*

COOKIE: There's rhyme there. That's true enough.

AMY: I . . . am . . . so . . . relieved.

COOKIE: Glad to have helped out . . .

AMY: It's the biggest fear I have.

COOKIE: Fences:?

AMY: (*Laughs, whoops.*) You are so *clever*, Cookie! You really are! (*Laughs.*) I haven't had a laugh like this in Christ knows how long! (*Laughs again, stops. Dries eyes.*) That was a good one.

COOKIE: (*Begins to laugh.*) I see. (*A deep laugh here.*) Whewwww! (*She joins his laugh with her own.*)

AMY: My sides!

COOKIE: Our sides! (*They both whoop again in laughter, looking across the space from table to table at one another. The laughter ends. They dry their eyes. There is a silence. They are lost in memory.*)

AMY: (*Breaking the long frozen silence.*) How were your grades?

COOKIE: (*Quickly.*) Not much.

AMY: Weren't they?

COOKIE: I didn't click into real concentration until . . . later on . . . later on in life.

AMY: Yes.

COOKIE: Your grades were excellent?

AMY: Quite good, yes.

COOKIE: B-pluses and A-minuses? That sort of thing?

AMY: Oh, yes. And then some.

COOKIE: Higher?

AMY: A bit.

COOKIE: A-minuses and A-s?

AMY: A-s and A-pluses, mostly.

COOKIE: Were you the . . .?

AMY: No . . .

COOKIE: I didn't think so . . .

AMY: . . . Bruce B. Webber . . .

COOKIE: . . . I remember that . . .

AMY: . . . Every A I got, he got an A-plus. Every A-plus I got, he matched . . .

COOKIE: Always higher . . .

AMY: On the average . . .

COOKIE: Must've bothered you . . .

AMY: Not at all.

COOKIE: Must have.

AMY: Not any more . . .

COOKIE: 'Course not . . .

AMY: Sixty years now . . .

COOKIE: Seventy-five!

AMY: Ah, yes . . .

COOKIE: That's why we're here . . .

AMY: Seventy-five . . . (*A pause.*) I remember being two.

COOKIE: Two years old?

AMY: I do. I have a memory. My mum . . . cuddling me.

COOKIE: Extraordinary mind you have.

AMY: Do you think so?

COOKIE: Oh, I do.

AMY: So much fed in.

COOKIE: Must be a burden . . .

AMY: Old age is supposed to dull it all . . .

COOKIE: Blend it together . . .

AMY: Not I.

COOKIE: Me neither . . . (*Pauses.*) Hell of a burden. (*Smiles.*) Whatever became of him?

AMY: Bruce B. Webber?

COOKIE: I'd heard Tech . . .

AMY: Tech?

COOKIE: M.I.T.

AMY: Oh, no! He quit there . . .

COOKIE: Really?

AMY: Quit during his first year. They say he was failing . . .

COOKIE: His *health?*

AMY: His grades!

COOKIE: You're joking!

AMY: Small fish, big pond . . . that sort of thing.

COOKIE: Bruce B. Webber? Failing? Doesn't seem possible, does it?

AMY: Smith girls often spent a weekend in Cambridge, Harvard, or M.I.T. Clara Ellison, from Great Neck, Long Island, New York, dated Bruce B. Webber's brother, Alfred, also an W.H.S. man . . .

COOKIE: Poor Alfred.

AMY: Oh, yes. Poor Alfred, indeed . . . you may remember . . .

COOKIE: Which of us could forget?

AMY: Clara brought the news of poor Alfred's brother, our own Bruce B. Webber . . .

COOKIE: And he was in fact failing?

AMY: And despairing, too!

COOKIE: Not drinking as well?

AMY: I don't think so . . . (*Pauses.*) Perhaps . . .

COOKIE: Who could have guessed?

AMY: Small fish.

COOKIE: But you certainly did well at Smith . . .

AMY: Quite well.

COOKIE: Same pond for both of you . . .

AMY: That's true enough. (*Smiles.*) Lake Quannapowitt.

COOKIE: Terrible, the pollution formed in that lake in seventy-five years!

AMY: Do you take walks?

COOKIE: Now, of course, with Route One-Twenty-Eight cutting right into my property, it's . . . well . . . it's not as nice, not as relaxing.

AMY: Noise can bury you!

COOKIE: You needn't say *that* above a whisper, I can tell you that! (*Leans in.*) I've foxed them.

AMY: Mmm?

COOKIE: The Route One-Twenty-Eight Commission. I've foxed them. (*Looks around room before he speaks.*) I requested, procured, and installed an absolutely official, state-provided sign for the road at my property-edge: "Blind Child." (*Smiles.*) Isn't that wicked clever?

AMY: (*Smiles.*) Blind child?

COOKIE: (*Chortles a while.*) Cut the noise to half . . .

AMY: Really?

COOKIE: You can see the cars and trucks visibly lose speed the moment they see the sign . . . feet loosen right off their accelerators! (*He chortles again.*) I'm very proud of *that* idea!

AMY: Do you own a great deal of property?

COOKIE: A modest amount.

AMY: How lucky for you.

COOKIE: I planned.

AMY: Good for you!

COOKIE: I bought the original parcel back about forty years now. At the time I first bought, I insisted on taking options on five adjoining parcels . . . (*Pauses.*) Or would I say "adjacent"?

AMY: You might. You might even say "contiguous" . . .

COOKIE: (*Somewhat "W.C. Fields."*) Ah, yes, contiguous parcels. That has a nice ring!

AMY: How clever of you! And you've managed to buy them all?

COOKIE: And then some.

AMY: Have you?

COOKIE: Twelve parcels in all.

AMY: My Lord!

COOKIE: It's an eyeful.

AMY: All near the highway, is it?

COOKIE: Oh, no. Just the tip of two. The bottom edges, you might say...

AMY: I see.

COOKIE: I've got a pond . . .

AMY: On your property?

COOKIE: It's very nice.

AMY: I love a small pond.

COOKIE: I wouldn't exactly call it a *small* pond. It's quite large . . .

AMY: Really?

COOKIE: Half-a-mile across in width; three-quarters-of-a-mile, in length . . .

AMY: Sounds enormous!

COOKIE: Very pleasant, I should say.

AMY: I should think so!

COOKIE: Stocked with pickerel . . .

AMY: Pickerel?

COOKIE: Pickerel are young pike. They like the deep, cool, fresh water . . . (*Smiles.*) They're quite a large, long fish.

AMY: How marvelous for you!

COOKIE: (*He returns to her table, sits. He talks quickly, confidentially.*) A bit saved every year and, by the time you hit my age . . .

AMY: Not I.

COOKIE: I'm sorry . . .

AMY: Never had a business head . . .

COOKIE: But you've got your pension . . .

AMY: Yes, that. But I never used it well . . .

COOKIE: Do you own or rent?

AMY: Rent.

COOKIE: Oh, I see. (*Pauses.*) Renting can be nice.

AMY: Not the same as owning.

COOKIE: I know many a happy renter . . .

AMY: I know a few . . .

COOKIE: I know many an unhappy owner . . .

AMY: Yes, I suppose . . . (*Smiles.*) You have a very pleasant way.

COOKIE: Do you think so?

AMY: I do.

COOKIE: Well, aren't you nice to say it . . . (*There is a pause. Cookie reaches across the table and touches Amy's hand. She smiles. Tableau. Cookie withdraws his hand. He smiles.*) Bruce B. Webber never impressed me much, I can tell you that!

AMY: Oh, I wouldn't sell him short . . .

COOKIE: I don't. I don't. But he did have an, arrogant streak!

AMY: You have to in this life. If you want to get ahead . . .

COOKIE: I don't agree!

AMY: I'm afraid it's true . . .

COOKIE: And where did it get Mr. Bruce B. Webber? . . .

AMY: I suppose . . .

COOKIE: All that drinking and despairing! . . .

AMY: I suppose . . .

COOKIE: As if that family didn't have enough trouble and grief, with poor Alfred's untimely end. . .

AMY: (*Shakes her head.*) There's no word invented for what that family did to Alfred L. Webber . . . not in Greek, not in Italian, probably not even in the Irish tongue . . .

COOKIE: Were you friendly with Alfred?

AMY: . . . L. Webber? Yes, I suppose I should say yes . . .

COOKIE: Were you close friends?

AMY: Which of us was, really? He was so . . . well . . .

COOKIE: Odd?

AMY: Odd's too harsh . . .

COOKIE: Despairing?

AMY: Yes, that too. And, of course, his problem . . .

COOKIE: The drinking . . .

AMY: Like a fish . . .

COOKIE: Awful to see . . .

AMY: Tried to stop him . . .

COOKIE: I'm sure you did . . .

AMY: Never could. . .

COOKIE: (*After a pause.*) You were *that* close, were you?

AMY: We took walks. In the afternoons. Not many, but they had quality . . . (*Smiles.*) He knew the lake like a friend . . . the wildflowers . . . by name . . . butterflies . . . by name, as well . . . the trees . . . (*Pauses.*) He was the first to make me see the beauty of the old headstones . . .

COOKIE: (*Amazed.*) In the cemetery?

AMY: Can you imagine? I was squeamish at first . . .

COOKIE: (*Increasingly amazed.*) The headstones in the cemetery?

AMY: We made rubbings.

COOKIE: (*Shocked.*) Of the headstones in the cemetery?

AMY: Some of them were quite beautiful . . . seventeenth century . . . very early Wakefield families . . .

COOKIE: This is a little difficult for me to follow . . . (*He is clearly amazed.*) You and Alfred . . . together . . . took walks in the cemetery? . . . and made rubbings of tombstones?

AMY: Yes, we did.

COOKIE: Christ!

AMY: I know it sounds a bit odd . . .

COOKIE: Odd? Weird, you mean.

AMY: Well, I . . .

COOKIE: (*Interrupting her.*) My entire family's buried there . . .

AMY: Not *that* cemetery.

COOKIE: Huh?

AMY: AMY: We did our rubbings in the other cemetery.

COOKIE: Oh, yes.

AMY: Near the Congo church . . .

COOKIE: Back of the Hartshorne House . . .

AMY: Precisely.

COOKIE: Alfred's as weird as they come.

AMY: (*Suddenly anger, after a pause.*) I think we've carried this subject to a conclusion, Mr. Silverstein. (*Pauses.*) I think this conversation of ours is . . . exhausted.

COOKIE: I didn't realize . . .

AMY: That we were close? (*Smiles.*) Yes, we were.

COOKIE: I'm really sorry.

AMY: I'm sure you are. (*Smiles.*) Alfred L. Webber was the gentlest man I have known in my entire ninety-three years of knowing men . . . and I have known many, sir, many. (*Pauses.*) I think we have touched, as they say, a ticklish spot.

COOKIE: I'm really sorry, Miss Chamberlain. I hope you can forgive me . . .

AMY: I do, I do. . . .(*Pauses.*) I'm a bit overprotective with my memories . . .

COOKIE: I understand . . .

AMY: So much of it has been so difficult . . .

COOKIE: Tragedy befalling you, over and over again . . .

AMY: (*Looks about room.*) Well . . . (*Smiles.*) I'm feeling a bit tired . . . (*Pauses.*) No one else expected. Just us, I suppose . . . (*Smiles.*) We didn't get an awful lot for our money, did we?

COOKIE: Oh! I have your money! (*Reaches in his pocket, finds check.*) Here!

AMY: On, not at all!

COOKIE: No, it's your check. I never cashed it. (*Pauses.*) Please. (*She takes check.*) When you failed to return the form, I assumed . . . (*Pauses.*) I only came myself on an outside chance that someone . . . (*Smiles.*) I'm very pleased I did . . .

AMY: (*Pocketing check.*) Yes. As am I . . .

COOKIE: I didn't order a meal, because . . .

AMY: I understand . . .

COOKIE: I canceled the caterer . . .

AMY: There was a caterer?

COOKIE: Oh, yes. I thought there might be as many as ten of us . . .

AMY: Really?

COOKIE: Tragic year for our class . . .

AMY: Perhaps next time . . .

COOKIE: What's that?

AMY: We'll keep the caterer.

COOKIE: And a proper dancing band!

AMY: A dancing band?

COOKIE: Easily arranged.

AMY: Dance band. I'm sure that's what you mean: a dance band.

COOKIE: Precisely!

AMY: Perhaps next time.

COOKIE: Should we wait the five years?

AMY: It's the tradition?

COOKIE: We might bend the tradition a bit . . .

AMY: In which way?

COOKIE: Why not wait just *one* year?

AMY: And have a seventy-sixth? I suppose. We could call it "The Spirit of Seventy-Six."

COOKIE: It certainly has a ring . . .

AMY: I wouldn't mind at all, really. Not at all . . . (*She stands.*) You have my address, don't you?

COOKIE: Twenty-seven Parker Road . . .

AMY: No, Thirty Gould . . .

COOKIE: Oh, yes!

AMY: Will you remember?

COOKIE: Etched on my brain already!

AMY: (*He helps her into her coat.*) Next year then? (*She smiles, extends her arm for a handshake.*)

COOKIE: (*Takes her hand, holds it a while.*) Could we do it next week?

AMY: Next week?

COOKIE: Next week. I would like that very much, Miss Chamberlain.

AMY: I suppose so. What would we call it?

COOKIE: Seventy-five-*A*.

AMY: Yes. Do you have a telephone?

COOKIE: I do. I do. I'll write out my address and number for you. (*He fishes for and finds a wallet with pad and gold pen, in his jacket's inside pocket.*) Here. I'll write it down. (*She is looking through her pocketbook.*)

AMY: I'm afraid I haven't a pencil . . . (*Sees his.*) Isn't that elegant?

COOKIE: (*Hands paper to her.*) That's my address and telephone there . . . may I ask yours?

AMY: I'll write it for you . . . (*She takes pen and paper and writes her address and telephone number upon paper.*) Wonderful pen . . .

COOKIE: Thank you . . . (*She hands pen and paper to him. He studies address.*) Ah, yes. Gould Street, Stoneham. I know it . . .

AMY: Just past where the scrap yard used to be . . .

COOKIE: You have lovely handwriting . . .

AMY: Do you think so?

COOKIE: Perfect Palmer Perfect . . . wonderful to see.

AMY: Not quite so perfect as it was . . .

COOKIE: Lovely . . . (*Pockets her address, his wallet, etc.*) I'll call you . . . when? . . . day after tomorrow? What's a good time of day for you?

AMY: Late afternoon. I've always enjoyed a telephone call in the late afternoon.

COOKIE: Four-thirty, day after tomorrow. You'll hear my ring.

AMY: I look forward to it.

COOKIE: Do you have a ride now? I could have my driver take you . .

AMY: You have a driver, do you?

COOKIE: Been with me for years now. Excellent driver. Highly skilled.

AMY: Do you have a limousine?

COOKIE: I do.

AMY: My goodness! (*She giggles.*) What a small world.

COOKIE: Could I arrange then for you to be driven? (*Smiles.*) I could ride along, if you'd like.

AMY: Thank you, but my ride is arranged. (*Looks at her watch.*) Well done by now, I should think. I'm nearly twenty minutes late. (*Smiles.*) Good company.

COOKIE: You're very kind to say that.

AMY: I can't promise you we'll meet next week, but we can discuss it . . . the possibility of our meeting . . .when you call.

COOKIE: I understand. Four-thirty. Day after tomorrow.

AMY: (*Extends hand again.*) Well, then . . .

COOKIE: I'll walk you to your car . . .

AMY: Please, don't! (*Smiles.*) I'm perfectly capable . . .

COOKIE: I know that. I just thought it would be nice . . .

AMY: I'd rather you didn't!

COOKIE: Fine. We'll say "Goodnight" here then . . . (*They shake hands.*) I'm very pleased to have met you . . . to have seen you again, I mean.

AMY: As am I . . . pleased to have met you again . . . Mr. Silverstein.

COOKIE: Cookie.

AMY: Goodnight. (*She exits. There is a silence. Cookie walks to the juke box and replugs electrical join to the wall outlet. The juke box lights relight. The music fades in again, winding up to full sound and speed, at the precise spot on the recording at which the plug was pulled earlier in the play. Cookie crosses to the chair, collects his coat, puts it on, stops a moment. He begins to exit, thinks better of it, returns to chair; sits. The music continues. Cookie sits at table, staring straight out, listening to music, lost in a fantasy. He taps his fingers on the tabletop, to the rhythm of the music. The lights fade out.*)

THE PLAY IS OVER.

A NOTE TO THE DIRECTOR OF *THE 75TH*

It is central to the play that the juke box be of the neon light-up variety, gaudy, in splendid contrast to the muted-tone tweed and wool clothing of Cookie and Amy. It is also recommended that the juke box be functional, if possible; the true source of the sound. Thus, when Amy pulls the electrical plug from the wall, the music will grind down and out. When Cookie replugs the juke box, at the closing of the play, the reverse will occur: the music will whirl up to tempo, until its conclusion.

If at all possible, older actors should be used for this play, thereby eliminating any need to act old age, allowing full rehearsal time for the development of the relationship between the two people. If younger actors are used for *The 75th*, do not allow the problem of aging the actors to consume valuable rehearsal time. Instead, merely indicate the age with costume and minimal use of makeup, and allow the lines of the play to take the actors to their correct age.

While *Hopscotch* seems to be a play about a pickup and instead reveals itself as a play about a reunion, *The 75th* completes the double-reverse: it appears to be a reunion, but becomes, in fact, a pickup.

The 75th is first and foremost a comedy, about a woman who has forgotten the phrase "lose my senses," and a man who learns to tap his fingers.

Israel Horovitz

New York, December, 1977

STAGE DIRECTIONS

For Edith Fournier

STAGE DIRECTIONS had its first public performance on May 31, 1976, at The Actors Studio, New York. It was directed by J. Ranelli with the following cast:

RICHARD .... Lenny Baker
RUTH .... Laura Esterman
RUBY .... Nancy Mette

Introduction

I'm often asked which play of mine is my favorite. In fact, it's almost always the one I'm in the midst of writing. Thus, *Stage Directions* remains, quite constantly, in second place. Yes, I think it's a good play.

I directed the French-language premiere of *Stage Directions* (*Didascalies*) in Paris, last season, and had a lovely time doing it...one of the best things of my life. *Stage Directions* was enormously successful, and I returned to Paris in the Spring of 1993, to film the play.

Stage Directions is a director's piece, best approached as chamber music played by three (tightly-wound) stringed instruments. The situation of the play is this: three grown siblings return from the grave of their parents to their childhood home...They are unable to speak to each other in conventional conversation. Instead, they announce their movement in the room...i.e.; "Richard enters, quietly. He crosses to the...". Thus, we hear only their stage-directions, their *didascalies.* The play alternates between funny and frightening, comic and tragic. Both masks must be attended to, carefully. The clear (to me) influences on *Stage Directions* were, once again, Euripides, and, once again, Beckett...perhaps, with an added touch of O'Neill. But, in the end, the invention was my own.

I first directed *Stage Directions,* some years ago, at The Actors Studio in NYC, with Laura Esterman, Lenny Baker and Nancy Mette playing the three siblings. Jack Hoffsiss then directed a full production at The New York Shakespeare Festival, in 1978, with Patti LuPone, Ellen Greene and John Glover. But, it was in Paris, last year, that the play first sang to me.

Jean-Pierre Stewart came back into my life through *Stage Directions.* He'd played in *The Primary English Class,* off-Broadway, during the mid-1970's, but, left America, shortly after the run ended, and settled his family in Paris. I'd seen J-P in Paris, from time to time, and observed that he'd grown into the perfect man to play Richard in *Stage Directions.* When I first started organizing my Paris production, I called Jean-Pierre from NYC, and asked him to join the cast. I then went to Paris, where I auditioned more than 100 actors for the remaining two roles. I settled on Anne-Lise Sabouret, a friend of J-P's, and a young, then-unknown actress, Laura Zichy. From day #1, they were, all three, brilliant...*vâchement génial!*

Because *Stage Directions* is such a technically-detailed play, I planned my production in advance, quite precisely. The stage was set by costumed stagehands, who, in blue light, in full view of the audience, ran across the stage with a huge white silk drop flowing over their heads, which they floated down onto the sofa and matching arm-chairs, covering them like objects in a house of the dead. While the stage was being set, a cellist played Bach, live. Black velour curtains were pulled aside, on cue, to reveal a mirrored wall, on one side of the stage, and a gold-framed photograph of the recently-dead parents, on the other wall.

As Jean-Pierre and I are both Actors Studio people, we were able to work quite internally for the first few weeks of rehearsal...and then, I began to lock in movement and sound. Anne-Lise Sabouret was superb as the steely-cold Ruth, and Laura Zichy was heart-breaking as the suicidal Ruby. But, it was Jean-Pierre Stewart who stole the show. He gave one of those once-in-a-lifetime, thank-God-I-was-there-to-see-it, standing-O performances, with a fully-tragic size to wring pity and terror from a grateful audience. I knew that Jean-Pierre would be good in *Stage Directions*, but, I was totally unprepared for the treasures he would mine from my odd, one-hour play.

Stage Directions chronicles, sort of, the absurdly tragic circumstance into which I was born. Shortly before my birth, my Grandfather died. My Grandmother, Aunt, and Cousin, flew to Arkansas to recover his body. Their plane crashed in the Ozark Mountains and they were all killed. Imagine: within a few days' passing, my Uncle Sam Horovitz had lost his father, mother, wife and son. Within weeks of these horrifying events, I was born. If Freud is to be believed, much of one's personality is formed in the first six months of life. If nothing else, my plays are quite casually tragic...as was the nature and condition of my entrance into this particular life.

If I were to choose one play to best represent my ferocious outpouring of work during the 1970's (20 plays in 10 years!), *Stage Directions* is the one. I've written earlier in these essays introducing my plays that I'd thought Creativity was God's gift to the suffering child. I should like to add, now, that, for me and for most artists I've known intimately, the suffering never stops...but, in the midst of creating the artistic product—the play, the painting, the dance, the *work*—the artist is almost never unhappy. But, when the work is done...

Characters

RICHARD A thin, hawklike man, forties.

RUTH A thin, hawklike woman, thirties.

RUBY A small, wrenlike woman, twenties.

Setting

Late afternoon, fall.
Living room, New England home,
overlooking Lake Quannapowitt, Wakefield, Mass.

NOTE The people of the play will speak only words that describe their activities and, on occasion, emotions. No other words or sounds are permitted. By definition, then, all activity and conveyed emotion must be born of spoken stage directions.

STAGE DIRECTIONS

Lights fade up. A cellist plays Bach, near the stage.
Sofa, slightly Right of room's Center.
Bar wagon and liquor, Upstage Right.
Overstuffed chairs, Right and Left of sofa, slightly Downstage.
Large framed mirror, 24" x 36", draped in black fabric, Upstage Left wall.
Equal-sized framed photograph, draped in black fabric as well, opposite wall, Upstage of Center of sofa.
China cabinet filled with bric-a-brac, wall beside Upstage chair, (Optional.)
Single door to room, Upstage Right wall.
Copious bookshelves and books, wherever space permits.
General feeling wanted that room belongs to bookish person.
Small desk Downstage Right. Writing stand, memo pad, stationery, on same. Wastebasket at Upstage front foot of desk.
Oriental carpet, subdued tones, under all of above.

RICHARD: (*Enters.*) Richard enters, quietly. Looks about room to see if he is alone. Certain he is, closes door. Click. He pauses, inhales, turns and leans his back against door, exhales, sobs once. He wipes his eyes on his cuff, notices black armband, which he removes and into which he blows his nose. He then stuffs armband into pocket of his overcoat which he then removes and folds somewhat fastidiously over back of sofa. He pauses, looking about room, taking a private moment: possibly adjusting his underwear and then discovering and dealing with a day-old insect bite in the pit behind his knee. A fly buzzes past his nose, breaking into his thoughts. He swats at fly, carelessly, but somehow manages to capture same in hand, which he brings down and then up close to his eye. He opens hand ever so slightly, watching fly awhile to determine its sex. Although it appears certain that he will open hand allowing fly *her* freedom, he suddenly smashes hands together, finishing fly and causing clap to sound in room. He walks to desk and using slip of memo paper from pad, he scrapes fly from palm and into wastebasket at foot of desk. He inspects stain on palm, lowers, hand to side, pauses, returns to chair, sobs once, sits, bows head, notices shoe, removes same, places single shoe in his lap, sobs again, searches for and finds lightly plaided handkerchief into which he blows nose enthusiastically, unclogging same and producing substantial honking sound in room. He settles back in chair, stares vacantly up at ceiling.

RUTH: (*Enters.*) Ruth enters, quietly, closing door with her heel. Click. She looks cautiously about room to see if she is alone, sees Richard sitting in chair.

RICHARD: Richard quickly bows his head and assumes somewhat grave look on his face, rather a studied vacant stare at his black-stockinged foot.

RUTH: Ruth smiles, as though she has been acknowledged.

RICHARD: Richard flashes a quick look at Ruth, to be certain it is she who has entered.

RUTH: Ruth catches Richard's glance and smiles again.

RICHARD: Richard is forced to return her smile and does. He then returns to former position in chair, head-bowed, eyes vacant, staring down toward black-stockinged foot.

RUTH: Ruth leans her back against door, exhales.

RICHARD: Richard adjusts his underwear, discreetly.

RUTH: Ruth sighs.

RICHARD: Richard wipes the palm of his hand behind the knee of his trouser-leg, accomplishing both a wipe and a rub of the day-old insect bite.

RUTH: Ruth touches her black armband to be certain it has not been lost; sighs again.

RICHARD: Richard glances at his hand to be certain now that fly stain has been completely removed. Satisfied, nonetheless, he wipes his hand on his trouser-leg again.

RUTH: Ruth pretends to be removing her overcoat while never removing her stare from the back of Richard's head. She slips her hand inside her coat and discreetly adjusts her brassière . . .

RICHARD: . . . just as Richard turns to her . . .

RUTH: She recoils quickly, pulling her hand from her coat.

RICHARD: Seeing that he has startled her, he turns away, reviving his former position, head bowed, vacantly staring at his black-stockinged foot.

RUTH: Ruth pauses a moment and then moves directly to bar and surveys liquor supply atop same.

RICHARD: Richard senses her presence at the bar and turns to look disapprovingly at Ruth.

RUTH: Ruth, sensing Richard's disapproval, quickly pours an inch of bourbon, which she downs in a gulp.

RICHARD: He continues his disapproving stare, while unconsciously touching his nose.

RUTH: She raises her glass toward him, nods: blatantly hostile. She smiles, unconsciously touching her nose as well.

RICHARD: She is smiling, deliberately handling her nose . . .

RUTH: He turns away, pompously . . . She clears her throat, attempting to regain his attention, but he remains unmoved, disapproving . . . She pulls open her coat and adjusts her brassière . . .

RICHARD: Raising his hip and thigh, slightly and quickly, he adjusts his briefs, scratches his day-old insect bite and then spits directly on to his palm and fly-stain, wipes his hand on his trouser knee, smiles . . . He turns now and faces her directly, but she is pretending not to notice, not to be paying attention to him. She searches for and finds a rather gaudy orange nylon handkerchief, into which she indelicately honks her hooked nose . . .

RUTH: He removes his sock and pulls at toes, playing with same . . .

RICHARD: She flings her coat sloppily over back of sofa . . . His other shoe off now and . . .

RUTH: (*Nota Bene Words and actions overlap competitively.*) Ruth removes her gloves . . . and hat . . .

RICHARD: (*Overlapping.*) . . . placing it precisely beside his first shoe.

RUTH: (*Overlapping.*) . . . tossing them in a heap on the sofa . . .

RICHARD: (*Overlapping.*) . . . He then peels of his other sock . . .

RUTH: (*Overlapping.*) . . . She then hoists her skirt and unhitches her stocking-top from the front and back garters on her garter-belt.

RICHARD: (*Overlapping.*) Richard averts his eyes!

RUTH: Ruth stares at the back of Richard's head, directly. The affect should be one of deep hostility. She is, however, surprised to notice that she is weeping.

RICHARD: As is Richard.

RUTH: There is a moment of absolute silence. (*Five count.*)

RICHARD: Sock clenched in fist, Richard will pound the arm of his chair, three times. He stares straight ahead, eyes unblinking. Three . . . dull . . . thuds . . . And then silence. (*Five count.*)

RUTH: Ruth approaches Ruby's chair, stands behind it a moment, pauses.

RICHARD: Richard turns to her and their eyes quietly meet.

RUTH: Ruth is the first to turn away.

RICHARD: Richard bows his head.

RUTH: Ruth walks quickly to the bar wagon and liquor supply, pours two inches of bourbon this time, tosses bottle cap on to floor and then returns to Ruby's chair.

RICHARD: Richard does not look up. He picks at a loose thread on his trouser-knee.

RUTH: Ruth sits, crosses legs, removes shoes, floors them.

RICHARD: Richard turns his body away from her, staring off, vacantly.

RUTH: Ruth notices now she wears one stocking pulled taut, the other dangling loose by her knee. She removes first stocking and allows it to stay on floor near her foot. She reaches under her skirt and unhitches other stocking from her garter-belt.

RICHARD: Richard glances at her, discreetly touching his nose.

RUTH: She senses his glance, but neither looks up nor acknowledges same. She instead removes stocking which she crunches and holds in same hand with glass of bourbon.

RICHARD: Richard suddenly stands, floors shoes, crosses room to bar.

RUTH: Ruth watches him, unconsciously touching her nose.

RICHARD: Richard searches for and finds small clear bottle of club soda, which he neatly uncaps, pouring liquid into small clear glass. He recaps bottle, replacing same precisely where it was found. Taking glass in hand, returns to chair, sits, sips.

RUTH: Ruth sips her bourbon and notices stockings crunched in hand. She reaches down and finds other stocking, joining both in loose knot, which she flings on to sofa seat.

RICHARD: Richard stares at her disapprovingly.

RUTH: Ruth remembers armband on coat. She stands, goes to it.

RICHARD: Richard stares after her.

RUTH: Ruth begins to remove armband, but, thinks better of it, returns to chair, begins to sit, thinks better of it, drains glass of its bourbon, returns to bar, pours three inches of fresh bourbon into same glass.

RICHARD: Richard turns away from her.

RUTH: Ruth glances at back of Richard's head.

RICHARD: Richard rubs his knee.

RUTH: Ruth tosses bottle, now empty, into wastebasket.

RICHARD: The sound startles Richard, who turns suddenly . . .

RUTH: . . . startling Ruth, who recoils, spill her drink . . . on the *rug*!

RICHARD: Richard stares at stain . . . on the *rug!*

RUTH: Ruth rubs stain with her toe.

RICHARD: Richard turns away.

RUTH: Ruth turns, cupping her forehead in the palm of her right hand. She then moves her hand down over her nose and mouth and sobs.

RICHARD: There is a moment of silence, which Richard breaks first by dropping his glass on to floor.

RUTH: Ruth looks quickly in direction of sound.

RICHARD: Richard is amazed. He grabs his nose.

RUTH: Ruth smiles.

RICHARD: Richard leans forward and picks up glass.

RUTH: Ruth drains her glass of its remaining bourbon, one gulp.

RICHARD: Richard wipes his stain on rug with his socks, never leaving his chair, but instead leaning forward to his stain.

RUTH: Ruth, for the first time, notices his body, now stretched forward. Her smile is gone.

RICHARD: Richard seems perplexed. He pulls at his earlobe.

RUTH: Ruth places glass atop bar. She searches for and finds dish towel, which she aims and pitches on to floor near Richard's stain.

RICHARD: Richard looks first at dish towel, then at Ruth disapprovingly. He then picks up dish towel and covers his stain with same.

RUTH: Ruth crosses to Ruby's chair, sits. She is weeping.

RICHARD: Richard, too, is weeping.

RUBY: (*Enters*) Ruby enters, somewhat noisily, clumsily.

RUTH: Ruth turns to her from chair, smiles.

RUBY: Ruby returns the smile.

RUTH: Ruth looks away.

RUBY: Ruby looks about the room until her eyes meet Richard's.

RICHARD: His expression is cold, the muscles of his face taut, his mouth thin-lipped, angry.

RUBY: Ruby nods to Richard.

RICHARD: Richard turns away, fists clenched on knees.

RUBY: Ruby closes door, bracing back against same.

RUTH: She has Richard's enormous Tel Avivian nose . . .

RICHARD: . . . Ruth's hawklike eyes, her hopelessly flat chest . . .

RUTH: . . . Richard's studied pomposity: his gravity . . .

RICHARD: . . . Ruth's self-consciously-correct posture . . .

RUBY: Rich girl's shoulders.

RICHARD: Richard loathes Ruby.

RUTH: As does Ruth.

RICHARD: Evident now in his stern glance.

RUTH: As in Ruth's sudden snap from warmth to disapproval: from passion to ice.

RUBY: Ruby moves four steps to center of room and then stops, suddenly, somewhat squashed by their staring.

(*Nota Bene: The following speeches are to be spoken as though interruptions, often overlapping, and often blending. No considerable movement wanted during this section.*)

RICHARD: Nota Bene. Richard was first to hear news of father's death . . .

RUTH: Nota Bene. Ruth heard news of plane crash and mother's death from Richard . . .

RUBY: Nota Bene Ruby was last to hear news of plane crash and mother's death . . .

RICHARD: . . . Mother's call put through by Betsy – the secretary – Mrs. Betsy Day, the secretary – Conference room, cigar smoke thick, business trouble, no time, distractions impossible . . .

RUTH: . . . Richard's phone call, Asian Studies Office, University of Vermont, town of Manchester, employed as nobody, researching nothing, touching no one . . .

RUBY: . . . Read news in Chicago *Sun-Times.* Heard same on FM station, midst of news, interrupting Bach's *Concerto in D Minor* for 3 harpsichords and orchestra, *Alla Siciliana,* my name, them famous, now dead, now famous death . . .

RICHARD: . . . Father's body must be gotten. Died in Hot Springs, Arkansas, getting cured . . .

RUTH: . . . Ruth had not known her father had died . . .

RUBY: Flew from O'Hare International to Logan International, United Air Lines, 707, morning flight, a clot of double-knit polyester leisure-suited business men, whispering loudly. Her second flight only, entire lifetime. . .

RICHARD: . . . Arranged for mother to fly to Hot Springs, Arkansas, to collect father's body, fly it home . . .

RUTH: . . . Ruth had not even known her father had been ill . . .

RUBY: . . . Her first flight was three years prior, visited father, first news of illness . . .

RICHARD: . . . Had reserved and paid for American Airlines First Class ticket. Had ticket hand-delivered to mother, two days prior . . .

RUTH: . . . Had years ago conquered fear of air travel. Had flown to and from all continents of the Earth . . .

RUBY: . . . Met with doctors, disease incurable, all hope lost . . .

RICHARD: . . . Had summoned surviving siblings to family home, New England September, all chill . . .

RUTH: . . . Had preferred Asia to all others. Had preferred living in countries possessing languages she could neither read nor speak . . .

RUBY: Brother Robert, gone as well, same disease, spared no pain, three years prior, family . . . curse . . .

RICHARD: . . . Had not spoken even one word to Ruth in four year's time, since her third divorce . . .

RUTH: . . . Had preferred most of all living within Cantonese dialect, Northern China, most difficult, words impossible to separate, blend together, word as din . . .

RUBY: . . . Missed brother Robert's funeral, fear of airplanes, trains too slow, Jewish custom, grave by sundown, arrived during night . . .

RICHARD: . . . Had not spoken even one word to Ruby in four year's time, since her first divorce . . .

RUTH: . . . Had stayed in room once, one full month, three years prior, Northern China, never straying, never speaking, not one word, not aloud, voice postponed . . .

RUBY: . . . Jewish Law, beat the sundown. Only mirrors, covered, missed her absence . . . All else saw . . .

RICHARD: . . . Had not spoken even one word to father in five year's time, since news of father's irreversible disease . . .

RUTH: . . . Ruth had loved her brother, Robert, deeply . . .

RUBY: . . . Family shocked by Ruby's absence, never forgiven, never heard . . .

RICHARD: . . . Richard was first to hear news of plane crash, second half of ticket, both together, Ozark Mountains, hillbillies found them, picked their clothing clean of money, pried their teeth clean of gold . . .

RUTH: . . . Mourned brother Robert's death, deeply, endlessly, silently . . .

RUBY: . . . Ruby, youngest, most degrees, Ph.D., Modern British, Joyce and Woolf her favored pair . . .

RICHARD: Pried their teeth clean of gold . . .

RUTH: . . . Never forgiven parents' not reaching her in time. Never said "Goodbye" to Robert . . . (*Nota Bene Overlapping ends here.*)

RUBY: . . . One brief marriage, to a surgeon . . .

RICHARD: . . . Mother's death . . .

RUTH: . . . Never reached her . . .

RUBY: . . . Engendered nothing, born barren, ovaries broken at birth . . .

RICHARD: . . . Richard feels responsible . . .

RUTH: . . . Ruth feels angry . . .

RUBY: . . . Ruby left husband; her, first to door, first to street, first to forget . . .

RICHARD: . . . Richard feels responsible . . .

RUTH: . . . Ruth feels angry . . .

RUBY: . . . Lived with friends, always male . . .

RICHARD: . . . Richard feels responsible . . .

RUTH: . . . Ruth feels angry . . .

RUBY: . . . Loved her brother, Robert, deeply. Mourned his death, not forgotten. Parents and siblings never forgiven, never forgave . . .

RICHARD: . . . Richard feels responsible for his parents' death . . .

RUTH: . . . Ruth feels angry at her parents' death . . .

RUBY: . . . Jet from Chicago, late as usual, missed their funeral, struck again. Ruby still stunned, unable to weep . . .

RICHARD: . . .Richard feels responsible for the death of his parents . . .

RUTH: . . . Ruth feels angry at the death of her parents . . .

RUBY: . . . Ruby is unable to weep at the death of her parents . . .

RICHARD: Nota Bene. All of above

RUBY: Nota Bene. All of above.

RICHARD: Richard glances at Ruby.

RUTH: Richard smiles, seeing Ruby's pain . . .

RUBY: Ruby regains her strength. She moves to the sofa where she flings her black coat, after tossing small Louis Vuitton weekend case to the floor beside sofa.

RICHARD: Richard is contemptuous of her gesture . . .

RUTH: As is Ruth, who is, however, somewhat amused at the same time and is surprised to find herself smiling. She adjusts her skirt.

RUBY: Ruby adjusts her skirt, re-tucks her blouse into skirt by reaching under skirt, pulls down blouse-ends from bottom, straightening blouse perfectly into skirt and, at the same time, pulling blouse tightly over her breasts.

RICHARD: Richard studies her breasts, certain there is no brassière supporting them.

RUTH: Ruth studies her breasts, certain there is no brassière supporting them.

RUBY: Ruby adjusts her brassière!

RUTH: Ruth adjusts her brassière!

RICHARD: Richard scratches his chest and coughs!

RUBY: Ruby moves to bar and pours glass full with ginger ale. She lifts brandy decanter from shelf, holds and studies same, somewhat lovingly.

RICHARD: Richard glances at dish towel on his stain . . . on rug near his foot.

RUTH: Ruth looks cautiously at her own stain.

RUBY: Ruby drops decanter . . . *accidentally!* It crashes down on bar top, causing loud noise to sound sharply in room.

RICHARD: Richard turns quickly to see what Ruby has done.

RUTH: As does Ruth!

RUBY: Ruby is amazed by what she has done! She takes the bar towel and feverishly wipes the spilled liquid.

RICHARD: Richard bows his head. He removes wallet from pocket, studies photograph of daughters and ex-wife, replaces wallet in pocket.

RUTH: Ruth bows her head. She pauses. She quietly slips from her chair and removes black veil from mirror. She studies her own image.

RUBY: Ruby moves discreetly behind Ruth, so that she is now able to see her own image in mirror as well.

RUTH: Ruth sees Ruby seeing herself and moves away from mirror, turning directly to face Ruby . . .

RUBY: . . . who is unable to meet the stare and turns her face downward, to the floor.

RUTH: Ruth smiles, crosses to sofa; sits.

RICHARD: Richard stands and walks directly to the mirror. He avoids looking at his reflected image, but instead recovers mirror with black fabric veil, moves to Ruby's chair; sits.

RUTH: Ruth crosses to Richard's chair and sits.

RUBY: Ruby clenches eyes closed, three count.

RICHARD: Richard adjusts his underwear.

RUTH: Ruth adjusts her underwear.

RUBY: Ruby crosses to what appears to be second veiled mirror and removes black fabric from it.

RICHARD: Richard averts his eyes from image . . .

RUTH: As does Ruth.

RUBY: Ruby exposes tinted photograph of parents, posed, taken on occasion of their 40th wedding anniversary. Ruby stares at photograph.

RICHARD: Richard is weeping. He silently mouths the word "Mama."

RUTH: As does Ruth.

RUBY: Ruby continues to stare at photograph a moment before taking two odd steps backwards, stiffly. She stops. She silently mouths the word "Papa."

RICHARD AND RUTH: (*Silently.*) Mama.

RUBY: (*Silently.*) Papa.

RUTH: Ruth glances at photograph and then at Ruby. She faces Richard, three count. She is openly contemptuous of her sister and brother.

RUBY: Ruby looks first at Richard and then at Ruth. She replaces veil over photograph. She moves to bar . . .

RICHARD: Richard follows her with his eyes, openly staring . . .

RUBY: . . . Ruby leans against bar, somewhat slumped, anguished . . .

RICHARD: . . . Richard coughs, turns away . . .

RUBY: . . . Ruby covers her eyes with palm of left hand. Right hand slides discreetly across stomach to waistband of skirt. She is adjusting and turning same.

RUTH: . . . Ruth remains silent, staring at stain on rug, lost in a memory . . .

RICHARD: . . . Richard strokes a tear from his cheek.

RUTH: Ruth stands, moves toward Ruby, tentatively: painfully slow, frightened. She plans to embrace her sister, but will not have the courage to do so.

RUBY: Ruby senses Ruth approaching, turns, faces her, smiles.

RUTH: Ruth is suddenly stopped.

RUBY: Ruby spies bottle-cap on floor, scoops it up, bending quickly, tosses same easily into wastebasket, leg of desk. Ruby turns, suddenly facing Richard . . .

RICHARD: . . . who has been discreetly admiring Ruby's upper thigh, made quite visible during her rapid bend and scoop . . .

RUBY: . . . Ruby giggles . . .

RICHARD: Richard turns quickly away from her, outraged.

RUBY: Ruby contrives a serious stare in his direction, but giggles again.

RUTH: Ruth is now holding her hand to her mouth, attempting unsuccessfully to contain a chortle.

RUBY: Ruby chortles openly.

RUTH: Ruth looks across stage to Ruby . . .

RUBY: . . . who looks across to Ruth.

RUTH: Ruth takes a step again in Ruby's direction.

RICHARD: Richard produces a wailing sound, suddenly, burying his face in his lap.

RUTH: Ruth turns to him and watches him awhile . . .

RICHARD: Richard is sobbing.

RUBY: Ruby walks to the back of Richard's chair, stops, reaches forward and allows her hand to rest a moment atop Richard's bowed head.

RUTH: Ruth watches, quietly, disapprovingly.

RICHARD: Richard seems unable to move. He neither turns toward Ruby nor away from her: he is instead frozen. His sobbing is now controlled: stopped, quenched.

RUBY: Ruby is embarrassed, sorry she negotiated the touching of Richard's head. She steps back now, three odd steps, stiffly; stops.

RUTH: Ruth stands staring at Ruby.

RUBY: Ruby looks directly at Ruth now. The sisters' eyes meet and hold an absolutely fixed stare.

RUTH: Ruth neither looks away, nor does she smile.

RUBY: Nor does Ruby.

RICHARD: Richard stands and moves directly to veiled photograph . . .

RUBY: . . . Ruby does not break her stare at Ruth . . .

RICHARD: . . . Richard pauses a moment, touching black fabric with the back of his hand . . .

RUTH: . . . Nor does Ruth break her stare at Ruby . . .

RICHARD: . . . Richard, carefully, silently, removes black fabric veil from photograph, allowing fabric to fall to floor beside his feet.

RUTH: Ruth is the first to break the stare between the sisters. She turns now to watch Richard.

RUBY: As does Ruby.

RICHARD: Richard stares intently at the photograph, reaching his left hand up and forward, touching the cheek of the man in the photograph. He rubs his finger gently across the face of the man, through the void between the man and the woman, finally allowing his finger to stop directly on the chin on the image of the woman in the photograph.

RUTH: Ruth stands, head bowed, silently mouths the word "Papa."

RUBY: Ruby stands, head bowed, silently mouths the word "Papa."

RICHARD: Richard turns, stares first at Ruth and then at Ruby. He points at the photograph, but then causes his pointing finger to fold back into his hand, which he clenches now into a fist, beating same, three times . . . *against* . . . *his* . . . *hip*. He relaxes. He silently mouths the word "Mama."

RUBY: Ruby moves to Richard's chair, sits, allowing her skirt to remain pleated open, high on her leg.

RICHARD: Richard notices her naked thigh.

RUTH: Ruth notices Richard noticing Ruby's naked thigh.

RICHARD: Richard notices that Ruth has noticed him.

RUBY: Ruby tugs her skirt down to her knee. With her left hand, she wipes a tear from her left cheek.

RICHARD: Richard moves to the bar. He studies the bottle of scotch whiskey a while before spilling five inches of the liquid into a fresh glass. He turns and faces Ruth, lifts his glass to her, then to his lips, drains it of its contents, drinking same.

RUTH: Ruth stares, silently amazed.

RUBY: Ruby bows her head and sobs.

RICHARD: Richard walks quietly to his shoes and socks and collects them. He sits on the sofa, center, and redresses his feet, sitting carelessly atop his sisters' outer garments.

RUTH: Ruth watches, standing straight now.

RUBY: Ruby notices the towel on the floor next to the chair in which she is sitting, rubs and moves same with her toe.

RICHARD: Richard looks up from tying his shoe to watch Ruby nudging his stain with her toe. He stares disapprovingly.

RUBY: Ruby senses Richard's disapproval and stops nudging at the stain. She instead leans forward and rubs the stain with her fingers, returning same to mouth, licking them with her tongue.

RUTH: Ruth gags.

RICHARD: Richard is *disgusted*! He completes tying his shoes hurriedly. He stands and tosses on his overcoat.

RUTH: Ruth takes three odd steps backwards, stiffly, stops.

RUBY: Ruby turns in her chair and stares openly at Richard.

RICHARD: Richard walks to bar, finds scotch whiskey bottle which he raises to his lips and drains, unflinchingly. Richard moves directly to position beneath photograph and stares at same, lifting bottle to image of mother and father.

RUBY: Ruby continues her stare at Richard, amazed.

RICHARD: Richard allows bottle to fall to floor near his feet. He touches photograph, precisely as he did before: man first, then woman. He then bows head, sobs.

RUTH: Ruth bows head, weeps, covering her eyes with palm of right hand.

RICHARD: Richard closes his coat fully now, lifting collar to back of his head. He discovers armband in pocket, removes it, clenching same in fist. He stares at Ruth, arm outstretched in her direction, fist pointing accusingly.

RUTH: Ruth glances up and then suddenly, down, averting eyes from Richard's but then looking up quickly, she stares directly into Richard's eyes.

RICHARD: He waits a moment, watching to see if she will have the strength to cross the room to him.

RUTH: Ruth moves one step toward Richard, not breaking their joined stare. But then she does. She stops. She lowers her eyes.

RUBY: Ruby stands, looks at Richard, but remains, unmoving, at the foot of her chair.

RICHARD: Richard watches Ruth a moment and then shifts his stare to Ruby.

RUBY: Ruby smiles.

RICHARD: Richard moves to door, opens same, pauses a moment, turns again into room, unclenches fist, allowing armband to drop to rug, pauses a moment, exits, never closing door.

RUBY: Ruby moves to door and closes same, leaning her back against it. She stares a moment at armband on rug.

RUTH: As does Ruth.

RUBY: Ruby moves to photograph and stares at same.

RUTH: Ruth finds shoes, slips quickly into same, moves to sofa, rapidly collecting her outer clothing.

RUBY: Ruby, suddenly realizing she might be left alone in room, moves, quickly, away from photograph, sees Ruth; stops, frozen.

RUTH: Ruth races to redress herself in her coat, jamming hat on to head, stockings in coat pocket.

RUBY: Ruby has her outer clothing now in her hands but realizes she is too late.

RUTH: Ruth has moved quickly and successfully, assuming an exit position at the door, coat buttoned closed.

RUBY: Ruby is stunned and allows her outer clothing to drop back down on to the sofa.

RUTH: Ruth smiles, touches doorknob.

RUBY: Ruby leans over sofa, her back to Ruth.

RUTH: Ruth stares at Ruby's youthful body, her thighs, her straight back, her rich girl's shoulders.

RUBY: Ruby lifts her face, but cannot turn to Ruth.

RUTH: Ruth glances at photograph, but cannot sustain look at same. She straightens her back, inhales, quietly opens door, exhales. She glances a final glance at Ruby. Exits.

RUBY: Ruby hears the door . . .

RUTH: (*Off.*) Click.

RUBY: . . . finally closed. She turns quickly. Certain now that Ruth has exited, Ruby stands frozen, sad-eyed, staring at the still closed door. She moves to bar and finds glass decanter on it, which she holds a moment before suddenly smashing same on bar. After shock of glass breaking, there is silence in the room. Ruby moves again to photograph, carrying jagged neck of glass decanter with her; considers destroying photograph, but instead softly caresses same with palm of right hand, touching first the image of the man, then the image of the woman and then again the image of the man. She moves to sofa, still carrying jagged remains of decanter with her. She thinks to sit but does not, instead turns, faces photograph, fully. Leaning forward over sofa, Ruby allows the weight of her body against the final point of the glass, causing the remains of the decanter to enter her body, just below the breast. She turns away from photograph, faces front, allows her body to relax on to sofa. Her hand unclenches. The jagged remains of the decanter fall. Blood drops from her hand, staining rug. Ruby faces front, pauses a moment. She opens her mouth, she screams, but there is no sound.

LIGHTS FADE TO BLACK.

THE PLAY IS OVER.

SPARED

For Lenny Baker

SPARED was first performed in a workshop at The Manhattan Theatre Club, New York City, during March and April, 1974, in preparation for its world premiere performances, April 17-27, 1974, at the Théâtre du Centre Culturel Américain, Paris, France. The play was directed by the author with the following cast:

MAN ....Lenny Baker

Subsequently, the American premiere of SPARED was presented by The Phoenix Theatre, in association with Brandeis University, at the Spingold Theatre, Brandeis University, Waltham, Mass., on November 15, 1975. The production was again directed by the author and again featured Mr. Baker.

Introduction

Sometime in the early 1970's, I'd discovered that I had made much more money than I needed. I'd written two Hollywood movies—*The Strawberry Statement* and *Believe In Me*. One of them was actually successful. I bought a townhouse in Greenwich Village—for cash—and still had some money left over. There was nothing else that I wanted to buy, particularly ... except an education.

My father had been a truck-driver until age 50, at which time he went to law school, nights, and made a lawyer of himself. When it was appropriate for me to go to university, the necessary tuition-money was being spent, understandably, on my father's late-life schooling. So, instead of going to a "name" university, I went to a nearly-free state-owned school, Massachusetts State Teachers College at Salem. I stayed at Salem Teachers for one year, but, I was bored sick. So, I quit school, and took a paying job. I worked for a life insurance agency, days, and wrote plays, nights. I saved my earnings, and, in the early 1960's, I sent myself to The Royal Academy of Dramatic Art.

Back home in America, in the mid-1970's, I grew to realize that my education was sadly lacking ... which is to say there were large gaping holes in my reading. So, I took my excessive Hollywood greenbacks, and, at age 30, negotiated an exchange of my new-found fame for a waiver of a required BA or better, and I enrolled in a Ph.D. Program in English Literature at the City University of New York. And then, for two wonderful years in a row, I read books much the way I imagine a starving man devours food: hungrily, selfishly, impolitely. My grades were A+'s and A's. For the first time in my life, I loved school. I even managed to teach myself enough French to pass the program's language exam.

But, at the end of the day (i.e.; the two years), I realized that the last thing I needed in life was a Ph.D. in English Literature. And the last thing I wanted to do with my life was to spend three more years away from daily disciplined play-writing, whilst, instead, writing a doctoral dissertation. So, I kissed my diss good-bye, and settled for an "enroute" M.A. in English Lit. I achieved this astonishing honor by handing over a longish paper I'd written on "Tragedy" to the powers-to-be at CUNY. To my delight, my paper was deemed acceptable as a Master's Thesis, which, along with my heroic coursework, qualified me for an M.A. Thus, I had proof of my two years' work, and back I tumbled, into the real world. Enough was enough.

But, when I went "A.B.D." (all but diss), I'd promised myself to find the time to something big, something significant ... something that would be as large and as complicated as my doctoral dissertation would have been. I constructed a detailed outline for a 7-play cycle, *The Wakefield Plays*, which I wrote during the following six years. *The Wakefield Plays* consists of a 9-act trilogy called *The Alfred Trilogy*: *Alfred the Great*, *Our Father's Failing*, and *Alfred Dies* ... plus, four inter-related short plays, *The Quannapowitt Quartet*: *Hopscotch*, *The 75th*, *Stage Directions*, and (finally, back to the point) *Spared*.

The Wakefield Plays is clearly the work of someone who's been through graduate school. The seven plays fairly burst with literary allusion ... which is to say, like *Finnegan's Wake*, they are brimming with dense highbrow thievery. (And there, all comparison ends.) Martin Esslin, the great and nice British drama critic, author of *The Theatre Of The Absurd*, called *The Wakefield Plays* "an American Orestia". Thornton Wilder, who was my mentor and friend, had something far different to say about *The Alfred Trilogy*, which I'd completed a year before the writing of *The Quannapowitt Quartet*. At the end of some lengthy and lavish praise ("You have created a masterpiece. The long plays are far too difficult. They'll almost never be produced, commercially, but, they are masterful!"). He then uttered a single sentence that altered the course of my playwriting from then till now ... "Of course, there's very little Wakefield in any of those plays." ... Spoken by the man who had created Grover's Corners, the world's most beloved New England town, I listened. And I thought. And I stewed. And soon, nervously, I set about writing *The Quannapowitt Quartet*: four plays that would be filled with real-life Wakefield, Massachusetts allusion. I was instantly thrilled by rediscovery of the dialect of my father and my father's father.

Soon after finishing the four short plays of *The Quannapowitt Quartet*, I began to write my eight Gloucester-based plays... *North Shore Fish, Park Your Car In Harvard Yard, Year Of The Duck, Strong Man's Weak Child, Sunday Runners In the Rain, Henry Lumper*, etc. But, my Gloucester plays are another story. Back to *Spared.*

Spared was written as the satyr-play of the Wakefield cycle. It was designed to undermine the seriousness, the pretentiousness of the entire undertaking. A satyr-play is a high-brow excuse for low-brow, sophomoric, pee-pee-poo-poo humor. In the simplest possible terms, after the dank and dire world of Alfred Webber and *The Alfred Trilogy*, I loved writing *Spared.*

Spared is one shaggy man's story, told at breakneck speed, as the man's life passes before his (and our) eyes in those last precious moments before death. Our hero has tried to commit suicide more than sixty different times. He has been, somehow, always, spared. This most recent attempt might be different.

A major component of the inspiration for *Spared* was an odd fact I'd learned about the human eye. I'd discovered that if the human eye is made to adjust to watching a poorly-lit object for a longish period of time, a image of that object imprints itself on the retina of the eye for as much as 48 hours following the essential squint. Thus, *Spared* was designed to be played in the dimmest possible light. Only the man's face is to be lit, and, by my rules, poorly so. Thus, if *Spared* is performed to my highest expectation, an image of the Actor will remain imprinted on the retina of the audience's eyes for up to a few days after they've seen my play. Of my fifty produced plays, *Spared* is, by far, my dirtiest trick.

Spared was painstakingly written and re-written, like my novel *Cappella*, in pen and ink, in five or six handsome notebooks, over a period of two or three years, pretty much non-stop. Samuel Beckett was the first humanoid to read the completed text of *Spared.* I got a note back from Mr. Beckett within a fortnight of sending him a copy of the MSS. "Dear Israel, Just read *Spared.* Bravo! Bravissimo! So glad. Love, Sam." So goes the fan-letter of my life.

With the nod from S.B. firmly in hand, I found the courage to show

Spared to a slightly larger world. I gave another copy of my manuscript to Lenny Baker, asking him if he would consider my directing him in the play. He read *Spared*, and quickly confessed to "total bewilderment" ... but, in the end, he said "yes", rather than "no". Lenny and I rehearsed *Spared* for about six months, and then began to play the thing for pretty much anybody who'd sit still and pay attention. And put up with the essential squint. My then-girlfriend, LuAnn Walther, claimed to have seen Lenny do Spared a hundred times. I remember auditioning *Spared* for Joe Papp, who said Lenny was too young ... and for Marshall Mason (Circle Rep), who said Lenny was too goofy. Both producers offered me NYC productions if I would agree to switch to other actors. Both got immediate turn-downs. Lenny Baker's performance in *Spared* was genius. It was Nureyev mid-leap, Horowitz one-handing Chopin, Cousey dribbling. It was *vâchement génial!* Lenny and Swoosie Kurtz and LuAnn and I traveled to Paris, where we opened a double-bill of *Spared* and *Hopscotch*, in English, at the old American Cultural Center, rue du Dragon. We rocked the joint. In the years after that, Lenny did *Spared* in a bunch of NYC venues, at Manhattan Theatre Club, at The Actors Studio ... in downtown lofts, in uptown basements ... wherever there was a human retina willing to put up with the necessary squint and strain.

In 1982, when Lenny was finally dying, he performed *Spared* in a small theatre in Los Angeles. He stayed in his bed six days a week, conserving his strength for a once-weekly performance of my 65-minute, dimly-lit, monologue. I am told by those who saw Lenny Baker's final performances of *Spared* in L.A., that he gave new meaning to the word "splendid".

Lenny Baker died of Cancer at age 37, with ten Horovitz plays, one Tony Award (*I Love My Wife*), and one Hollywood lead (*Next Stop, Greenwich Village*) under his belt. He would have a great Broadway and Hollywood career. He didn't. He died. But, for me and many theatre-goers, Lenny Baker is imprinted on the retina of our hearts ... forever.

ADDENDUM #1: After Lenny Baker's death, I retired *Spared*; hung it up like my old track-spikes. A few years ago, William Hickey stopped me on the street in front of my house the Village, and asked if he could tackle *Spared.* As I could not imagine a better replacement for Lenny Baker than Bill Hickey, I said "Yes", rather than "No". Bill and I have been rehearsing *Spared* for the last two years, or so. We're not quite ready to open, but, we're getting closer.

ADDENDUM #2: *Spared* has been beautifully translated into French by Samuel Beckett's friend and protégé Édith Fournier. I may direct a French production of *Spared* (*le Rescapé*) next season, with my old pal Jean-Pierre Stewart starring in the dim light. I directed Jean-Pierre in *Didascalies* (*Stage Directions*), in Paris, last season. But, in the end, I may not ever actually open *Spared*, again. I still cannot get Lenny's voice out of my head. Perhaps, *Spared* has been, for my lifetime, done? Perhaps, for me, *Spared* is best left as a beautiful memory. What I do know is this: we human types spend far too much time in life fearing our own deaths. Our own deaths are painless. It is the deaths of those we love that hurt beyond our worst and wildest dreams.

ADDENDUM #3: To my amazement, a few years ago, Massachusetts State [Teachers] College at Salem gave me an honorary Ph.D.

Characters

MAN, ancient.

Setting

Outdoors; near Lake Quannapowitt, Wakefield, Mass.
The present.

SPARED

Auditorium dark. Silence.
Curtain. Lights to soft glow, revealing man suspended in space considerably higher than audience level of auditorium. He has a pistol pressed to his temple.
But for soft glow, there is darkness and infinite space all around Man squints into glow, is at first silent, but then awakens and speaks.

MAN: (*Points to pistol pressed to temple: speaks clearly.*) I have tried to destroy myself more than sixty different times. (*Pulls trigger. Click. No gunshot. He shrugs.*) Always spared. (*He lowers gun at his side now. Pulls trigger. Blam! Gunshot. Man is amazed, Blackout. Auditorium and stage in darkness. Man's voice heard, high-pitched, manic. Speaks rapidly, almost unintelligibly at first: A tiny child's singsong voice.*) Five, the first time. Didn't know why. Children happy. Laughter all around. Me outside. (*Pauses.*) Father then moving. Mother all ears. Hugs abundant. Talk endless. Food, as talk. Sister, wide-eyed, adoring. Didn't know why. (*Pauses.*) Knife on table, eyebrow-high. Watched it, tiptoe. Sounds all empty. Colors mute. Smells to rancid. Tiny chest thumping. (*Pauses.*) Curled in fingers. Sounds, colors, smells, all gone. (*Pauses.*) Point pricked, no rain. Full thrust, no blood. Eyes clenched, no scream.

VOICE: (*Speaker No. 1.*) Poor child.

VOICE: (*Speaker No. 2.*) Poor child.

VOICE: (*Speaker. No. 3.*) Poor child.

VOICE: (*Speaker No. 4.*) Poor child.

VOICE: (*Speaker No. 5.*) Poor child.

VOICE: (*Speaker No. 6. Shrill scream.*)

(*Lights restore to soft glow. Man wears white shirt, enormously outsized pinstriped suit, fat necktie. He stiffens, squints. His arms are outstretched, dangling down into darkness. Legs same, feet over edge of playing platform. Sense that chair and man are suspended in space, floating, is wanted. Voice changes in age, dependent on text. Amplification needed. Speakers surround audience, placed in six positions: one in corner of auditorium, one above audience, one in darkness above man's head.*

Interruptions marked "Voice" are taped by man, but sound womanly, always kindly and sympathetic. When "shrill scream" called for, sound should again be produced by taped voice of man, but for this occasion childlike scream is wanted: shrill, sustained, anguished, breathless only after count of ten. Accent, if distinguishable, Boston. Man's face unflinchingly confident: head rarely bowed. He looks up and realizes audience is watching him. He smiles and speaks.)

MAN: Fifteen, the second. Thanksgiving Thursday. Aunts scrubbing, cigar smoke uncles. Fat Charlotte, the cousin, all green and sick.

VOICE: (*Speaker No. 1.*) Poor Child.

MAN: Skeleton turkey, once dead, now eaten. Laughter all around. (*Pauses.*) Three uncles, back from fishing. Cracked the early ice. Three pickerel. (*Voice to harsh.*) Easy catch. Frozen solid. In the surface. Eyes open. Still stiff. Mouths open. Still, as well. Caught together. Near the top. Chipped free. Grave to grave. (*Voice to innocent, young again.*) Watched them thaw. Early evening. Never thinking. Eye to eye. (*Pauses.*) Turkey carcass, winter treasure. All still. No scream. (*Pauses.*) Apple-bobbing. All cousins. Heads plunged, eyes clenched, mouths plugged, stuffed, reward. Me, outside. Ever-wondering, still, unspeaking. (*Pauses.*) Stood in archway, top curved, me tall, head bowed. All eyes on me, pull me in, push me under, no control, all gone. (*Pauses.*) No ice, no flow, easy now, do nothing. Eyes open. Life to play? (*His voice suddenly shifts to experienced voice.*) All lies! Only apples bobbing by! No breath, no sound, no voice, no scream.

(*Nota Bene: Man will hear voices that follow, now, and be frightened by them. He will recognize some as his own.*)

VOICE: (*Speaker No. 1.*) Poor child.

VOICE: (*Speaker No. 2.*) Poor child.

VOICE: (*Speaker No. 3.*) Poor child. (*Sound reverberates.*)

VOICE: (*Speaker Nos. 4 and 5. Sustained shrill scream.*)

MAN: Four years slid. Women now. All in that . . . what's the word? Chokes me still. All in . . . (*Chokes three times, L-sound, sudden return to young voice.*) All in *love.* Silent then. Not a sound. Eyes all voice. Never closed. Not a blink. Ears a team. Never clogged. Girls all blab. Heard them come, watched them go. Countless thrills! Well . . . fifty-nine. Love her even now. What's her name?

Not to worry. Love her still. WHAT'S HER NAME?

VOICES: (*Speakers Nos. 3 and 5.*) Poor child.

VOICES: (*Speakers Nos. 4 and 6.*) Poor child.

MAN: Mary! No. Mae it was. May in June. 12th. I think. Two o'clock. Veteran's Field. Sun still high. Number sixty. Mae was chilled, all regret. Me still dumb, staring through. Not to worry . . .WHAT'S HER NAME?

VOICES: (*Speakers Nos. 1, 2, 3, 4.*) Poor child. (*Sound reverberates.*)

MAN: Made a pact, Mae and me. Leave together – from the rocks. Climbed them, smiling. July the Fourth. Parade below. Independence. Father's friends as Indians, marching. John Kennedy, too. Senator then. All applause. Us, above it, bound to leap. Children laughing, balloons wound tight. Mother down there. Then still moving. Aunts and uncles, bellies full. (*Pause.*) From our perch, we watched them watching. Silent now, our hands ungripped. (*Pauses.*) Mae edged closer, never talking. Hair was brown, her loose blouse white. (*Pause.*) Runaway balloon floating up to us, past us, then beyond I followed with my eye. When I thought of Mae again, I was alone. She was gone.

VOICE: (*Speaker No. 3.*) Poor child (*Sound reverberates.*)

MAN: She was broken near a 4-H float. Not a sound. No cry, no scream.

VOICE: (*Speaker No. 1.*) Poor child.

MAN: No plan . . .

VOICE: (*Speaker No. 3.*) Poor child.

MAN: No desire . . .

VOICE: (*Speaker No. 5.*) Poor child.

MAN: . . . No scream.

VOICE: (*Speaker No. 6. Sustained scream.*)

MAN: (*Voice again confident, cynical.*) When I was twenty-two, I played a game called Houyhnhnm Roulette. (*Pauses.*) All cylinders of the pistol were filled, but for one. (*Pauses.*) Played the game each night for five consecutive nights. (*Pauses.*) Finally, my nerves gave out. Had to stop playing. (*Pauses.*) Never been much of a good-loser. (*Pauses.*) Played another game, six months later. (*Pauses.*) A big talent scout passed through town and picked me for his television quiz show, in Boston. Boston's first. (*Pauses.*) Heartbreak. (*Pauses.*) That was the name of the show: Heartbreak. (*Pauses.*) By answering twenty obvious questions in my choice category, Romantic poetry, specifically Blake, I won more than $18,000. Cash. (*Pauses.*) All of America watched me win. (*Pauses.*) Outside the studio, I was mugged four times. (*Pauses.*) Twice more at the subway. (*Pauses.*) In the parlor car on the Boston & Maine to Wakefield, the rear pockets were ripped from my trousers. (*Pauses.*) Before leaving the train, a series of Bud-liners hooked together, I was mugged and interferred with, seventeen different times. (*Pauses.*) The most bizarre attempt was a sad old lady, who filled a Hefty Bag full with water and then threw it at me. While my trousers were drying, she stole them. (*Pauses.*) I was naked upon arrival in Wakefield. (*Pauses.*) The remainder of the year passed without incident. (*Pauses.*) Twenty-three. All repaired. Emily then. Our town. One son. Brown hair and eyes. Nose mine, enormous. (*Pauses.*) No. No son. Never could.

VOICES: (*Speakers Nos. 1 and 3. Shrill scream. Man whacks his head against padded chair-back in failed attempt at suicide.*)

MAN: She stayed with me nine years. No point going on. My fault. She was . . . normal. (*Pauses.*) She left as she first came, but nine years older. Neither of us had grown taller. Nothing visibly good had sprung from it. I wonder why we tried?

VOICE: (*Speaker No. 3. Female laughing.*)

MAN: (*Voice normal again.*) I grew narrow. (*Pauses.*) My clothes never fit again. Not ever. (*Pauses.*) During the final month of my 32nd year, I lost more than 100 pounds of weight. Never tried to. Did the opposite in fact. Ate like a horse. Also *ate* a horse. Cooked, of course. (*Pauses.*) I lost precisely 3.3 pounds per day for 30 consecutive days. No matter what I ate, I couldn't stop losing weight. (*Pauses.*) Tapeworms. Two of them. (*Pauses.*) Lucky for me they hated each other. (*Pauses.*) On the 31st day of the 12th month of my 32nd year, I lost one pound by noon and then no more. (*Pauses.*) The problems seemed to, well, *pass.* (*Pauses.*) No one knows to this day why the tapeworms attacked, nibbled at and destroyed each other instead of me, but they did. I was spared. (*Pauses.*) Jealousy, perhaps. Maybe just hunger. (*Smiles.*) My weight has never changed again not an ounce, not in any of the years that followed, right up until today . . . and including today. (*Pauses.*) Which is, I suppose, only to say that in all these years, I've lost . . . well . . .

VOICE: (*All speakers. Female laughing.*)

MAN: . . . nothing! (*Has been somewhat anxious. Changes attitude, sensing that audience has sensed his anxiety. He is now quite cool.*) During my 33rd year, I quit all major religions. (*He looks up, suddenly frightened. He genuflects, then, rocks back and forth a moment, as might an old Jew. He looks out at the audience and is once again suddenly confident. He gestures a shrug with his hand.*) Pppppptttttt! (*Pauses. Young man's voice used here.*) Thirty-four, cleaning dishes for the Hazelwood Cottage on Main. One-fifty an hour. *Selling out.* (*Pauses.*) My first earned room. Chestnut Street, top floor right. Cold in winter, warm in summer. No pets permitted, not that I would have. (*Pauses.*) All the Hazelwood food a man might dare. A bit soggy, a trifle – well – *touched.* (*Pauses.*) Food and a room. Never happier. (*Pauses.*) Gus, the short-order German, said I had style. Brought a certain *je ne sais quoi* into the old rathole. Easy for Gus, nose dripping in the *soupe du jour.* (*Pauses.*) I said little, of course, always certain to be caught brooding. These lines in the face, even then. All that *practice!* Never saw wisdom in all that gravity—just couldn't control myself—couldn't stop squinting. Reading books again. (*Pauses.*) My room was perfect to me. Amazing sun in the morning. Sunsets through the window by the stove. (*Pauses.*) Nancy was the first to visit there. Beautiful thing, Nancy. Long, straight hair, dark brown. Wonderful legs: thick and tight with muscles from her walks. (*Pauses, voice changes to old age.*) Wonderful leg, I should say. I never actually saw both of them, together. Within one . . . viewing. (*Pauses.*) I never actually saw her walk, either. (*Pauses, voice younger.*) I'm sure she must have. How else could she have gotten into my room? (*Pauses.*) She had one leg or the other bundled in a quilt most of the time. Maybe *all* of the time. Certainly *most* of the time. *All* of the time *I* was nearby, which is, strictly speaking, *most* of the time. (*Pauses.*) There was *some*thing going on under the quilt. (*Pauses*) I keep my distance. (*Pauses.*) Warmed her belly with pots of Lapsang Souchong tea I'd read in Boswell, bought in Boston. (*Pauses.*) She loved me for every ounce of it. (*Pauses.*) We had a gentle time, at first. A lot of reading. Blake: all of *Jerusalem.* Me, in my orange bathrobe, in the easy chair, reclining. (*Pauses.*) I never liked sitting much then. Standing either: I especially avoided standing. The recline suited me best. (*Pauses.*) The less said about Nancy's body, the better. (*Pauses.*) My Hazelwood days were numbered from the moment I reflected upon the stack. I counted: three hundred dishes, two hundred cups, the same in saucers, and roughly, countless spoons. (*Pauses.*) I couldn't. I didn't. (*Pauses.*) "Gus," I said, "I've got the dread disease." "Gott bless you," he belched. (*Pauses.*) I left immediately. He'd never asked me *which* disease. (*Pauses.*) He trusted me, old Gus. God bless him. (*Pauses.*) She stuck it out with me five months, until the money ran out. First hers, then mine. (*Pauses.*) Hers actually ran out just before I'd met her. Which is to say, just before I found her in my room. (*Pauses.*) That's not quite the case, either. (*Pauses.*) I found the room with Nancy in it. It was a furnished place: easy chair, Murphy-bed, naturally, table, silverware and dishes, the usual, plus a plump book of verse, quilt and, of course Nancy, herself. (*Pauses.*) She said she'd worked the year before in the B.P.L. (*Pauses.*) I believed her. (*Pauses.*) A woman wouldn't lie about working in a *library.* (*Pauses.*) We kept our little idyll, as they say, *up,* until my ignominious parting from Hazelwood and money. (*Pauses.*) Her note said she'd found work in England. (*Pauses.*) I must not have wanted to follow her, because I didn't. (*Pauses.*) I wonder. (*Pauses.*) In all that time together, we never once raised our voices in anger or regret.

VOICES: (*All speakers. Female laughing.*)

MAN: Actually, we never much raised our voices at all, I don't really remember much talk beyond the reading. *Jerusalem.* (*Pauses.*) I never warmed to the didactical or the symbolical. (*Pauses.*) Thirty-six. Changed rooms. Alone again. Took a smaller one, top floor, down on West Water. Cheaper. (*Pauses.*) Not the only reason. (*Pauses.*) Couldn't stop finding *her* in the old room. Bits and scraps: nothing solid. I mean, nothing like the original find of the quilt and, of course, Nancy, herself. A bobby-pin once, dozens of emery boards, a plump book of verse. (*Pauses.*) The painful letter was in it. Tucked. (*Pauses.*) "Dear Nancy. I copied your name and address from your notebook cover. I hope you don't find it too froward [sic] of me, but I found you to be so lovely. I have to try. Would you see me? Perhaps a film together?" (*Pauses.*) His address next, then his telephone, then his name: Blake. (*Pauses.*) What was the honorable thing to do? (*Pauses.*) I telephoned the pompous son-of-a-bitch during the middle of each successive night for thirty consecutive nights. Woke him up. Gave *him* something to think about. (*Pauses.*) I never spoke, of course. (*Pauses.*) He sounded lonely, our Mr. Blake. Jim. He sounded lonely. Always home when I called. Probably firing off his letters. (*Pauses.*) I wrote to him in March, asking for a meeting. Signed a woman's name – Aphra Behn. I thought it might be nice to have a look. Waited nearly an hour. He didn't show. (*Pauses.*) Burned the letter, finally. Nothing solid. Nothing to keep, certainly not to lug around. (*Pauses.*) I moved. Forty. Went with Evelyn to Utah. Her people were there. Born there and stayed. Three generations of them. (*Pauses.*) Not Evelyn. She was spunky. Met her at Hazelwood, where she dunked and downed her morning cruller, daily. She'd come East for money. Worked at the copy-center, Lakeside Office Park. (*Pauses.*) Evelyn was quite something. Straight back. Rich girl's shoulders. Fantastically limber legs: two of them. (*Pauses.*) She talked me into the trip westward *a la puriste.* She'd wanted us to walk to Utah, but once I'd remembered that walking trips were all the rage among romantic poets, I had to pass. (*Pauses.*) We settled on a covered wagon and two donkeys: a lamentable choice in every way imaginable. (*Pauses.*) Less than 100 miles from Wakefield, we discovered our donkeys were sexually opposed, which is to say, a man and a woman. (*Pauses.*) They were shameless, even as donkeys go. (*Pauses.*) We stopped for ten minutes out of every hour, so "Get Off the Rug" and "You Too" could have their goes . . . (*Pauses.*) Those were their names: "Get Off The Rug" and "You Too." Evelyn had quite a gift for the odd moniker. (*Pauses.*) Had to arrange for an illegal abortion for "Get Off The Rug" in Kansas. (*Pauses.*) At the Utah Border a band of hostile Mormons attacked and shot the poor dumb ass herself. Killed her as well. (*Pauses.*) "You Too" was desolate upon arrival at the Great Salt Lake. (*Pauses.*) Once there, Evelyn was somewhat anxious: frightened of how her folks would take to me. Baptists, they were. I reminded her that I'd grown up with Baptists on all sides. Wakefield was a hotbed of Baptist thought. (*Pauses.*) She warned me about the Grace ritual . . . not to take down any of their food without thanking God, first. (*Pauses.*) I hated her for telling me that. (*Pauses.*) Her old man gave me a brandy and water. I blessed it. "Dear Lord, bless this brandy-and-water and cause it to bring peace into this strange land." Then, I sang *Rock of Ages.* A half-hour later, I prayed over her mother's clam dip and Fritos, and then, an hour later, I blessed the

Puss'n'Boots they put out for their cats. (*Pauses.*) Dinner went down without so much as a nod to God. (*Pauses.*) Left Utah, but stayed West. Forty-three, talking more than ever. Not saying much, but speaking well. Easterners grow ten times more learned west of the Mississippi. (*Pauses.*) Found Los Angeles, and a job. Names from my childhood, to my amazement, here and well known. Mine, as always, an unheard-of thing, never pronounced as written, always misspelled, never listened to, thus, never remembered. (*Pauses.*) One face from fifth grade appeared on my television screen. The nose known as target of frequent successful pickings, Warren School, thirty-seven years before, now wrinkled, perplexed. Above serious lips, speaking of politics and honesty. Concerned words. (*Looks around.*) No scream? (*Pauses, voice gangsterish.*) I never wanted a *social* life, exactly, but, I had hoped for a *life.* (*Pauses, voice again normal.*) My job was counting. I worked for an inventory service, supermarkets our specialty, meat and poultry mine. (*Pauses.*) I met Ethel there, in the counting. She worked spices. We met in early morning, one Monday, just before absolute totals. (*Pauses.*) She was fifty, old Ethel. Amazing tits and ass. She'd been married before. Widowed young. Three sons, not yet grown. I had my first with her. Happened so fast, I can't remember deciding to. (*Laughs.*) Must have, though. (*Pauses.*) We named him Alfred, after Ethel's father, Alfred, who was not quite deceased, which is to say, still alive. (*Pauses.*) He was in Chevrolets, Ethel's father, Alfred. Near a major freeway. Can't remember the name of his place – just the brand. (*Pauses.*) He was extraordinarily loyal. (*Pauses.*) Owned four Chevrolets: one for the missus, one for himself, one for Ethel's retarded brother, Alfred – oh, yes, the brother was Alfred, too. Alfred III, actually. My poor Alfred was at the end of a long – as they say – *line!* (*Pauses.*) Ethel got the coupe. They were not a family of what you might call your major-league drivers. (*Pauses.*) Ethel's father, Alfred I, was, well, grateful. Old Alfred the grateful. He never liked me much, but he was full of shhh . . . well . . .gratitude. Ethel wasn't what you'd call much of a bargain, what with her three imbecile children and her awful malady. (*Pauses.*) Hiccups. Ethel had hiccups. Had them nearly thirty years before I met her. (*Pauses.*) It was funny at first. Cute, I suppose. A large woman, wonderful tits and ass, hiccuping through every sentence. (*Pauses.*) I learned to loathe every hic and belch. After five years, I thought of . . . well . . . destroying her. (*Pauses.*) I tried every known method of cure. Jumping out of closets was kid stuff for me and old Ethel. I once drove the coupe straight off Laurel Canyon Road. Mulholland, actually. Through the white fence and straight over the side. (*Pauses.*) I didn't do it on purpose. I was day-dreaming. Thinking of ways to end her hiccing. (*Pauses.*) Ethel figured it was just another ploy to shut her up – so she wasn't scared at all. (*Pauses.*) She didn't even believe my blood on my face. Or, afterward, this scar. (*Pauses.*) I did it. (*Pauses.*) I did. (*Pauses.*) I could not stand the hiccing . . . or worse yet, I could not stand what came between: the endless babble, the endless babble of Ethel's words. (*Pauses.*) I downshifted the coupe into second gear, pulled left into the fence, drove through, and then threw it into neutral. Ethel landed on my shoulders. I carried her on my shoulders, all the way down. Bizarre. It became a sort of St. Christopher act of self-destruction. (*He hiccups. Pauses: voice now as child's.*) This purple scar on my face. That's all. (*He hiccups again. Attitude changes again.*)

VOICE: (*Speakers Nos. 2 and 4.*) Poor child.

VOICE: (*Speakers Nos. 3 and 5.*) Poor child. (*He begins to attempt suicide by choking himself and then whacking his head, violently, against back of his chair and then choking himself again. When he fails again to die, he will simply shrug.*)

MAN: We divorced immediately. I took nothing, she took the rest. (*Pauses.*) Most of all, old Alfred hated me for wrecking his car. (*Pauses.*) At the airport, all alone. No sound. . . .

VOICE: (*All speakers.*) Poor child.

MAN: . . . no scream.

VOICE: (*All speakers. Sharp shrill scream.*)

MAN: (*Voice old again.*) East, again. The Big Apple. Got a job selling life insurance. Twenty-payment life my specialty. Made a fortune. Bought a car: a Ford. (*Pauses.*) Thirty-five thousand miles the first year and never left New York for one of them. (*Pauses.*) Just as many dollars as miles that year and no end in sight. (*Pauses.*) Never happier. (*Pauses.*) Sold an Executive Planner Policy, Tarrytown, Tuesday, May 8th. Two hundred fifty thousand, face value. Borrow cash value, increasing term rider: very neat. (*Pauses, voice younger.*) Can't remember the street. Wooded, dark. (*Pauses.*) When I got back to my Ford L.T.D., there was a small Oriental man in the back seat. Saying nothing. Worse: not speaking. I asked him to leave. He wouldn't answer. (*Pauses.*) I asked him his name. He wouldn't answer. (*Pauses, bows and smiles.*) Sobbing, I did what a man in my position had to do: I handed my keys to him and left the car. He drove away! (*Pauses, bows, smiles inscrutably, as an Oriental. He pantomimes driving away in car.*) Good car, the L.T.D. (*Pauses, voice old again. Very confident.*) Fifty-six and back in Boston. Marlborough Street, just before Kenmore. (*Pauses.*) Old ground. (*Pauses.*) Very confident. (*Pauses.*) Sold the old policy again out of an office in Chestnut Hill over Stop and Shop. Very seedy, compared to my old Gramercy Park operation. (*Pauses.*) Millionaire's Club in six months and more than forty thousand for me, after taxes. (*Pauses.*) Never happier. (*Pauses.*) Couldn't be. (*Pauses.*) It became more than a job for me, really. Selling the twenty-payment became . . . well . . . a mission. (*Pauses.*) Most of my clients actually died. That doesn't *sound* astonishing, but it was. Of the hundred and twelve Metropolitan men in my ordinary district, I was the only one who actually had a client die. (*Pauses.*) My rate was three a week. (*Pauses.*) No one who knew my reputation would ever buy a policy from me. (*Pauses.*) I had to watch my step. I changed my name several times. Most men my age would be squeamish about changing names – that late in the game and all. Didn't bother me at all. Still doesn't. (*Pauses.*) It did present some minor problems now and again. When I delivered the widow's-money, I'd often have to do a bit of research to find out exactly who I was at the time of the sale. (*Pauses.*) It was also difficult when I sold to family. But those who bought died and the problem came to a natural conclusion. (*Pauses.*) I sold to everyone in my family, parents included. (*Pauses.*) Eventually, by the age of sixty-one I'd come into a great deal of money. Quite an embarrassment for a man of my years. (*Pauses.*) Three and a half-million, precisely. (*Pauses.*) No friends. (*pauses.*) No family, of course (*Pauses.*) No complaints from me . . . no time. (*Pauses.*) No scream.

VOICE: (*Speakers Nos. 1 and 2.*) Poor child.

VOICE: (*Speakers Nos. 3 and 4.*) Poor child.

VOICE: (*Speakers Nos. 5 and 6.*) Poor child.

VOICE: (*All speakers. Sharp shrill scream. He grabs necktie as a noose and tries to strangle himself. He fails. He shrugs.*)

MAN: (*Pauses: tone brightens, straightens tie.*) When I first spoke – first learned – I was very close with people. In the beginning. (*Pauses.*) I asked him, my father, why I was born: what purpose he'd had in mind for me. (*Pauses.*) He slapped me. (*Pauses.*) I asked my mother. She told me to ask my father. I never brought the question up again. No need. No purpose to it. No scream. I began trying then. (*Pauses.*) I've tried . . . to destroy myself . . . more than sixty different times. (*Suddenly, he tries to choke himself with his own hands, fails, shrugs to audience, in disgust.*) Always spared. (*Pauses. Voice old again, confident.*) When I was 4-foot-2, I swallowed a bottle of pills. My mistake, vitamins: E and B12. (*Pauses.*) I grew a foot in seven months, which is to say, I became 12 inches taller. (*Pauses.*) That next year, at 5-foot-2, I hurled myself into Lake Quannapowitt. The water was 4-foot-2, I was a year late. (*Pauses.*) Caught an awful head cold. (*Pauses.*) The next year I tried fire. (*Pauses.*) Burned all the woods by the West Ward School. (*Pauses.*) Nearly got the little red prison itself. (*Pauses.*) The tree I'd tied myself to was the only one left intact. (*Pauses.*) Horse-chestnut tree. (*Pauses.*) The firemen found me. Bound to it. (*Pauses.*) They wouldn't believe me when I said I'd tied myself. (*Pauses.*) Neither did the police. (*Pauses.*) Neither did the Wakefield Daily *Item* or the Boston *Post* or *Traveler*. (*Pauses.*) Once the rock of scandal rolls out of control, logic and truth present no worthy obstacle. (*Pauses.*) Tried that too. (*Pauses.*) Tied myself to an enormous boulder and tried to roll the West Ward hill. (*Pauses.*) Never got the stone out of the mud. (*Pauses.*) Ropes held them too. Didn't surprise me any when all papers, local and national, passed the second story by. (*Pauses.*) Spent one whole night lying tied in front of a parked Sears and Roebuck trailer-truck. Driver finally came out in the morning. Backed up. (*Pauses.*) He couldn't imagine who had tied up a kid in front of his truck. He would have called the papers except he didn't much care to have the world know where he'd spent the night. (*Pauses.*) Me neither. (*Pauses.*) No regrets now. Not really. (*Pauses.*) The next year, on March 31st, my birthday, I tied myself to the train track, northbound side. (*Pauses.*) Twenty-two hours, freezing all night, sweating all day. (*Pauses.*) The Boston and Maine was on strike. Fare increase threat. Trains didn't run again for six weeks. (*Pauses.*) Took me the full twenty-two hours to get my hands free. (*Pauses.*) Opened the knots, finally, mid-day, April 1st. (Voice to old.) April Fool's Fay. Never stopped trying. (*Voice to young.*) Simply never, well, succeeded. (*Pauses.*) Hardly failed. Money, children, wives, travel, books, several foreign tongues. God *knows* I've still got my health. (*Pauses.*) I'm an international ideal. (*Pauses, voice of gangster's.*) Sixty-two and my reputation's spread beyond repair. I couldn't have sold a policy to a dying man – *especially* a dying man. (*Pauses, voice to old.*) Kiss of death. (*Pauses.*) That's what they called me; kiss of death. Benjy was the first. At an awards dinner in Boston. The district agent was handing me my twenty-eighth medal for excellence. He was searching for an adjective, I suppose. From the audience, down below, Benjy's voice came booming up: (*Squeaky voice here.*) "Kiss of death! That's what the ghoulish son-of-a-bitch is: kiss of death!" (*Voice to normal.*) The audience laughed first Then they clapped. Everybody knew me. I was a legend all over the country. (*Pauses.*) Kiss of death. (*Pauses.*) I worked another six months after that, but once a problem has a label that's easy to remember, it's instantly solved, or incurable. (*Pauses.*) Mine was incurable. Everybody knew who I was – and now – *what* I was. (*Pause.*) No point in going on with it. (*Pauses.*) None. (*Pauses.*) I missed a few. I missed a couple I'd like to have sold. (*Pauses.*) Benjy. I'd pay his premiums myself. Over now. What's the point? (*Pauses, voice of gangster.*) When I was sixty-four, I met a twenty-three-year-old girl who said she loved me. (*Pauses, voice to old.*) Just me and a Cairn terrier. (*Pauses, looks around his feet for dog.*) Never knew an animal to be so faithful. Always with me. Wakes when I wake, sleeps when I sleep, eats when I eat. Walks with me. Watches me constantly. (*Pauses.*) I do nothing to deserve such handsome treatment. He certainly doesn't know I'm wealthy. I mean, he can't be in it for the money (*Pauses. Suddenly shocked, remembers dog is dead.*) Gone now. Hit twice by a Chevrolet. Once wasn't enough. The old lunatic had to back up to see what he'd done. (*Pauses.*) I'd like to think Murphy didn't know what hit him. He did. He knew. (*Pauses.*) Took him sixty-eight days to die. (*Pauses.*) One day for every year. (*Pauses.*) Sixty-eight now. Me. (*Pauses, voice now childlike again, innocent.*) All that time dying. Not fair.

VOICES: (*All speakers.*) Poor child. (*Laughs, scream.*)

MAN: (Voice now old.) During my sixty-fifth year I survived eight known incurable diseases. (*Pauses.*) The most bizarre was called *la Maladie Charcot.* (*Pauses.*) The first hint came on March 31st, the first day of my first Medicare year. (*Pauses. He struggles with sneaker and succeeds finally in removing it from foot.*) The big toe on my left foot went numb. I wouldn't have known, but for the way I tend my toenails. I've always used that very toe as my barometer. (*Pauses.*) When the nail of my left-hand big toe reaches the innermost point of my left hand shoe, I clip them all. (*Pauses, makes spitting sound.*) Pttttttttt . . . (*Sentimental again.*) I was given then to Adidas sneakers, the all-white variety. (*Holds up sneaker next to his face as product in television commercial. Pauses.*) Wore them twenty-four hours a day. Simultaneously, I was rarely given to cleaning my toenails, except during manicure. Which is to say *pedicure.* On Tuesday, March 31st, at 2:30 P.M., precisely, I kicked my alarm clock (*Pauses.*) and heard the most peculiar sound, like the sound of a toenail striking a plastic clockface. (*Pauses.*) My left-hand toenail had poked through my left white Adidas sneaker. I had heard the sound, but felt nothing. Although the nail was in every way tip-top, the toe was dead. (*Pauses.*) What faced me was the dread disease. (*Pauses, removes sock.*) Thirty days later, the last in April, my left foot was dead to the knee. By the end of May, my entire leg to my chest. The whole right leg joined in one fantastic overnight freeze, in July. By the start of September, I could do no more than blink my left eyelid for yes and my right eyelid for *no.* (*Pauses, winks left eyelid first, then right.*) Rather flirtatious messages for a man in my condition. (*Pauses.*) My young doctor, Johnson, attempted euthanasia. And succeeded. (*To audience.*) Not me. The hag across the hall. (*Pauses.*) He injected air into an artery – at least, that's what the paper said. He was found innocent, of course, and quickly. (*Pauses.*) On September 30th, the last, he bent over as if to hear my breath. (*Pauses.*) "Do you want a shot?" I blinked my left lid. (*Pauses, to see if audience remembers code.*) As soon as the air hit my brain, all limbs unlocked. (*Pauses.*) Without malice of forethought, my elbow joint constricted, causing my fingers to clench into a fist, causing, in Dr. Johnson's groin, a hernia of almost landmark proportions. (*Pauses.*) When the dust, as they say, settled, Johnson was unconscious, and every muscle in my entire body was absolutely functional, except for those controlling the lids to my left and right eye. (*Pauses.*) To this day,

I don't blink. I can *force* a blink but the normal everyday state of my eyes is . . . wide open. (*Pauses.*) The other diseases are hardly worth a mention. (*Pause, voice is younger.*) If I could have been a cucumber. [*Nota Bene: Actor will supply own fresh words here for each performance. Example. "If I could have been a large vibrating egg." Or, "Cookie . . ." Or "Cupcake . . ." Chosen words should not be repeated during run of play. I.H.] (Pauses, voice returns to normal age.*) Benjy reappeared not more than a year ago. He'd aged; been awfully sick. (*Pauses.*) He wanted me to sell him a policy. I don't know how the hell he found me all the way up here but he did. My reputation, probably. (*Pauses.*) *He* should have known. (*Pauses.*) He named it. (*Pauses.*) I could have. But now that he wanted one I couldn't. To tell you the truth, I was pleased to see his old face. Not that we'd ever actually drunk together, let alone talked. Still and all, there was a face there I'd seen before. And a name with it. (*Pauses.*) I asked him to stay. He did. Three months. Stayed in the back bedroom. Didn't stray out from it much. Stayed in bed, I guess. (*Pauses*) That's where I found him. Buried him myself out in back. (*Pauses.*) Wasn't much of a talker, Benjy. Never was. Never will be. (*Pauses.*) The thing about Benjy that intrigued me was his height. He had almost none. Couldn't have been more than three-nine, maybe three-ten. (*Pauses.*) Benjy's problem in the insurance game was doorbells. (*Pauses.*) Winters too. Snow banks. It's hard to imagine what it would feel; like to sink in up to your eyes. (*Pauses.*) He had a big heart, Benjy. Never saw a little woman-chaser like that before. Had a lot of style, especially with the tall ones. They used to mother him. (*Pauses.*) Sixty years old and he'd ask 'em if he could sit on their laps. So he could hear better. (*Pauses.*) They loved it. (*Pauses.*) He carried a big knife, Benjy. (*Pauses.*) People used to like to hurt him. Never saw anything like it. I hated to walk on the street with him. People used to come up, out of nowhere, and pinch his cheeks, or poke his arm. (*Pause.*) "How'd you get so little fella? Didn'tcha' drink your milk?" (*Pauses.*) Then he'd show them his big knife. They moved on. Nobody really liked the sight of a little man with such a big knife. (*Pauses.*) *Kiss of death*, he called me. (*Pauses.*) I did. (*Bows head.*) I did it. (*Pauses, voice now young.*) So small. Everything born, dies. Once you see the thing itself, you can't pretend. (*Pauses.*) I never had a son. How could I? (*Pauses.*) Over the years, I lost track of what was real and what was imagined. The distinctions between the two became . . . unimportant. Style was another matter. (*Pauses.*) I'd hoped to tell it well. The beginning was . . . well . . . not bad. (*Pauses.*) I wish it might have continued that way. Oh, I suffered. But no more, no less, than . . . well . . . him. He was my father and, as such, naturally, got to the best and worst of it *before* I could. But no more, no less, really. (*Pauses.*) It's all the same.

VOICE: (*All speakers. Shrill scream.*)

MAN: (*Suddenly whacks himself on head with Adidas sneaker several times in still another suicide attempt. He fails to die. In shrugged disgust, he throws sneakers away. He suddenly realizes that he is high on platform in space and that sneaker is out of reach, low on ground:*

gone. Pauses; voice again old.) Two days ago, all my things were stolen. Everything I owned, gone. (*Pauses.*) Caruso. The handyman. He did it. (*Pauses.*) I knew right away. He was the one to tell me about the first break-in. He was shaking. (*Pauses.*) I came home. He was there, in my living room, with his wife. (*Pauses.*) Bald. (*Pauses.*) His wife. Erica. Stone bald. (*Pauses.*) She was standing behind him, with mannish, muscular arms folded across her enormous décolletage. Quite a contradiction to consider, this union of Caruso and Erica. (*Pauses.*) Caruso was shaking. He couldn't look at me. His eyes always kept darting about the room. He couldn't look at me. (*Pauses.*) The window-shutters were whacking and thumping – the way they do in Yugoslavian movies. (*Pauses.*) The sofa was gone. So was the chaise-lounge, the desk, the desk chair, the bookcases and all books but for a plump book of verse. (*Pauses.*) Caruso was sweating. "You've been robbed," he said. Then she punched his arm. They looked deeply into each other's eyes. Then they either kissed or talked intimately: I couldn't be sure in that surprisingly inferior lighting. Then, Erica, the bald wife, sang an awful aria in that horrid coloratura soprano voice of hers. She punched his arm again, they laughed and left. Later, I noticed that all my lamps had left as well. (*Pauses.*) The next night, all bric-a-brac; rugs and carpets, occasional tables, long tables, three end tables, new, by Drexel. Paintings by all prominent landscapists, trash-can and ash-can Americans and by God, an early Lipshitz. (*Pauses.*) Four Van Velde lithographs. Etchings by Baskin, Robbins, Wells, Rich and Green, Lestrille's famous gouaches, obscure Amy Vanderbilt dècoupage, old lady watercolors. Copious aquatints. Frames for everything mentioned, except the Lipshitz, which was, of course, a large bulbous statue. (*Pauses.*) No mirrors. Never. Not ever. No need. (*Pauses.*) Insurance trophies-hundreds of them. Some gold, some silver, come copper, some bronze, and a slew in lucite. All gone. (*Pauses.*) I needn't mention the appliances or every shred of identity – passport and driver's licenses, birth certificate and childhood locks of hair. All gone. (*Pauses.*) Every scrap moved from its natural place. All order broken. All gone. (*Pauses.*) Sixty-eight years of careful accumulation, moved in a mere twenty-one days. (*Pauses.*) The rhythm boggles the brain. (*Pauses.*) Caruso and Erica. (*Pauses.*) They must have been obsessed.

VOICE: (*All speakers. Female laugh.*)

MAN: By the night of the tenth day, there was nothing left in the house, but my bed and this small revolver, .32 calibre. (*Pauses.*) This morning, shortly after I woke, Caruso and Erica took my bed. They said nothing. They simply walked into my room and she took it. (*Pauses.*) I gave up trying to reason with them, days ago. I don't think Caruso would steal from me if he weren't pushed to it – by her – the bald wife. (*Pauses.*) I can only guess at what time the bed left. I haven't had a clock in any form for more than a week. Ten-thirty, maybe eleven. At noon or half past twelve, Caruso came into the bathroom, where I was . . . sitting. He still had trouble looking at me. "Somebody took your bed," he said. I spat at him. (*He spits.*) He said it again. (*He spits again.*) "Somebody took your bed." (*Pause.*) He was crying when she came in. They carried me out of my house and left me there, at the trell's. I heard them bolt the door locked, from the inside. (*Pauses.*) The gun was in my pants pocket. (*Pauses.*) There was no reasoning with them. (*Pauses.*) I said I was sorry. God only knows what it was I did. They didn't care. (*Pauses.*) I tried again. (*Pauses.*) No sense to it. Point pressed to chest. Inside thumping up to it. Finger still fighting, after all. (*Pauses.*) Waited for life to pass in front of eyes. Legend faulty. Never did. (*Pauses.*) Four years old. Woke all shivers. Mid-July. Nearing dawn. (*Pauses.*) Before me, I stood. I and my father. Face to face. (*Pauses: voice to old again.*) Both sixty-eight, both spoiled, both exactly as I am before you now. I and my father. Face to face. We touched. (*Pauses, voice again normal.*) Eyes again open. Mother there.

Then, still moving. I: all words. (*Pauses, voice child's.*) "Kiss me, Mama. Hold me gentle." (*Pauses.*) Down she smiled. Poor child," she said. (*Nota Bene: "Poor child" should now sound exactly as it did on tape. Pauses; voice young.*) I then screamed, so shrill and sudden, all sound stopped, all colors bled. (*Turns away: screams exactly as on tape.*) Mother's pity joined my scream. Those two sounds would never leave me. Those and all other sounds would only float momentarily away. All sounds floating to and from me, at will, their will, not mine. (*Pauses.*) I could not continue to hear my returning ignorancies without end. Voice without end. Sound without end. No pardon. No amen. No matter how I tried, I could not end it. (*Pauses.; Nota Bene: laughs exactly as on tape.*) Trying since beginning. Five, the first time. Didn't know why. Children happy. Laughter all around. Me outside. (*Pauses.*) Father then moving. Mother all ears. Hugs abundant. Talk endless. Food, as talk. Sister, wide-eyed adoring. Didn't know why. Gun in pocket, eyes open. Felt the weight of it. Pushed it in as if to stab. (*Pauses.*) Sounds all empty. Colors mute. Smells to rancid. Tiny chest thumping. (*Pauses.*) Lump pricked through. No pain. Full thrust, no blood. Eyes clenched, no scream. (*Pauses.*) Always spared. (*Pauses. Voice gangster's.*) Spared. (*Pauses, voice child's.*) Spared. (*Pauses. voice hushed, a whisper.*) Spared.

VOICE: (*All speakers, a whisper.*) Spared.

LIGHTS FADE TO BLACK.

THE PLAY IS OVER.

AUTHOR'S NOTE

Voices on tape to be prerecorded by the actor, using high-pitched voice. Laughter and scream both sustained, breathy. Words to be recorded once only, spliced together and repeated without pause. Frequency as noted in text.

When actor imitates mother's words, scream and laugh, imitation must reveal taped voice as his.

Four distinct voices must be developed for performance: old man's narrative voice, harsh, deep, cynical; young man's sincere voice; boy's innocent voice, and gangsterish, rather comic voice. These voices should work as warring contraries whenever possible, within sections, even within sentences and phrases. Thus, whenever Man seems to contradict himself, correct himself, contrary voices need be chosen to personalized conflict.

Dependent on size of theatre, platform should be built of the maximum possible height to hold actor's face within sight-lines, but to create sense of maximum distance from audience-floor. Two instruments for lighting: one straight above, straight down; the second slightly above the first, focused on center of actor's face. Thus, channel of light created to allow actor to lean forward to audience during more intimate moments. Lights must be low level, soft glow, no edges, focused evenly so that no lighting changes occur with actor's forward movement.

Sense of infinite blackness and space, all around.

If house-curtain is used, lights to be preset for start of play, switched off after gunshot, faded in softly after opening monologue and left on throughout rest of play. House curtain can close to end play.

Recommend, however, that final cue be slow fade out of lights to blackness, as after-image in dark useful.

Opening moments of play to be musical images, not slowed in tempo for recognition of narrative. Closing moments opposite.

FAITH

FAITH, HOPE AND CHARITY was presented by Max Daniels, in association with Hospital Audiences, Inc. at the South Street Theatre in New York City on December 15, 1988. It was directed by Edward Berkeley; the sets were by Patricia Woodbridge; the lighting was by Jane Reisman; the costumes were by Martin Pakledinaz; the sound design was by Paul Bang; and the production stage manager was Tom Roberts. The cast of FAITH, in order of appearance, was as follows:

JACKIE .... Claiborne Cary
TED .... Rodney Scott Hudson
FAITH .... Angela Nevard
AGATHA .... Marilyn Sokol
ROGER .... John Rothman

Introduction

More than twenty years after *Morning, Noon and Night* was done on Broadway, Terrence McNally, Leonard Melfi and I decided to have a reunion ... on stage. The result was our second triptych, *Faith, Hope and Charity.*

Short-term memory is the oddest thing. I have practically no memory of when and/or how and/or why we decided to do this project. Yet, by contrast, I can remember finite detail of the *Morning, Noon and Night* experience. I do remember pulling the long match and getting *Faith* as my assignment. And I do recall contributing the stage-setting to *Faith, Hope and Charity.* I'd many times run past a statue in Central park that never failed to make me smile. It is an overly elaborate tribute to a great Polish warrior. I suggested that all three plays be set in Central Park, at the foot of the statue. Terrence and Leonard, both reasonable men, agreed.

Faith was written in Australia, in the early '90's. For a couple of winters in a row, my wife Gill and I exchanged houses with novelist Peter Carey and his wife, stage-director Alison Summers. They came to snowy Manhattan; we went to sunny Sydney. *Faith* was my writing project for Down Under, Christmas, 1991.

I'd long wanted to write about '60's people. I thought a *Morning, Noon and Night* reunion might well embrace a play that was a '60's reunion. *Faith*, among other matters, contrasts post–AIDS–scarey sex of the 1990's with no-problem–simple-passion sex of the 1960's. The narrator of the play, Faith, is the aftermath of her once-hippie-now-yuppie mother. I wanted to write an outrageous play for *Faith, Hope* and *Charity,* as I had, years before, with *Morning,* for *Morning, Noon and Night. Faith* didn't work out quite the way I'd hoped it would. In fact, I ended up writing a rather silly and sad play. I don't know why I did, really. Perhaps, the Australian sunshine made Life seem too Prozac-perfect?

Perhaps, Terrence, Leonard and I should have left *Morning, Noon and Night* in our memories? In the end, the entire triptych *Faith, Hope and Charity* was a sad. Ed Berkeley, who'd earlier directed the NYC premieres of my plays Dr. Hero and *The Primary English Class,* directed *Faith, Hope and Charity.* Ed gave *Faith, Hope and Charity* a serviceable production. Not bad, just not inspired. The reviews for *Faith, Hope and Charity* reflected this. Mel Gussow, writing in the NY Times, said he liked the show, but, somehow "expected more from these three playwrights". As did Terrence, Leonard and I.

Things do somehow happen in their own correct time, don't they? At our best, we mortals are like Keatsean heroes, leaving the Earth, from time to time, for superb, elated moments. But, then, when we return to Earth, we are changed. And when we try to get back to where we were, we can't. It is the essence of Ionesco's Absurd. It is the most exciting and frightening thing I know about Life: we can never again be what we just were. Life is constantly changing. And superb moments of great elation can often be, like orgasm, little deaths.

Characters

TED Black and balding; looking at 40, maybe less.

JACKIE Somewhat, uh, stocky; same age as Ted. Might also be black.

FAITH Waspy, leggy and 18; by comparison, Lolita is frumpy.

AGATHA Same age as Ted and Jackie, but slightly thinner and enormously louder.

ROGER Oldest of all; an hirsute anachronism (Hippie).

Setting

In front of the statue of Polish warrior,
southeasterly section of Central Park, New York City.
Morning, the present.

FAITH

Scene 1

Central Park, New York City, morning. The lights fade up on the statue of Polish warrior. A stiatapigeous woman, Jackie, waits at the foot of the statue, putting on make-up. Jackie uses a tiny, rectangular mirror to check the progress of her make-up application. And then she attempts to use the same mirror to check her more than ample body. She wears a huge cape-like coat, white, which blankets her like snow on Everest. Ted, a black man, her age, enters quietly, opposite side of statue, checking her checking herself over. He wears a baggy trenchcoat, tweed cap, gloves and scarf.

TED: Excuse me . . .

JACKIE: (*Terrified.*) Let me just say this *straight out*: I've got no money, but I do have a kick, I do have a *gun*, I do have a set of lungs that will wake the fuckin' dead! So dick with me, asshole, and you are rib-roast covered with flies! Is this established?

TED: Jackie? . . .

JACKIE: Ted?

TED: Yup.

JACKIE: My God!

TED: Well . . . you look . . . *Fabulous*!

JACKIE: You look . . . well . . . God! It's been a couple of years, huh?

TED: Twenty. That's why we're here.

JACKIE: I didn't recognize you . . . not right away. (*Still doesn't.*) You're Ted?

TED: Cut my hair.

JACKIE: You recognized me right away, huh? No problem?

TED: Uh, well . . . not much.

JACKIE: I've gained some weight.

TED: Oh, yuh, me too . . .

JACKIE: I kept the same weight for 25 years, since high school, until I got divorced.

TED: Marriage didn't work out, huh? That's tough.

JACKIE: A killer.

TED: I can see why it didn't work, though. Truthfully, bluntly, I never liked him much. I always thought he was . . . if you'll forgive me, really . . . I always thought he was a total bullshitter. A pompous, self-righteous, nowhere *asshole.*

JACKIE: You knew Morgan?

TED: I knew Morris.

JACKIE: Morris died.

TED: Morris *died*?

JACKIE: His heart . . . on the tennis court . . . right here in the park. 37 years old, not a sick day in his life.

TED: Oh, God, that's awful. . . (*Pauses.*) He was a hell of a guy: Morris. (*Pauses.*) Who's Morgan?

JACKIE: My ex-husband. I know you're supposed to say "former" 'cause it's gentler . . . kinder . . . so, I would just like to make a point here of calling him "ex," if you follow my drift.

TED: (*Smiles.*) I think I do, yuh . . . (*Laughs.*) Big breakup, huh?

JACKIE: It was nothing to me. (*Changes subject.*) We haven't seen each other in a long time, huh, Ted?

TED: (*Whistles.*) Lonnnggg time!

JACKIE: (*Looks around, focuses on statue. Laughs.*) Leave it to Roger to set up our reunion under a statue of a Polish warrior! (*Looks at Ted, smiles.*) What memories, huh? . . . Let's see . . . Ted, Ted, Ted, Ted . . . you were seein' somebody, back then . . . who was that? A wispy, Waspy little tart . . . who was that?

TED: Agatha Footes . . . (*Rhymes with boots.*)

JACKIE: Agatha Footes! She wrote the story about the pigs fucking . . .

TED: Cows fucking.

JACKIE: Pigs.

TED: Cows. I helped her cut it down, before class. I remember . . . cows.

JACKIE: How could it have been cows? Cows are female. Cows give milk. Right? I mean, *pigs* fucking is weird enough, but that would have been *bizarre:* Lesbianism among *farm animals!*

TED: It was cows. Boy cows and girl cows.

JACKIE: (*Jackie looks at him for a while.*) Boy cows and girl cows?

TED: You know what I mean: A cow and a steer, uh, a bull . . .what do I know about this stuff? I live on West End Avenue. (*They both laugh.*) Agatha and Morris kind of had a thing.

JACKIE: With each other? (*Thinks.*) Oh, my Goddd, that is riiiight! (*Thinks further.*) Before me or after me?

TED: Before you and after me . . . (*Pauses.*) during me, actually.

During me and after me, but before you. You know what I'm saying?

JACKIE: Sure. 'Course I do. He had something: Morris, didn't he?

TED: I never saw it myself.

JACKIE: Every single female in the workshop, including Perthe McDonald . . .

TED: I'm not sure I remember her . . .

JACKIE: She was the Australian poetess they brought in to team-teach us . . .

TED: A bag of bones . . . mousey . . .

JACKIE: That's her!

TED: I never could understand a fuckin' thing she said! She use'ta'call me "mite" I always thought she meant the little white things that kill your house plants.

JACKIE: All those sensitive Australian-pride poems about snakes and bugs. (*She laughs; suddenly goes sad.*) She was teaching us the day of the night Bobby Kennedy got shot . . .

TED: Oh, right. Miserable fuckin' night that was. That was right in the middle of the Agatha/Morris thing . . . (*A delayed double-take.*) Morris was schtooping Perth McDonald?!

JACKIE: Well, I don't know if he was *schtooping* her, but, they would, from time to time, take off their clothes and she would lie down in Missionary Fashion and he . . . (*Ted suddenly kisses Jackie.*) What are you doing? (*He kisses her again. It is a long, deep, wonderful kiss. They break from it and look at each other. They both smile.*)

TED: I'm so glad to see you, Jackie. I really am. This reunion was a great idea! (*The lights fade out.*)

END OF SCENE 1

Scene 2

In the darkness, we hear a Neil Young/Buffalo Springfield song. Lights up on Faith, a thin, athletic 18-year-old. She has one leg up on the crossbar of her bike. She has just begun a conversation with Jackie and Ted.

TED: . . . Faith?

FAITH: My sister got worse.

JACKIE: Hope?

TED: Charity?

FAITH: Close, Chastity . . .

TED: Same as Cher's baby . . .

FAITH: What's his face, Alice Cooper, he named his Moon Doo-doo…

TED: It was Frank Zappa. He named his baby Moon-Walk Zappa, 'counta . . .

FAITH: You think Moon Doo-doo Zappa's *bad* and Moon-Walk Zappa's *good?* Who's the pothead, what's-his-name? . . .(*Sings.*) Electric banana . . . Is going to be the very next craze . . .

TED: Donovan!

FAITH: Donovan! He named his baby Lemon Peel, didn't he?

TED: Ione Skye Leitch. She's beautiful.

FAITH: Breaks my heart I wasn't alive then to see it for myself. I would have *laughed* and *laughed.*

JACKIE: (*Studying Faith intently.*) Your mother's who?

FAITH: Agatha Footes. (*Jackie and Ted exchange a knowing glance.*) (*Lights fade. Music restores.*)

END OF SCENE 2

Scene 3

Lights up on Jackie, Ted, Faith & Agatha. Music fades under again.

TED: (*Ogling Agatha.*) You look very well, Agatha. (*And that she does. Agatha, like Ted & Jackie, wears a long, long coat. Faith by contrast, is wearing shorts and a t-shirt.*)

AGATHA: Why shouldn't I look well? I'm smart, I'm rich and I'm not married. (*Looks at statue.*) I have jogged on this path for 15 minutes every morning of my life for the past ten years and I have never *once* seen this fucking statue! Who would have guessed that Poland was named for some guy named Poland? I always thought it was "the land of the Po" or something.

FAITH: Like Lapland?

AGATHA: What do I know? Shut up! This is my reunion. (*To Ted.*) Who are you?

TED: Ted.

AGATHA: You are joking! Ted was a skinny little baby-faced *rogue* with a huge Afro . . .

TED: I cut my hair.

AGATHA: You're not kidding? You're really Ted? (*Agatha whoops with laughter; spots Jackie.*) My Jesus, Ted, you look awful! What have they done to you to make you look so awful? Have you been beaten?

TED: I . . . I've had some bad luck from time to time.

AGATHA: I should say you have! (*Agatha whoops with laughter; spots Jackie.*) Who did you used to be?

JACKIE: (*After a long pause.*) Jackie.

AGATHA: (*Tries not to speak in words. Instead, she does a sort of Dance-Of-Amazement, physically expressing such thought as "I cannot believe my eyes! This cannot be true! This is one of Life's Seven Wonders! Etc." Jackie, Ted, and Faith stand and watch Agatha's ritualistic moves, her flailing arms, her forehead-slapping amazement. When it is over, Agatha speaks to Jackie as if none of the above has happened: She speaks simply, dryly.*) Nice to see you again, Jackie . . . been a long time. (*Agatha whoops with laughter.*)

FAITH: My mother lost 35 pounds for this reunion. She dieted and jogged double-sessions for nearly six weeks. She told me forty or fifty *thousand* times "If you think, after 20 years, I'm gonna let those motherfuckers see me *fat,* you are off your gourd. Suzie-Q, *off your gourd!*

AGATHA: (*Agatha stops laughing; faces her daughter.*) Are you trying to humiliate me in front of my friends"

FAITH: When my mother got her divorce judgment against my father, she had an announcement card engraved at Tiffany's that she sent out to everyone she knew: "Mrs. Jack Rubin takes great pleasure in announcing that she is no longer Mrs. Jack Rubin" . . .

TED: That was *you?* I thought Jack Rubin married Betsy Ackerman before she died?

AGATHA: Of course, he married her *before* she died! You think he married her *after* she died? You were always a bit slow on the uptake, Ted, but ole' Sister Time has slowed you right down to a fucking *crawl, hasn't she?* (*To Faith.*) Can you believe it? I had a huge thing with this one. . . a huge thing! (*Pauses; laughs to herself.*) Drugs. (*Laughs again.*) I can remember going to this party with you, Ted, up near City College, somewhere, in some filthy, *dreadful hovel* . . . milk crates for furniture . . . early Che Guevara décor . . . positively *scrofuloso!* Our host was this hippie-dippy-Yippie with this hair out to *here* . . . scrawny . . . it's weird I can't remember his name, 'cause I think I actually went out with him a couple of times . . . anyway, you and I, Ted, were very, very very fucking mellow, 'cause we had smoked *bananas* or God knows what, and then sniffed yellow paint and snorted Rice Crispies or somesuch . . . anyway, if you can *believe* this, Faithie, this one and I got incredibly horny . . . I mean incredibly horny and we start in doin' it! Dozens of hippie-dippies around, smoking, drinking, dancing . . . the TV blaring in the middle of the room 'cause of the elections . . . Ted and I really and truly into it an alls'a sudden there's this screaming and yelling and the whole thing *turns.* I mean turns. Bobby Kennedy has been shot. Talk about Bad Sex!

TED: That was me: your host. You weren't there *with* me. You were *supposed* to be. I mean, we were a *thing* up until then. That was Morris Aaronson from our workshop. You met him on the corner by my house and you did some drugs together before you got there . . . I mean, you were both pretty zonked when you got there. That was Morris.

AGATHA: I think you're right. (*Blackout.*)

END OF SCENE 3

Scene 4

In the darkness, a Donovan tune. Lights up on Agatha, Faith, Ted and Jackie, in a line, facing Roger. Faith is shaking Roger's hand as the scene begins. Her handshake grip lingers a bit flirtatiously.

FAITH: I *begged* my mother to let me come to this reunion with her. I've been *desperate* to meet you people, really. I've heard about you, *endlessly* . . . especially you, Roger. I mean, truthfully, I talk about you so often in my sessions with Dr. Schwartzman, I'm *amazed* that we're just now really meeting for the very first time! I mean, I am, after all, meeting the minds that . . . well . . .

spawned me! (*Smiles.*) You're much younger and better looking than I thought you'd be. (*Roger is an aging hippie. He is thin, athletic/Yogic, long-grey-haired, bespectacled-Granny-glasses variety, extremely apt to smile and say positive things. He, too, wears a long raincoat over his clothing.*)

ROGER: This is so great . . . this is so *fucking great!* This like totally blows my mind! Ted, man, I cannot believe this . . . (*Roger hugs Ted.*) I just can't . . . like *wow*, right?

TED: It's very, very nice to see you, again, too, Roger. You really haven't changed much at all . . . *really.*

ROGER: A little snow on the roof . . .

TED: Hardly noticeable.

ROGER: I feel good. I feel strong . . . full of plans . . . (*Sees Jackie.*) Jacqueline, look, at *you!* (*Hugs her.*) This is such an amazing treat! I'm just . . . God! . . . *choked up*, here, really! OOOoooOOOoo, you still *feel so good*, too!

JACKIE: You look great, Roger. You do. God! (*They hug again. Jackie then holds Roger out at arm's length.*) You seemed older to me, back then. Now you seem like you're our age . . . maybe even younger.

ROGER: I feel good. I really do. (*Sees Agatha.*) I will never forget that fabulous story you wrote for me about the monkeys fucking . . .

TED: Cows fucking . . .

JACKIE: Pigs fucking . . .

FAITH: What's this?

AGATHA: That wasn't me. That was Amanda Vogel. It was about a pig and a cow.

ROGER: Really. I remember a monkey story.

AGATHA: I once wrote a warm-up poem for class, about a monkey-house . . . maybe that's what you remember.

ROGER: It touched me. I still think about it. Monkeys are like us . . . great stuff! Like . . . wow.

TED: Amanda, uh, *died*, didn't she? I think I heard something.

ROGER: (*Pantomimes a dive with his right hand.*) Nineteenth floor, straight down . . .

JACKIE: That was ages ago . . .

AGATHA: Must be 16, 17 years . . .

ROGER: 18 years . . . right after I left New York.

AGATHA: 18 years . . . I knew she would. She always wanted to fly.

JACKIE: Whew! The chemicals that went through that girl's brain . . .

ROGER: She was seized by some savage God . . .

TED: So . . . how's California, Rog?

ROGER: Oh, I haven't taught out there for 10, 12, 13 years . . . 13, nearly 14. Typical thing: you go out there, it's all bare feet and pick-your-own-courses. Next thing you know, they're assigning you 19th century autobiography and hiring suits-and-ties from Princeton, so fuck that, right? On to Honolulu. Five years stoned out of my gourd, teaching 6 sections of poetry a day . . . all free form, mostly to wives of military personnel. I didn't feel I was growing at all, so I came back to the mainland. A year in a straight job in Denver, which is when my hair turned grey. Six months of sports-coats: grey. Took me another six months to get my shit together, and here I am . . . here *we* are . . . together again! (*Smiles.*) Took me *ages* to track you all down. (*Pauses.*) There is some bum-you-right-out type news. (*Pauses.*) We're *it*.

AGATHA: (*After a pause in which they all exchange a glance.*) It's uh, a little hard to follow your syntax, Rog. We're "it" in what sense?

ROGER: We're it in the sense that everybody else isn't coming kind of thing . . .

TED: No interest kind of thing? Or moved away kind of thing?

ROGER: Dead kind of thing. Amanda was 1st . . . then, Fat Charlie and Brenda, not more than a month later.

TED: Together?

JACKIE: Didn't you know?

TED: Maybe I forgot . . .

ROGER: Car wreck . . . Woodstock . . . I heard the news from Perthe McDonald . . . Perthe's gone too. Snakebite. Ironic: Makes it all the way from the Australian Outback . . . gets herself bitten by a snake in upstate New York!

JACKIE: I can visualize the classroom: me, Ted, Morris is gone . . . Amanda, Betsy Ackerman, Agatha, Fat Charlie, Brenda . . . Rog and Perthe up front . . . what about the tall guy? . . . always sat in the back row, wore a serape . . .

TED: Jimmy Reilly? You didn't hear. Big big big drugger . . . (*Points to her arm-veins, indicating needle-in-the-arm.*) He used'ta nod off in the middle of a sentence.

JACKIE: That's right! I went out with Jimmy Reilly three or four times, but he never finished a fucking sentence! And then I started seeing Morris.

TED: Me.

AGATHA: Hm?

TED: You started seeing me. I took you away from Jimmy Reilly. You took me away from Jackie.

JACKIE: And I started going with Morris. (*Suddenly; annoyed by Faith, who has been taking notes all through the scene.*) Why is she taking notes?

FAITH: For Dr. Schwartzman. He thinks that you all aren't the children of the 60's: it's me . . . me and Lemon Peel and Moon Doo Doo . . . that's what Dr. Schwartzman thinks. He says we're the drug deaths, not you . . . we're the ones with Faith in nothing . . . she names me "Faith" – hah! We've got no Faith. That's why we're such money-grubbers. Anyway, that's what Dr. Schwartzman thinks: that you all really wrecked the planet Earth with all your drug-taking and your phony love is all you need tripe. I'm just taking notes, so I can see for myself. (*Looks up; smiles.*) Go ahead . . . (*Glances at her notes.*) you were talking about Jimmy Reilly being dead, too. (*Everybody glances at everybody else. Faith smiles brightly. The light fades out.*)

END OF SCENE 4

Scene 5

In the darkness, music: possibly Hot Tuna or Grand Funk. Lights fade up on Roger and Jackie, back of Statue. The Statue has turned around, so we have a new perspective. The others – Agatha, Faith and Ted – are chatting, upstage, front of statue, backs to audience.

JACKIE: Rog, why exactly did you call this reunion? It's great seeing everybody . . . those of us who lived . . . but, why, Rog? It's so, I dunno', so . . . weird. I mean, look at me: fat, depressed, unsuccessful. Look at Agatha: thin, depressed, successful. Look at both of us: We've been divorced more times than we've been married. And Ted, Rog, look at Ted. Remember skinny little Ted with the big mother Afro? Fist in the air, all the time. He could boogaloo and chicken-back so wild, man, you wanted to go down on him without hesitation! (*Embarrassed.*) Sorry . . . an unguarded moment of throw-back, there . . . (*Softly.*) and you,

Rog . . . Look at you.

ROGER: My hair's greying.

JACKIE: You're hair's not "greying", Roger: it's grey.

ROGER: I suppose it is.

JACKIE: Why did you really call this reunion, Rog? So, we can all peek around the corner, together, into the valley of the shadow of death?

ROGER: I want to put our group back together, Jackie. I want us to be short-story artists again . . . to meet and look at life, twice a week, maybe three times. I want to get back to what we were.

JACKIE: Oh. (*Music under, softly: possibly "Eleanor Rigby."*)

ROGER: Before anybody says "no", let's check out the alternatives. Ted?

TED: What?

ROGER: What have you got going?

TED: In what sense, Rog?

ROGER: In every sense. In life . . .

TED: I don't really follow . . .

ROGER: What happens when you get up in the morning? Where do you live? Where do you work? Who are you, Ted? We all remember who you *were*. Tell us who you *are*, at the moment.

TED: (*There is a healthy pause. All eyes are on Ted. He laughs nervously.*) I thought this was going to be different, our getting together again . . . this *reunion* . . . funny costumes . . . search out and find a goddamn *Poland* statue to meet at! (*Laughs nervously, again.*)

ROGER: What kind of work do you do, Ted?

TED: I sell insurance.

ROGER: You like it?

TED: Selling insurance? Do I *like* it?

ROGER: Any reason why you wouldn't want to resume our short-story workshop, Ted?

TED: I haven't written anything in 15 years, Rog, maybe more. I haven't read anything in about 10 years . . . except maybe the *Post*.

ROGER: So?

TED: So, why not? (*Smiles.*)

ROGER: Jackie?

JACKIE: What?

ROGER: Who are you?

JACKIE. Oh, come on! (*Roger smiles. Says nothing.*) Morris and I lived together 'til I got pregnant, then we got married and he started going to law school, nights, down at NYU. We lived out in Forest Hills with four other couples in a natural-foods commune. We planted everything you could think of in the backyard, but nothing much grew. Except me. I gained 75 pounds. I had twins. I went to this granola-feminist birthing center in Ozone Park . . . tall women with hairy legs and armpits, the whole shot . . . (*Pauses.*) Morris and I had dropped way too much acid. I stopped as soon as I knew I was pregnant . . . well, pretty soon after . . . but, it was way too late. One of the twins was born dead and the other one lived . . . but she wasn't very bright. She was nice . . . I had to put her in a home and Morris left me 'cause I was too depressing, and, also, 'cause he met this girl at NYU . . .

TED: I never liked Morris Aaronson. I always thought he was an arrogant prick!

JACKIE: One day, I was down in the Village looking at an apartment to possibly rent for myself, over on McDougal Street, and this salesman guy who was showing me around, who I'd known for about six-and-a-half *minutes*, starts puttin' major moves on me. We made it on the sofa in that place and then we made it again a half hour later in some amazing fuckin' penthouse on Christopher Street he also had the keys to for renting-purposes. (*Smiles.*) That was Morgan. We got married down at City Hall two weeks later and we stayed together for almost 15 years, 'til recently when Morgan, uh, found interests elsewhere. (*Pauses.*) I've got no reason not to try writing stories again with you guys. What the hell, huh? Maybe write some poetry? Why not? (*Ted and Jackie exchange a smile, squeeze each other's hands. Roger smiles at Agatha.*)

AGATHA: What? *Me?* The movie takes a turn here, 'cause I can't relate to you *depresso's!* You want a hear a poem I wrote? (*Shrugs.*) I'm *svelte* and I've got *gelt* . . . (*Smiles.*) nobody ever talks about it, really . . . what it really was. (*Pauses.*) We were young. We were beautiful. And when you're young and beautiful, you never think it's gonna' turn to *this* . . . (*Motions to all of them, herself included.*) you look back at it and you think "That wasn't me: that was a movie I was in . . ." You remember a movie or you remember a life: what's the difference, really? It's all happening in your head . . . (*Pauses.*) I remember being 18 years old and going to this friend's house on East 68th Street and Fifth, looking into the Park . . . (*Points.*) Just about *there* . . . She went to City College, 'cause she got thrown out'ta Antioch and Bennington. Now, that should tell you something about this girl! Anyway . . . I sit down at the dinner table with this girl and her mother and out comes this hippie butler with this enormous Royal Doulton soup-tureen filled with pills. Every kind of pill you can imagine: tabs of acid, MSG, PVC, BVD – who the fuck remembers the names? – and the mother says "We'll start with a light salad." That was it: the salad: the bowl of pills . . . (*Pauses.*) First, the mother takes a spoonful, puts it on her plate. The butler comes around, very proper, offers me the next helping. I'm 18. What do I know? I take a spoonful, put it on my plate. Then my friend. Then, we nibble away and we chat. Uptown East Side shit . . . "Where's the best rum-raisin ice cream? Serendipity is overtaking Rumpelmeyer's – that kind of world import. (*Pauses.*) About an hour later, I perceive that we are all naked and doing things in a padded pit with this butler. There is a live sitarist squatting in a corner, chanting some sort of gibberish and *I am not making this up: I lived this!* (*Pauses; then to Roger and others.*) You want to go back to that? Do you? I'm supposed to *think* "These are my *fond memories!??*" What are you all: *demented?* (*Pauses.*) I vote "no". You wanna' meet twice a week with Timothy Leary here, you do that. (*Music, possibly, Crosby, Stills and Nash "Our House (is a very, very, very, fine house)," plays under the action. Everybody has brought small picnic hampers. Agatha opens hers and eats a pita-bread sandwich, turns away from the others. Roger lights up a joint, offers it around, after taking a giant drag, uh, toke, uh, hit, for himself.*)

ROGER: (*Without exhaling.*) Jackie? . . .

JACKIE: Uh, no, thanks, Rog. I'm high enough . . . I'll have a ham and Swiss, instead. (*Laughs. She takes a sandwich from her picnic hamper, eats.*)

TED: (*Roger offers joint to Ted.*) Oh, yuh, me, too, Rog. I'm tripping. I dropped acid on my way across the park . . . (*Holds up doughnut from his picnic hamper; playacts being stoned.*) Whoa, lookit this cream-cruller! *Farr outtt!*

ROGER: You're just kidding old Roger, right, Ted? You didn't drop acid, did you?

TED: Oh, that's right, Rog. I'm just kidding. I haven't dropped acid since the week I spent in Mt. Sinai trying to get the quarter out of my nose. (*Roger starts to offer joint to Agatha, but never gets the words out.*)

AGATHA: Don't waste your breath, Rog. And don't even think about offering you-know-what to you-know-who . . . (*All look at Faith.*)

ROGER: That's cool.

FAITH: When I was in 6th grade, the entire class was doing coke . . . not just some of us: everybody. Some kids were skin-popping. (*Smiles.*) Every single kid I knew had a mother or a father or both who had been druggies. And everybody's parents were saying the same thing: "Don't do it!" "Drugs are dumb!" (*Laughs.*) It's not what you say, you know: it's what you *do* . . .

JACKIE: (*Vague confidentially.*) Agatha, I hope you take this in the right spirit, it is incredibly annoying to have your daughter scrutinizing us in this particular way.

AGATHA: Why? You think I don't know? You think I like having Lois fucking Lane from the Daily fucking Planet resident in my miserable fucking life?

FAITH: You ever notice that we rarely, if ever, use the "f" word, but you all use it, constantly, as though there were some amazing mystery around it. I prefer *doing* it to *saying* it . . . if you follow my drift.

ROGER: Listening to you all, stoned, is *sooo amazing!*

AGATHA: Blow it out your ass!

FAITH: That's my mom and I love her.

AGATHA: I was eighteen years old, and this one tells me if I can't open up to him, sexually, I'll never be a great writer . . .

ROGER: (*He smiles.*) We were younger.

AGATHA: I was younger.

TED: So, did you?

AGATHA: Did I what?

TED: Open up to him . . . sexually.

JACKIE: God, Ted, what's with you?

TED: I'm just interested.

JACKIE: So? Did you?

AGATHA: Why? You *didn't?*

JACKIE: Me, with Rog? I did. Not a lot. Once or twice a week . . . maybe three times, some weeks.

AGATHA: That, by you, is not a lot? I've got friends that would establish Personal Records with those statistics!

JACKIE: These are not recent figures.

ROGER: I'm still doing it once or twice a day, sometimes. I never miss. (*Puffs on his joint, so to speak.*)

FAITH: He asked me to slip over to the bandstand with him. He said he knows a bush.

AGATHA: Uh, Rog, we're talking 5-to-10 for Child Abuse . . .

TED: Nice, Rog . . . She's just a kid.

FAITH: It may just shock and amaze you all, but I am not in the slightest sexually attracted to this "brilliant little fucker" . . . isn't that what you used to call your college short story writing workshop teacher, mother? "Brilliant little fucker"?

AGATHA: It was a private little joke that just didn't translate particularly well after the 1960's . . .

FAITH: I wasn't born in the 1960's. I couldn't have heard it then. I must have heard it in the 1970's or 1980's. How come you kept telling a joke that never got any *laughs*? (*To all.*) Dr. Schwartzman said you ruined sex for us, too . . . with your middle class money and your free love and your drugs and needles, you spread every killer virus known to Western Civilization. You know how *incredibly romantic* it is in the throes of body heat to face what you set up for me? (*Playacts body heat throes.*) "Oh, oh, ohhh, Oliverrr . . . yes, oh yes, oh yes . . . have you been AIDS-tested? Yes, me, too. Yes oh yes oh yes . . . have you slept with anybody *since* you were AIDS-tested? Oh, God, oh, good, oh yes oh yes oh yes. Have you had any sort of intravenous injections or blood replacement? Oh God, thank God oh yes oh yes oh yes! Have you traveled in Africa or South Asia? Oh God thank God thank God! Have you got a minimum .6 millimeters-thickness major-brand condom? It's alright, it's alright! I have a stock in my purse! Would you mind terribly if we used two? Oh God thank God thank God . . . yes oh yes oh yes NOWWWW Oliver NOWWWW! (*To Ted.*) And how come you said "Nice, Rog . . . she's only a kid" when you heard he asked me to hop in the bush with him? Didn't you ask me to go over to the boathouse with you?

TED: Just to chat!

FAITH: If it's chat you want, keep your hands off my breasts and my bottom, *d'accord?* Every time he comes near me, this one, he's touchie-feelie . . .

TED: (*Sickly smile.*) She's making this up . . .

ROGER: That is *great!* I'm really *thrilled!* When was the last time you groped a girl, Ted, huh? Ten years ago? Twelve years ago?

TED: Off my case, will ya', Rog? Read my lips: Anita Hill.

ROGER: Who's gonna be our next vice president, Jackie? What's his stance on human rights? How does he feel about military spending? Does he give a shit about Nicaragua? What page do you read first when you read the paper, Jackie? Hmmmm?

JACKIE: I go straight to Page Six. I haven't watched the news on television, intentionally, for over ten years. Once in a while, if I'm flipping from channel-to-channel, something on the news'll catch my eye . . . a plane crash . . . a big fire . . . some disaster . . . (*Softly.*) I used to have a lot of energy and I miss it, Rog. I do. (*Pauses.*) I feel like I died, but I'm not dead. I'm still moving around and I don't know what for. (*Pauses.*) I miss it. I do. (*Pauses.*) It wasn't just the being young. It was the being tough.

TED: I was tough. First in the air. Bandanna tied, *just so,* over my eyes, highlighting this big fucking explosion of hair . . . (*Nearly weeps; saves himself.*) What happened? How'd I lose it?

ROGER: I haven't lost a thing. (*Offers joint to Jackie again.*) Jackie?

JACKIE: I haven't put smoke in my lungs in ten years. I quit. I . . . no, thanks . . .

ROGER: Ted?

TED: Same here, I quit.

ROGER: Why? (*To Agatha.*) Ag?

AGATHA: It took me six years to quit smoking. I went to Smokenders clinics in five countries. I spent over $100,000 learning to not smoke. You think I would maybe just try a couple'a tokes for oldtime's sake? I don't think so, Rog.

ROGER: Why? Why'd you all quit something you all enjoyed?

JACKIE: Uh, Rog, I know it's tough getting all the information, when you basically live under a rock, but . . . a whole lot of people aren't smoking anymore.

TED: (*Ted is practically inaudible.*) We're afraid to die.

ROGER: What? I couldn't hear you, Ted.

TED: (*Audibly.*) I said "We're afraid to die!"

ROGER: I think you're afraid to live.

AGATHA: Ahhh. I forgot about *that!* . . . The way they got you with a well-turned aphorism . . . a sly little catch-phrase . . . even a rabble-rousing bit of jingo like "Dump the Hump!" I was up there, on this stage, fist in the air, screaming "Dump the Hump!

Dump the Hump!" There were maybe 50 kids up there with me, yelling the same shit, over and over, pumping the audience – about a thousand more kids – into a frenzy. We're all screamin' Dump the Hump!" Me, one of the *leaders* . . . I didn't have a clue who the "Hump" was! Not a clue. I was stoned for four straight years, just worrying about staying focused long enough to cross on the green and wait on the red! . . . (*Truthfully.*) Aww, what's the diff? He would have died in office, anyway?

JACKIE: He wouldn't have died in office. He died from a broken heart, probably . . .

TED: You don't know that! We had some effect . . .

JACKIE: Like what?

TED: Viet Nam . . .

JACKIE: What effect? They're still fighting! Look at the facts, Ted: we changed the face of *nothing!* If anything happened, it got *worse!* Johnson, Nixon, Ford, Carter, Reagan . . . *What fucking effect?* You want to hear a sociological overview of Western man's Ruling Class in the past four decades? Hep, Hip, Hippie, Yippie, Yuppie . . . Cool, Hot, In, Far-Out, Fresh, Chill, Def! *Nice, huh? Great fucking effect!*

AGATHA: I loved my life, then. I really did. I really loved it. I loved Yoga class . . . the Stones, Paul and Artie . . . Mary Travis was sooo perfect . . . (*Pauses.*) I had Faith. It's true. That's why I picked her name. It was the thing in my life that was missing and I wanted it back . . . I had Faith in the world that I could be as critical and outrageous as I wanted, and the world would still have me . . .

TED: It's true. That's the truth. You could get bashed by a cop 'cause you called him a "pig," but it all only went so far . . . you got bashed but you didn't get killed . . . and the Cop thought about things . . . and so did you. Maybe you even talked to a Cop. I did. I confronted this big fucking ape of a Cop up on like 187th street . . . (*Laughs*) I can't believe I had the balls to do that! I'm 19, looking at a 38" stick in one of his hands and a .38 calibre pistol in the other. And I know he ain't gonna shoot! And I keep talking . . . about bein' Black . . . about Columbia owning all our land, uptown . . . about John Lindsay and Nam and, oh, yuh Cambodia. I was very into Cambodia . . . (*Laughs again.*) he bought me a beer. Then, we went out back of the barroom and smoked a joint together. And I felt a shitload better about Cops and he felt a shitload better about kids. (*Pauses.*) I look at Cops, now, and I marvel at the fact that somebody's actually still doin' that for a livin'. I wouldn't. I wouldn't have the guts. (*Sadly.*) I loved my life, then, too. I don't now. I truly don't. I'm just marking time. I don't smoke. I don't drink, much. I don't know the name of a single song in the Top 40, and that's a fact. I don't bother women. I avoid the mirror as much as possible. Like Aggie says, I got no faith in anything. But, worst of all, I've got no friends. (*Pauses.*) You think if I had friends, I would've showed up at something like this?

JACKIE: You've got me, Ted. Remember when we said we were "soulmates forever?"

TED: (*Laughs.*) I . . . I'm not sure I do remember that. It sounds like something I might have said to a couple of girls. (*Ted suddenly kisses Jackie. Everybody else stares and smiles. They break from kiss, hold each other at arm's length. Music in: Carole King's "You've Got A Friend".*) If I said it, I meant it.

JACKIE: Pick a night, Ted. I won't probably have to cancel much . . . (*Laughs, bravely.*)

AGATHA: I used to talk to maybe ten different friends on the phone every night of my life, even if I had to start making the calls at midnight. "Ruthie: Ag. Sorry to wake you up, but I couldn't call earlier. Go back to sleep. Call me in the morning . . ." "Mary Beth? Ag. Listen, go back to sleep . . . " (*Laughs.*) So many friends.

JACKIE: It wasn't just 'cause we were young. It was because we were *different* . . . We were friendlier.

ROGER: So, can we do it?

AGATHA: Do what, Rog?

ROGER: Meet up, say, Tuesdays and Thursday . . . We'll write short stories and poems and we'll talk to each other on the phone every day and if you guys don't wanna smoke, that's cool, really. More Boo for The Boss . . . (*Pauses.*) I've missed you all so much, really . . .

TED: Sure.

JACKIE: Why not?

AGATHA: Can we add in a couple of other people . . . just so, you know, we have . . . a couple of other people! (*Laughs.*)

ROGER: Sure. I'll bet we each know two or three other people we could call . . . people who might get off on this kind of thing.

JACKIE: I probably know two . . .

TED: I'll have to track 'em down, but I've got a good hunch . . .

AGATHA: (*Laughing; playacts making a phone call.*) "Ruthie . . . listen, I know it's midnight and it's been twenty years, but, I got in late . . ." (*Sincerely.*) I know at least four people I'd be happy to call.

ROGER: Good.

TED: Good.

JACKIE: Good.

AGATHA: Good. (*Smiles.*) We gonna' show off our clothes, or what? I didn't lose 35 pounds to fit back into this stuff without getting to show it off . . . (*To Roger.*) That was the brilliant part of your invitation, Rog. That was the part that got me here, really . . . (*Quotes invitation to Reunion.*) "Wear What You Wore The Last Time You Did The Chicken-Back." (*Smiles.*) I'm ready.

ROGER: I'm exposed, already. It's up to you two chicks, and you, man . . . (*Ted, Agatha, and Jackie stand and ready themselves. One-by-one, they remove their long coats and reveal outrageous 1960's outfits: what they wore the last time they danced the Chicken-Back. They laugh. They dance: Jackie with Ted; Agatha with Roger. The Statue rotates, faces upstage now. They all shift with Statue, their backs to audience. With Statue in new position, back to Audience, we see that Statue, too, wears 1960's "gear": denim jacket with peace symbol appliquéed; ponytail hangs from warrior's head, tied at bottom with shocking pink ribbon; Horse's tail gets same treatment; horse's hip painted with legend "OUT OF CAMBODIA!" Etc. All, but for Faith, dance the Frug in background. Faith moves downstage, talks directly to Audience.*)

FAITH: It was murder getting my mother to come here . . . to meet up with everybody, again. She was fat and depressed. Frightened to go anywhere. But, she's cool, my mom. She's got guts . . . Dr. Schwartzman says that we can never again be what we were. He says that that's the very worst thing about life and the very best thing about life: change upon change upon change. We've got to keep fighting. We've got to have Faith. (*Pauses. She looks at others.*) Life's great, isn't it? (*The lights fade. The music swells.*)

THE PLAY IS OVER.